Children's Nature

AMERICAN HISTORY AND CULTURE
General Editors: Neil Foley, Kevin Gaines,
Martha Hodes, and Scott Sandage

*Guess Who's Coming to Dinner Now?
Multicultural Conservatism in America*
Angela D. Dillard

One Nation Underground: A History of the Fallout Shelter
Kenneth D. Rose

*The Body Electric: How Strange Machines Built the
Modern American*
Carolyn Thomas de la Peña

*Black and Brown: African Americans and the
Mexican Revolution, 1910–1920*
Gerald Horne

Impossible to Hold: Women and Culture in the 1960s
Edited by Avital H. Bloch and Lauri Umansky

Provincetown: From Pilgrim Landing to Gay Resort
Karen Christel Krahulik

*A Feeling of Belonging: Asian American Women's
Public Culture, 1930–1960*
Shirley Jennifer Lim

Newark: A History of Race, Rights, and Riots in America
Kevin Mumford

Children's Nature: The Rise of the American Summer Camp
Leslie Paris

Children's Nature

The Rise of the American Summer Camp

Leslie Paris

NEW YORK UNIVERSITY PRESS

New York and London

NEW YORK UNIVERSITY PRESS
New York and London
www.nyupress.org

₵ Epigraph sources: Putnam Easton, quoted in a letter from his
⟨ mother, Emma Easton, in Camp Winnisquam brochure (1910), 37,
NHHS; Camp Larry Scrapbook, 1938, 2, folder 11, box 3, August
Meier Papers, NYPL-SCH.

Library of Congress Cataloging-in-Publication Data
Paris, Leslie.
Children's nature : the rise of the American summer camp /
Leslie Paris.
p.   cm. — (American history and culture)
Includes bibliographical references and index.
ISBN-13: 978-0-8147-6707-8 (cloth : alk. paper)
ISBN-10: 0-8147-6707-9 (cloth : alk. paper)
1. Camps—United States—History. 2. Children—United States—
History.   I. Title.
GV192.8P37 2007
796.54'20973—dc22   2007028474

New York University Press books are printed on acid-free paper,
and their binding materials are chosen for strength and durability.

Manufactured in the United States of America
10 9 8 7 6 5 4 3 2 1

I know one thing—I wish I were to begin the summer all over again to-morrow A.M.

> —boy from Boston, Massachusetts, circa 1909, when his mother
> asked him if he had enjoyed his vacation at a
> private New Hampshire camp

I still have three days, and I don't want to go home. Guess I'll have to though but I'm going to miss Mike blowing the bugle and Bob to climb up on and George to throw me around and Brownie to tell me to keep quiet and go to sleep. And I'm going to miss everybody, even Dopie.

> —girl from Durham, North Carolina, 1938, writing in the camp
> newspaper of the unionist Pioneer Youth of America's
> Camp Larry, North Carolina

Contents

Acknowledgments

I am deeply grateful to the many people who have helped me to conceptualize this book, suggested sources, provided first-hand accounts of their own camping histories, or otherwise smoothed my way. Special thanks are due to Regina Morantz-Sanchez for her astute historiographical advice, to David Scobey for his insights about narrative, to Susan Johnson for her thoughtful readings, and to Susan Douglas for her expertise in twentieth-century popular culture. In New York City, the members of two writing groups provided much-appreciated scholarly companionship: many thanks to Bridget Brown, Sandie Friedman, and Rebekah Kowal, and to Ruth Abusch-Magder, Libby Garland, Alexander Molot, and Jane Rothstein. In Vancouver, Mary Chapman, Karen Ferguson, Erin Hurley, and Paul Krause read numerous chapter drafts. At various stages, Joan Jacobs Brumberg, Paula Fass, Miriam Forman-Brunell, Jenna Weissman Joselit, Lisa Jacobson, and Bill Tuttle generously took the time (over dinners, correspondence, and even a car ride into the Adirondacks) to think through this project with me. More generally, I am grateful to the growing community of children's history and youth studies scholars, who have made my own work that much more gratifying.

Outside academic circles, I am indebted to the camp directors, past and present, who shared their knowledge, facilitated my use of private archives, and in some cases provided meals and lodging in the days when I was traveling frugally through the mountains: Chris Clements of Adirondack Woodcraft Camp; Karen Meltzer of Brant Lake Camp; Aaron Mitroni of Bronx House; Mel and Ruth Wortman of Camp Che-Na-Wah; Brian Mahoney, Wheaton Griffin, Jon Appleyard, and Peggy Bolster of Camp Dudley; Phil and Gary Confer of Forest Lake Camp; Frances McIntyre and Jehanne McIntyre Edwards of Camp Jeanne D'Arc; Peter Gucker of North Country Camps; Jack Swan of Camp Pok-O'-Moonshine; Adele and Joe Janovski of Camp Redwing; Tad

Welch and Ali Schultheis of Tanager Lodge; Brad Konkler of Camp Treetops; and Althea Ballentine of Camp Kehonka. Librarians and curators at numerous repositories aided me in locating useful materials. Special thanks are due to Jim Meehan and Jerry Pepper at the Adirondack Museum; Steven Siegel at the 92nd Street YMHA; Ameeta Kumar and Mary Levey at the Girl Scouts of the USA's National Historic Preservation Center; Dorrie Hanna at the Mystic River Historical Society; Doug Brown at the Groton School; Loris Clark at the Schroon–North Hudson Historical Society; and to the staffs of the Library of Congress, the New Hampshire Historical Society, the New Hampshire State Library, the Indiana Historical Society, the American Camp Association in Martinsville, Indiana, and various special collections including those of Columbia University, New York University, the University of Minnesota, Smith College, the University of Maine, Orono, and the Schlesinger Library at the Radcliffe Institute of Harvard University. Heartfelt thanks are due to the many former campers, counselors, and camp directors who shared their memories with me, loaned me photographs and other camp memorabilia, and were invaluable sources for the "unofficial" stories of camp life.

This research was made possible by a variety of grants. At the University of Michigan, the Horace H. Rackam School of Graduate Studies, the Program in American Culture, and Women's Studies together provided several years of initial support. I later expanded the scope of the project with the aid of postdoctoral fellowships from the Gilder Lehrman Institute of American History in New York, St. Mary's University in Halifax, the University of British Columbia in Vancouver, and the Social Sciences and Humanities Research Council of Canada.

Several articles based on this research are in print: "The Adventures of Peanut and Bo: Summer Camps and Early-Twentieth-Century American Girlhood," *Journal of Women's History* 12, no. 4 (winter 2001): 47–76; "'A Home Though Away from Home': Brooklyn Jews and Interwar Children's Summer Camps," in Ilana Abramovitch and Séan Galvin, eds., *Jews of Brooklyn* (Boston: University Press of New England/Brandeis University Press, 2001), 242–249; "'Please Let Me Come Home': Homesickness and Family Ties at Early-Twentieth-Century Summer Camps," in Caroline F. Levander and Carol Singley, eds., *The American Child: A Cultural Studies Reader* (New Brunswick, N.J.: Rutgers University Press, 2003), 246–261; and "Tradition and Transition at Adirondack Summer Camps," in Hallie Bond, Joan Jacobs Brumberg, and Leslie Paris, *A Paradise for Boys and Girls: Adirondack Summer Camps* (Syracuse and Blue Mountain Lake, N.Y.: Syracuse University Press, 2006), 1–12.

I was lucky to find a research topic of which I never tired. But I could never have taken on this work without the support of friends and family. Particular thanks are due to my parents, Roz and Joel Paris, and my sister, Nancy Paris. Finally, I am deeply grateful to my husband, John Pitcher, for his encouragement, homemade pizza, and astute editorial advice.

Introduction

A Warm History of Modern Childhood

Just a short letter to thank you for getting me into *CAMP LEMON* and for being so kind. I had a wonderful time. I went swimming twice a day during the first week an part of the second. It did not rain and the lake didn't flow. The lake became pollouted so we coudn't go swiming. I got quite tan. Once again I THANK YOU.

—former Camp Lehman camper to the executive director of the 92nd Street Young Men's Hebrew Association, 1939 (all spelling original)[1]

In 1927, Jerome Hyman, a twenty-two-year-old Harvard Law School student, spent the summer as director of Camp Lehman. The camp, run by the 92nd Street Young Men's Hebrew Association (YMHA) near Port Chester, New York, served working-class Jewish boys from New York City. At the end of the summer, when Hyman reflected on the summer that had just come to a close, he felt that he faced a nearly impossible task: recapturing in language the ephemeral joys and dissatisfactions of the camp season. "And now the dusty files must be fed, and a Report written," he mused.

To what avail? Who has the pictorial genius to revivify and immortalize camp life? Who can perpetuate the happy babel of boys swimming or the brightness of a day's fun or the inevitable sigh of homesickness? . . . The following Report sets down in cold type the warm history of two hundred boys, rescued from the rough thoroughfares of city life and tucked away in the haven of rest which is known as Camp Lehman. It is the fervent hope of the writer that those who read this history will find the sympathetic imagination to supply those human feelings and emotions which, because of the poverty of language, it is impossible to describe.[2]

When I came across Hyman's report seventy years after he wrote it, I immediately understood his predicament. How can cold type ever adequately represent as warm a history as that of camps, which offered experiences at once so intense and so fleeting? Nonetheless, I take up what I see as Hyman's two-part challenge: first, to approach the history of American children's summer camps with "sympathetic imagination" and, second, to make this seasonal world intelligible and compelling. What follows is a history of American summer camps, the aspirations of the adults who created them, and the experiences of the children who attended them, from the industry's inception in the late nineteenth century through its expansion in the first four decades of the twentieth century.

For well over a century, summer camps have provided many American children's first experience of community beyond their immediate family and home neighborhoods. The fact that the camp season is inherently time-limited has only enhanced its power. Decades later, adults often vividly recall details and feelings associated with their summer camp years. Camps' importance in American popular culture has become such that even for those who never attended them, the term conjures up nostalgic images of children singing around a campfire and watching marshmallows turn golden over the flames (or, alternatively, of campers sneaking out of their bunks after lights out).

This book explores how camps came to matter so greatly to so many Americans, both young and old. Summer camps helped to consolidate the notion of childhood as a time apart, at once protected and playful, which required age-appropriate, adult-monitored leisure in the company of select peers. Camp leaders promised that their clients would be physically and morally invigorated by fresh mountain air, simple food, daily swimming, and group living, and thus better fit for the year to come. But camps were so important not simply because adults designed them but because children delighted in them, helped to shape them, and felt transformed by them. "I am now a healthy boy who gained a lot of weight and looks very brown," wrote Henry F. in 1940, after a vacation at Camp Lehman.[3] At camps across the nation, millions of other children found the experience of attending a camp revelatory and formative.

In the 1880s, a small number of camps served several hundred middle- and upper-class Protestant boys. In the five decades that followed, the industry expanded rapidly as adults adopted the idea for other constituencies: girls, new immigrants, members of religious, political, and sometimes racial minorities. Camps were transformed from experimental institutions to mainstays of mass culture. Urban newspapers and parent-friendly magazines printed paeans to the industry each summer, children's fiction writers used camp settings for their stories, and motion pictures vividly represented camps' adventurous possibilities. By the interwar years, thousands of camps served more than a million children each summer, each camp promising, in the words of a typical private boys' camp brochure, that "camping is not a vacation of idleness and trivial pleasures, but an institution to teach the child to employ the leisure of its entire life in a healthful, cultural, and constructive manner and to teach future generations to do likewise."[4]

Parents proved receptive to this message. They subscribed to the idea that camps were educational. They believed that "country air" had important health benefits and that their children's play had important social consequences. They accepted the advice of a new stratum of professionals, in this case recreation and child-study experts, whose ideas they gave increasing weight on matters pertaining to family life.[5] They hoped that their families might actually gain from being temporarily dismantled. Most parents also welcomed camps as personally liberating. Parenthood could be both financially and emotionally taxing, and camps offered freedom to caregivers, who, depending on their family finances, were either temporarily freed to take their own summer vacations or, like the overworked mother of two boys who sent one to Camp Lehman, found in camps some relief from the pressing demands of child care: "I can't afford to entertain them in the things they want, so if one goes away its [*sic*] restful for me too."[6] At the end of the summer, Camp Lehman parents were typical of parents of all classes in hoping to find their children looking sturdier and happier. In a letter to the YMHA, one mother noted, "My two boys Frank and John came home . . . both of them looking and feeling fine and gained on weight, which made me and my husband very happy for the opportunity you gave our boys to be in the country."[7]

This transformative project, so enthusiastically endorsed by adults, was also taken up by children themselves, for whom camp life represented a dramatic change from the regular routine. Again, Camp Lehman is illustrative. Founded in 1916, the camp was located in Westchester, about an hour north of New York City. For working-class boys who had never before ventured beyond city limits, it felt like a world apart.[8] At camp, the boys encountered new kinds of freedom and adventure. Sleeping in tents, diving into the "swimming hole," taking turns at kitchen duty—all of these activities were new to boys more used to crowded tenement buildings and bustling neighborhoods than campfires and forest hikes. As they faced camp challenges and opportunities—whether learning to swim or simply making it through what were initially bewildering days—many campers felt that they were developing muscles and maturity. As one camper wrote in 1923, "Who said Camp Lehman can't make men out of us? Look what it did for Sam N——? When he came to Camp, all he did was cry. Now, three days later, he is a different boy. He almost won the contest in trying to see how long we could keep under water, and he's always ready to help others, and he never cries at all."[9] Of course, these success stories were not universal; Hyman noted "the inevitable sigh of homesickness," and some children loathed their camp experiences. But at their best, camps could feel like magical spaces, fundamentally unexplainable to outsiders, where pleasure and improvement were conjoined.

Late-nineteenth and early-twentieth-century camps were among the most visible expressions of the rising idea that childhood should be a time apart, protected from "adult" culture. Young people were the targets of new laws that restricted child labor, made school attendance mandatory for longer periods, and proposed to keep young people (especially girls) sexually pure. Children also constituted a new and important constituency for municipal agencies, urban reform professionals, educators, the emergent fields of pediatrics and psychology, and child study organizations, all of which recognized the intensifying social value of young people and promised to address their special, age-specific needs.[10] Play, education, freedom from productive labor, a degree of "innocence" in the world—all of these, a new cadre of child-care professionals asserted, were fundamental rights of childhood.[11]

Middle-class children, most of whom grew up in towns and cities, were far more likely to enjoy such protections than were their rural or working-class peers, as beneficiaries of a more companionate childrearing ideal. Companionate parenting, characterized by extended financial support and a more effusively affectionate parenting style, first took hold among nineteenth-century middle-class parents, whose ability to

Camp Lehman group, 1925 (Courtesy 92nd St. YMHA, New York)

provide advanced education and cultural opportunities to their children signaled their own class status as well as their parental affection.[12] The majority of nineteenth-century and early-twentieth-century American parents did not have the means to fully enact this ideal. Many depended financially on the contributions of their children, especially older children. For this reason, millions of children entered the workforce in their teens or even earlier, whether on farms, on factory floors, or in other workplaces.[13] Many urban children attended schools but lived in cramped housing in overcrowded neighborhoods lacking parks and playgrounds. Jerome Hyman alluded to these urban conditions when he characterized his campers, most of whom came from low-income immigrant families, as having been "rescued from the rough thoroughfares of city life and tucked away in the haven of rest which is known as Camp Lehman."

By the turn of the century a greater range of children was benefiting from extended childhood. Progressive reformers enacted legislation that restricted children's labor and made longer periods of schooling mandatory across classes. The decline of farming meant that fewer children labored at home. As their economic worth declined, children of all kinds came to become, in the words of scholar Viviana Zelizer, emotionally "priceless."[14] Their attendance at summer camps was one measure of these gains. Some of the Camp Lehman boys came from families so poor (especially after Lehman became a full-scholarship camp in the late 1930s) that if they took blankets to camp, they left their families with no bedcovers at home.[15] Yet they too attended camps.

In effect, campers were among the first beneficiaries of the relative democratization of children's leisure. In the 1880s, far more children worked in the summer months than took vacations. By the early twentieth century, Camp Lehman boys had holiday opportunities similar to (if not as fancy or extensive as) those of their better-off peers. As a result, their expectations of summer fun widened long before their parents could reasonably expect to take their own summer holidays.[16] Camps prepared an increasingly diverse range of children to expect vacations and gave them a lexicon for leisure that would serve them over the course of their lives.

Only a minority of American children attended camps: perhaps a few thousand in total in the 1880s and as many as 15 percent of children nationwide by the interwar years. Camps served those who lived at the center of the new industrial order in the nation's largest cities far more than those at its periphery in small towns or rural farms. Middle- and upper-class children attended more often than working-class children. Boys, who were the subject of more serious attention on the part of adult reformers, attended the first camps in significantly greater numbers than their sisters did, although by the early twentieth century a growing number of girls had camping opportunities as well. For members of the northeastern elite, the camp experience became an expected rite of passage; by 1930, two-thirds of the young women who were incoming undergraduates at Vassar College in Poughkeepsie, New York, had attended camps.[17] In contrast, perhaps one thousand out of fifty thousand black children living in New York City attended a camp in 1931, and not a single child profiled in a study of one hundred midwestern farm children attended a camp that summer.[18] These differences suggest, as historian Elliott West has pointed out, that "telling *the* story of American children is impossible."[19] Inasmuch as camps were spaces of children's leisure, they make visible the lives of those children who actually had vacation time in the summer months and had parents and local organizations able and willing to support these kinds of experiences. For this reason, camp histories are disproportionately those of white, urban children.

However, the camping cohort was growing with each decade, making this childhood experience increasingly common. Rural communities continued to contract and cities continued to grow in size, while the idea that children had a particular right to vacations grew more influential. Boys and girls, recent immigrants and the native-born; the children of union activists, socialists, and progressive educators; Protestants, Jews, and Catholics; and children of all races and classes—to varying degrees, by the early twentieth century all of them went to camp. Widely disparate groups of adults came to share the belief that rural spaces were healthier and safer for children than cities were, and they proposed that camps were especially suited to teach children the arts of social acculturation and good citizenship.

As camps moved into the cultural mainstream, a wider range of early-twentieth-century parents and children shared in this annual rite of summer. However, individual camps remained strikingly segregated spaces, designed to reflect or "uplift" particular constituencies. The parents sending their boys to Camp Lehman, for instance, were all working-class Jews. At a time when many leisure institutions discriminated against Jews, Jewish camps arose as counterparts to the Christian camping movement. Not all Jewish campers attended Jewish-only camps; some organizational camps, and a smaller number of private camps, were interfaith. But many Lehman parents specifically sought out Jewish camp environments for their boys. The widowed mother who wrote to the 92nd Street YMHA to explain that "we are Hebrew and naturally would prefer a Jewish organization" was expressing a widespread sentiment: that leisure was preferable, as the father of one prospective Lehman camper put the matter, among "our own people."[20] The leaders of camps who promised Christian-only clienteles, or who charged fees so high that only the elite would think to apply, similarly aspired to create privatized public spaces, providing common experiences but not shared campsites.

In effect, camps were far more socially exclusive than was urban leisure. Late-nineteenth- and early-twentieth-century cities, however much they were divided into ethnic- and class-based neighborhoods, were almost always marked by some degree of overlap and mixing across lines of difference. Camps reflected the urban networks through which children circulated—to attend Camp Lehman, for instance, a boy had to be or become a member of the YMHA—but they made possible a degree of ethnic, racial, and religious homogeneity that could not be achieved in cities, the kind of imagined "village" intimacy that the adults who organized camps feared had waned in the heterogeneous modern age.[21]

However, the degree to which camps segregated children diminished somewhat over time, as some of the social barriers long upheld by camps—especially differences of religion, gender, and race—began to fall. In the interwar years, a small number of adults consciously founded nonecumenical, coeducational, and interracial camps. Although differences of religion, gender, and race continued to define individual children's opportunities, these camps presaged an age in which such differences were imagined to be somewhat less consequential.

In 1934, in a *New York Times* article on camps, journalist Eunice Fuller Barnard reflected that "it is no coincidence that the skyscraper, for example, and the Summer camp are practically coeval."[22] This juxtaposition might initially seem odd, for if both were products of the late nineteenth century, skyscrapers exemplified the bold technologies of the industrial age, the metropolitan density that sent land prices soaring in business districts, and the corporate financing that made large-scale construction possible. In an age of steel, camp leaders housed campers in purposefully rustic surroundings made of canvas, wood, and stone. In an era of corporate consolidation, most summer camps were founded by individuals and organizations with more enthusiasm than money. During a period of technological upheaval, camp staff taught children nostalgic skills, such as canoeing and cooking over campfires, which derived their cultural capital from their apparently antiquated status.

For the leaders of the early camps, the new industry represented an important test case for the promise and perils of modernity. Change itself was a constant throughout the generations, but the rate of change —indeed, a culture of change—appeared to be intensifying rapidly by the late nineteenth century. Many adults feared that something vital had been lost in the transition: a familiarity with the natural world, a slower pace, a rootedness in the land. In 1924, when Porter Sargent responded to the growing consumer interest in camps by publishing his first annual *Handbook of Summer Camps* (a spin-off of his series on American private schools), he promised his largely urban parental audience that camps were helping children to develop by "getting back to the root of things."[23] This nostalgia was critical to camps' appeal among the adults who founded and promoted them. Criticizing the "artificiality" and "speeded-up" pace of contemporary life, camp leaders claimed to better socialize the next generation by returning them, if to a limited degree, to a simpler way of life, what Sargent termed "the sturdier training of our forebears under more primitive conditions on the farm or the frontier."[24]

In the days when the United States was a mainly rural nation, children's labor had been critical to agricultural production during the summer months. Now, the long summer vacation, a nineteenth-century educational innovation, created opportunities for productivity or for idleness. If rural children remained physically active in the summer months, urban children appeared at particular risk of becoming bored, listless, and susceptible to unsavory influences. Reiterating an argument that philosopher Jean-Jacques Rousseau had popularized in the eighteenth century, camp leaders envisioned children as closer to nature by virtue of their yet-unblemished characters. Camps, they promised, would socialize modern children in appropriately bucolic settings.

Yet camps' arcadian fantasies were distinctively modern, inspired by many adults' anxious reaction to urbanization, to the millions of new immigrants who made the nation more ethnically, racially, and religiously heterogeneous, and to the new technologies and commercial markets that were transforming the American economy. More precisely, what the men and women who brought urban children into the woods envisioned was a kind of nostalgic countermodern that conjoined traditional aesthetics and modern sensibilities. They represented their work both as an antidote to modernity's ills and as an expression of the latest leisure and childrearing practices. Sheltering children from the wilderness that they extolled, and providing comforts and recreational facilities as quickly as they could afford them, camp leaders supplied not wild but rather controlled nature, safe places for modern youth. Moreover, the industry's success rested on its leaders' ability to tap into a widening range of urban (and, with the growth of suburbs, suburban) networks, to market themselves successfully to prospective clients, and to lay claim to a modern style of professional child-centered expertise. Camps were hybrid cultural spaces, middle grounds where pioneer cabins sometimes coexisted with miniature golf courses, where children "played Indian" one day and dressed as film stars the next. Their return to an imagined past was only thinkable in relation to the industrializing present with which their leaders and clients were in constant dialogue.[25]

Camps' juxtaposition of Arcadian nostalgia and contemporary culture was revealing of how modernity was actually lived: not as an endless parade of new technologies and consumer products but as a back-and-forth between tradition and innovation. As camp life demonstrates, the modern was inherently plural and untidy, and it was experienced as such both by adults and by children.

Despite the prominent place of camping in American popular culture, when I began this study a decade ago I found little scholarship on which to draw. Summer camp history has long been the province of enthusiastic former campers writing memoirs of their postwar camp experiences or histories of their own specific camps. For earlier decades, I had access to an extensive but incomplete (and sometimes inaccurate) interwar literature. Camps were relatively unregulated, a minority of camp owners joined the industry organizations that sprang up in the early twentieth century, and few camp directors kept detailed records.[26] As camps came and went, many were lost to history. By the beginning of the century, early camp leaders could only hazard an educated guess as to the size of the movement, the number of children involved, and the percentage who returned for several seasons. By 1936, when camp director Henry Gibson published one of the first major overviews of the movement's history in *Camping*, many of its early details were already lost.[27]

In order to surmount some of these gaps, I grounded my own research in the records of many more camps than actually appear in this book: perhaps fifty camps with significant archives and hundreds of others I explored in lesser detail. Because the camping ideal crossed so many lines of difference, I chose to explore the widest possible range of camping constituencies rather than focusing specifically on any one. I looked at private camps, most of which were segregated by religion, and at organization-run or "organizational" camps, some of which were run by youth groups, others by community centers, and an important subset by charities. I focused on the camp mainstream: "sleepaway" summer camps. By definition, at these institutions children spent their nights as well as their days away from home. Almost all sleepaway camps had sessions of at least a week, rather than a night or two. To preserve my focus, I did not examine shorter-term excursions, nor did I treat the few winter camps that served as holiday camps during this period, the "family" camps that served parents with their children, or those charitable camps that sheltered working-class children under the supervision of their mothers. All of these would make interesting studies, but they do not typify the children's camp experience.

The United States is where children's camps began and where they achieved their greatest success. Drawing on longstanding national ideologies and iconography, especially the idea of entrepreneurial individuals forging communities in frontier (or at least rural) conditions, they represented a particularly American solution to the question of children's socialization in modernity as traditional systems of socialization became less powerful in shaping young people's lives. Although camps were founded across the country by the 1890s, the industry began, developed most extensively, and grew largest and most diverse in the Northeast, near most of the nation's largest cities. A book focused on midwestern camps might emphasize canoeing to a greater degree. A history of Colorado "ranch" camps would have more to say about horseback riding. But although children camped near palm trees and in arid terrain, nowhere did the industry develop more extensively than within a day's journey from New York City. Indeed, by one (perhaps enthusiastic) estimate, by the 1930s as many as half the nation's paying campers lived in the greater New York metropolitan area.[28] My focus is thus on northeastern camps, at the industry's rapidly growing center.

This book is divided into two parts. The first four chapters explore the ideological, economic, physical, and social landscape of summer camps from the late nineteenth century onward. Chapter 1 examines the first camps' ideological and institutional foundations and considers the industry's expansion in the first decades of the twentieth century. By tracing the commercial, institutional, local, and personal networks through which prospective campers and their parents circulated, chapter 2 considers how children found their way to particular camps. Chapter 3 follows children into camps, exploring the personal and collective practices through which children became campers. Chapter 4 reflects on communal intimacy and explores the limits of and intergenerational tensions particular to camp "family."

As these chapters demonstrate, many camp rituals, routines, and ideals that were developed in the late nineteenth century became standard practice in the decades to come. As children's camps entered the American mainstream, so did a fairly consistent idea of what that experience entailed: group living away from parents but under adult guidance, outdoor activities, regular evening campfires, a greater appreciation for the natural world, and tests of skill and independence. The experience of attending a labor-affiliated camp of the 1930s was similar in many important respects to that of a YMCA camp of the 1880s, even though each had its own particular clienteles and goals.

Over the decades, however, camps did sustain important differences. The second part of the book focuses primarily on the interwar years, a period of consolidation for the industry but also a time of changing ideals and expectations. These chapters investigate camps' growing importance as purveyors of modern and nostalgic experience and consider various challenges to these traditions. Chapter 5 explores how industry leaders tried to reconcile progress and camp conventions in the increasingly commercial world of which camps were a part. Chapter 6 analyzes the centrality of racialized, nostalgic primitivism to camp life and explores camps' slowly shifting color line. Chapter 7 traces the emergence of a more permissive "child-centered" ideal and considers the implications of this shift for children's culture more broadly. As these chapters suggest, the shift to a more democratic ethos was slow and incomplete, but it took many forms, from the beginnings of racially integrated camping to greater validation of children's own decision-making.

In choosing as the title of my book "Children's Nature," I mean to highlight the historical constitution of childhood as well as of nature. Childhood is a biological and developmental category, but what it has meant to be a child (or to care for one) has been historically variable. The story that follows explores how age-bound identities have been produced, regulated, and disputed by adults and by children. Some summer camps served children as young as four and as old as eighteen, but most drew campers between the ages of eight and fourteen. This age range encompassed significant developmental and social differences. Camps ritualized these distinctions, allowing children different degrees of power and new group identities, activities, and opportunities as they aged. As important spaces of intergenerational negotiation, camps allow us to see childhood and youth as they were produced in conversation between different age groups, and even between children of different ages.

Because children have not had the same relation to power or public life as their adult counterparts, their voices can be difficult to recuperate. They have left behind few of the documents that historians might normally use as evidence, such as laws or published speeches. Their views cannot be extrapolated through a study of voting or political and religious leadership. They often have had little say about where they lived, worked, or went to school. The historical record is particularly unrevealing of the hopes and feelings of younger children, while it has much to say about the expectations and desires of the adults who wrote about and cared for them. But although adults' perspectives and organizing efforts are far better documented than those of children, to describe the intended organization of camp life is not to describe its emotional effects. Campers had inner lives at camp beyond the purview or ideological reach of adults, and while adults ran camps, children made their own meanings out of what was offered to them. They subscribed to the ideal of playful transformation and participated in the ideological project of camp life, but they did so from their own, child-centered perspective. Certain aspects of children's culture made many camp leaders uncomfortable: sexual curiosity, casual cruelty, even in some instances an open refusal to adhere to adult demands. Camps were important adult-run institutions of social instruction, ideology, and indoctrination designed to reinforce the values of the communities that sponsored them. But campers did not always follow the rules, nor were they always motivated by their leaders' ideals. Adults praised camps for "getting back to the root of things," but children generally did not arrive at camp driven by ambivalence toward the modern age. In fact, camp was often where boys and girls learned nostalgia for an era that they were too young to recall.

To convey some of the texture of campers' experience, I have worked with a wide range of historical sources in which children's voices (some more and some less mediated) appear: children's writings in camp newspapers, diaries, and scrapbooks; letters home; written reminiscences and oral histories of former campers; the records of religious institutions, settlement houses, youth groups, and scholars of the period; commercial brochures, photographs, and amateur films of camp life; industry books and magazines; and government reports. These varied sources allow me to better explain camps as intergenerational phenomena shaped by the mutual will of children and adults. Although the challenge of writing the simultaneous history of childhood ideology and children's experience remains, wherever possible I have worked to set adult intentions into conversation with children's own observations.

Children's own participation in intergenerational community is one of the central themes of this book. Children did not shape their own camp culture on their own terms, and their power was semiautonomous at best. But neither were they the passive recipients of adult ideas. Young people responded to, adapted to, supplemented, and sometimes challenged the camp project. Camps offered them unparalleled opportunities for freedom, adventure, self-exploration, and, to an important extent, youthful self-determination. Although adults had more power, children's desires had to be considered if camps were to be successful. Thus, as compared to more repressive institutions such as juvenile courts and schoolrooms, camps were sites of children's agency. Whether children enjoyed the experience of attending a camp or not, they recognized that it was different: more intense, more concentrated, more demanding, sometimes more painful, and often more rewarding than their everyday lives. Many campers felt that camp was truly "theirs" because they were collaborators in the camp experience. In the pages that follow, I have made every effort to be inclusive of their own perspectives and ideas.

I recognize that I am writing on a topic about which many readers may have personal experience. To those adults who attended camps of the 1940s onward, I must add a caveat: you may not recognize every aspect of the world that I sketch out in these pages. If your childhood experience of camp includes having sung "Little Rabbit Foo Foo" or Al Sherman's 1963 classic "Hello Mudduh, Hello Fadduh," then you are younger than the generations whose experiences I chronicle here. Still, you will undoubtedly recognize many camp rituals that are well over a century old, such as the use of the term "counselor," the importance of camp songs, and the variety of activities.[29] For over a century, children have experienced the pain of homesickness, learned to swim, and sat around campfires at night. Generations of American adults have imagined camps to be critical venues for children's socialization. Generations of children have found in them important sites of community. In my exploration of this terrain, I make no claims to what former camp director Jerome Hyman termed "pictorial genius." No degree of writerly brilliance could bring any of us back to childhood, or to the hot days and star-filled nights of the summer camp season. But I take up Hyman's challenge, and the following chapters will try to bring this special and emotionally resonant world to life.

PART I

At Work and at Play
The Making of Camp "Family"

1

Small Islands
The First Summer Camps

Pull boys, pull! Hoorah for Camp Chocorua!
Steady on the stroke; we soon shall reach the shore.
Finished is our work until the bright tomorrow.
Friends we shall be, both now and evermore . . .
We, one and all, with happy, honest faces
Shall strive to do our duty and bid farewell to care.
    —Camp Chocorua song, Squam Lake, New Hampshire, 1880s[1]

In June 1881, Ernest Berkeley Balch, having recently completed his sophomore year at Dartmouth College, was rowing along New Hampshire's Squam Lake when he happened upon Burnt Island. The island was rocky and relatively flat, much like the twenty or so others that dotted the lake. Most of its three acres were covered in pine, birch, oak, and poplar trees. At the island's northern end, through a cluster of silver birches, Balch could see the majestic Chocorua Mountain about thirty miles to the northeast. On the south side of the island he found a white sand beach. He also noted a protected cove suitable for boaters and canoeists. For Balch, this uninhabited plot of land seemed almost divinely ordained for what he had in mind: a summer camp for adolescent boys. The camp he founded that summer at the age of twenty-one was, he later wrote, almost an inevitable consequence of the island's own perfection: "I felt sometimes it had been designed from the beginning of all things for such a camp as I dreamed of."[2]

Balch's was both an individual act of manly self-assertion and an extension of an American project: the creation of empire.[3] To discover and take possession of an island, as did Balch, was to lay claim to one of the central parables of American history: the story of virtuous pioneers, guided by manifest destiny, who forged new communities on virgin land. This story was, however, more revealing of pioneer nostalgia than of the actual pioneer past. Earlier generations of Euro-American settlers had found camping less romantic than inconvenient, uncomfortable, and sometimes dangerous. Pressing west and south, they had resigned themselves to the temporary inconvenience of living out of tents, to their unnerving proximity to the wild world around them, and to the violence that attended the forcible displacement of Native Americans.

By the late nineteenth century, the days of continental expansion had come to a close. Squam Lake itself was becoming a popular summer resort district, drawing middle- and upper-class northeasterners to its picturesque hotels and cottages. Other vacationers ventured further into the woods. As the era of necessary camping faded, recreational camping acquired an aura of health and rejuvenation, providing campers a sense of connection to a romantic American tradition. Many wilderness enthusiasts had grown up on farms or in small towns, and they bemoaned the gradual loss of a farming culture, but they were particularly thrilled by the thought of wild spaces untouched by market utility, human occupation, or the recent agrarian past.[4] For those men who could afford the travel and the time away from paid labor, camping beckoned as a means of recapturing, however briefly, the early pioneers' bravery and independence.

Cultural innovators, the founders of the first children's summer camps translated these antimodern anxieties into youth-specific terms. Camp Chocorua, one of the first American summer camps, represented the early industry's key themes: a manufactured peer group of older boys gathered under men's guidance for outdoor recreation, health and physical activity, and character development. Several decades before the concept of adolescence came into popular parlance, the leaders of the nascent camping industry were architects of a new style of leisure designed to make better citizens of older boys. They did so by addressing what they took to be their campers' age-specific recreational needs, including the importance of peer groups. The "twelve–sixteen" years were, Balch posited, "the golden age of a man" when "the foundations are laid and the shape of the building determined," when boys were neither too plastic nor too fully formed.[5]

The subsequent proliferation of camps, on Squam Lake and elsewhere, attested to the success of the summer camp ideal. Only a handful of boys attended Chocorua in 1881. By 1889, the camp's final season,

Balch had an enrollment of about twenty-five or thirty boys, ranging in age from eight to fifteen, with five men on the "faculty" to guide them. Two of Balch's peers, inspired by his example, opened similar boys' camps on the shores of the same lake: Algonquin (founded in 1886) and Asquam (1887). Then the Squam Lake summer camp scene became appreciably more diverse. Three former Asquam campers were inspired to found the Groton School Camp (1893), a charitable camp for working-class boys from Boston and New York, on another of the Squam Lake islands. This camp gave elite boys attending Groton School (a Connecticut boarding school), who supported and worked at the camp, a taste of "missionary" work.[6] Hale House, an early settlement house (progenitor of today's community centers) based in Boston's impoverished South End, began at the beginning of the new century to send groups of working-class children to Camp Hale on Squam Lake. There, mostly Jewish boys and girls enjoyed separate two-week vacations.[7] The lake was already a center for children's camping when in 1902 a Miss Muñoz founded Camp Pinelands, one of the first private American girls' camps, near Camp Asquam.[8]

In the first decades of the twentieth century, adults of all kinds—reformers and parents, wealthy and poor, women as well as men—began to value the camp ideal, convinced not only that rural recreation was a desirable antidote to city life but also that a broader range of children should benefit from its opportunities. Late-nineteenth-century adults had founded perhaps twenty-five small private camps, and a few hundred others were organized by churches, Young Men's Christian Associations (YMCAs), urban settlements, and charities. Most were boys' camps founded by idealistic men of Balch's background, who saw in the outdoors a manly testing ground away from the purportedly effeminizing influences of "civilization." The great majority of these camps operated for only a few years and served no more than a few dozen children at any given time. By the turn of the century, however, the summer camp movement was growing rapidly, and its leaders' aspirations and their clients were increasingly diverse.

Balch's brand of virile Protestant manhood, and his fear of what he called "weakening feminine influences," suggested one of these countering forces.[9] Tradition had long dictated that well-to-do women should focus their energies on the home. But a growing number of such women attended colleges, worked in the professions, campaigned for woman suffrage, and participated in sports and outdoor activities including camping expeditions.[10] Some of these pioneers of a new model of female physicality, and a few similarly inclined men, founded the first camps for girls at the turn of the twentieth century. Meanwhile, new camps for working-class and immigrant children reflected their parents' growing political clout at the municipal level, as well as Progressive reformers' eagerness to alleviate the deprivation of the poor and better socialize and Americanize new immigrants.

Most of these early camps remained sites of social consolidation, where children of similar backgrounds were invited to form cooperative cultures away from "other" influences.[11] Camp leaders claimed to be returning children to a healthier, more natural way of life, but they generally reiterated urban social and class divisions. Figuratively (as well as literally, in certain cases) the first summer camps were islands, illustrating the limits of democratic inclusion and the degree to which American culture was deeply fragmented.

The Summer Vacation and the Natural World

Ernest Balch, born in Newport, Rhode Island, to Reverend Lewis P. W. Balch and his second wife, Emily, spent much of his adolescence and young adulthood in small New Hampshire towns: at the family home in Holderness, only a few miles from Squam Lake; at Phillips Exeter Academy, the elite boys' boarding school in Exeter; and at Dartmouth College in Hanover, where he entered with the class of 1883. In his first year at Dartmouth, when he began to reflect on the possibilities of camping for adolescent boys, he turned to the region he knew best. In the summer of 1880, he and his Dartmouth friend Charles Applegate took two boys—Balch's twelve-year-old brother, Stephen Elliott Balch, and Stephen's friend Henry "Toby" Blair—on a short camping expedition to "Camp Nirvana," a campsite on the Squam lakeshore owned by Dartmouth friends. This outing was a happy one, and Balch was encouraged, in the year that followed, to consider a more permanent camp in the woods for boys.[12]

Balch believed that elite summer resorts were far too luxurious to provide the kinds of rugged and masculine experiences that boys, especially older boys, required. "America was getting soft," Balch later recalled. Boys from better-off families, who enjoyed many luxuries as a matter of course, were in particular need of fortifying and vigorous outdoor experiences if they were to grow up to lead the nation and protect women and children or, in his words, "to hold this Republic safe against the forces of evil and keep the soft hearted and soft headed safe in their homes."[13] In the words of the Chocorua camp song, he expected his campers to be "steady on the stroke," that is, to put into practice habits of virtuous physicality, collective labor, and moral character.

Balch's camp was pioneering, but his reasoning was not. Increasing numbers of Americans identified a return to nature as a palliative to the increasingly industrial world: restorative, both physically and spiritually, for modern men living overly regimented lives. At midcentury, Harvard University graduate Henry David Thoreau chose to live for several years in a rustic Massachusetts cabin. As he explained in his memoir, *Walden,* published in 1854, "I wanted to live deep and suck out all the marrow of life."[14] In the second half of the century, nature enthusiasts experienced the modern world around them as one of rapid, sometimes confusing, and potentially deleterious changes and responded with nostalgia for what had been lost in the transition. In 1893, the young historian Frederick Jackson Turner postulated that the American frontier had provided a testing ground for new immigrants, making them into virtuous citizens as successive generations pressed further west. Now that the frontier was closed, Turner concluded, the safety net that had once forged American men's character had vanished.[15] In the face of these losses, camping enthusiasts saw salubrious possibilities. For Balch and a growing number of his contemporaries, the wilderness lifestyle of an earlier era offered exactly the kind of rugged, primal experience that would enhance manhood in the modern age.[16]

Balch's desire to make of the summer months something useful and productive was congruent with an older American tradition. In the early nineteenth century, only the wealthiest Americans could afford the time and money for what they termed "the fashionable tour." While some upper-class Americans traveled to East Coast cities and urban attractions, increasing numbers chose rural destinations where they could bathe by the sea, breathe mountain air, view picturesque landscapes, or "take the waters" at mineral springs. At the new summer resorts, these rural tourists spent much of their time engaged in a genteel social whirl of activities such as promenading, bathing, and taking carriage rides. Religious camp meetings offered less-wealthy and rural vacationers a similar mix of pleasure and purpose: friendly recreational opportunities as well as periods of group prayer and reflection. This emphasis on virtuous leisure was far more pronounced in the northern states, where early-nineteenth-century Americans tended to justify travel as healthful or spiritually restorative, serving a higher purpose than mere amusement or status display. Such misgivings were less entrenched in the South, where the local gentry had long proved their place in the social hierarchy through luxurious and conspicuous entertainments.

None of these early travelers would have termed his or her experience a "vacation." This term, and the ideology underlying it, swept into broader usage in the 1850s. At midcentury, doctors, religious leaders, and the popular press began increasingly to promote vacationing, especially as a tonic for urban men caught up in the rising industrial economy. Although women of the middle and upper classes were presumed to have greater leisure and a degree of protection from the marketplace, they too were imagined to benefit from the healthful effects of nature.[17] So eagerly did middle-class Americans of the second half of the nineteenth century embrace this message that the ability to take an annual holiday quickly became a marker of class status.[18] After all, most Americans could not travel for pleasure. Rural farm-dwellers put in long hours during the spring planting and the fall harvesting, most attended to livestock year-round, and few could afford extensive vacation travel. For working-class Americans, a vacation was similarly out of reach; not only was the cost of travel prohibitive, but since many urban families lived from paycheck to paycheck, the loss of a week's wages could be calamitous. Even among middle- and upper-class families, women were more likely to take the children on extended summer holidays while their professional husbands worked and visited their vacationing families from time to time.

For those urban Americans who could afford rural tourism, summer vacations appeared to address a multitude of social and health concerns. In an era before air conditioning, cities often became oppressively hot and humid in the heat of July and August. The smell of rotting produce, horse manure, and untreated sewage was most intense, and the threat of such infectious diseases as cholera and typhoid was at its height. The cool air of the mountains and the refreshment of ocean breezes appeared particularly restorative and healthful by comparison, rural roads were more passable in the warmer months, and the weather was better suited to outdoor pursuits. Meanwhile, over the course of the nineteenth century the extended school vacation in July and August became standard, ending the tradition of the summer school term.

Working-class and rural parents often relied on their children's labor, especially when school was not in session, whereas urban middle-class parents had to consider how best to fill those summer hours.[19] For all these reasons, the months of July and August became the focal point of the American vacation season.

As the new vacationers traveled toward nature's "simpler pleasures," they took advantage of a growing infrastructure of ferries, roads, and railroads, transportation technologies that were reshaping rural as well as urban life. In 1850s New Hampshire, for instance, developers built railroads in order to move finished goods and natural resources more quickly and efficiently between industrial port cities and the more rural northern regions of the state. These same trains passed through the White Mountains, making possible the expansion of tourism into relatively remote areas.[20] Loggers, miners, farmers, and fishermen had long exploited the region's natural resources. Now, in increasing numbers, tourists consumed the beauty of vacation communities such as Squam Lake.

Two different but equally nostalgic forms of rural appreciation attracted visitors. The first was an agrarian impulse. During the latter half of the century, thousands of tourists paid to board on working farms in order to experience first-hand the benefits of farm-fresh food and country air and to witness (but not to join in) hardy, virtuous labor. The second was a preagricultural wilderness ideal, which valued the spiritual and aesthetic possibilities of "uncivilized" nature over any utilitarian importance. This enthusiasm was enshrined in the late-nineteenth-century popular press in specialized magazines for sportsmen such as *Forest and Stream* (1873), *Outing* (1885), and *Outdoor Life* (1897) and in the movement to create national parks and other protected spaces outside the reach of industrial and agricultural sprawl. Balch stood firmly in this second faction. Farmers toiled along the shores of Squam Lake, but they did not figure into his fantasies. Nor, as he saw it, did they share his vision of how nature might be used: they were afraid of the lake, were unable to swim, owned boats of poor quality, and, he later argued, "For the exquisite beauty of Asquam it was rare to surprise a trace of feeling."[21]

Although many urban Americans were attracted to the idea of wilderness vacations, in practice most preferred a more mediated encounter with nature. Many readers were taken, for instance, with Boston clergyman William H. H. "Adirondack" Murray's romantic portrayal of his camping trips, *Adventures in the Wilderness; or, Camp-Life in the Adirondacks* (1869).[22] The book achieved an extravagant popularity and inspired a sudden rush of visitors to this Upstate New York region. But few tourists actually were prepared to tough it out in the woods. So many came so quickly to a region unequipped to provide them with adequate guides and hotels that they were dubbed "Murray's Fools." Within a decade, the local economy had caught up to vacationers' desires. Now, Adirondack tourists could choose from among a fair number of lodges and fancy resorts complete with eight-course menus. The very wealthiest visitors acquired lavish countryplaces, called "Great Camps," which combined an aesthetic of rusticity with significant luxury. Up and down the East Coast (and to a lesser degree, in the upper Midwest and the mountains of the Southeast) the same dynamic was repeated. Developers created new resort communities within traveling range of the nation's larger cities, while some of the simplest religious campsites of earlier years became more elaborate vacation centers.[23]

As the tourist economy developed, those Anglo-American middle- and upper-class men who preferred more strenuous hunting and fishing expeditions set off for the woods, sometimes in the company of hired local guides who knew the terrain, carried provisions, set up camp, and made dinner each night. These wilderness excursions were driven by specific class- and gender-based aspirations and anxieties. Many men feared that the rising market economy threatened traditions of independent manhood and self-sufficiency. In the apprenticeship system of an earlier era, laborers might have expected to become skilled enough at trades to set up their own shops. Now, their urban, middle-class social equivalents worked more often in middle management, which generally did not lead to business ownership, and at a pace increasingly marked by the clock instead of the season. Many men further fretted that modern society was overly "feminized," meaning that women exerted too strong an influence in cultural life, the church, and even at home (especially in spoiling or overprotecting their sons).

In the late nineteenth and early twentieth centuries, these fears were voiced most loudly by proponents of what was termed "muscular Christianity." Muscular Christians feared that the Protestant church, and American culture more broadly, had become weak, sentimental, and feminized, and they called on Protestant men to recapture a more virile Christianity. A vigorous spiritual practice, they believed, required a strong and healthy body; in wartime, men might prove their valor on the battlefield, and in times of peace, strenuous activities such as competitive sports and wilderness trips improved bodily vigor and provided the basis for higher moral development.[24] The YMCA movement, founded in England in 1844 and then organized in the United States from 1851 onward, exemplified the muscular Christian cause with its focus on the physical and spiritual needs of young men coming into cities from more rural communities.[25] Theodore Roosevelt personally embodied the ideal. A hunter, soldier, historian, Progressive reformer, and, from 1901 through 1908, the nation's president, he extolled camping and hunting as necessary counterpoints to the effete tendencies of civilized life. After building himself up physically as an adult, he presented a striking example of what in 1899 (in the wake of his much-publicized heroism in the Spanish-American War) he famously termed "the strenuous life": a show of male strength, bravery, and righteousness in the service of the nation.[26]

To a significant degree, the rise of wilderness camping turned on the problems and possibilities of modern civilization. In both industrial and imperial terms, the late-nineteenth-century United States was an empire ascendant. New technologies and an influx of immigrant workers propelled what would be, by the turn of the century, the largest mercantile economy in the world. Achievements such as the seventy-foot-tall Corliss Steam Engine, which powered the exhibits in Machinery Hall in 1876 at the Centennial World's Fair in Philadelphia, appeared to presage a new era of American might. While the continental frontier was closing, an American empire beyond the continental United States was beginning to take shape. By the end of the century, in the wake of the American victory in the Spanish-American War of 1898, the United States gained control of a number of Central American and Pacific nations and territories. This development, many American observers of the period argued, proved the superiority of Anglo-Saxon American men.

Despite these proofs, many American men, Balch and Roosevelt among them, worried that an excess of civilized living threatened the men who ought to lead by virtue of their class and race. Ironically, civilization, by "softening" elite men, seemed to contain within itself the seeds of its own destruction.[27] Moreover, the nation's cities were becoming more heterogeneous. Increasing numbers of men and women who had grown up in rural areas were propelled into the cities in search of work, either unable or unwilling to stay on farms. Millions of new immigrants to the United States, many of them desperately poor and neither

Protestant nor English-speaking, were settling in urban areas. For those who had grown up in more culturally homogeneous American villages and towns, the relative anonymity of urban life, its size, and its ethnic and racial diversity all engendered anxiety.

For all these contradictions, rural tourists expressed a genuine desire for rugged experiences in the wake of rapid social and economic change. Many Americans of the latter half of the century worried that an important connection to the land was being lost, and with it, the traditional locus of republican character. American traditions, they felt, had been bred of frontier conditions that tested one's mettle, and American morals had grown out of rural soil. Camping, an act seemingly at the heart of the historical national experience, appeared to offer a temporary reprieve from the perils attendant to modernity.

The Child and Nature

The summer camp ideal conjoined this strain of antimodern anxiety to new ideas about childhood and childrearing. In an agricultural economy, men, women, and children all worked in and around the home, although each had gender-specific tasks. The expanding industrial economy drew working-class Americans of all ages into factories, because family survival often depended on the financial contributions of wives and children. Middle-class women and children, in contrast, were shielded from paid employment by definition of their class. Professional husbands and fathers drew high enough salaries to support their wives and children at home and to protect them from what was imagined to be the chaotic, morally suspect world of labor. Middle-class domestic ideology extolled the home as a safe and protected space outside the market economy, a space to which men could retreat at the end of the work day into the loving embrace of their families.[28]

In practice, the conditions of middle-class life were more ambiguous. Women continued to supplement the family economy through housework, even if this work was not financially remunerated. The work of shopping for the family drew women outside the home and into the market as consumers. Moreover, by the late nineteenth century a significant minority of middle-class Americans never married or had children. Still, the middle-class domestic ideal, within which mothers created domestic havens, fathers supported extended educations, and children enjoyed extended childhoods, powerfully shaped these families' aspirations. Parents who had seen the economic and social value of higher education in their own lives willingly supported their children through extended periods of dependency, believing that formal schooling into adolescence and even beyond would help their sons enter into professional careers and their daughters prepare for advantageous marriages.

Although middle-class children possessed little economic value to their parents, they were at the heart of new ideologies of home life. Parents of this class adopted a more companionate model of family relations: more affectionate and emotionally intense than earlier generations, less hierarchical, and with fathers participating more actively in childrearing. Although contraception was still unreliable (and, after the social-purity campaigns of the 1870s, difficult or even illegal to obtain), better-off Americans were also consciously practicing sexual restraint in an effort to have fewer children. As a result, by the end of the century the middle-class birthrate plummeted by half, to about three children per family instead of six. Observers such as Theodore Roosevelt feared that the predominantly white nation was headed toward "race suicide" (in the sense that "race" denoted ethnicity and national origin as well as skin color) because white, native-born Americans were having fewer children than immigrant and working-class parents were. Less prosperous Americans tended to have more children, sometimes for religious and cultural reasons, or for lack of access to birth control, but also often because they relied on their children's labor. Rural children on farms helped to weed, to plant and pick crops, and to care for animals. Urban, working-class children took up a range of labor: selling newspapers on the streets after school, working in textile mills, or watching over younger siblings while their mothers went off to work. The new ideal of protected childhood was fully possible only for the mainly urban, middle-class minority.

Nonetheless, the emergence of a more sentimental approach to childhood in the late nineteenth and early twentieth centuries affected children of all kinds. Foremost, child-labor laws and extended compulsory education legislated a separate, noncommercial space for a broader range of children. The rise of the public high school, which middle- and upper-class adolescents attended in growing numbers, reinforced this notion of extended childhood and was pivotal to the emergence of adolescence as a separate peer group (albeit one still defined at the time by class). A variety of modern professions and subspecialties further demarcated childhood and adolescence from adulthood. By the turn of the century, a new cohort of play-experts, psychologists, and child-welfare activists justified in increasingly "scientific" terms the impulses that once had driven Balch toward boys' work.

Particularly influential was the work of G. Stanley Hall, a Clark University professor who pioneered in psychology and child study beginning in the 1880s. In his central theory of "recapitulation," Hall proposed that childhood play occurred in developmental stages, each of which corresponded to a stage in the history of the human race. Recreation was not mere relaxation or idleness, he argued, but a critical facet of children's work toward the next level of development. In *Adolescence, Its Psychology and Its Relation to Physiology, Anthropology, Sociology, Sex, Crime, Religion, and Education* (1904), Hall explained that each stage had its own mandates.[29] Early on, boys and girls adopted separate developmental paths. Girls learned motherly caretaking skills in a "feudal" phase, while in their "primitive" stage, boys needed to pull away more tangibly from adult society. Boys' adolescence was inherently more rife with turmoil, both for the "race" (as Hall termed racial and ethnic differences) and for the individual, before the settling-down phase of adulthood. To repress the natural impulses of any stage of development, Hall warned, would lead to incomplete maturation. By this logic, adults must respect adolescent assertions of autonomy and accept the fundamental value of the child's peer group.

Many youth-oriented professionals of the day concurred. Instead of looking at "boy culture" as troublesome, they began reinterpreting gangs and pranks as healthy evidence of manly growth. As clergyman William Byron Forbush argued in *The Boy Problem* in 1901, "to get together, to work off physical energy, to roam, to contest, to gather treasures and meet new experiences . . . are not in of themselves mischievous desires." The question was how to direct boys' energies in a direction susceptible to adult influence; the solution, for Forbush and many others, was to gather boys into adult-sponsored organizations "just before their own social development tends to become dangerous, at about 10, . . . until the organizing craze is over and the years of adolescence are well past."[30] Instead of fearing boys' rowdy gang life, "boys' work" advocates worked to steer it in character-building directions.

Much of this new literature on adolescence celebrated the adventures of boyhood rather than the supposedly more restrained maturation of girlhood. Because social conventions and domestic responsibilities tended to keep girls, especially older girls, more firmly under adult supervision, girls generally had fewer opportunities to roam or act out than did their brothers.[31] Recapitulation theory indicated not only the greater visibility of male adolescence but also its seemingly more exciting contours. In this sense, Hall's theory was essentially a male narrative of progress and civilization.[32] Like Hall, most youth workers of the period focused primarily on boys and their needs. The number of adults engaged in "boys' work" was as much as twenty times higher than the number doing "girls' work."[33]

Hall's narrative of childhood development was also explicitly racialized. Recapitulation theory assumed that each generation passed on its "racial" improvement to the next, so that only the members of advanced races could attain the highest level of civilization. According to Hall, the mixing of northern Euro-Americans (with their British, German, and Scandinavian racial roots) made for greater stress at adolescence but ultimately led to a superior form of civilization, whereas other racial groups could only advance past the lower level set by their own race. A primitive sojourn into savagery appeared particularly critical to white boys' development, after which point these young men could rise to their rightful stature as heirs to civilization.[34]

This ideological terrain was somewhat more ambiguous than it might first appear. Claims that boys would become better men through virile wilderness retreats exerted a powerful cultural appeal, yet youth workers embraced only a touristic version of primitivism: worth a trip, but within boundaries, as a necessary additive to civilized life. Youth leaders wished to build boys into strong, manly men, but men who would understand chivalry and self-denial as well as their physical impulses. They described the city as rushed, dirty, and industrial and yet also as overly feminizing and domestic. Civilization was the pinnacle of human history, but it had unhealthy softening characteristics. If white manhood was politically and socially dominant in American life, the parameters of maleness, primitivism, and civilization were ambivalent and never fully determined. In this sense, Hall's recapitulation theory, which attempted to ground gender and racial conventions in "nature," can be read not only as a reflection of the gendering of power but also as a symptom of cultural anxiety occasioned by the emergence of new models for manhood and womanhood and by the increasingly visible immigration of non-Northern Europeans.

Like many antimodernists of his day, Hall felt that cities were dan-

gerous to children's development. In the romantic tradition of philosopher Jean-Jacques Rousseau, he imagined that children were "primitives" who should only gradually be introduced to "advanced" civilization. In 1905, shortly after *Adolescence* was published, Hall personally
endorsed the summer camp ideal, telling a group of summer camp directors gathered in Boston that "the child is a wonderful reflex epitome
of the whole macrocosm of the whole universe. . . . ought it not to be a
rule for children to go to the country—country for children, city for
adults. City life in every race is developed much later than country life.
Primitive man is essentially sylvan, not urban but rural. . . . the city is a
forcing house, it is a hothouse, it brings everything to maturity before
its time."[35]

The success of Camp Chocorua and of other late-nineteenth-century
camps serving middle- and upper-class boys situates *Adolescence* in the
context of a larger youth movement. More than two decades before
Adolescence was published, many of its central ideas—antimodern anxiety, the rising social value of childhood, the ideal of developmentally
age-specific play for growing boys, and the sense that rural environments were better for children—inflected the early summer camp movement. The middle- and upper-class urban boys who attended camps like
Chocorua were among this movement's first beneficiaries.

The Earliest Boys' Camps

In 1861, Frederick William Gunn, headmaster of his own private boarding school for boys in Washington, Connecticut, established a two-week
excursion, the Gunnery Camp, during the summer term. That first year,
sixty Gunnery boys hiked four miles to nearby Milford for two weeks
of sleeping in tents, boating, sailing, fishing, marching, and tramping
(that is to say, hiking with camping gear) on Long Island Sound. The
first group of boys was eager to simulate the life of Civil War soldiers.
The end of the war did not dampen their enthusiasm for camping;
through the summer of 1879, Gunnery boys traveled to Lake Wara-
maug, several miles away from the school, for their annual two-week
holiday. The Gunnery Camp was not exactly a children's summer camp.
Although designed for rural recreation and training, it was part of the
school year, and it had the looser structure of an intergenerational family camp. Adult friends of the school, including Frederick's wife, Abi-

Dr. Joseph Trimble Rothrock with 1876 campers at his School of Physical Culture. (Photo originally published courtesy David S. Keiser, in Henry W. Gibson, *Camp Management: A Manual on Organized Camping* [New York: Greenberg, 1923, rev. 1939])

gail Brinsmade Gunn, and other women and men, frequently joined the group. When the Gunns reorganized the school calendar and instituted a long summer vacation, the Gunnery Camp ceased to exist.[36]

Dr. Joseph Trimble Rothrock's North Mountain School of Physical Culture, founded in 1876 at Lake Ganago, near Wilkes-Barre, Pennsylvania, was more properly a summer camp, bringing together boys who were not already living together and specifically for the purpose of health and outdoor recreation. Rothrock, a native Pennsylvanian, Harvard graduate, and Civil War veteran, was thirty-eight years old and already established as a doctor, professor, conservationist, and botanist when he founded the North Mountain School adjacent to a hotel, the North Mountain House. He himself had been unwell as a child and had spent time in the outdoors as part of his recovery. Now he advertised a camp for "weakly boys" at the considerable cost of two hundred dollars for four months. Eighteen boys aged twelve and older from the cities of Philadelphia and Wilkes-Barre attended Rothrock's "School," where they took part in swimming, rowing, walks in the woods, fishing, and shooting expeditions. Several hours each day were spent in instruction of some kind. Rothrock lectured on aspects of natural history, and others among the staff taught the science of storms and clouds, drawing, surveying, and "physical culture" (or the art of exercise). The next summer, Rothrock moved on to new research projects. Other men carried on the camp work through the summer of 1878, at which point the project was abandoned.[37]

In 1880, Reverend George W. Hinckley of West Hartford, Connecticut, founded the first church-sponsored boys' camp. As a young adult in the 1870s, Hinckley had rebelled against religion after he was unable to attend Yale College and Yale Theological Seminary. As he later recalled, he became a self-indulgent young dandy, gambling at the racetrack and smoking cigars, but he was fundamentally unhappy until he finally "surrendered" to God.[38] In the late 1870s, while teaching boys in Kingston, Rhode Island, in preparation for a pastoral career, he encouraged his students to spend time with him in active leisure pursuits. Upon becoming a pastor in 1879, Hinckley determined to organize a camping trip for the sons of his new parish. During the summers of 1880 and 1881, Hinckley brought a number of boys from his parish (and, more unusually, three students from China who were attending a Hartford high school) to camp out on an island near Wakefield, Rhode Island. The camp day combined religious services, recreation periods, swimming, and evening campfires.[39]

Decades later, Hinckley expressed frustration that the camping movement recognized Ernest Balch, and not himself, as the leader of the first organized summer camp. After all, Balch was not the first man of his time to bring a group of boys to camp together for moral and physical betterment. But Balch operated Chocorua for nine years, making it one of the longest-lasting early camps. Over the course of those years, he developed the summer camp idea much further than his predecessors, directly inspiring the leaders of several other early summer camps, and his camp was unusually well documented in its day. Two of Balch's elder siblings published articles about Chocorua in national, middle-class periodicals: Elizabeth in 1886 in *St. Nicholas,* a magazine for children, and Albert in 1893 in *McClure's.*[40]

Balch's camp began somewhat inauspiciously. In the summer of 1881, Balch, his friend and recent Dartmouth alumnus Charles Applegate, and Stephen Balch and "Toby" Blair were putting up their first building when one of the island's owners happened to row by. He was

Ernest Balch (seated, upper right) with campers and one of
his sisters, 1881. (Courtesy Chocorua Island Association and
the descendants of the sister of Ernest Balch)

shocked to find Balch and his crew engaged in construction work. Balch
was surprised to find out that he had been trespassing, since he assumed
the uninhabited island had no owner. He purchased Burnt Island for
forty dollars, renaming it Chocorua Island in honor of the mountain.

Over the course of that first summer, five other Christian boys from
well-to-do Boston and Washington, D.C., families joined the original
group. They swam in the lake, hiked in the mountains, made their own
canoes, shared in communal chores, and participated in the camp choir.
At Chocorua, the Balches related, the boys were busy from morning
until night. Daily activities focused on water sports: swimming, diving, boat work, sailing, and canoeing. The campers also played baseball (at a site on the mainland), sang together, fished, took part in races,

and did carpentry. They wrote letters home, had pillow fights and water fights, listened to stories, performed plays, wrote for the camp newspaper, the "Golden Rod," and attended weekly Sunday services at their own outdoor chapel at the north end of the island. Together they paddled a flatbed scow, named *Icthyosaurus,* around the lake. Special events included a Water Sports day, an annual "Long Walk" away from the camp, and the occasional "liberty day" without oversight. Their days, as Ernest Balch (known as "Mr. Ernest" to his campers) later described them, were a "rushing driving life, full to the brim."[41]

Chocorua was notable for Balch's efforts to foster a democratic culture in which each boy began on relatively equal ground. He instituted a uniform of gray flannel shirts and short trousers for everyday use, with the addition of scarlet stockings and caps for Sunday services. The boys tucked the official camp flower, the goldenrod, into their caps and aspired toward a special camp medal, the silver "C.C." pin, which represented the highest degree of character and achievement.[42] More unusually, Balch ran the camp without servants or a professional cook because he believed that boys must develop self-reliance and learn the value of work. In place of servants he developed an elaborate system of labor. The boys washed their own plates on the sandy beach, and they were members of work "crews" that rotated through kitchen, "police" (or general clean-up around the camp), and dish duties.[43] Each crew was led by a boy "stroke," who in turn was supervised by a member of the "faculty," or adult staff. An adult could issue an order to a stroke, but only the stroke had the right to order his crew to work. To maintain their own coveted positions in the work hierarchy, the strokes had to lead their underlings by example. Discipline emanated from within the camper ranks, not merely from above; as Alfred Balch explained, "It was a cardinal principle in Camp Chocorua that the boys should govern the boys."[44]

Ernest Balch was eager to teach these sons of prosperous families the value of money as well as honest labor. As he noted with amazement, many of his clients had no idea what their fathers did in their offices all day long. In fact, he later recalled, "the boy was apt to answer that his father did no work."[45] In the woods, Chocorua campers learned not only about nature but also about capitalism, market values, buying on credit, hiring themselves out, and paying for the labor of others—skills with applications in the environments from which they came and to which they would soon return. The boys began with equal personal assets: an allowance of twenty-five cents per week each to spend as they wished. Any boy seeking more money had to work as a "slave," a term the boys themselves instituted to describe the practice of selling their labor. Boys made money by washing dishes or clothes for others or by doing construction projects around the camp, and the price their labor commanded varied with the market.

Within a few years, the "contract" system had grown to encompass fairly sophisticated financial and legal traditions. Experienced campers ran contracting companies that bid on large projects such as the construction of new buildings. They subcontracted other campers to help them to complete the labor. New campers with good credit but without capital borrowed money from the camp bank to make large purchases of their own. Occasionally, boys reneged on these promises or were unable to complete contracts for which they had successfully bid; for five cents and the cost of legal counsel, any member of the camp could bring a claim against another to the camp court, where the matter was settled in front of a judge, and sometimes a jury.[46] Chocorua was physically set apart from modern "civilization," but the camp was deeply implicated in its workings, with its own labor codes, structures of law and order, financial institutions, and systems of legal redress.

Over the course of nine years, Chocorua's market economy developed particularly around the culture of canoeing. Before a boy could use a canoe (or what was actually more of a sailing kayak), he first had to prove his skill in swimming and diving, skills that many urban boys of the period did not possess and had to learn at camp. Once he was a "water dog," in camp parlance, he then had to earn the money to build or purchase his own canoe. Canoeing was, for Balch, a means of advancing both the boy's physical development and his work ethic. "It was delightful," Balch recalled, "to overhear a boy of eleven explain to another the mysteries of finance by which you could buy a canoe and have it when you had no money."[47] By the time a camper paddled off on the lake, he had mastered fiscal prudence in addition to technical water skills.

Balch's ideas exerted significant influence over his peers. Two students from the Cambridge Theological Seminary of Massachusetts opened Camp Harvard at Rindge, New Hampshire, in 1885 after corresponding with Balch; two years later, under the leadership of Winthrop Tisdale Talbot of Boston, the camp was moved to Squam Lake and was renamed Camp Asquam.[48] In 1886, Boston educator Edwin DeMerritte founded Camp Algonquin on the same lake.[49] The three camps were informally linked through occasional water-sports competitions and baseball games. These camps influenced others in turn. In 1905, former Chocorua campers Oliver Huntington and Stephen Elliott Balch founded Camp Cloyne on Squam Lake.[50] In 1894, New York City resident and Yale University graduate Edward Wilson spent a summer as a member of the Asquam Camp Council (the origin of the term *counselor*), before founding his own camp, Camp Pasquaney, at Newfound Lake, New Hampshire, the following summer.[51] Dr. Edward Schubmehl also worked at Camp Asquam before opening his own Sherwood Forest Camp in 1903, taking with him many of Talbot's campers and staff.[52] Former Asquam campers founded the charitable Groton School Camp in 1893.[53]

Through these personal and regional networks, many elements of Chocorua culture were incorporated into other boys' camps: special uniforms, the "contract" system, a rotating list of chores, Water Sports Day, and the idea of an extended camping trip away from camp.[54] However, each camp had its own distinctive traditions, lore, jargon, and songs. None of Balch's close peers took up his vision of a camp run entirely without servants. In an attempt to guarantee meals of higher quality, the leaders of other private boys' camps hired professional cooks. Perhaps Balch's idealism served him ill in this regard; although at Chocorua the boys scrubbed their dirty tin plates clean in the sand and then presented them for inspection, in the final camp season of 1889 typhoid fever swept through the camp.[55]

The early camps blended experiential and formal education to differing degrees. At Chocorua, Balch emphasized participatory activity rather than academic lessons. Other camp innovators imagined "schools of science" where campers would undertake formal instruction of some kind. Rothrock, for instance, gave lectures in natural science to his campers. Pasquaney's Ned Wilson bristled if anyone called his camp a "school," but he lectured to the campers based on notes he had taken while an undergraduate at Yale.[56] Many private boys' camp leaders offered tutoring, although they generally limited such work to an hour or so each day.

By the turn of the century, camp leaders began increasingly to draw a distinction between experiential and school-based learning. Educator C. Hanford Henderson, when he founded Camp Marienfeld on the Upper Delaware River in 1896, planned a "study camp" that would combine a formal curriculum with outdoor recreation. Over time, he later wrote, he realized what a "novel and magnificent educational opportunity" camps represented and shifted the emphasis to nature expeditions.[57] Many other private camp leaders retained tutoring as an optional part of the curriculum but gave it less weight over time. Parents and campers may have encouraged the shift. Edward Schubmehl successfully recruited many of the Asquam campers to his own Camp Sherwood Forest in the wake of Talbot's decision to lecture more often to the boys.[58]

Although the camping movement was open to varied interpretations, the pioneering summer camp leaders shared much in common. Educated, native-born, and often quite young, the men who founded the first camps were idealists committed to countering the seeming enfeeblement, depletion, and degeneration of middle- and upper-class American boys.[59] Their camps' success rested on their own commanding personalities. Teddy Jackson, an 1895 Pasquaney camper, recalled of the man they called "Mr. Ned" that "to say he was beloved is not enough—the fact is that we worshipped him, each and every one of us."[60] Ironically, many of these private camps were also commercial failures. Dr. Rothrock's North Mountain School of Physical Culture barely broke even despite the substantial fee.[61] Talbot was so deeply in debt by 1907 that he was forced to shut down Camp Asquam.[62] Ernest Balch charged $175 for the summer season in the mid-1880s, but despite the relatively high fee and his own ingenious efforts to teach his campers about the capitalist marketplace, he had amassed a debt of eight thousand dollars by the time he closed Chocorua after the 1889 season.[63]

These early leaders were driven by other, more personal rewards: the opportunity to do work of substance on their own terms, to inspire loyalty and affection, and to create communities of lasting value to their members. Camp Pasquaney founder Ned Wilson, for instance, spent his early adulthood plagued by self-doubt, physical fatigue, and bouts of depression. He drifted for years after graduating from Yale in 1885. After beginning medical studies at Columbia University, he decided not to pursue the profession. He then became a private tutor to boys and took up creative writing. "Still sick at heart and disgusted with myself and everything else, and I wish I were dead," he wrote in his diary in 1887. "I shall never amount to anything. I am a total failure in every way."[64] Perhaps his concern that elite boys were idly wasting their summers was exacerbated by his sense that he too had been frittering away his own time.[65] In any event, when he heard about Camp Asquam, he had the sudden conviction that he too should start up his own camp. "My very soul cried out," he wrote; "I felt this must be a call."[66]

The first camp directors evidently took enormous satisfaction from the experience of leading boys in the woods, and away from idleness and dissipation. One can only speculate about the affective lives of Ernest Balch and Ned Wilson, men who devoted themselves to boys' work while remaining bachelors. They were among a significant minority of late-nineteenth-century adults who remained unwed. What is clear is that for these men the opportunity to mentor boys beyond the confines of the traditional nuclear family represented an important source of intimacy and self-esteem.[67]

Given their own search for meaning, it is no surprise that many of the first camp leaders went on to other, similarly idealistic enterprises. Rothrock became a prominent Pennsylvania forest conservationist for whom a state park was later named. Hinckley moved to Bangor, Maine, to organize Sunday schools, continued to lead boys' camping expeditions, and in 1899 founded Good Will Farm, a year-round home for orphans and other needy boys.[68] Winthrop Talbot eventually moved to New York City and took up the problem of immigrant illiteracy.[69] Balch pursued a range of projects. He never returned to Dartmouth, and after his first summer at Chocorua he supported himself in the winter months by tutoring boys. He closed Chocorua for good after the 1889 season. Not only was he in debt, but his beloved sister Emily, who had helped him to recruit campers and had served as the camp's choir director, died after the 1889 season. Balch sold Chocorua Island to a few former campers.[70] He then spent many years in Mexico and Venezuela working in the cordage industry, in real estate, and in oil speculation. Driven out of Mexico in 1914 by regime change, he moved back to the Northeast and returned to his earlier interest in boys' work: he tried to develop the idea of winter camps, he wrote *Amateur Circus Life* (1916) for youth leaders, and he mentored and provided financial support to a number of impoverished boys.[71] In his latter years he lived in squalor in Brooklyn, New York, as a near recluse. He died in 1938, survived by his brother Stephen, Chocorua's first camper, and was buried in the Balch family plot at a Holderness church cemetery a few miles from the camp he had founded. By then, the movement he had helped to found recognized him as an early leader, and the *New York Times* eulogized him as a "pioneer in developing camps."[72]

In the late nineteenth century, when private camps were few and far between, it was still possible for an individual to imagine that he was inventing the summer camp idea. Henderson later claimed that when he founded Marienfeld in 1896, he had not heard of any other camp; in his effort to keep his students from the "boyish tragedy" of "slipping backward" during the summer vacation, he "fancied [himself] a veritable pioneer."[73] Most Americans still knew nothing about this experimental vacation movement, and perhaps fewer than a thousand boys nationally attended private camps each summer. But Henderson, who moved his camp to Chesham, New Hampshire, in 1898, was typical of the prevailing mold. These muscular Christians led camps by the force of their own enthusiastic personalities. Suspicious of mothers' influence (what Henderson in 1916 called "soft effeminate home life"), dissatisfied with boys' summer opportunities, and ambitious to try out new ideas, they found in rural settings a remarkable degree of freedom to try to socialize boys as they saw fit.[74]

Organizational Summer Camps

During the last two decades of the nineteenth century, perhaps twenty-five private camps were founded, the great majority of these in New Hampshire, Maine, New York, Connecticut, and Vermont, with a few in Pennsylvania and the South.[75] As late as the 1910s, when hundreds of private camps were in operation, fully 90 percent were located in the Northeast.[76] Most were situated in relatively remote locations such as northern New England and the Adirondack Mountains of New York, within a day's journey of such large cities as New York and Boston. The journey to camp was expensive and time-consuming, but this was proof of their exclusivity and remove from urban life.

The boys' camp founded by the Natural History Society of Worcester, Massachusetts, on nearby Lake Quinsigamond in 1885 was a different kind of enterprise. Whereas most private camps were founded by individuals as stand-alone projects, the Natural History Society Camp represented the extension into camping of a group already engaged in other projects. Whereas private camps were private fiefdoms, organizational camps tended to be collaboratively run, inasmuch as their directors often rotated in and out of the camp leadership. Private camps often brought boys together for a single, eight- or ten-week period of moral and physical improvement, whereas many organizational camps offered

shorter, one- or two-week sessions. Whereas private camps promised social and geographical exclusivity, organizational camps tended to offer
relative convenience and inclusivity. The Natural History Society's camp
was so close to Worcester that the campers could walk from home to
the Lake Quinsigamond campsite, and at camp they could hear the
distant sound of city bells. With the help of Worcester benefactors, this
camp was planned to be affordable to middle-class families.[77] Still, private and organizational camps overlapped considerably in intent. Their
leaders shared the concern, as the Worcester society expressed it in the
camp's 1892 brochure, "that the months of July and August are largely
a period of idle or of undirected and purpseless [*sic*] activity on the part
of numbers of boys." Their activities were also fundamentally the same;
the Worcester boys took optional instruction in botany, ornithology, and
astronomy, as well as swimming, rowing, carpentry, and military drill.[78]

By the turn of the twentieth century, hundreds of organizational
camps served many thousands of boys, far more than the number who
attended private camps.[79] As the idea that adolescent boys required
rugged peer-group experience came into vogue, organizations that conducted "boys' work" began to see camps as extensions of their year-
round efforts to mold better boys. These camps represented a middle-
class and occasionally working-class alternative to elite private camps.
By one estimate, the average private camp of 1900 charged about $150
for a ten-week season.[80] YMCA camps of the same period charged between $3.50 and $5.25 per week. Such a fee would have represented a
considerable sum at a time when the average unskilled worker's annual
wage in the northern states was $460 per year, but it was relatively ac-
cessible to middle-class families, whose average annual income was over
$1,500.[81] By keeping their prices lower, YMCAs were able to serve (and
thus, their leaders hoped, to potentially influence) many more boys.[82]

Sumner Francis Dudley, founder of one of the first American YMCA
summer camps in 1885, was typical of the first generation of organizational camp leaders. Born in 1854 in Worcester, Massachusetts, he became active in his local YMCA at the age of thirteen. By the mid-1880s
he was living in New Jersey, working for the Dudley family's surgical
supply company, and volunteering at the South Orange, New Jersey,
YMCA, where he was eager to expand the organization's offerings to
adolescent boys. In 1885, YMCA activist George Sanford asked Dudley
to lead a group of seven boys, all but one from the Newburgh, New
York, YMCA, on an eight-day excursion to nearby Orange Lake.[83] Sim-

Sumner Dudley and campers, 1894. (Courtesy Camp Dudley)

ilar camp excursions had already been ventured by YMCA leaders in Detroit, Michigan, in 1882, and Richmond, Virginia, in 1883.[84]

Dudley supplied Camp Bald Head (a facetious reference to the fact that the boys had their hair shorn very short before they left for camp) with little more than a borrowed tent and a rented boat. Despite the mosquitoes and the rocky ground on which the boys slept, the enterprise was an immediate success, inspiring Dudley to write,

> I have just returned from eight days in camp, conscious of having one of the most delightful and profitable times of my life. . . . Weather: delightful, just enough rain to add variety; fishing—very moderate; swimming—three times a day; health—good; accidents—none; appetites—ravenous; hearty, manly, fun—any quantity; good nature—largely developed.[85]

Every evening, Dudley, Sanford, and the boys rowed out onto the lake at sunset for evening prayers, which one 1885 Dudley camper later recalled as "earnest" and deeply meaningful: "the confessions and resolutions were so honestly made, a word for Christ was spoken from some lips for the first time and thanks be to God, those lips are still speaking for him."[86]

The muscular Christians who founded the first YMCA camps valued physical improvement and picturesque surroundings as a means to a nobler end. Their ultimate goal was the religious awakening of boys and their "conversion" to Christ.[87] This blend of outdoor recreation and Bible study attracted twenty-three boys during its second year, when Dudley moved the group to Lake Wawayanda, New Jersey, and eighty-three boys by 1891, the year the camp moved to Lake Champlain. By then, so many boys wished to attend what had become known as the Boys Camp Society, or BCS, that prospective campers had to pay fifteen cents for the application packet, prove their knowledge of the Bible, and promise to study Bible passages.[88] Around the evening campfire, in the intimacy of their closed circle, YMCA leaders encouraged boys to make stronger religious commitments. As Henry Gibson, then-director of the state Massachusetts and Rhode Island YMCA camps, boasted in 1906, "Over fifty boys last season made the decision to accept Jesus Christ as their Saviour and Friend. . . . Hundreds of boys date the beginning of their religious life to the camps."[89]

Camp Dudley's early success reflected its founder's devotion to boys. Dudley paid all his camp's expenses in its early years. In 1887 he gave up his business to devote himself full-time to YMCA work. When he died in 1897, at the age of forty-three, he left his camp equipment to the New York State YMCA, which promptly renamed the camp after him.[90] In his desk was found evidence of correspondence with over two hundred boys.[91] In later years, YMCA camps' success reflected the growing importance of "boys' work" for the organization. By the turn of the twentieth century, camps were a staple of YMCA outreach efforts, and new camps were being founded every year. In 1901, there were 167 YMCA camps nationwide, most clustered near northeastern cities. Four years later, there were 300 such camps.[92]

The expansion of youth work inspired the creation of new organizations focused exclusively on adolescent and preadolescent boys. Of these, Ernest Thompson Seton's Woodcraft Indians and Daniel Beard's Sons of Daniel Boone were the most influential, offering complementary but competing variants on the theme of American boyhood adventure. The Woodcraft Indians originated in 1901, when Seton, attempting to manage the problem of young trespassers on his Connecticut estate, led the boys in Indian stories and camping out. Seton, already a writer and naturalist, documented the group's activities in the *Ladies' Home Journal* in 1902. He then further popularized "woodcraft," the appreciation and study of nature, in his autobiographical *Two Little Savages,* published the next year.[93] Seton's Woodcraft Indians, later the Woodcraft League, situated woodcraft within Native American traditions. His was a veritable smorgasbord of tribal legends, games, songs, dances, crafts, and religious rituals from across North America. Seton's versions of Native American rituals such as evening Council Fires and the Omaha Tribal Greeting soon circulated widely at camps. For Seton, the "Red Man" was a perfect patriotic symbol of the rugged outdoors, and Native American cultures represented an appealing respite from modernity's time constraints, its urban mixings, and its displacements of artisanal skill and tradition. So-called primitive life was not a savage precursor to civilization, as G. Stanley Hall would have it, but a worthwhile end in and of itself.[94]

Beard's Sons of Daniel Boone, founded in 1905, articulated a contrasting American iconography, that of the frontier pioneers who had skillfully supplanted Native American peoples. In Beard's organization, boys took on the roles of Daniel Boone, Davy Crockett, and Kit Carson. Beard, like Seton, aimed to bring boys' "natural" instinct for rugged, primitive adventure under adult guidance. However, the two men jockeyed for professional and symbolic prestige. The Indian, in harmony with nature, and the colonist, the ingenious successor on the land, embodied very different perspectives on the meaning of American history. Seton's antimodernism, along with his distrust of modern industrial capitalism, stood in opposition to Beard's optimistic depiction of modern technologies as the logical extension of the pioneer past. If the Woodcraft Indians achieved a greater success, this was due only in part to Seton's charisma and organizational skills. The antimodernism that Seton expressed, and his insistence on a fundamental rupture between the frontier past and the modern present, resonated more deeply with the anxieties of the age.[95]

Both Seton and Beard were active in summer camp circles. Seton visited many camps to teach woodcraft, among them Camp Dudley.[96] Dan Beard also traveled the summer camp circuit before founding his own camps: first a woodcraft camp for boys in Culver, Indiana, beginning in 1911, and then the Dan Beard School in Hawley, Pennsylvania, which he established in 1915.[97] Many American boys knew these men by reputation and were enthusiastic to meet them. As one of Beard's former campers enthused in 1915, "I got your postal a week or two ago and felt so good to have a postal from 'Dan Beard' whom everybody knows all over the world."[98]

In the 1910s, many of Seton's and Beard's ideas were subsumed in a new organization, the Boy Scouts, which reflected their shared interest in primitive adventure. Both men were initially active in the Boy Scout leadership.[99] Like the YMCA movement, Boy Scouting began in England. British General Robert S. S. Baden-Powell (known popularly as B-P) had served for years in colonial South Africa. He gained renown at the turn of the century during the Boer War, for his successful defense of the town of Mafeking. In 1899, B-P wrote up the first version of "Aids to Scouting," a handbook explaining how to train soldiers in the field.[100] B-P later brought this colonial experience to bear on an experimental boys' camp held on an island off the Dorset coast in 1907. Here, he tried out his "Scouting" material with a group of twenty-one boys from thirteen to sixteen years of age of varied socioeconomic backgrounds. B-P divided the boys into four patrols named for animals; lectured on British patriotism, chivalry, and empire; told stories of his adventurous past; and taught a Zulu marching chant. To add to the colonial drama, B-P flew a Union Jack riddled with Boer bullets that he had saved from his Mafeking days, and the boys woke each morning to the sound of their leader's kudu horn, a spoil of an earlier campaign.[101] In Britain, as in the United States, male adventure entailed a primitive rite of passage from the colonial past. Although scouting appealed to boys' enthusiasm for the rugged outdoors, it aimed to tame them by teaching patriotism, woodcraft skills, and obedience to authority.[102]

B-P's *Scouting for Boys* (1908), which borrowed heavily from Seton's Woodcraft program and manuals, met with immediate success, paving the way for the rapid appearance of a transatlantic movement.[103] By 1910, the first American troops were promising, in the American version of the Scout pledge, to remain "physically strong, mentally awake, and morally straight." That same summer, a few of them attended camps. Ernest Thompson Seton and YMCA leader William Murray ran one experimental Boy Scout camp at Silver Bay, New York, where under Seton's Woodcraft influence, the boys lived in tepees, did their

Bugler at Hunter's Island Boy Scout Camp, Bronx, New York, circa 1911–15. (Courtesy Ten Mile River Scout Museum)

own cooking, and had a council fire at night.[104] Daniel Beard made a brief appearance there as well.[105] Within a year, camps for Boy Scouts from across the cities and suburbs of the Northeast and Midwest were founded, many of them less expensive than YMCA camps.[106] These camps attracted many boys to the Boy Scout movement.[107] By 1920, almost 45 percent of all Boy Scouts, or over 160,000 boys, spent at least a week at camp in the summertime.[108]

Like their private camp counterparts, most organizational camp leaders were idealists with powerful personalities. George Peck, who attended Dudley's 1885 camp and took on the camp's directorship after his mentor's death, reflected that Dudley was the "man, who, next to my parents, was the dearest friend I had in the world."[109] But whereas private camps served only a small number of boys, organizational camps made the camp movement far more affordable, mainstream, and national. Parents were drawn to the idea of supervised rural activities and to the promise of useful learning, patriotism, and daily Bible study. Their sons, meanwhile, actively sought out organizations that offered outdoor adventure. Authentically intergenerational in their appeal, boys' summer camps were becoming an American phenomenon.

Girls' Camps

In the summer of 1902, high school teacher Laura Mattoon brought eight girls, students of hers at New York City's private Veltin School, to camp out on Lake Wentworth, in New Hampshire.[110] When Mattoon, a Wellesley College graduate and avid weekend camper, founded Camp Kehonka, hers was one of only a handful of girls' camps nationwide.[111] The girls, or "Kehonka geese" as they playfully called themselves, dressed in bifurcated bloomers instead of long skirts. They slept in tents with earth floors, built their own beds out of tree-trunk frames, filled their mattresses with fir balsam, swam in the lake, and hiked through the area.[112] Aside from the bloomers, the Kehonka girls lived much like boys at camp.

To live like boys was adventurous in itself, an implicit rebuke to those male youth leaders who focused on the perils of adolescent boyhood and who generally did not conceive of girls' adolescence as equally exploratory.[113] From the perspective of child-study experts such as G. Stanley Hall, domesticity advanced adolescent girls' development, but it threatened that of boys. And although women played important supportive roles at some early boys' camps, as did Emily Balch at Camp Chocorua, the men who led early boys' camps generally aimed to provide a masculine counterpoint to feminine influence in the home. In 1914, C. Hanford Henderson of Camp Marienfeld reflected that "the best women are always missed, and any company is the poorer for their absence. And yet a summer camp is, I think, better off without them, for the life is so much simpler and freer."[114] Still, the idea that girls might camp separately did find favor with some muscular Christians, since girls would grow up to become, as Theodore Roosevelt proposed in 1899, "the wise and fearless mother[s] of many healthy children."[115] To do so, they themselves had to be healthy.

Camp Kehonka camper, 1920s. (Collection of author)

The new girls' camp directors, most of whom were educated, middle-class women, deployed traditional maternalist ideologies, representing themselves as the nurturing leaders of children, but they also saw themselves as "New Women" who could speak to such traditionally male domains as politics, the professions, and higher education.[116] If the twentieth century was to be, as one influential book termed it, the "century of the child," these women expected to play important roles in advancing children's welfare.[117]

At the turn of the century, female teachers with camping experience were unusual but not exceptional. Mattoon was like many of her college-educated female peers in remaining unmarried, devoting herself to an exciting professional life as a science teacher, and trying out new outdoor activities. She was no great athlete. In fact, according to one of her early counselors, she never learned to swim.[118] But she found in camping a venue for her aspirations, becoming one of the most important early leaders of the national camping movement. Her camp (which moved to Lake Winnipesaukee in 1906) would become nationally known.

Exceptionally, the first two private camps in New York State offered programs for girls soon after they were founded in the early 1890s.[119] Another camp, the French Recreation Class for Girls, was founded by

1896. Few others followed suit. At the turn of the century, when the YMCA was expanding its camping programs for boys, the leaders of the Young Women's Christian Association (YWCA) did not embark on similar efforts for adolescent girls, although they did found a camp in 1898 at Altamont, New York, for working adolescent girls and young women of limited means. In 1903, when Winthrop Talbot of Camp Asquam organized a large Camp Conference in Boston, one hundred men attended. Only two women joined them, one of whom, Isabel Barrows, ran a family (or intergenerational) camp, not a girls' camp. The other woman, Elizabeth Ford Holt of Cambridge, Massachusetts, had founded Camp Redcroft for girls in 1900 on Newfound Lake, New Hampshire, and was in the process of launching Camp Mowglis, a camp for preadolescent boys, nearby.[120] As the report that came out of the camp conference, entitled "How to Help Boys," suggested, girls' camps were still quite marginal to the larger camping enterprise.

Although muscular Christians often characterized women and girls as the "weaker sex," girls' camp directors could use this line of thought to argue that girls were in particular need of camping excursions. In 1903, speaking to her peers in Boston, Holt explained that "it seemed to me that health was the greatest blessing our girls can enjoy and if athletic sports are good for boys, I did not see why they should not be for girls. Certainly we have a great many pale girls in our schools, and have a great many break down from nervous prostration and exhaustion."[121] Other early leaders of girls' camps tacked between traditional and emergent notions of femininity. As the brochure for Peekskill, New York's Camp Idlewood enthused in 1904, "We aim to develop superb womanhood, to give to girls a perfect body, complete symmetrical physical development, a strong physical organism, to make their bodies fitting temples for their souls."[122]

At the turn of the twentieth century, new private camps for girls celebrated the emergence of a more adventurous (but still protected) female adolescence: in New Hampshire, Camp Pinelands (1902), the Pasquaney Nature Club (also known as Mrs. Hassan's Camp, 1904), and the Kareless Klub (1904); in Maine, the Wyonegonic Camps (1902); in Vermont, Camp Barnard (1903) and Camp Aloha (1905); and in Massachusetts, Camp Quanset (1904).[123] By the 1910s, increasing numbers of college-educated women (sometimes called "directresses") and a few men and married couples were opening camps for girls similar to those that boys had enjoyed for two decades. These camps met with an enthusiastic response. By one estimate, about one hundred were in operation by 1915.[124] By another estimate, new camps for girls were actually established at a higher rate than those for boys in the 1914–16 period.[125] Camp Chinqueka, a new private girls' camp in Bantam Lake, Connecticut, could fairly proclaim in 1915 that "camp life for girls is no longer an experiment."[126]

As girls gained increased access to "the primitive life," they did so on slightly different terms than their brothers did. Whereas the early boys' camps expressed the necessity, however ambivalent in practice, of a rustic removal from civilization, the early girls' private camps promised traditional feminine gentility as well as female physicality. The 1896 brochure for the French Recreation Class for Girls promised that under the tutelage of Mademoiselle Debray-Longchamp, the campers would participate in outdoor exercise, walking and rowing (always "suitably accompanied"), daily French study, optional classes in botany and sketching, and special college-preparatory courses. The girls would breathe invigorating outdoor air but sleep in comfortably furnished camp buildings.[127] The 1904 Camp Idlewood brochure promised somewhat more ambivalently that girls could choose to live in an eleven-room cottage or a tent.[128] At a time when many boys camped in wooden buildings, the Camp Kehonka tents were particularly rugged in this regard.

In the 1910s, the idea that girls were entitled to adventurous recreation found further expression in new girls' youth groups. Only a few years after the American Boy Scout movement was inaugurated, two similar organizations for girls, the Camp Fire Girls (1911) and the Girl Scouts (1912), followed suit, each of them broadening girls' camping opportunities. The Camp Fire Girls began as an extension of Dr. Luther Gulick and his wife Charlotte Gulick's interest in recreation and youth. Luther Gulick had made his mark in physical education and playground reform, as the first director of physical education in the New York City public school system; the editor of the journal *American Physical Education Review*; co-founder of the Public Schools Athletic League that served New York City boys; first president of the Playground Association; and, by the 1910s, director of Child Hygiene for the Russell Sage Foundation. Charlotte Gulick had studied briefly under G. Stanley Hall.

In 1910, William Chancy Langdon put together the first Camp Fire Girls group while organizing a pageant to celebrate the 150th anniver sary of the town of Thetford, Vermont. He brought in a troop of local Boy Scouts to help with some scenes, and then with Luther Gulick's help he founded a group for local girls who wished to participate in the pageant but who had no youth group of their own.[129] Luther Gulick then took the idea of a girls' group to friends, among them G. Stanley Hall, Ernest Thompson Seton, and James West, executive secretary of the Boy Scouts—youth activists who had made their mark in "boys' work" and most of whom lived in and around New York City. The Camp Fire Girls program, which like most similar programs for boys was pitched primarily to middle-class children, met with an enthusiastic response across the nation. By December 1913, it boasted an estimated sixty thousand members, thousands of whom began to attend affordable local camps.[130]

The Gulicks were part of a family active in girls' camps. Charlotte Gulick's sister-in-law Harriet Farnsworth Gulick and Harriet's husband, Edward Leeds Gulick, founded Camp Aloha in Fairlee, Vermont, in 1905. Three years later, Harriet's brother Charles Farnsworth and his wife, Ellen, launched the Hanoum Camps at Thetford, Vermont. These pioneering Upper Connecticut Valley camps formed the nucleus of an important regional center of early elite girls' camps. From 1888, Luther and Charlotte vacationed near New London, Connecticut, along the Thames River with as many as seventy-five others, camping in family groups. Occasionally, the Gulick daughters brought along a few paying friends.[131] In 1910, Luther and Charlotte Gulick founded their own girls' summer camp in Raymond, Maine, with their older daughters becoming counselors. Charlotte took primary responsibility for Camp WoHeLo, where the couple developed the "Work, Health and Love" (or "Wo-He-Lo") philosophy that would guide the Camp Fire Girls.

Although the Camp Fire program furthered the notion that outdoor adventure benefited girls, it did not represent a radical shift in gender expectations. It explicitly tied participation in outdoor life to older ideologies of maternal devotion and domestic inclination, justifying female vigor as a means to enrich childbearing and nurturing capabilities, and camping as a means to buttress traditional female skills. Luther Gulick acknowledged that a few men and women were adapted to untraditional gender pursuits. But generally, he proclaimed in 1911, "we hate manly women and womanly men. . . . The bearing and rearing of children has always been the first duty of most women, and that must always continue to be. This involves service, constant service, self-forget-fulness and always service."[132] The organization aimed to romanticize women's traditional labor through song, pageantry, and dance, not to supplant the domestic sphere. The fire of the Camp Fire Girls, Gulick pronounced, was not wild and untamed; it was symbolic of the domestic hearth. The program's focus on Indian ritual and costuming had a similarly gendered spin. By making their own dresses, and decorating them with individualized Indian-style insignia, girls could simultaneously put on primitive personae, explore the creativity of dressmaking, and learn useful sewing skills. In other words, the Gulicks encouraged girls to use Indian cultural elements so as to become gracefully domestic in the modern world, not to explore the possibilities of "savagery."

The Girl Scouts, founded in 1912 by Juliette Gordon Low, also conjoined traditional domestic skills and adventurous physical activity. In 1911, Low was living in England when she met Sir Robert Baden-Powell, whose sister Agnes had recently started a parallel British group for girls, the Girl Guides. Low helped to establish several Girl Guide troops, and upon her return to Savannah, Georgia, she founded the first American troop with eighteen girls in 1912. The following year she changed the name of the organization to Girl Scouts. In the early years Low, like Hinckley and Dudley before her, funded her innovative group herself. By 1920, there were about fifty thousand members nationwide, many of them attracted to the organization's widely publicized national service during the First World War. By the 1930s, the Girl Scout membership exceeded that of the Camp Fire Girls.[133]

The gender politics of the Girl Scouts were equivocal. The Girl Scouts' khaki uniforms and their adoption of military drill threatened the Boy Scouts' leader, James West, who considered the Camp Fire Girls a more appropriately gendered counterpart. West railed particularly against the Girl Scouts' use of the term "scout," fearing that if the term became feminized it would become unsuitable for boys' adventure. The Girl Scouts, however, was not an explicitly feminist organization. When the issue of suffrage was being debated nationally in the 1910s, Low never took a public stand. Many of the girls' badges, unlike those for boys, rewarded domestic labor like nursing and laundry.[134] The Girl Scouts' war work and their adoption of military-style uniforms proclaimed that girls, along with women, occupied important public roles, but their actual work usually traded on traditionally gendered skills such as knitting for soldiers overseas. A typical 1917 Girl Scout manual warned girls against physically overexerting themselves through gender-inappropriate sports such as high jumping, distance running, and basketball, and it asserted that girls, more than boys, needed to learn teamwork.[135]

Still, Girl Scout camps exemplified new possibilities for women and girls in outdoor recreation and, more generally, as active players in American life. In 1912, the first Savannah Girl Scout troop left on a camping vacation decorously dressed in skirts. Once out of the public eye, they stripped down to long bloomers, swam, cooked for themselves along the Savannah River, and slept on the sand. During the First World War, Girl Scout campers, much like their male counterparts, slept in tents and spent their days engaged in practicing drill formations, learning first aid, signaling, swimming, knot-tying, and rowing on the lake.[136] In 1917, the Girl Scout magazine, the *Rally*, critiqued gender conventions that stifled female energy and enthusiasm: "the old-time education of girls kept them too much under cover, too much confined to books, too little free to engage in sports that might spoil their clothes. All healthy, normal girls have resented this violently, and endured the title of 'tomboy,' if only they could have the chance of the tomboy's free movements and fresh air." Representing the gendering of adventure as constructed, not biological, the *Rally* posited that "primitive women knew all about [outdoor living] quite as well as primitive men."[137] Through camps, the organization deployed American antimodern nostalgia to very modern ends.

Girls' camps extended girls' worlds without explicitly challenging the ideal of separate socialization. Boys and girls at neighboring camps met with, but generally did not test themselves directly against, one another. On one unusual occasion in 1916, a group of Kehonka girls traveled to Camp Winnipesaukee, a neighboring boys' camp, to watch the boys play baseball against the boys of Hill Camp. When the Hill Camp boys failed to show up, the Kehonka girls played two innings against the Winnipesaukee boys. The game was called off when the girls were leading by a score of twelve to five (whether for lack of time or because the girls were so superior to the boys is unknown).[138] Camps like Kehonka gave girls opportunities to acquire the same athletic skills as their brothers, helping to create a shared leisure culture across gender lines and to challenge the assumptions undergirding the turn-of-the-century child-study movement.

Camps for Working-Class Children

In the late nineteenth century, urban reformers began to develop a range of vacation ideas for working-class children. As reformers noted, few of these families had the means to flee the heat, the health risks attendant to their overcrowded, ill-ventilated homes, or the bustle of city life. Children (and particularly boys, who had more freedom than their sisters) appeared particularly vulnerable inasmuch as they played and sometimes worked on city stoops and streets without adult supervision and spent their spare pennies in commercial venues designed primarily for adults.[139]

Initially, reformers focused less on age-specific children's recreation than on simply removing urban children from city streets. Some of the first charitable ventures included holidays at urban beaches, private homes, farms, and vacant country estates donated by their wealthy patrons. These holidays often served the so-called worthy poor (those who could not be expected to provide for themselves, like women, children, and the sick) in intergenerational settings, where mothers were expected to help watch over their children. In some cases, children and adult visitors unknown to one another were sent out to live together with rural families under nominal agency supervision.[140]

Like private camps, many of these early programs were founded by individuals unhappy about urban children's summer opportunities. In 1877, for instance, Reverend Willard Parsons began organizing rural vacations for impoverished urban children. Parsons had recently moved from a working-class parish on the Lower East Side of Manhattan, at that time the most populous and immigrant-filled neighborhood in the city, to Sherman, Pennsylvania, a relatively rural parish. In New York, he had been struck by the paucity of healthful leisure opportunities during the summer months. Once in Sherman, he convinced members of the community to become volunteer hosts to children from his old parish. Sixty children enjoyed a summer vacation that year, and within a few years the *New York Herald Tribune* was raising funds and public awareness on behalf of the program. Other newspapers followed suit with their own Fresh Air programs.

When New York City businessman William George first read about Fresh Air work in 1890, he had already been exploring the city's so-called slum districts, befriending the boys and a few of the girls he met there and organizing boys' clubs and baseball teams. He resolved to take a group of forty boys and ten girls away on a holiday near his western New York hometown. It is a measure of public enthusiasm for Fresh Air projects that his rural neighbors in Freeville, New York, willingly housed the girls and provided gifts and entertainment to the boys camping nearby. It is also striking that many New York City parents were so eager to secure rural vacations for their children that they allowed their children to participate in an experiment with a man most of them hardly could have known. The project was a success, and within two years George's camp served almost five hundred campers.

Whereas Ernest Balch sought to toughen the elite, George aspired to uplift the poor. George worried, as he later reflected, that his campers "were reckoning their good time according to the amount of clothing and general produce that they might be able to take back to the city upon their return. I felt certain that they were claiming charity as a right."[141] So from 1894 onward, he began to put into place an elaborate system of camp governance designed to instill more virtuous behavior. He made campers "pay" for their own food and shelter by laboring around the camp, and he worked to develop a village system with its own legislative, executive, and judiciary branches: "Our Glorious Republic in miniature—a Junior Republic."[142] Like Balch, George envisioned a self-sufficient community in which children would learn to labor for their pleasure and in which camp life would teach virtuous American citizenship.

The Junior Republic ideal emerged in the context of a new cultural movement: Progressive reform.[143] Progressives of the late nineteenth and early twentieth centuries took a variety of sometimes contradictory approaches to effecting change. Broadly speaking, they turned both to government solutions and private philanthropy to respond to social problems specific to modernity. Most lived in and focused their attention on urban areas. They advocated for better public health programs and better housing for the urban poor. They worked to integrate and assist new immigrants. In a reflection of many reformers' nativist fears of native-born "race suicide," they also sought to ensure that these new arrivals would "Americanize," that is, accommodate to middle-class American values.

Frequently, reformers' efforts took the form of advocacy on behalf of children: the pursuit of laws and organizations to govern the quality of food and drugs, the reduction or termination of children's labor, the improvement of young people's access to education, and the conditions of children's play. Some reformers subscribed to the eugenic idea that certain ethnic and racial groups were more advanced than others. However, reformers also believed that children's character was not altogether inherent but could be developed, for good or for harm, through life experiences and appropriate adult interventions. As Ernest Thompson Seton explained in 1910, "Boys have their badness thrust upon them. They are made bad by evil surroundings during the formative period between school and manhood; between twelve and twenty years of age."[144] Children's physical and social environments were thus of enormous import.

Progressivism is best known as a movement of the first two decades of the twentieth century. As earlier Fresh Air work suggests, similar efforts were under way decades earlier. One of the most successful Progressive ideas was the settlement-house movement, modeled on Toynbee Hall, established in 1884 in London's impoverished East End as a residential space of learning and reform work. In 1886, American philosopher and Ethical Culture Society leader Stanton Coit opened the first American settlement, Neighborhood Guild (later, University Settlement) on New York's immigrant Lower East Side. By the end of the century, settlement houses in major American cities offered an array of services to underprivileged city residents, including health clinics, vocational training, English-language study, children's playgrounds, legal clinics, libraries, public baths, and evening entertainments.

Progressives had a particular interest in "uplifting" urban working-class and immigrant communities through leisure. In addition to Fresh Air programs, by the mid-1890s reformers had turned to the establishment of adult-supervised playgrounds to teach immigrant children American games and American values. Team sports, for instance, were imagined to lessen interethnic tensions and reinforce "appropriate" group skills. Children were also expected to function as emissaries of American culture, bringing new values home to their less pliant parents. In 1906, many of these reform efforts coalesced in the establishment of a national organization, the Playground Association of America, later the National Recreation Association.

At the turn of the twentieth century, the leaders of established charitable organizations and settlement houses began to found summer camps as extensions of their urban work and as opportunities to more intensively socialize young people. As Lillian Wald, one of the founders of the Henry Street Settlement on the Lower East Side of Manhattan, explained in 1915, "the possibility of giving direction at critical periods of character-formation, particularly during adolescence, and of discovering clews to deep-lying causes of disturbance, makes the country life a valuable extension of the organized social work of the settlement."[145] Like most camps of the period, the first camps specifically for working-class children served boys, a reflection of reformers' concern that working-class boys represented a greater threat to the social order and their belief that boys had a particular need for outdoor adventure. Camps for girls followed, especially from the 1910s onward, as girls' camps became more common.

As at private camps, campers at charitable and low-cost camps hiked, learned to play team sports and to swim, and helped to cook and clean up. However, these camps differed in several important respects. The accommodations and equipment at charitable camps were often more basic. Many private campers arrived with some experience of rural resorts, but few Hale House or Groton School campers had so much as taken a train outside the city. If wealthy families could choose among camps, poorer ones could not count on a camp vacation. The ideological underpinnings of these two kinds of camps were also somewhat different. Whereas men like Balch focused on the threats of idleness and overcivilization to the sons of the wealthy, urban reformers feared that urban poverty would lead working-class boys to delinquency and moral corruption. Through their camps, reformers aspired to instill middle-class habits and American values in their campers as well as to amuse them. Each of the impoverished Boston boys who attended Camp Hale, for instance, had to bring a toothbrush to camp and use it every morning (the boys were encouraged but not forced to use their toothbrushes in the evening as well).[146] The boys learned to drink fresh milk in large quantities. Their camp leaders also tried to inspire them to praise particularly lovely vistas and to be kind to chipmunks rather than to throw rocks at them. All in all, this was a civilizing mission in the woods.[147]

During the First World War and in the immediate postwar years, when fears of radical activism and political instability at home and in Europe fed anti-immigrant sentiment, charitable and settlement-house camps made a particular point of Americanization. "Alien Children Are to Be Schooled This Year in Patriotism" at summer camps, promised a 1915 *Washington Post* headline.[148] Moral oversight could be exercised secretly, reformers hoped, far from the corrupting city streets and "the radical and the enemy that is so ready to play upon the impressionable young minds with abominable theories of politics and government," as the New York Children's Aid Society warned in 1921.[149]

Late-nineteenth- and early-twentieth-century working-class Americans enjoyed some success in controlling the conditions of their own leisure hours. At the city park, the ethnic community hall, the church dinner, and the saloon, workers asserted their social standing, affirmed their ethnic ties, and expressed their support for their own communities' cultural norms. They did not have paid vacations, but the work week was contracting, allowing them more time to devote to leisure pursuits. If reformers saw in leisure a choice between "preferred" and "degenerate" values, American workers of all classes were coming to see leisure on their own terms, not as an occasional privilege but rather as a necessity, indeed as central to their rights as Americans.[150]

Charitable and settlement-house summer camps suggest the limits of this control. Few working-class families could afford to pay for their children's camps, and few chose from among many camp options. Their camps represented the physical expansion of the philanthropic domain, not working-class families' specific aspirations. Many Fresh Air homes, for instance, rejected Jewish children whose parents insisted on kosher food.[151] Many other settlement-house and charitable camps were ethnically varied, and their leaders hoped to effect a "melting-pot" effect. However, some parents were upset to find out that their children had shared beds at camp with campers from different ethnic groups.[152] Others tried to keep their children out of mixed camps. As one native-born Protestant explained in a letter to the New York Association for the Improvement of the Condition of the Poor (AICP), the families of his New York parish "are a proud class, and would rather see their children suffer from the summer heat than be sent to mix with Italians and Jews and other immigrants." The organization was able to suggest a few groups, such as the *Tribune*'s Fresh Air fund, which sometimes sent out parties from which Jews and Italian immigrants were excluded.[153] Poor children generally attended camps less on their own families' terms than on those of the charitable organizations that sponsored them.

Still, settlement and welfare camps were never simply expressions of elite hegemony. Progressive organizations' recreation plans were successful inasmuch as they responded to their clients' needs and aspirations. When reform ideas did not meet with community approval, they were less effective. For example, many urban children were reluctant to attend playgrounds far from their own homes and ethnic enclaves. Charitable and low-cost camps succeeded because they provided parents relief from the burden of caring for children at home during the school vacation, catered to their aspirations for their children's health and well-being, and offered children exciting opportunities for adventure.

As ethnic, immigrant, and religious minorities gained power, many founded their own summer camps. Like their Protestant counterparts, Catholic youth leaders saw in camping programs a means of strengthening their sphere of influence; the Marist Brothers of Saint Ann's Academy in New York City organized the first private Catholic camp for boys, St. Ann's, on Lake Champlain in 1892.[154] In the face of anti-Semitic restrictions—most Christian-owned private camps, like the majority of resort hotels, either specified or implied a Christian-only clientele—acculturated, middle- and upper-class Reform Jews whose ancestors had settled in the United States generations earlier also founded early private camps.[155] Catholic and Jewish reformers also began founding camps for working-class and immigrant children of their faith. New Hampshire's Camp Hale, for instance, served a primarily Orthodox Jewish clientele, and although the food was not officially kosher, meat was not served, an important concession to the clientele.[156]

Very few children from minority racial groups attended camps before the interwar years. Policies of racial segregation and outright exclusion gained strength in the late nineteenth century; the 1882 Exclusion Act, the first national immigration exclusion act based on country of origin, severely limited Chinese immigration in the decades to come, and the 1896 Supreme Court decision in *Plessy v. Ferguson* legalized the segregation of African Americans in the South. Further, the early movement was strongest in cities where immigrant European populations were more significant; urban African Americans, Latinos, and Asian Americans were more likely to live in the South, the Southwest, and on the West Coast, regions where the camp movement was less developed. In 1880, when Hinckley included three visiting Chinese boys among his campers, his was an unusual choice that caused some consternation among his white campers.[157] Perhaps Hinckley was more willing to accept Chinese campers because there were relatively few Chinese and Chinese Americans in the Hartford area. Similarly, in the years before the First World War, when few black Americans lived in Boston, the Groton School Camp accepted a few black campers. As cities grew more racially diverse, these occasional practices disappeared.

For those working-class children who did attend camps, the experience offered a dramatic widening of the world. "We thank you very much for sending us out here," one New York City boy wrote in 1910 to his camp's charitable sponsor. "We sleep out in open air tents. We had a picnic Thursday and I won a prize, we are also going to have another one Monday. We are always playing ball out here. . . . we pick blackberries and people give us pears and apples."[158] These were new experiences for children who had never before left city limits. No wonder, as one working-class fourteen-year-old, who with her younger sister had attended a camp run by the AICP, wrote in 1917, "the children that went home Monday cried as if their hearts would break at the thought of leaving behind the time of their lives."[159]

The summer camp industry was exceptional in providing a broad range of urban children access to rural vacations. Decades before extended vacations became standard among working-class parents, many social-service organizations expressly sought out some of the least fortunate urban children, providing weeks of camping to them free of charge. Children of all classes benefited, albeit unequally, from the idea that children were deserving of special pleasures and that camps were important staging-grounds for better citizenship.

"A few shanties on a lovely island in an exquisite lake. Several inexperienced and enthusiastic young men. A lot of fine boys."[160] So Balch extolled his old summer camp in the first of Porter Sargent's *Handbook of Summer Camps* in 1924. In Balch's telling, Camp Chocorua exemplified a modern version of the American pioneer tradition. The group was characterized by the relative equality of all participating members. Everyone contributed and thrived according to his own ability, and he "slaved" in his own best interest as well as that of the larger community. Chocorua was a hierarchical meritocracy, in this telling, where the brightest and most hard-working were most successful. Yet this vision of democracy was necessarily limited, the early camp leaders suggested, to groups of suitable compatriots—in Balch's case, Christian white boys from well-to-do families. For the most part, camps were deeply segregated spaces, far more effectively segregated than the urban constituencies that sponsored them. Whereas urbanites were constantly reminded of a world beyond their own communities' borders, camps reflected the divisions of American society at large, socializing children in the ways of segregated democratic culture.

Camps were not wholly self-contained, however, nor were the constituencies that they served. Each group interacted to some degree with the next. The Asquam boys played baseball against their Groton School counterparts, and boys from Andover, the elite Massachusetts boarding school, sometimes camped alongside boys from Hale House.[161] The terms on which the boys met were not equal; the elite boys were being trained to their roles as social leaders uplifting the less fortunate. Perhaps future president Franklin Delano Roosevelt, who as a teenager volunteered at the Groton School Camp, was inspired to contemplate poverty and opportunity. The unusual proximity of very different kinds of camps along Squam Lake provoked Edwin DeMerritte, director of Camp Algonquin, to reflect on differences of class; as he contended, the Groton School Camp boys whom he could hear out on the water from his own camp a half-mile away were true " 'gentlemen' . . . a little slangy, as is apt to be among boys of that class, [but] nothing was heard that would shock a lady." The same was not always true, he added, of the well-to-do boys who visited his own campers.[162]

As the range of camps on Squam Lake suggests, the ideological foundation of children's camps quickly extended to serve girls, children of the working classes, and members of religious (and occasionally racial) minorities. Although camp leaders' motivations and their programs differed according to their clienteles, overall the participation in camping of new groups challenged the traditional notion that wilderness adventure was the prerogative of elite, native-born males. The net result was the limited but rising democratization of urban children's vacation leisure.

2

"A Home Though Away from Home"

How Parents, Camp Owners, and Children Forged Camp Networks

At Camp the boy mingles with boys of his own age and standing; perhaps with boys of greater attainment and talent, boys who are born to lead.

—Schroon Lake Camp brochure, 1926[1]

In 1923, Mike Hessberg traveled by train from Flatbush, a middle-class Brooklyn neighborhood of tree-lined streets, to attend Schroon Lake Camp for the first time. He felt anxious, as he recalled later that summer: "I did not enjoy the camp so much because of strangeness and the usual difficulty in getting things started."[2] He was, however, already a veteran of the local camp scene, having attended a neighboring camp in the southeastern Adirondacks the previous year. In Mike Hessberg's day, the region was known for its elite Jewish private camps, including Schroon Lake, Idlewood, Cayuga, and Pine Tree for boys, and Paradox, Nawita, Woodmere, Red Wing, Severance, and Rondack for girls, and for the hotels and resorts that served campers' vacationing parents.

Schroon Lake Camp, among the first private camps for Jews in the nation, exemplified the extension of the summer camp ideal at the turn of the century. In 1905, Rabbi Isaac Moses, writer of a popular Reform prayer book and leader of the Reformed Central Synagogue of Manhattan, purchased a farmer's field along the rocky shore of Schroon Lake. The next summer, Moses opened a camp for his son Eugene and eleven other boys from his congregation.[3] The camp was an immediate success.

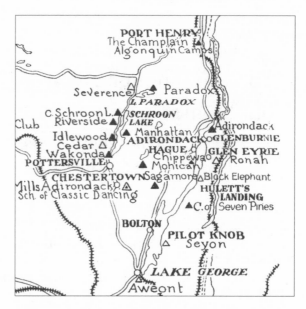

Detail from Adirondack summer camp map. (Originally published in Porter E. Sargent, *A Handbook of Summer Camps*
[Boston: P. Sargent, 1924])

Within three years, fifty boys attended, and by the early 1920s, by
which time Eugene Moses (known to the boys as "Uncle" Gene) was
running the camp, the enrollment exceeded one hundred boys per year.[4]

Mike Hessberg was among a growing minority of American children
who attended camps. Perhaps one million children were sent to camp
each summer in the 1920s. In 1924, when Porter Sargent began to pub-
lish his annual *Handbook of Summer Camps*, he estimated that about
one thousand private camps were operating nationwide, 60 percent of
which served boys and 40 percent girls.[5] Five years later, there were
anywhere from thirteen hundred to twenty-two hundred private camps.
The organizational-camp sector was growing even more rapidly. By
1930, there were anywhere from five to seven thousand camps nationwide, the majority of which were run by youth groups, settlements, and
charities. By one estimate, organizational camps provided vacations to
750,000 children, while private camps served only 100,000. The industry continued to expand through the 1930s, by which time perhaps two
million children attended camps each year out of a school-age popula-

tion of thirty million.[6] Most campers attended for only one or two summers, so the overall percentage of interwar youth who attended camps was substantially higher, especially in many urban areas. In the late 1920s, one study of Brooklyn youth (most between the ages of twelve and sixteen) found that 25 percent of the boys and 16.5 percent of the girls had attended a camp within the past two years.[7]

By the interwar years the camp industry had come of age, achieving significant national visibility and acclaim. Across the country, urban newspapers printed annual tributes to camps, describing the pale and lethargic city children who returned tanned and vigorous at the end of the summer. In magazines such as *Parents'*, founded in 1926 for a national middle-class audience, child-study experts argued for camps' importance in children's development. Owners of private camps advertised in a variety of other magazines with middle- and upper-class audiences, some of which, such as *Atlantic Monthly, Harper's Bazaar, Redbook, and Vanity Fair*, established camp information services of their own.[8] Major urban department stores offered seasonal exhibitions of camp craft, songs, and dances tied to their own camp departments.[9]

This attention was one measure of camps' appeal. Mass culture does not, however, serve to explain the processes through which individual families found their camps. Friends and neighbors, schools and social clubs, and families' political, religious, and racial identifications all played as decisive a role as money, and a far more important role than advertising, in determining children's access to and consumption of this leisure form. Many camp leaders advertised very little in print sources and found their clients mainly through personal contacts and recommendations.[10] Even the wealthiest families considered specific camps within a limited range determined by their region, religion, race, and the gender of their child, as well as their class. Very few Christian-owned camps would have welcomed Mike Hessberg, for instance, nor would his parents have been likely to choose a camp outside the Northeast camping corridor. The Hessbergs were probably attracted to Schroon Lake Camp's longstanding reputation among well-to-do Reform Jews and the area's reputation for welcoming Jewish vacationers. The family may well have known other Schroon Lake Camp clients in the neighborhood; in 1923, Hessberg was among twenty-three Brooklyn boys attending the camp, a number of them from Flatbush.[11]

As the evidence of camps suggests, Americans' experience of consumer culture was shaped by distinctive variations.[12] Choosing a camp

Tents at Schroon Lake Camp, 1918. (Courtesy Schroon–North Hudson Historical Society)

was a particularly intimate act of consumerism. To temporarily relinquish control over their children's day-to-day lives, parents had to identify with (or, in the case of some working-class families, at least minimally accept) the sponsoring organization or a camp leader's vision of community life. Parents expected their own values to be fortified or, in the case of charitable camps' clients, at least not usurped by the camp socialization process. Children themselves preferred environments where they might anticipate feeling understood and appreciated. Across the generations, local networks provided a sense of security, at times perhaps too much so given that the industry was essentially unregulated. Camps extended and reinforced the mainly urban communities that supported them, and these personal networks, more than the industry's success at large, persuaded parents and children to have faith in their choices.

The Interwar Camp Market

Private camp directors such as Isaac and Eugene Moses put considerable effort into maintaining and extending their client networks. Isaac

Moses, who remained a figurehead director until his death in 1926, had many contacts in Reform Jewish circles, in and beyond New York City. Eugene Moses, who worked at the camp for a decade before becoming the sole director, cultivated his own network, keeping notes on the friends, cousins, schoolmates, and younger siblings of current clients and city acquaintances; after one conversation with a client parent in 1923, Eugene Moses wrote in his journal that he "spoke to Mrs. B on phone. Sister has boy. Phone again."[13] Many private camp directors were teachers and school principals who had time off during the school holidays and regular year-round contacts with young people. In the 1920s, Schroon Lake Camp's long-time head counselor, John Green, served with Eugene as an associate director while working in administration at Brooklyn's Manual Training High School.[14]

For private camp directors, advertisements represented only one additional source of clients. Some hired counselors or took on partners, with the explicit expectation that these staff members had their own clienteles or could persuade a certain number of youth to enroll.[15] Others paid commissions to counselors who found campers for them. Through the interwar years, the average such commission at private camps was twenty-five dollars per child, a significant financial incentive given that most counselors earned well under one hundred dollars per season, and sometimes only a third that much.[16]

The work of finding new clients and retaining alumni went on year-round. During the school year, private camp directors wooed prospects through telephone calls and home visits. During the camp season, they worked to consolidate these relationships. As William Abbott, director of Adirondack Woodcraft Camp, a camp for Christian boys, suggested in 1940, "Clever is the camp that publishes a newspaper during the camp season, preferably by the campers themselves, and sees to it that copies of the publication find their way into the hands of the parents. [It is] another subtle form of selling." Birthday cakes for campers with summer birthdays offered the chance to impress parents: "underneath the frosting of the cake there is a good deal of fine, subtle selling." The same was true of the birthday cards addressed to campers during the school year, the miniature calendars sent to families at the beginning of a new year, and the camp reunions commonly held during the winter— all, Abbott contended, perfect occasions to reinforce the fun of camp times.[17] Despite these personal enticements, however, a significant number of families waited until weeks before the camp season started to enroll their children. It was not unusual for Isaac and Eugene Moses to advertise their own camp as late as early June.[18]

In the 1920s, as more Americans achieved middle-class incomes, they supported a greater number of private camps. In 1916, Porter Sargent counted over 300 such camps, of which he had specific information on 180 for boys and 144 for girls.[19] By 1929, the industry journal *Camp Life* claimed 2,200 private camps, ten times as many.[20] Steadily increasing fees were another measure of private camps' success. In 1916, most private camp directors charged between $135 and $250 for the summer season.[21] By the end of the 1920s, the leaders of particularly exclusive camps were asking as much as $400, with small discounts for siblings.[22] The owners of the oldest camps with well-established reputations tended to charge the most, as did those in regions with particular camping cachet. Few camp directors in the Catskills, for instance, charged as much as those in the Berkshire Mountains of Massachusetts, the Adirondack Mountains of New York, and the Maine lake regions. Private girls' camps were generally more expensive, but so were the costs associated with these camps; they generally had a higher staff-to-camper ratio and fewer campers overall, allowing their leaders to promise better chaperonage.[23] To put these prices into perspective, in 1920 about half of New York City families had incomes below two thousand dollars per year, another 30 percent earned between two and three thousand dollars, and the top 20 percent earned over three thousand.[24] A summer at Schroon Lake Camp, at a cost of two hundred dollars in 1924, was too expensive for all but the top 20 percent.[25]

As nonessential luxuries, private camps were vulnerable to short-term economic fluctuations. After the recession of 1920–21, for instance, the 1922 camp season was a time of retrenchment, when many boys' camps shrunk in size and fees dropped slightly.[26] Dr. Eugene Swan, director since 1909 of one of Maine's oldest and best-known boys' camps, Pine Island Camp, fretted in early June 1922 that "to date, we have one dozen less boys than last year and I am sending out—an S.O.S. call to everyone to see if out of some dim corner they can not discover A BOY. All camps are having a difficult time this year—and many have closed."[27] Even in prosperous times, established private camp directors could not afford to rest on their laurels. Every year, some children grew too old to attend camp, and others dropped out due to lack of interest or competing summer plans. Many middle-class children participated in youth groups like the Boy Scouts, which ran their own camps. And a thriving industry inspired competitors to try to enlist the same children. In the early 1910s, for instance, Isaac Moses was forced to rebuild his client base after staff member Edward Goldwater left to found nearby Camp Paradox, taking with him a significant number of Moses's clients.[28]

Most private camps struggled during the Great Depression, an era when the unemployment rate reached as high as 25 percent.[29] At Schroon Lake Camp, for instance, business fell off dramatically, from 126 campers in 1929 to 50 in 1932. Nationally, *Camp Life* estimated that the number of private camps and campers fell by over a third during this same time period.[30] Some camp leaders responded by undercutting their competitors or by privately offering discounts, or "concessions," to individual families. Others paid higher commissions than usual to anyone who could find new clients. Some children found themselves moving between different kinds of camps as their parents' fortunes changed. Even so, there were enough well-to-do families during the Depression years to keep the private camp industry afloat. Enrollments began to rise again by middecade, when the worst of the Depression had passed, and in 1935, Eugene Moses attracted 105 boys to his camp.[31] By the end of the decade, private camp directors were able to raise their fees. They still charged less than they had in 1929, but their new rates indicated a renewed confidence due to their clients' improved finances.[32]

The industry owed much of its continued expansion to less costly organizational camps. In the search for clients, youth-group and settlement-house leaders had three advantages over individuals running private camps: their fees were lower, they had year-round opportunities to build interest in camps, and active members of youth groups were already accustomed to enjoying themselves as a group. Children who participated in youth groups were far more likely than other children to attend camps. In Brooklyn in the late 1920s, for instance, more than a third of boys affiliated with adult-supervised clubs attended camps. One thirteen-year-old Catholic Polish American boy, who was queried as to his camp experience, replied astutely that "I don't belong to no club so I didn't go to no place."[33] Youth group members already "belonged," and camping together consolidated their sense of membership.

Most organizational camps offered fewer specialized activities and a higher ratio of campers to counselors than their private counterparts. In 1930, by one estimate, private camps hired 30,000 counselors for

100,000 campers, whereas organizational camps hired 40,000 to manage 750,000.[34] Some organizations rented campsites at state parks and forests; others built swimming pools on landlocked properties. Through these varied means, interwar youth groups kept their costs down to about seven to fifteen dollars per week, less than half and sometimes a quarter of the weekly cost of a private camp. As the brochure for the New York City YWCA's Camp Quannacut promised, nothing essential was missing: "it is possible to find more expensive camps . . . more elaborate camps . . . but camps with no higher qualities of program and leadership, of health and happiness."[35]

In the 1930s, many parents who could no longer afford private camps found organizational camps a more reasonable alternative. Porter Sargent's annual handbook, which had long focused on private camps, noted in 1932 that "the center of gravity is shifting. The organizational camps are coming forward."[36] That same year, *Camp Life* observed that what it termed "public and semi-public" camps "materially increased in number" and that "the general demand for camping vacations taxed their facilities to the limit. More than a million children went to these camps this past summer."[37] Some organizational camps struggled to finance their camps, and others sold their properties.[38] But in a sign of the sector's growing prominence, more organizational camp directors joined the Camp Directors' Association, which had formerly been dominated by leaders of private camps. Day camps, though still relatively novel, also increased steadily in numbers in the 1930s as organizations attempted to provide for children whose parents could not afford overnight camps.

Charitable camps reflected a different set of networks. Children often came to the attention of charitable camp providers at moments of personal or familial crisis: for instance, if they were identified as underweight at school health exams, or they appeared in juvenile court, or their parents received public assistance.[39] In New York City, the Community Service Society (CSS) first intervened in the B. family in the fall of 1940. The family was in some disarray. One of the children had been sick, the father had been fired from a work-relief program after he consistently failed to report to work, and the mother was experiencing discomfort with her wooden leg, having gained thirty pounds since it was first fitted. An agency nurse assigned to the family insisted that Mrs. B. should lose weight, told her to keep a record of what she ate, and warned her to avoid sweets. Mrs. B. may well have found such advice invasive or even coercive. On the other hand, the agency also referred her nine-year-old daughter, the eldest of five children, to a Fresh Air camp in the summer of 1941.[40]

The quality of charitable camps varied widely. When, in 1925, Professor Lloyd Sharp of Columbia University's Teachers College was invited to help revise Life Fresh Air camp programs, he found that "conditions existing in many of these charity camps were of such a very low standard that they should not have been permitted to continue."[41] In the mid-1920s, New York City's Children's Welfare Federation (CWF) came to a similar conclusion. Many of their camps lacked bath tubs and showers and had no trained health personnel on site. The average counselor-camper ratio was 1:16, with counselors at some member camps supervising as many as twenty-five children apiece. Most member camps failed even to provide organized activities or "nature work" (woodcraft and environmental education) to the campers.[42] Their leaders held themselves to a lower standard, perceiving themselves to be serving children simply by taking them away from impoverished city neighborhoods. Parents sometimes complained if their children appeared uncared for. However, those who paid the least (or, in the case of charitable camps, nothing at all) had little power to shape their children's camp experiences, other than to keep their children at home; camps represented unusual leisure opportunities for their children.[43]

Outside the paid camp market, families found camps largely on the basis of personal connections and their ability to navigate social services. The Stoopenkoff family, Christian Russian Orthodox émigrés who had settled on the Upper East Side of Manhattan, were too poor to own a radio or to afford a heated apartment. In the winter, they sat around a kerosene stove, listening to Mrs. Stoopenkoff read stories in Russian. But in the mid-1930s, through a family connection, their daughter Lydia attended a settlement-house camp.[44] In a few cases, parents' assertive efforts to find camps for their children dismayed charitable camp providers. In 1936, one Brooklyn mother wrote to the Jewish Vacation Association (JVA), a charitable camp clearinghouse for New York City Jews, complaining that her two children were living in desperate circumstances. A home visit made to determine the family's actual need revealed that the family lived in a comfortable apartment on a wide street near a city park, that the father had been steadily employed (if at a low wage) during the Depression, and that the children were "well-nourished and nicely clothed. The mother freely admitted that they were in no desperate need of a vacation but that because it was so hot, she had hoped they could get away for a few weeks."[45] The mother's plea was rejected. Still, the JVA noted with dismay that some families successfully evaded its mandates. The organization estimated that at least 2 percent of low-income parents were signing up their children at more than one agency in an attempt to accrue additional vacation time, and it acknowledged that agency workers usually knew nothing about their clients' varied contacts.[46]

For most working-class Americans, rural holidays remained out of reach. One Muncie, Indiana, resident told visiting sociologists in 1925, "Never had a vacation in my life, honey!"[47] Interwar children who attended low-cost and charitable camps continued to have vacation opportunities unavailable to their elders. Working-class parents could not, however, assure their children a vacation, as the demand for free camps consistently exceeded the supply. Each year, some children signed up and underwent health exams, only to be disappointed when no space was found for a child of their age or gender. Some parents made significant compromises in their search for a camp. Writer Chaim Potok, recalling his Depression-era childhood, noted that his family's desire to protect him from dangerous urban polio epidemics overrode their religious principles, including the observance of Jewish dietary laws. As a boy he attended nonkosher Jewish camps, "the only free camps available to us."[48] Camp providers, not parents, had the final say in determining camp placements. In the 1930s, increased competition made the challenge of finding free camps that much more acute.[49]

Factors other than class also significantly influenced the likelihood of a particular child attending camp. Early-twentieth-century boys more often participated in afterschool clubs and youth groups than did girls. They benefited from the greater number of urban organizations that focused on boys' leisure needs, and they had greater awareness of camp opportunities and organizational ties to groups providing camp vacations. They further benefited from the persistence of traditional ideas about their purportedly greater need for "primitive" adventure. Adults' preference for sending boys away to camps was particularly clear when families' resources were scarce. In 1931, the director of Camp Guilford Bower, a coeducational camp serving African American girls and boys north of New York City, noted that "in a year of depression parents are more likely to keep their girls at home."[50] Similarly, in 1938, a Jewish uncle hoping to obtain a vacation for his nephew at the YMHA's Camp

Lehman explained that none of his nieces had been away from the city, but "as this is a man's world, the girls will have to stay at home."[51]

Boys' opportunities to attend camps reflected greater freedom at home as well. Although parents complained about daughters who were out at all hours, girls were statistically less likely than their brothers to roam freely or even to see films of their choice unchaperoned by their parents. Working-class girls and eldest daughters were also more likely to shoulder domestic chores such as the oversight of younger siblings, responsibilities that kept some girls in the city.[52] When, in 1942, the "B." family's daughter, now ten years old, asked to return to the free camp that she had enjoyed the previous summer, her parents said no. As the family's case report noted, her mother was pregnant, and "parents have since decided that they would rather have her at home to assist with the care of the younger children."[53]

These gendered distinctions varied by religious and ethnic group. For instance, Jewish girls attended camps in numbers well above the national average. Many urban Jewish parents and organizations perceived camps for both sexes as emblems of their own success, as well as a sign of their integration into American cultural practices (even though many Jews attended Jewish-only camps). In a study of Brooklyn children in the late 1920s, about 30 percent of Jewish and Protestant boys attended camps, but Jewish girls were more likely than their Protestant or Catholic peers to attend camps, at a rate of over 22 percent.[54] In contrast, urban Italian American girls and boys attended camps at rates of approximately 4 percent and 9 percent, respectively.[55] Although some Italian American children attended church-run camps, many of their parents had little interest in girls' camps. As one researcher investigating working-class Italian American girls living in New York in the early 1930s contended, "Those few girls who had had the privilege of a summer camp were girls sent to the country by the social agencies for mental or physical health reasons. . . . the traditional boast of never having slept a night from under the parental roof until the wedding night is hard to combat."[56] When girls were active in afterschool clubs and youth groups, they had more opportunities to attend camps. When family honor depended on female purity, girls were kept close to home.

At the beginning of the century, many camp brochures promised "health and strength and true Christian manliness" as outcomes of the camp experience.[57] In the interwar period, the self-sacrificing and high-minded rhetoric of muscular Christianity dropped out of most camp brochures as the movement came to seem old-fashioned and, in the wake of the carnage of the First World War, even distastefully militaristic. As Americans became less religiously observant, many camp leaders adopted more ecumenical programs that stressed morals over religiosity. The range of religious rituals at both Christian and Jewish camps of the early twentieth century reflected the growing diversity of American communities. Although some Jewish camps and many Catholic and YMCA and YWCA camps offered intensive religious programing, religion generally became less prominent in camp culture as part of the larger trend of secularization. Nevertheless, Christian and Jewish children rarely mingled at private camps, bastions of greater exclusivity. Although many interwar camps continued to promise "Christian influence" and "select Christian clienteles," these terms were increasingly code words for ethnic and religious exclusivity, not appeals to muscular Christianity per se.[58]

Race remained another important factor in interwar camp admissions. A small number of middle- and upper-class minority children attended elite private camps. In the Adirondacks, a number of wealthy Central American and Puerto Rican students who were enrolled at an Upstate New York boarding school and were unable to return home during their summer vacation were some of Camp Pok-O'-Moonshine's first clients in 1905, and a few Asian Americans attended Camp Riverdale in the 1930s.[59] In 1916, the roster of Connecticut's Camp Mystic included Kapiolani and Liliuokalani Kawananakoa of Washington, D.C., the daughters of well-to-do Hawaiian princess David Kawananakoa.[60] These were exceptional cases. Relatively few Latinos lived in the Northeast when Camp Pok-O'-Moonshine was founded; the presence of a small number of wealthy foreigners at camp did not threaten white clients' sense that the camp was exclusive.

Across the country, black children were not welcome at private, white-owned summer camps, regardless of their family income. In the South, white leaders of youth groups such as the Girl Scouts sometimes blocked African American children from joining their organizations and thus from attending their camps.[61] Few segregated alternatives existed; as late as 1940, when fifty-six children's camps were operating in Georgia, only three segregated camps enrolled African Americans.[62] In the North, the majority of organizational camps were also segregated, and few organizational camps served the growing black populations of northeastern and midwestern cities. In the late 1910s during the war years, hundreds of thousands of African Americans moved from the rural South to cities of the Northeast and Midwest in search of better employment opportunities and an escape from the South's discriminatory Jim Crow laws. This trend continued through the 1920s. A number of urban black churches founded camps, but few owned their own campsites. Two that did, and that became well-known in elite black circles, were Camp Atwater (1921), founded as St. John's Camp in North Brookfield, Massachusetts, by the St. John's Congregational Church of Springfield, Massachusetts (and later affiliated with the Urban League), and Camp Guilford Bower (1928), founded by St. Philip's Church of New York City in New Paltz, New York. Black families of means from the Midwest and the South as well as New England and New York patronized the two camps.[63]

Region strongly influenced camp enrollments as well. Although interwar children across the country attended organizational and charitable camp, the vast majority of campers were urban and attended camps within a day's journey of their homes. Generally speaking, Boston children were sent to camps in Maine, New Hampshire, and Massachusetts. New York parents chose camps along a corridor from Pennsylvania to Maine. Chicago and Detroit parents sent their children to camps along the Great Lakes in Minnesota, Wisconsin, and Michigan. Southern families chose the cooler mountain air of the Smokies, the Alleghenies, and especially the mountains of western North Carolina.[64] Out west there were smaller clusters of camps in the mountains of Colorado and along the Southern California coast. Most campers stayed within their region, but some private western ranch-style camps attracted wealthy easterners, and midwestern and northeastern campers also occasionally attended private camps in Ontario, Canada. Only parents of means could afford to send their children so far away; most chose camps closer to home and more convenient to visit during their own vacations.

In the Northeast, New York State became the center of the national camp industry by the late 1920s. Whereas Maine's and New Hampshire's private camp clusters dominated the industry at the beginning of the century, New York's camp scene grew larger and more diverse. Approximately four hundred camps were operating within its borders, just over half of which were privately run and the others organized by leaders of area youth groups and charities.[65] Over the course of the 1930s, when organizational camping grew more rapidly than private camping, New York State extended its dominance of the industry with about eight hundred camps.⁶⁶ The range and diversity of camps in and around the state was unparalleled.

In contrast, relatively few West Coast children attended camps. The region was significantly less urban than the Northeast and Midwest. Further, many Anglo-American migrants to western cities felt themselves already to have escaped the worst of industrial modernity, so the middle-class adults who were most likely to found camps and to send their children to camps often experienced city life as less "unnatural."⁶⁷ "We have a problem in the West not found in the East," reported Rosalind Cassidy, chairman of the Department of Physical Education at Mills College near Los Angeles and an activist in girls' camp counselor training, in 1930. "The growth in the number of camps has been much slower because parents are not convinced that the child should be sent to camp as a necessary part of his education."⁶⁸ Further up the coast, the story was much the same. From a camping standpoint, for instance, Washington State was blessed with many lakes, mountains, and ocean beaches. One of the earlier "muscular Christian" camps, Kamp Kontent, was founded for Seattle boys in 1890 by a local minister. But in the decades to come, the summer camp tradition did not take hold in the same way as it had back east. Seattle residents promoted their city's natural assets: the relative cleanliness of the water and the air, the beauty of nearby mountains and ocean, and the fact that one could canoe, swim, or fish not far from the downtown core. A state government survey of the late 1930s concluded that "in the Pacific Northwest the appeal [of camps] to parents from recreational and health viewpoints is not so great as it is in the congested cities of the East." Fewer than twenty-five thousand children, mostly from the cities of Seattle and Tacoma, attended camps in the state, mostly organizational camps.⁶⁹

Access to camps grew dramatically in the interwar years; as the *New York Times* enthused in 1930, camps served "tenement waifs and hearty young suburbanites, Boy Scouts and tiny cripples, State wards and scions of Park Avenue."⁷⁰ Individual children's access to summer camps was a more complicated matter. Their families' opportunities, priorities, and political, religious, ethnic, and regional identifications made possible some choices and precluded others. For any individual family, the importance of some of these factors changed over the years. Consider the girl who was sent first to the progressive, labor-affiliated Pioneer Youth Camp and then to a traditional private girls' camp in Maine.⁷¹ These choices appear somewhat incongruous, but if a private girls' camp was a more conventional expression of a family's resources, the Pioneer Youth Camp was well-known in certain liberal middle-class circles. More often, families chose camps within a limited range, if they chose at all, such that their children camped with others of similar backgrounds. This isolation remained integral to camps' appeal.

The Family Marketplace

In an expanding industry, camp owners and advocates addressed parents as thoughtful consumers of child-centered goods and services. The good parent was one who could, as Porter Sargent's *Handbook of Summer Camps* proposed in 1924, "consider the child's personality, his temperament, his psychological reactions, and his physical condition."[72] Harriet Gulick, founder of Camp Aloha in Vermont and member of the prominent Gulick camping clan, told readers of *Parents'* magazine in 1935 to consider their children's particular stage of physical and emotional development before making any summer plans: "Does your son or daughter need to develop [the] ability to make choices? Does he perhaps need many leisure hours to follow creative impulses?" There were camps to suit every need: a small one for the shy child, a larger one for the more aggressive child. The wrong camp was potentially as detrimental as the right camp was helpful, Gulick argued, and the responsibility for good camp consumption fell squarely on individual parents' shoulders: "From time to time we hear of sad accidents in poorly planned and carelessly conducted camps, few as I hope such are. Severe as the arraignment of such camps should be, don't forget that they exist because some parents were not painstaking enough in finding out about them before entrusting children to them."[73] Such advice presupposed not only parental acumen but also consumer clout, and it assumed middle- and upper-class parents who could pick and choose among a range of options.

Like their predecessors, interwar camp leaders reconciled a more traditional vocabulary of improvement—the idea that camps would shape better children—with the emergent language of consumer gratification. In the 1880s, when Ernest Balch advertised Camp Chocorua he promised "swimming, rowing, and fishing, and the practical work of Camp Life" and "a natural and complete outdoor life for boys . . . while their parents can feel they are under competent care and supervision."[74]

Interwar camp leaders continued to combine romantic prose, promises of healthful and happy outdoor experiences, and claims of professional care and expertise. In the Schroon Lake Camp yearbook of 1934, for instance, Eugene Moses counted among his camp's achievements character development, self-reliance, a wholesome enjoyment of fun, training in leadership and unselfish service, love of the outdoors, and "a careful and skillful development of the human body."[75]

In the context of this consumerist ethos, private camp catalogues were replete with photographs of campers diving into the water, canoeing, playing baseball, dancing (if a girls' camp), engaged in pageantry, lined up in front of their cabins, and on hikes away from camp. Photographs of the tents and cabins, of modern kitchens, rustic boathouses and dining halls, and picturesque views of the lake at sunset or at the evening campfire also made the case for beauty, healthfulness, and athletic opportunity. Some brochures included "before and after" photographs demonstrating that children had grown stronger and larger after a summer at camp.[76] Testimonials from satisfied parents added a personal touch: "Before entering your camp my boy was under a doctor's care, he was underweight and somewhat nervous; now he has gained eight pounds, has a wonderful color and [is] full of life," wrote one Detroit father after the 1925 Schroon Lake Camp season, in a letter published in the 1926 brochure.[77]

Parents who could afford private camps expected these camps to reflect their own values and achievements. Some parents were attracted to specific promises and attractions: flexible scheduling or military order, "all-around" camping or a particular emphasis on horses or canoeing. Others hoped their children would experience "primitive camping" or hesitated when they saw such words in camp brochures.[78] "The campers and parents are constantly comparing their camp to other camps," Eugene Lehman, director of Highland Nature Camp, a private camp for Jewish girls in South Naples, Maine, noted in 1932, "and the director is forced to satisfy his patrons just as a merchant is forced to please his customers."[79] At Schroon Lake Camp, each summer brought improvements to the physical plant: a sand beach, new water-sports facilities, a stage with scenery and footlights, and upgraded tennis and basketball courts.

Camp leaders had to decide how best to market their camps. However, many camp brochures resembled one another so closely that as *Parents'* magazine contributing writer Gertrude Middleditch Platt jokingly related in 1932, choosing her own daughter's camp entailed the seemingly endless perusal of near-identical pages: "I came to the place where shining photographs of pine trees haunted my waking hours, and my nights seemed filled with an endless procession of smiling children clad in white middy blouses, neckties tied just so, and legs encased in woolen bloomers."[80] The middle-class readers of *Parents* were learning to trust a modern form of recreation that few of them had enjoyed in their own youth, but which now appeared desirable. As consumers, they had many options. How to choose?

To entice and reassure parents, camp leaders tried to position themselves as objective, professional child experts. Those parents considering Vermont's Camp Winnahkee in 1920, for instance, were promised that "even a single summer at camp will do more to develop the finer, sweeter, healthier qualities of girlhood than years of indulgent or stern parental guidance."[81] Camp brochures also warned that camps were critical to children's future success. The 1919 brochure for Connecticut's Camp Wonposet for boys praised

> the open air, the woods, the fishing, the outdoor sports and exercises and the living and sleeping close to the heart of nature [which] make sound, sturdy, erect and vigorous young men out of boys who would otherwise be round-shouldered, thin, narrow-chested, and timid and indecisive. . . . It should be borne in mind that nowadays without these things, no boy can achieve a large measure of success and fulfill the hopes and aspirations of his parents.[82]

Even the best parents, camp directors claimed, could not possibly meet their child's need for a separate peer group or teach skills that required specially trained leadership. Sending one's child off to camp was not an abdication of parental duty, industry leaders argued, but an extension of the loving, companionate family; even the happiest, best-adjusted child would profit from this short-term separation.

Camp leaders' promises resonated with a parental audience at once anxious about childrearing, able and eager to afford their children special opportunities, and receptive to the argument that camps were necessary adjuncts to home life.[83] At a time when professional expertise came to exert an increasingly influential role in childrearing, many parents responded with enthusiasm and relief to the prospect of camp leaders molding their children. Charlie Stanwood first attended New

Hampshire's Camp Pasquaney in 1921, at the age of eleven. His mother, desperate to resolve what she saw as her son's behavioral problems, had traveled to New York City to ask the advice of Morgan Shepard, editor of *John Martin's Book,* a children's magazine. Shepard recommended Pasquaney to her. Although she had never heard of summer camps, she eagerly enrolled Charlie.[84] Other parents turned to camp directors for support in resolving specific family issues. In 1939, the father of a Camp Dudley boy explained, in a letter to director Herman Beckman, that his son "is a little bit self-centered and inclined to overeat. If it is not too much trouble will you tell his leaders to work on him in these two particulars?"[85] Another father wrote in 1940 that "the querying age seems to have arrived rather sooner than normal and [his fourteen-year-old son] has been quite a dissenter and absentee. . . . Any spiritual stimulation that you inspire Dan with will be quite desirable."[86] Part of what parents purchased, when they had the means to choose a camp, was the idea of objective professional expertise. As one mother explained in a letter to camp director Dan Beard in 1932, "I think it most helpful for parents to get the point of view of someone outside of the family—and I am a parent who can stand it."[87]

Of course, parents' aspirations did not always correspond to those of their children. The mother of the son under Beard's care was disappointed to find that her child was more interested in writing for the camp newspaper than participating in active sports. Others misjudged their children's interests and abilities. In 1934, after the leaders of the Girl Scouts' Camp Andree, a New York camp for adolescent Scouts, asked parents to fill out a "Camper's Interest" form, one bemused staff member noted that "one girl's mother wished her to realize the beauty of her voice, but the girl was not musical, not interested in singing, and does not have a good voice. . . . One girl's parents wished her to gain confidence in her ability to do things. [The] Girl was quite self-confident, and the idea that she wasn't was entirely her mother's."[88] However misguided, such requests demonstrated parents' investment in the idea of camp as a space in which their children were simultaneously to enjoy themselves and be transformed.

Even as reform ambitions continued to shape the interwar child-recreation movement, American adults were becoming concerned less with the traditional values of "character" and self-control than with personal gratification. Recreation was increasingly accepted as a worthwhile pleasure in itself rather than justified as a means toward self-reform. The most obvious pleasure-seekers were the nation's "flaming youth": the middle-class adolescents and college students of the 1920s whose vibrant, heterosocial youth culture (drawing on elements of working-class youth culture) signaled their emancipation from more restrictive traditions.[89] Older adults frequently criticized this youth culture, but they too had more leisure time and more ways to enjoy it: motion pictures and amusement parks, pleasure rides in automobiles, and opportunities for tennis, boating, and swimming at municipal parks.[90]

From the late nineteenth century onward, some well-to-do parents considered camps convenient repositories for their children when private boarding schools were not in session. By the interwar years, the ascendant ideal of companionate marriage justified middle-class parents' need to renew their own relationships while camps were in session. As the *New York Times* suggested in 1923, "The boys' and girls' camp have opened up a new vista of enjoyment and education for middle age as well as youth."[91] Meanwhile, working-class parents who could not afford to stay at home to supervise their children during summer vacations were grateful for camps' responsible adult supervision. Many parents turned to camps at particularly stressful moments in family life, such as a mother's pregnancy or the birth of a younger sibling.[92] A few parents took advantage of the privacy afforded by their children's absence to end their marriages.[93]

Most interwar children of camping age were too young to participate fully in the youth culture that was dominated by older adolescents and young adults, but they were increasingly powerful as consumers. Vendors increasingly targeted children for age-specific marketing campaigns. By the interwar years, year-round toy departments had become standard in urban centers, and advertisers, department stores, and magazines such as *Parents* all turned with increased attention to children as customers and as recipients of parental largesse.[94]

In an era in which children exerted growing power in family decision-making, many parents considered their children's opinions and those of other children with care. In 1927, a child who was a neighborhood friend of Libby Raynes recommended Camp Greylock, an Adirondack camp for Jewish girls; the Raynes parents sent Libby and their other daughter, Ruth, to Camp Greylock for several summers.[95] Few interwar parents had themselves attended camps in their youth, and fewer still visited specific camps in season before making their selections. Brochures and meetings with camp leaders helped to allay their concerns, but the personal recommendations of trusted friends, neighbors, and children themselves were even more reassuring.

Children actively recruited new campers among their peers at home. C. Mifflin "Miff" Frothingham later recalled that after he and his fellow campers attended Camp Pasquaney back in 1895, they returned to their homes eager to praise the camp: "You couldn't stop a camper from talking about it. . . . at school, and in their daily themes, it was camp—camp!—camp!!!—and the Lake!"[96] It was not unusual for a younger child to arrive at camp already familiar with all the songs and various other details of daily life, or for a younger sibling to feel like an old camper, having already heard so much about the camp.[97] Camp directors tried to mobilize this influence toward their own ends. In their communication with children, they frequently exhorted current campers to recruit new ones. As the alumni bulletin for Camp Jeanne D'Arc, a private camp for Catholic girls, suggested, those who helped to recruit would "prove . . . your Camp spirit."[98]

Some of the poorest children took matters into their own hands, negotiating directly with social workers and settlement-house staff or working in a settlement house in exchange for a vacation.[99] In 1935, the JVA worked to find a joint placement for two boys who had each been offered separate camp vacations. The brothers asked to be sent together on the basis of their emotional attachment to each other. Once this was settled, they asked to go later in the summer on a trip of longer duration than the agency could afford. "The whole matter was left in abeyance," the JVA reported, "when suddenly [the first boy] turned up at life camp [the Life Fresh Air Camp] having been sent by a third agency —one which has practically no Jewish clientele and the last place in the world with which one would expect the boy to have a contact."[100] Even the boy who refused a social agency's free camp placement because he had not enjoyed the camp in previous years was asserting some control over his vacation experience.[101]

Camps were part of an expanding child-centered consumer realm, in which parents and children both made choices. The idea that children's leisure should be productive and useful continued to hold sway among parents and camp leaders even as American culture more broadly became more pleasure-driven. Yet children were not simply pawns of adult improvement projects. Few could afford to pay their own camp fees, and none was admitted without parental consent. But as the structure of American family life became more democratic, children's influence in selecting camps was increasingly significant.

Camp Standards and the Growth of Camp Associations

The interwar camp industry's rapid growth attested in part to a lack of regulatory oversight. Some states' health departments enforced minimal health and safety standards, and organizations such as the Girl Scouts set up their own national camping guidelines in the interwar years, but decisions about food quality, counselor-camper ratios, and adherence to new interwar Red Cross standards at waterfronts rested largely in the hands of individual leaders. Again and again, camp leaders noted the ease with which anyone could start up a camp, regardless of qualifications. In 1916, Alcott Farrar Elwell, assistant camp director of New Hampshire's Camp Mowglis, argued that "it has been easy for a person having a free summer to start a camp—throw up a few tents—gather what children he could and while business was good, continue—to disappear if difficulties came."[102] Two decades later, the refrain was much the same. A typical 1939 article in *Camping* complained that "anyone who has the cash and the urge, regardless of qualification or training can secure a site, erect a cabin or two, get up a fancy folder and presto! advertise an ideal, high grade summer camp."[103]

That so many of these camps were successful was a sign of consumers' enthusiasm for the camp project. But as the industry grew, some camp leaders began to suggest that parents were overly trusting. In 1936, Hedley Dimock, leader of an annual conference in Chicago for midwestern camp directors, concluded that in "the years of our own reckless glorification of the values of the summer camp—any summer camp—we helped to produce a naive, trusting public who too easily caught or accepted our enthusiasm for the summer camp in general, undifferentiated by such qualifying and discriminating factors as standards."[104] Only the market set standards, in that the majority of camp directors adhered fairly closely to the practices of comparable camps of their type.

High prices were no guarantee of high-quality vacation experiences. The Raynes parents of New York City could afford private camps in the 1920s for their daughters, Ruth and Libby. They chose within certain bounds: private Jewish camps with kosher-style, if not kosher, food. By the ages of eleven and thirteen, respectively, Libby and Ruth Raynes were veterans of one camp where the lake water had leeches and another where the owner turned out to be an alcoholic.[105] In a similar vein, when Henry Wellington Wack, founder of *Field and Stream* magazine, undertook a series of investigative tours of camps in the mid-1920s, he noted that one girls' camp near Asheville, North Carolina, appeared to be "a roadside tea hut with someone's mountain cottage and a few outhouses behind it . . . [with] a dilapidated tennis net and an unmade, overgrown court, a dismal area of dustladen underbrush, unkempt young men and women and a flea-larded dog."[106]

Even the happiest and most prestigious camps could be dangerous places. The majority of the adult staff at Rothrock's North Mountain School in Pennsylvania became sick with typhoid fever in 1876.[107] In the decades to come, camps with poor hygiene or inadequately supervised waterfronts and campfires put campers at risk. On Squam Lake alone, one new camper drowned at Camp Asquam in 1896 after taking out a boat without staff supervision, an eighteen-year-old Groton School Camp counselor of 1906 died of cramps while swimming in the lake, and two Camp Cloyne boys exploring a cave in a sandbank in 1907 suffocated when the cave collapsed on them.[108] When J. Edward Sanders, a doctoral student at Columbia University's Teachers College, surveyed 114 camps in 1929, he noted one fatal drowning and at least five near-drownings, three of which he witnessed personally during his own short visits. Burns were commonplace at camps because campers frequently lit campfires and lanterns with kerosene. At one camp in the study, a child was burned to death, and at several others campers were hospitalized with serious burns. As Sanders concluded, "merely living in a rural environment does not of itself guarantee health."[109]

Every year, there were preventable injuries and accidents, some of them fatal, at summer camps. For instance, at Camp Tabor, a private camp for Jewish girls in Lakewood, Pennsylvania, a number of campers became ill with typhoid fever in 1927. The cause of the infection turned out to be the camp cook, who had not been screened prior to beginning work. When she returned in 1929, another fifty members of the camp were infected and several girls died.[110] Camp Tabor was not unusual. Sanders discovered that almost 80 percent of camps did not require stool and urine tests of their kitchen staff to check for typhoid.[111]

From the beginning of the century onward, groups of camp directors met in an effort to build a more professional association and discuss camp standards. The directors of boys' camps first came together in significant numbers through the initiative of Winthrop Talbot, who organized a small meeting of camp leaders in 1899 at Camp Asquam.[112] Three years later, the Association of Organized Workers with Boys met at the New York City YMCA's Harlem branch (which then served a mainly white ethnic neighborhood). At this meeting, held in April 1902, Talbot participated in a discussion titled "Summer Camps and Outings for Boys," speaking so compellingly about the need for a camp organization that his peers authorized him to promote a camping conference for the following spring.[113] In April 1903, at the first large-scale meeting of camp directors in Boston, approximately one hundred men compared notes on programing, facilities, and their respective histories. The participants included prominent private camp directors like C. Hanford Henderson, founder of New Hampshire's Camp Marienfeld; men affiliated with various YMCAs and boys' work organizations; and two women camp directors.[114] A second meeting, in 1905, drew northeastern camp leaders including Winthrop Talbot of Camp Asquam, Edwin DeMerritte of Camp Algonquin, Henry Sawyer of Boston's Hale House, and various YMCA camp leaders. G. Stanley Hall was invited as a guest speaker.[115]

Boys' camp leaders did not meet together again in significant numbers to discuss their work until 1910, by which point Talbot's camp had failed and he had retreated from the camping field. This time, the impetus came from Allen Williams, director of the Reptile Study Society of America. Williams was personally acquainted with many camp directors, since he lectured frequently at boys' camps on the topic of snakes. Although he felt that camps should be educational rather than commercial ventures, he came up with the idea of publicizing boys' camps within a commercial context: a Sportmen's Show in New York City for which he had been hired to organize the publicity. In advance of the 1911 show—where wilderness guides and their patrons would meet, plan trips, and view the latest guns, fishing tackles, and camping equipment—Williams gathered together a group of about twenty YMCA and private camp directors at the 23rd Street YMCA in New York City in 1910. They proved interested not only in sponsoring a boys' camp exhibit at the Sportmen's Show but also in founding an organization, the Camp Directors Association of America (CDAA) to promote their collective interests.[116]

A few girls' camp leaders gathered with similar intentions. In 1912, nine women camp directors, including Laura Mattoon, met informally in New York City to discuss camp standards.[117] In 1916, a larger group of women and men met to found the National Association of Directors of Girls' Camps (NADGC). They elected as their first leader Charlotte Gulick, co-founder of the Camp Fire Girls and Camp Wohelo in Maine.[118] Over the next eight years, women and men shared the NADGC leadership. In 1924, the NADGC and the CDAA merged to form the new Camp Directors Association (CDA), a sign of the increasingly important place of girls' camps. Laura Mattoon was the group's first treasurer and paid employee, as well as one of the most vocal female voices within the mostly male-led organization.

These various associations had national ambitions, but in their early years they mostly reflected the industry's northeastern orientation. The CDAA's first president, Charles R. Scott of Newark, had founded the New Jersey YMCA State Camp for boys at Wawayanda in 1901, when New Jersey boys stopped attending Camp Dudley in the Adirondacks.[119] Over the next decade, most of Scott's successors were educators from New York or New Jersey who worked at prestigious area high schools and who directed northeastern camps. In the winter they met regularly in New York City to discuss their experiences.[120] The active members of the NADGC also knew one another through social and regional (and sometimes, as in the case of the Gulick clan, familial) networks.

By 1930, the CDA had become more national. It had nine regional branches, including the Mid-Atlantic Section, Midwestern Section, Rocky Mountain Section, and Pacific Section, reflecting the spread of camps across the country. Maine-born, Chicago-based John Perley Sprague, the founder and director of Wisconsin's private Camp Minocqua (1905), had been elected president of the CDA. Still, two regions dominated the membership and the industry literature: the New York Section, the most populous and most heterogeneous camping region, and the home base for the greatest number of national child-welfare and youth organizations, and the New England Section, largely though not exclusively the province of private camp directors. Despite some grumbling from directors in other regions who complained about the CDA's northeastern focus, these two regions remained most influential.[121]

In no region of the country were professional organizations able to regulate the industry or to establish "brand-name" loyalty, either among parents or camp directors. Membership in a professional association did not ensure a camp leader's success, nor did abstention from membership necessarily preclude it, and most early-twentieth-century camps remained unaffiliated with regional and national camp organizations. When, in 1935, the CDA was renamed the American Camping Association (ACA), the organization had a membership of only two hundred camps, out of many thousands operating.[122] Only in the postwar era did the ACA grow more substantially, beginning to enforce minimum standards among its own members (but not the industry at large) in 1948 with a new program of accreditation.

The interwar CDA/ACA, having failed to "brand" the industry or to shape its practices, acted as an agent of moral suasion rather than as a policing body. Its leaders saw themselves as engaged in educational work, wished to advance a more professional organization, and worried about the low quality of some camps. Lacking the clout to set standards, they remained frustrated. State health departments made annual visits to camps but rarely shut them down, even when inspectors noted lax sanitary standards.[123] When a drowning or typhoid epidemic made newspaper headlines, CDA/ACA leaders could do little but fret about the possible damage such publicity posed to the industry as a whole, even when the camp in question was unaffiliated with them.

The growing range and diversity of camps further compounded the problem of weak national oversight. How could the CDA/ACA respond to the concerns of camp leaders with radically different, even oppositional, ideals? What advocacy group could speak for the directors of camps serving the children of radical labor organizers, middle-class Zionists, wealthy conservative Christians, and local Girl Scout troops? How could camp directors who abhorred commercialism and those who celebrated modern commercial trends both be accommodated? Many of the camp directors who had founded earlier summer camps expressed mixed feelings about the interwar industry's expansion. They were pleased to see parents responding so eagerly to the camping idea, but they feared that the industry's commercialization and its disorganization would tarnish their own loftier goals. As Edwin DeMerritte, who had founded Camp Algonquin in 1886, complained in the pages of *Camping* in 1929, many newer camps were both too big adequately to care for their individual campers and too profit-oriented. "Now is the time," he concluded, "to stand shoulder to shoulder and save a noble work from decay."[124] Camp leaders who were attracted to this "purist" message often joined the CDA. Those who ran the kinds of programs

that *Camping* derided as overly commercial generally did not. Ultimately, parents were responsible for ensuring that their children's camps
were good and healthful.

Brooklyn Jews: A Case Study

At the turn of the twentieth century, very few Jewish children attended
camps. Within two decades, they were among the industry's most enthusiastic supporters, at the epicenter of the summer camp marketplace.
Jewish parents were atypical in that they sent their children to camps in
disproportionate numbers as compared to their Christian peers. Yet the
Jewish camp experience is richly revealing both of the rise of a diverse
camp market and of the processes through which families navigated this
market. Like other groups, American Jews' camp choices proclaimed
specific community identities while establishing connections to American culture more broadly.

Most early-twentieth-century American Jews lived in the urban
Northeast, where camps were becoming most popular. Jews were also
particularly enthusiastic about vacationing. In the late nineteenth and
early twentieth centuries, a wide range of Jewish-owned resorts emerged
in the face of the anti-Semitic restrictions endemic at Christian-owned
resorts. Jewish resorts proclaimed their clients' success, allowing recent
immigrants brief and humble retreats from the heat and noise of urban
summers, while providing wealthier Jews a means to affirm their class
status and respectability at fancier resorts.[125] In the same vein, specifically Jewish camps provided community alternatives to the many Christian-owned summer camps that explicitly advertised restricted Christian
clienteles as a component of their elite status.[126]

Most important, summer camps allowed American Jews to balance
ethnic community and their children's acculturation into American life.
Jewish camps represented independent social networks, but the industry more generally appeared modern and American. Given that many
Jewish immigrants had fled anti-Semitism and fears of violence in their
home countries, the impetus to assimilate was significant; American
Jews tended to be particularly eager to provide to their children what
appeared to be "American" experiences.

In the first decades of the twentieth century, traditional modes of
Jewishness gradually became less forceful in establishing community.

After the First World War, American anxiety about foreign-born radicals spurred new immigration restrictions, bringing the migration of eastern and southern Europeans nearly to an end in the 1920s. Most of those already in the United States distanced themselves from the traditions of the immigrant generation, including regular synagogue attendance and strict observance of ritual laws. Yet American Jews remained sentimentally attached to the world of their parents. Their children were, as a group, considerably less likely to attend religious services than their Protestant and Catholic peers, and their sons often stopped going to synagogue after they turned thirteen, the age of symbolic manhood within Jewish religious tradition, but parents sought out other ways to socialize their second-generation children as Jews.[127]

Even in areas of extensive Jewish in-migration, children of diverse religious and cultural backgrounds shared local resources. The majority of Jewish American children attended public schools, where they studied among youth from different ethnic groups, and many Jews attended ethnically and religiously mixed youth clubs as well.[128] When parents attempted to secure Jewish-led vacations for their children, they were hoping for the kinds of "village" Jewish community experiences that were impossible to achieve in heterogeneous cities. As one parent of a son active in his local YMCA explained, "I would like him to go to a Jewish (American) camp."[129]

Like piano lessons and Chanukah presents, camps provided American Jewish parents with a tangible means to demonstrate their parental affection and investment, to celebrate their children's potential and their own improving place in American life.[130] At a time when the most prestigious universities restricted Jewish enrollment, camps offered a safe staging-ground for Jewish American success. At Schroon Lake Camp, the boys aspired to join the camp honor society, Beta Rho, and they played in the "HYPN" baseball league, with teams named for Harvard, Yale, Princeton, and Notre Dame (the latter, a prominent Catholic university, might seem an odd choice for a Jewish camp except that it was well-known in college athletics).[131] Jewish summer camps promised a modern mixture of pleasure and ethnic connection, opportunities for social improvement, and a model of Jewish physicality (an implicit rejoinder to the idea that Jews lacked athletic prowess).

These activities served the cause of assimilation into American practices, while solidifying a new brand of ethnic Americanism. The creation of specifically Jewish camps reflected the exclusionary realities of many Christian camps and of Christian-dominated institutions more generally, but they also represented a kind of privilege: the ability to stay within ethnic networks and to create Jewish culture (in a variety of forms, from kosher food to Yiddish to Zionism) in new places, while participating in activities deemed desirable by a broader spectrum of Americans. Whether or not specifically Jewish summer camps offered formal Jewish education, kosher food, or Sabbath services, they melded the imperatives of assimilation and of ethnic persistence.[132] Many parents, whether their impulses were religious or social or both, wished to reinforce their children's connections to Jewish community. Judaism, these camps proclaimed, was entirely compatible with a summer of fun.

The meaning and degree of camps' "Jewishness," whether defined in religious or ethnic terms, varied considerably. Within Brooklyn's Jewish community, parents chose from among a range of camps: private, institutional, and charitable; kosher and nonkosher; Orthodox, Conservative, Reform, and unaffiliated; Yiddish-speaking, Zionist, and socialist; exclusively Jewish and religiously mixed. Some families sought exclusively or primarily Jewish settings, whereas others willingly patronized camps where campers of several religions lived and played together. Summer camps reflected the breadth of ways in which parents raised their children.

Because private camps tended to operate along a religious/ethnic divide, Jews who attended them generally found themselves in wholly or almost exclusively Jewish spaces, at least where the campers were concerned. But what made Jewish camps Jewish, other than their clienteles, was open to debate. Most of the private camps around Schroon Lake served relatively acculturated families. The food at these camps was either not kosher or it was "kosher-style." No Orthodox Jew would have sent a child to Schroon Lake Camp, for instance, where lard, a traditionally nonkosher food, was on Eugene Moses's shopping list.[133] Schroon Lake camp communities observed the Sabbath with prayers, but services were usually simple and abbreviated, and were even more so as time went by. Still, the children at these camps lived in a Jewish world, surrounded by other Jews: the parents who came to visit and who stayed at area resorts and hotels and hundreds of other Jewish children attending area camps. While downplaying traditional religious practices, such camps allowed their clientele the comfort and pleasure of ethnic fraternal socializing in a fairly secular setting.

Jewish Boy Scout at Kanawauke Scout Camps, circa 1920s.
(Courtesy Palisades Interstate Park Commission Archives)

Jewish parents had reason to prefer camps and camping regions where they were not a small minority. Where Jewish children were few in number, they were more likely to face anti-Semitism at camp. For instance, Jews could attend many YMCA camps, and a small number did, but casual anti-Semitism was not only tolerated at YMCA camps; it was sometimes a source of formal entertainment, as when camp staff impersonated Jews to comic effect.[134] One set of Jewish sisters attending a Christian settlement camp in Connecticut, who were made to go to the camp chapel on Sundays, sing hymns, and kneel, practiced a small form of resistance; as one of them later recalled, "We made it a point of honor not to kneel, but to squat down."[135] Other Jews at religiously mixed camps felt anxious to prove themselves in sports competitions.[136] Just as the concentrated dispersal of Jews to specific city neighborhoods created relatively sheltered urban environments, Jewish camps and those with a significant Jewish presence shielded children from interethnic antagonism.

Yet a significant number of Jewish families of means did not choose Jewish-only camps. During the late 1920s, the Boy Scouts of America, which ran religiously integrated camps, was the single most popular camping option among Brooklynites. In New York City, one of every eight twelve-year-old boys was enrolled in the Boy Scouts organization in 1926, and of these, about half attended a Boy Scout camp.[137] Of the Brooklyn boys who attended agency camps that year, about half attended Boy Scout camps, at a cost of about eight to ten dollars per week. Even well-to-do families who could afford private camps often chose this less costly option because of their boys' prior involvement with the organization.[138] Many Jewish parents saw their children's participation in nondenominational organizations as a sign of their families' successful integration into American life. In 1924, a reporter from the *Brooklyn Jewish Chronicle,* visiting the camp at Tuxedo, New York, observed that Jews and gentiles played and lived happily together. Perhaps, the *Chronicle* suggested, Boy Scout camping constituted a meaningful bridge to the emergence of a new and unprejudiced generation.[139]

Mixed camps were one reflection of an urban culture that inevitably crossed ethnic boundaries, at least some of the time. Yet Scouting also provided opportunities for Jewish communal activity. Perhaps more important than the question of whether Jews attended mixed camps was the question of how they did so. Nationally, by 1936 almost 4 percent of Boy Scout troops were chartered by Jewish organizations.[140] Across Brooklyn, for instance, thousands of Jewish boys and girls participated in Scout troops hosted by local settlement houses, Jewish centers, synagogues, Hebrew schools, and Jewish orphan asylums, where they experienced Scouting in the context of Jewish communal life. The Brooklyn Council's Boy Scout Camp perpetuated these connections. The camp was ethnically diverse, but Jewish boys often arrived with friends from their own neighborhood synagogue or community center and camp policy dictated that local troops remain together as a group.

Based on their degree of acculturation and religious observance, Brooklyn Boy Scouts could opt for full or only partial integration into mainstream camp culture. Some camped in special troops with a kosher kitchen and dining room.[141] All campers, whether Jewish, Protestant, or Catholic, attended Sabbath services. Campers in kosher units, however, had a more intensively Jewish cultural experience, including daily services held in a clearing in the woods on sunny days, campfires where the boys sang Yiddish folksongs and Hebrew melodies, Friday-night meals with white tablecloths and Sabbath candles, fasting on the morning of Tisha B'Ab (a holiday commemorating the destruction of the Second Temple in Jerusalem and the subsequent exile of the Jews), and even the occasional Bar Mitzvah. The United Synagogue, the central congregational organization for Conservative Judaism, was particularly active in organizing Jewish Scouting activities, both in the city and at camp. Arguing that "camp should be the place in which the Scout's Jewish training should find expression," its Boy Scout extension bureau provided rabbis for the New York kosher camping units and between 1928 and 1932 published the *Scout Menorah* free of charge for Jewish Scouts.[142] Kosher services grew over the course of the era; by 1940, when over half the Brooklyn campers were Jewish, their parents chose the kosher division more than three times as often as the regular one.[143] It is likely that many parents who did not keep kosher at home chose this option for the Jewish fraternal experience. As the *Scout Menorah* proclaimed of its Boy Scout camping efforts, "It is a home though away from home."[144]

For Jewish boys, attending a mixed camp was not necessarily a leap into uncharted waters, nor did it constitute a rejection of traditional Jewish life or of Jewish community. Just as most interwar Brooklyn Jews chose to live in areas with a significant Jewish presence, the majority sent their children to camp alongside other Jews. Sometimes, however, the desire to participate in nonsectarian activities necessitated distressing compromises. The camping needs of observant Jewish Girl Scouts from Brooklyn were not well served by the local Girl Scout Council camp. The camp itself was often described by visiting members of the national staff as poorly run. More to the point, it made no provision for kosher meals despite the fact that almost half the campers were Jewish and that a third of the Jewish campers came from kosher homes. The camp's leadership resisted a change that might segregate campers at meals and raise costs. Some Orthodox parents and a local Jewish women's group complained, but many continued to send their daughters back year after year.[145]

The range of camps that American Jews supported reflected the complexity and internal divisions of a single ethnic community. Some families had to make significant concessions, but at the center of the nation's most diverse camp market even unusual communities often had numerous choices. For instance, only a small minority of interwar Jews self-identified as communists or socialists, but in the New York City area these families could choose among many summer camp options, among them Camp Kinderland (founded in 1925) and Camp Wo-Chi-Ca, the Workers' Children's Camp (1936), affiliated with Communist-led fraternal orders, and the Pioneer Youth Camp (1924) and Camp Woodland (1938), which represented the efforts of progressive educators and activists. Wo-Chi-Ca, Woodland, and the Pioneer Youth Camp emphasized interracial cooperation rather than the particularities of Jewish experience. Other camps, like the Sholem Aleichem Folk Institute's Camp Boiberik (1919), Kinderland, and Camp Kinder Ring (1927), combined political goals with Yiddish culture, and the Labor Zionist Habonim camps (1932) attracted adolescents and young adults who were considering settling in Palestine.[146]

Like Boy Scout and Camp Fire Girl camps, progressive and radical camps represented social extensions of their clients' home lives. In the 1930s, young Esther Israeloff's New York City family was devoted to socialism and Yiddish culture. Her father, a line-typist at the *Jewish Forward*, a Yiddish-language socialist paper, organized near the family's home a local Workman's Circle school (called a *shul* in Workman's Circle parlance), where Esther studied both Yiddish and English during the school year. In the 1930s, when Esther arrived at the organization's Camp Kinder Ring at Sylvan Lake, New York, she already knew many of her fellow campers through school and the Young Circle League.[147] And just as Boy Scouts met weekly during the school year to practice their skills, Camp Wo-Chi-Ca campers traveled from all over the city to International Workers Order halls, where they took classes and participated in baseball games.[148]

Private camps often began with local clienteles known to their directors, then branched out regionally as they grew better-known. Schroon Lake Camp attracted families from well beyond New York City, many of them Reform Jews who knew Rabbi Moses by reputation. By the 1920s, numerous Jewish parents in Ohio, a regional center for the Jewish Reform movement, sent sons to Schroon Lake Camp. One boy traveled to Schroon Lake all the way from Waco, Texas. Around their Adirondack campfire, where the Schroon Lake campers literally faced inward for reflection, discussion, and song, the boys' parochialism came up against a wider Jewish world. The friends whom Mike Hessberg made at camp likely expanded his sense of community and provided a counterpoint to Jewish life as he knew it at home.

American Jews were particularly enthusiastic consumers of camps, but the search for camps attuned to one's own cultural and religious heritage was not uniquely Jewish. Varied constituencies forged their own camp "villages," sometimes traveling significant distances if there were few local options. In the first decade of the century, New Hampshire's Camp Pinelands (1902), one of the first private girls' camps, attracted clients from across the eastern seaboard, a few from Montreal, and at least one from California.[149] Camp Dixie (1915), in the mountains near Wiley, Georgia, drew southern white Christian families both from nearby Atlanta and from Texas, Florida, and Louisiana, southern states with little private camping.[150] Camp Atwater and Camp Guilford Bower served African American children from across the eastern seaboard and beyond. The German American Camp Brosius (1935), on Wisconsin's Elkhart Lake, served German American campers from several midwestern cities.[151]

All these camps shared certain basic, nondenominational rituals such as swimming, hikes, and campfires, but the industry prospered through its ability to serve specific constituencies, to advance community fraternalism, and to help bind specific ethnic, religious, racial, political, and class ties. Camps represented the outer limits of metropolitan networks, even more so at those camps where children from a particular city or club were grouped together in the same tent or cabin. At the same time, camps broadened children's circles of connection, enabling them to make friends with others from outside their own neighborhoods and sometimes their own ethnic and religious group.

Mike Hessberg adored Schroon Lake Camp. "When the end of the season approached," he wrote in 1923, "all of us decided that we had had a corking time, and we went home happy and contented, our only sorrow being that the season had ended. There was one consolation, however. That was—'Look at the time we'll have next year.' Hot dawgs!"[152] Hessberg's parents enrolled Mike for the following three summers. His attendance at Schroon Lake Camp was a sign of their

Schroon Lake Camp race, circa 1920s–1930s. (Courtesy
Schroon–North Hudson Historical Society)

own financial success and their ambitions for their son; Mr. Hessberg,
in a testimonial letter that appeared in the camp's 1926 brochure, expressed his own satisfaction with his son's "association with boys of
a select type" at Schroon Lake.[153] Mike was also highly successful at
camp. He was elected to the honor society in 1924 and won the Best
All-Around Camper's Cup as a Senior camper in 1926. He then returned one last summer as a counselor.[154]

Such stories of personal and community development resonated with
parents across a broad ethnic, religious, and ideological spectrum. In an
age when many traditional ethnic and religious groups were increasingly dispersed in heterogeneous urban settings, camps promised cultural capital to their clients—not only new skills but also new connec-

tions and forms of fraternalism that would strengthen community at home. In a wide-open camp market, these promises helped parents to feel more secure that their children's camps would reflect their own values. The process of mutual selection demanded identification and trust, themes that camps would then reinforce in the summer months.

3

Rituals of the Season
The Organization of Camp Community

A sound breaks the silence—oddest of squawks,
Trills, runs, then a scale, and ends in a cough;
The bugle to wake us! That's what it is!
Some one deny it! Ask Ed, it's his biz.
A bell and a whistle, we breathe loud and long,
We watch Chief's contortions and follow them wrong,
And when our insides are nicely upset,
We rush to the house some breakfast to get.
"Save all the spoons, girls," "Now, hot, wet or dry?"
We eat. Maud swallows a third on the sly.
Service begins, which the dogs both enjoy,
They growl and they scratch, and us songsters annoy.
And now our committees! We candles renew,
And pick up all scraps with a grunt and a "goo,"
We pluck ferns and flowers for porch and the table,
And arrange them artistically, if we are able.
So on and on till all work is done,
Then we swim and we dive and we roast in the sun.
    —Kehonka camper Marguerite De Buys, from a poem published
        in the Camp Kehonka newspaper, *Goose Quills*, July 1916[1]

At the beginning of the 1917 camp season, just after six o'clock in the evening, a group of about thirty Camp Kehonka girls stepped off the train at Wolfeboro, New Hampshire. They had spent a long day traveling up the coast from their northeastern homes, and their train had arrived an hour behind schedule. Still, they were in good spirits as they boarded the camp boat, the *Kehonka IV*, for the last leg of their journey across Lake Winnipesaukee to the Alton lakeshore. The "old girls," those who had already attended the camp, knew that soon they would see the wooden lodge at the water's edge where they would eat their meals, the woods of pine, spruce, and hemlock that rose into the hills, the brook that flowed down along the edge of the property to the beach, and the canvas tents set on wooden platforms that would be their homes for the next two months. The "new girls" knew the camp only from photographs or what others had told them, and they likely admired the confidence with which one of the returning campers offered to steer the boat under the watchful eye of staff member and craft instructor Almyr "Bally" Ballentine.[2]

As the girls reached the camp, they could pick out members of the staff who had gathered to greet them at the shore. At the group's symbolic center stood camp director Laura Mattoon: slim, often dressed in knickers, her long dark hair pinned on top of her head, and large round spectacles perched on her nose. Mattoon, Camp Kehonka's director from 1902 until her death in 1945, was well situated to consider the girls' passage into camp life. One of the most active participants in the national camping movement, she was a member of the National Association of Directors of Girls' Camps (NADGC), its treasurer from 1921–24, and, after the NADGC merged with its boys' camp counterpart in 1924, the Camp Directors Association's (CDA) first elected secretary-treasurer and first salaried executive.[3] In the pages of industry journal *Camping* and at regional and national conventions, Mattoon spoke out for simplicity and "old-fashioned" values in camping. At her own camp, she worked to instill in the girls a practical and spiritual appreciation of the outdoors, physical prowess, and greater independence. "The entire camp environment," as she argued in the *Granite State News* in 1933, was "planned so as to inspire and foster in the campers rational habits of health, of joyous work, of wholesome fun, of esthetic appreciation and reverence."[4]

In choosing this camp, the Kehonka girls' parents had already participated in a process of selection along gender, class, racial, ethnic, and religious lines. The girls who now stood along the Winnipesaukee shore were white, Christian, middle- and upper-class girls from cities, towns, and suburbs along the Northeast corridor. Such similarities of experience enabled the girls to identify more easily with one another and with their camp director. But these shared attributes did not in themselves ensure that the camp community would be cohesive. It was the social organization of camp life—the making of camp cohorts, the structuring of

Camp Kehonka dock, 1920s. (Collection of author)

space, the ordering of time, and children's immersion in varied activities —that truly made girls, in Kehonka parlance, into "goslings."

The trip to camp was the first of many journeys, both physical and emotional, that the girls would take that summer. Camp culture comprised a series of rites of passage, some more formal or explicit than others, designed to foster children's sense of participating in a transformative enterprise. New campers began as "greenhorns," a term that denoted awkward newcomers both at camp and in American culture more broadly. Like recent immigrants to the United States, beginning campers enjoyed protection but not full citizenship. Their passage into citizenship required that they learn a new set of cultural references: the geography of the lake and camp grounds; special songs, expressions, and foods; new hierarchies and social expectations; camp nicknames; and appropriate dress. New social groups, daily routines, and forms of authority temporarily reconfigured their lives. New smells, sounds, tastes, and sights made clear their distance from home. Regular assessments of their skills and their bodies propelled them to consider how they were learning and growing over time. These differences allowed camps to feel like miniature worlds apart from the everyday, worlds where life was lived fully and intensely.

The relative homogeneity of individual camps allowed children to meet on terms of relative equality: dressed alike or nearly so, living in near-identical tents or cabins, and eating the same food. Early-twentieth-century camp leaders made much of the idea that camps were democratic spaces, where children achieved according to their own talents rather than external status markers.[5] Yet like citizens of any nation, campers had unequal access to power and prestige. Even after new campers made the initial adjustment to their surroundings, camp culture continued to divide them, primarily by age and skill. In a sense, camps were modern bureaucracies, characterized by their differentiation of (mostly age-based) peer groups and their emphasis on productive leisure. In this sense, if camps reoriented the social order, they did not turn it upside down. Campers arrived at camp already conscious of their own differences from one another. Camps' rituals of incorporation did not make all campers equal but provided them a variety of ways successfully to integrate themselves into the community.

Off to Camp: "Greenhorns" and Returning Campers

Long before children arrived at camp, their experiences began in the realm of the imagination. Those who had never before attended a camp gleaned information from their parents or friends, while happy veterans grew increasingly excited as the date of departure neared. In the 1930s, Helen Weisgal of New York City was a regular camper at Camp Carmelia, a private Jewish camp. As she later recalled,

> The great moment of the year came in June when my mother took down the camp trunks from the high shelf in the big closet. The smell of camphor balls and the sight of the "inventory," pasted on the inside of the trunk and consisting of a list of all the clothes and personal gear I took with me, gave me a high (although the word didn't exist in that sense then). I was in a continual fever (and/or fervor) from then until the day, a few weeks later, when we were taken on the Weehawken Ferry to the railway station in New Jersey.[6]

What preparing for camp entailed differed along class lines. The leaders of private camps expected parents to purchase long lists of required clothing and encouraged them to pack a tennis racket or a musical instrument in their child's trunk as well. Parents of Kehonka girls purchased for their daughters a typical private girls' camp uniform: white middie shirts with sailor-style collars, accessorized by dark, loosely knotted ties that were tucked under the collar in back and that hung down the chest in front; black knee-length bloomers; and dark knee socks. In the 1910s, a few younger boys attended Kehonka as well. They likely wore a standard early-twentieth-century boys' camp uniform of sleeveless or short-sleeved cotton tops, woolen sweaters, and khaki shorts or pants.

The leaders of charitable camps, in marked contrast, often found it necessary to provide sheets and toothbrushes as well as clothing to their impoverished clients.[7] Despite their limited resources, many working-class children found ways to express their anticipation. Before attending New York's Hebrew Orphan Asylum (HOA) Camp Wakitan in the 1930s, Hy Kampel, a resident of the orphanage, made a point of going to Woolworth's to purchase his own bar of soap and a ten-cent cardboard suitcase. Unlike some of the other boys from the asylum, he was pleased to consider, he would not have to pack his belongings in an ordinary bag.[8]

The actual journey to camp tended further to differentiate clients of private, full-season camps from those of less elite camps. Private camp clients often began their trips by train at the end of June or the beginning of July, departing in such great numbers from major cities of the Northeast and Midwest that railroad companies had to add extra train cars to handle the spike in traffic. Children attending organizational and charitable camps often spent only a few weeks instead of a full two months at camp, and their periodic departures over the course of the summer, whether by train, ferry, bus, or private automobile, created far less public impact. But for campers themselves, all such trips were substantial ones, especially the first time around. One group of working-class New York City boys on their way to a charitable camp sponsored by the Association for the Improvement of the Condition of the Poor in the late 1910s were "alight with eagerness" and full of questions (which the organization rendered in dialect in one of its fundraising brochures, all the better to express the boys' rough-edged, childish enthusiasm): "W'ere's de place we'se goin to stop?" "Do we sleep in tents?" "Will we go swimmin every day?" and "Do we have to wear swimmin tites?"[9]

If New York City was, by the early twentieth century, the industry's

Boy Scouts traveling to Camp Manhattan, 1937. (Courtesy Ten Mile River Scout Museum)

client epicenter, Grand Central Station was at the symbolic heart of its most spectacular goodbyes. Soon, the adults and children whose lives were affected by camping would scatter: the adults back to their homes or their own summer vacations, and the children to relatively secluded locations far from the public eye. For a brief moment, the departure of so many children at one time from one train station showcased the camp industry's rising cultural importance. In the 1920s, A. E. Hamilton, the son-in-law of Luther and Charlotte Gulick who took over the directorship of their Camp Wohelo in Maine, described with enthusiasm the "ten thousand boys and girls gathered together on one June day in the Grand Central Station. Lettered banners above their heads, bags and paddles in their hands, smiles on their faces, tears in their parents' eyes."[10] More caustically, New Yorker (and later, novelist) Herman Wouk, who attended Camp Barrington in Massachusetts during that same decade, would recall "boiling knots of perspiring, peevish city children."[11] The *New York Times* gave front-page coverage to the "din," which was "deafening," and to the chaotic scene: "Youngsters wandered away, only to be rounded up and bustled back by watchful group attendants."[12] Parents drifted from one area to another looking for the appropriate camp banner, children followed, often dressed in formal travel outfits, and counselors and camp directors fretted about the campers who had not yet shown up.

This noisy, disorienting scene undoubtedly added to the stress inherent in these farewells, not only for first-time campers but also for parents, who were often handing over their children to strangers. Some goodbyes were tearful or extended.[13] One mother, anxious to spend a final moment with her child, sneaked onto the train and had to leap back onto the platform as the train departed.[14] Others, in an effort to avoid emotional displays, made a joke of what could have been an awkward moment; the mother of Ruth and Libby Raynes, dropping her girls off at Grand Central Station, always teased them by saying "Good riddance to bad rubbish!"[15]

Traveling into the countryside, learning camp songs as the scenery rolled by, children became congregants in a shared culture. Especially for first-time campers and those who had never before left city limits, the act of traveling to camp was itself a rite of passage into another world. Camp routines were, however, not yet fully in play. As counselors noted with exasperation, children on their way to camp were often difficult to manage. Especially on overnight trips, incoming campers often stayed up late talking excitedly among themselves despite adults' attempts to keep them quiet. Some engaged in pillow fights, water-pistol play, and pranks as they headed toward the lakes and mountains, signs of their high spirits, anxiety, or even boredom on the long train trips.[16]

The rules of camp life were only beginning to be put into place when children first passed by the camp sign along a rural road or under a wooden archway with the camp name spelled out in block letters at the entrance to camp. Like new immigrants, the newcomers had much to learn about the landscape and community around them. Official rituals of initiation such as welcoming talks and first-night campfires provided some sense of the daily schedule and the rules. Returning campers were another source of information. A new boy at Camp Pasquaney in 1897 might well have asked why returning campers referred to one camp building as Mump Hall; an experienced camper could have explained that the year before, half the campers had lived in quarantine in this building during a mumps epidemic.[17] As a newcomer learned to use this term with confidence, and to find his way to Mump Hall, he too became a Pasquaney boy.

Camp campuses were diverse. New camps often had the bare essentials: sleeping quarters, a grassy area for play, and a dining hall (often a converted summer house or barn) for meals and shelter from rain. Some camps were designed like military encampments, with tents laid out around the sides of a central field and a "mess hall" in lieu of a dining hall. This layout was especially popular at boys' camps during the First World War. More established camps, and private camps more particularly, were often designed like bucolic miniature villages, with paths instead of streets and rows of tents or attractive wooden bungalows in lieu of houses. As camps grew, their organization of space became increasingly specialized. Paths wound through the woods, down to the waterfront, up to clusters of tents, and past specialty cabins for crafts or the boathouse. Permanent campfires often had logs arrayed in a circle or semicircle so campers could more comfortably sit facing the fire. Many spaces served multiple purposes. Grassy fields were used for religious services, plays, and morning calisthenics. Dining halls brought campers together for meals, evening entertainments, dances, and rainy-day activities.

Like the layout of camp space, camp architecture suggested a middle ground between the natural world and civilization. The main buildings were generally built of local materials, especially wood and stone. Purposefully rustic, they were by no means plain. They often had high ceilings, shaded porches, and various artistic flourishes. The Kehonka lodge typified this bucolic style. Built in 1910, it contained a living room with a large stone fireplace, a dining room, and a veranda from which campers could look out over the lake toward the Ossipee mountain range and the foothills of the White Mountains. A live pine tree grew from a hole in the floor of the dining room, whimsically bringing nature into this sheltered space, and the campers decorated the tables with ferns and flowers, domesticating and beautifying their dining hall. "The house somehow satisfied the tired traveler from the city—simple, restful, artistic, giving clues to the camp history in its adornment," wrote one Kehonka newcomer in 1916.[18] Beyond the lodge, an outdoor walkway led to the kitchen and the icehouse, work spaces set apart from the campers' lives.

Whereas lodges and dining halls emphasized the group as a whole, sleeping quarters privileged small-scale group intimacy. New campers were each assigned a cot and a shelf or floor space for their luggage, but there was little room for personal belongings or privacy. As at many early-twentieth-century camps, the Kehonka tents were raised on platform boards to keep the floors dry. Two layers of canvas overhead protected against wind and rain, and the girls could open the side flaps in sunny weather. For campers who shared a bedroom at home (or, in the case of some working-class children, a single bed), such tents might have felt relatively spacious; for the Kehonka girls, many of whom likely had bedrooms of their own at home filled with their own possessions, the accommodations were unusually intimate. Campers sometimes slept in beds a foot apart from one another—some even shared a bed at charitable camps—and often showered and bathed as a group.

For many new campers, the scent of pine trees, the smoke of the evening campfire, the smell of mildew on wool blankets, the charred caramel taste of toasted marshmallows, the brightness of the sky filled with stars at night, and the rustle of crickets and chipmunks were all novel sensory experiences. Some found the rural quiet positively unnerving after the bustle of urban life.[19] Others were frightened by insects. Camp food was a particular source of novelty and sometimes of anxiety. At one settlement-house camp of the 1930s, Lydia Stoopenkoff got in line to enter the mess hall and was "hit in the face" by the heat from the kitchen: "heat that smelled *awful*—boiled beans. We never ate beans at home."[20]

During the first few days of camp, veterans had opportunities to exploit their greater knowledge through pranks that demarcated them from the greenhorns. In a sign of the more explicitly aggressive nature of boys' culture, hazing rites, both official and unofficial, appear to have been far more prevalent at boys' camps. At interwar Camp Dudley, "old-timers" regularly asked new campers to water the tent pegs or to find cans of striped paint, ridiculous or impossible tasks. Official initiation rituals also emphasized newcomers' vulnerability. At the Adirondack Woodcraft Camp, new boys were blindfolded after dark and led, holding on to one another in a blind processional, to the camp council circle to answer questions from the "Dragon" and his "guards." Although the questions themselves were banal (among them, "Do you believe in Santa Claus?" and "Are you afraid?"), the ordeal likely engendered anxiety among newcomers, as well as pleasure and relief among returning campers who were spared this embarrassment.[21]

At boys' camps around the nation, the most common hazing ritual was the snipe hunt, a kind of wild goose chase for newcomers. In preparation for the hunt, counselors and "old boys" gave earnest advice about how to catch this waterfowl, then sent the newcomers off on a fruitless expedition. In 1940, camper Andre Laureys was among the new boys at Camp Riverdale, a private Adirondack camp, who were taken to a nearby island to catch snipe for the next night's dinner. The counselors left the boys, promising to scare the snipe out from hiding on the other side of the island, and rowed away. When the campers did not hear the "snipe beaters" at work, they gradually became suspicious and walked to the other side of the island. As Laureys related in the camp newspaper, "The 'beaters' had 'beaten it,' and we were left with only two rowboats and one oar!" Finally, the counselors returned for the boys and brought them back to camp, where the others cheered and teased them (and, as Laureys soon found out, where his bed had been "pied," or short-sheeted, in his absence). By the end of the summer, when one of the members of the ill-fated expedition delivered a sparkling account of the hunt, all the boys were in on the joke. Campers like Laureys could now look forward with enthusiasm to putting new arrivals through the same embarrassing ordeal the following year.[22]

Children's initiation into camp culture took more generous forms as well. Consider the practice of camp nicknames, which (like pranks) stood between official and unofficial camp culture. In 1937, the Camp Andree girls on a canoe trip included Van, Scotty, Ditt, Mugs, Chippy, Marie, Ellen, and Shelly, and the counselors they called Rush and Scamper. A good number of the Andree girls renamed themselves and one another, sometimes more than once. Van (perhaps Vanessa at home) explained that when Scotty (whose nickname might have attested to Scottish heritage or to her last name) stuck her head out of Van's green blanket one morning, she "looked so much like a turtle that we promptly named her 'Turtle.'"[23] Special camp names testified to new identities and experiences, asserting children's disjunction from ordinary life while illustrating their active participation in making camps into special spaces of personal transformation. Nicknames also ritualized new ways of thinking about family and kinship outside traditional bounds. At many camps, the counselors became "Aunt" or "Uncle," and the youngest children were under the care of a "Camp Mother." Nicknames remained bound by hierarchy and power relations. Some Camp Andree girls found, to their displeasure, that they were not allowed to rename the adults around them.[24] Still, the regular social order had been temporarily reoriented, and much seemed possible.

What made a camper into an "old boy" or "old girl" was less a matter of age than of experience. The category encompassed veterans who had attended the camp before as well as those who had arrived earlier in the summer and stayed on through a second session when newcomers arrived. Veteran campers who had enjoyed their camp generally returned with confidence and delight. In 1909, camper Bess Hartshorne of the Pasquaney Nature Club, writing in the camp log, described her newly returned campmates rushing around exclaiming, "Oh don't you remember this, that, and the other thing?"[25] Even adults who were new to camp could feel like "greenhorns" as compared to experienced campers. As a new counselor at the Girl Scouts' Camp Andree complained after the 1927 season, three of the older girls "knew more about things than I did." Such girls returned to camp with a sense of entitlement and were more likely, the counselor wrote in her evaluative report, to try "to run affairs to suit themselves."[26]

However, no camp was entirely static from year to year. Camp Kehonka occupied a few campsites from 1902 through 1910 before Mattoon found a permanent home for her camp. She briefly enrolled a small number of younger boys, who had their own separate activities. She regularly planned new buildings such as the "Treasure House" (the natural history museum), a Loom House, a Craft Shop, a Boat House, and a smaller lodge designed as a social space for the younger campers. Mattoon was forced to undertake repairs after a September 1938 hurricane toppled seventy trees against the lodge. Every year the mix of campers and staff was unique.[27] Kehonka camper Margaret De Buys attended from 1910 through 1916, but this "old gosling" did not return the following year. By the 1920s, few campers would remember her.

Those who returned to camp found themselves occupying slightly different places in the social order. At Kehonka, the youngest girls lived at one end of a tent line, and the oldest girls at the other, so returning campers had tangible evidence of their changing status. Some friends and counselors from previous seasons were likely back, but others were not. A returning camper might be assigned to a new group as well, depending on the size of his or her camp and the age range of its campers: at various camps, those who had been Indians became Juniors, Midgets became Seniors, and Bluebirds became Parrots.[28] Although prior experience gave some children a degree of initial privilege, even those "old-timers" who had superior knowledge of camp places and traditions inevitably renewed their claims on camps from fresh vantage points.

Over the course of the first days and weeks, distinctions between new and returning campers subsided as newcomers found their footing. As they learned to find their way from one space to another, to sing with the group, and to use camp slang, they became part of the larger community. But these participatory and playful communities would remain hierarchical, emphasizing certain differences even as they integrated newcomers into collective life.

Age Cohorts and Intergenerational Community

At a general level, camps were worlds of age hierarchy. Adults asserted the authority to organize children's time, activities, bodies, and access to various spaces: monitoring campers to make sure they brushed their teeth, wore clean clothing, and were in bed at night by the time the last bell struck; planning their days; and forbidding them from wandering into camp kitchens or swimming in the lake without adult supervision. Kehonka girls had much greater opportunities for outdoor adventure than did most girls of their era, and they had some degree of autonomy at Kehonka in helping to plan the camp day, but they were always expected to defer to adults. If girls wished to go into the town of Wolfeboro, or to pick strawberries for dinner, or to take a boat out on Lake Winnipesaukee, they had to ask permission of Miss Mattoon (or, as they sometimes affectionately called her, Mother Goose).[29] Any camper who disobeyed adult leadership risked being sent home.

From their arrival, and sometimes on the train ride to camp, children were separated into smaller age-based cohorts that marked their more specific place in the camp at large.[30] Some of these divisions were imposed by adults; others were identified by children themselves. At Camp Chocorua, for instance, the youngest and oldest campers were at different developmental stages. Ernest Balch's later recollections of the camp give the impression that he enrolled early and middle adolescents aged twelve to sixteen, old enough to benefit from camp but impressionable enough to mold.[31] However, some of his actual clients were much younger. His brother Alfred later recalled that the Chocorua clientele ranged "from eight to fourteen years." At Chocorua the older campers were more likely to run camp businesses, while some of the youngest campers were so inexperienced in taking care of themselves that they could not properly dress themselves or lace their own shoes. Scorned as

Two Boy Scouts, Kanawauke Scout Camps, circa 1920s. (Courtesy Palisades Interstate Park Commission Archives)

"Incapables" by their fellow campers, these younger boys struggled to catch up.[32] Each summer the very youngest boy at Chocorua was nicknamed the "infant" and had special rights befitting a pampered youngest son, including the right to eat ice cream whether or not he had helped to make it.[33]

At early-twentieth-century camps, most campers were still on the cusp of early adolescence, and the average camper was about twelve or thirteen years old.[34] Increasing numbers of parents sent even younger boys (and, as girls' camps expanded, young girls) to camps, an indication that these institutions no longer appeared particularly experimental or risky. Some parents, whether eager to have their own time freed from child care or believing strongly in the camp ideal, enrolled children as young as four or five. In 1902, Mattoon first set out to camp with eight adolescent girls, students at the private New York City high school where she was head of the science department. By the mid-1920s, when she enrolled fifty girls per summer, the Kehonka tent line included sections for girls from six to ten, eleven to thirteen, and fourteen to eighteen years old.[35]

Successful camp directors marked age differences more systematically as their camps grew, incorporating campers into the larger group not only as children but as members of age-specific cohorts with their own names, special spaces, developmental needs, and rights. All campers swam, hiked, and attended campfires, but at many camps the youngest children had their own play spaces, a higher counselor-camper ratio, and the attention of a "Camp Mother" (often the wife or mother of the camp director), while the oldest children enjoyed special privileges such as later bedtimes or intercamp dances. In 1923, Ruth Saslov, a "Midget" camper at Camp Che-Na-Wah, a private Adirondack camp for Jewish girls, noted mournfully in her camp newspaper that "when the Seniors had a barn dance, the rest of the campers had a marshmallow roast. When we got to the Lodge, we had only two marshmallows, and we had to go to bed. That is the life of a Midget."[36] To be a Senior (or, for that matter, a counselor) at Camp Che-Na-Wah was to exist on a more rarified plane, a zone of greater privilege, authority, and even the possibility of romance.

The number of adolescents over the age of sixteen who attended camps as paying clients was always low, and by the interwar years it was negligible.[37] Most older youth withdrew from the groups that sponsored camp vacations. Some were obliged or preferred to work for pay during the summer. Many were no longer attracted to the idea of recreation under adult oversight. A distinctive adolescent peer culture was growing, especially among high school students. As the proportion of fourteen- to seventeen-year-olds attending high school rose from under 10 percent in 1900 to almost 80 percent in 1940, adolescents were increasingly likely to spend their days with their peers rather than in mixed-age work environments.[38] Those who continued to fraternize with younger children, meanwhile, often suffered socially. In 1935, a group of Camp Andree girls, all of them Girl Scouts fourteen years of age or older, contended that they had paid a price for remaining in the Girl Scouts past the age at which most other girls dropped out to pursue

other interests. The uniform, which they had to wear to meetings during the school year, was, they felt, "unbecoming"; more important,
they faced significant peer pressure from their non-Scouting peers, who
taunted them, calling them "good little girls" and "Girl Frights." These
girls chose a camp designed specifically for adolescents fourteen years of
age or older, and they specifically requested greater autonomy and a
program better attuned to their needs.[39]

As older adolescents began increasingly to resist spending their summers with younger children, camp leaders worked to find new roles
for older campers that would acknowledge their special status and retain their interest while keeping them under adult oversight. As early as
1915, Camp Dudley policy encouraged older boys to become "junior
leaders," and Camp Andree was founded in 1921 specifically with the
needs of older Girl Scouts in mind.[40] By the 1930s, the demands of
campers too old to enjoy the same old roles and too young to be staff,
along with adult acknowledgment of their fundamental difference from
younger children, stimulated the development of junior-counselor and
counselor-in-training (CIT) programs at camps across the country. Well
before the Second World War, the era when many merchants began particularly to target adolescents through specialty teen clothing lines and
magazines such as *Seventeen* (1944), a distinctive "teenage" culture was
already under development at summer camps.[41]

The organization of camp age cohorts began at the most intimate
level, that of tent and cabin assignments. These living units constituted
campers' closest "family" for the weeks or months to come and were a
matter of some importance. Whether campers belonged to a tent or
cabin group of four, eight, or twelve, they generally ate at the same dining room table, pursued most of their activities as a group throughout
the course of the day, performed chores together, and shared a counselor or two who served as their most intimate quasi-parental authority.
If a Camp Dudley boy received a food package from home, celebrated
his birthday with a cake, or caught a fish of any size, his group shared
in his good fortune. If he received too many "sinkers" for bad behavior, the rest of the group would also suffer.[42] A camp "family" might encompass children as young as four and as old as seventeen, but each age
cohort had its particular spaces and routines and to some extent its own
social life. Many tent and cabin groups developed their own nicknames
and private jokes, while close friendships (and sometimes bitter rivalries) were forged within these shared quarters.

Age-based camp cohorts were shaped by children as well as adults. The distance from Kitten to Bluebird, or Junior to Senior, did, after all, span critical developmental and cultural differences. Consider the experience of Lydia Stoopenkoff, born in 1930 in New York City to a working-class family of Russian, Eastern Orthodox immigrants. At the age of five, she attended a settlement-house camp, where she was mortified to have her bedwetting made public: "my older sister, in the dorm next to mine . . . would hang my wet sheet on the line. . . . It was like a banner of shame. But I also felt great love for my sister for protecting me from all those people out there." By her early teens, Lydia's interests and concerns had changed dramatically. She now attended a private camp organized for a Russian American clientele. No longer a bedwetter, she had a crush on Donat, the young male counselor: "when he wore his bathing suit we would fall apart. We would never stare when he was looking, and we would giggle if anyone would refer to 'his secret package.'" More thoughtful, Lydia watched her mother labor in the hot camp kitchen to pay for her vacation and felt, for the first time, how hard adult life could be.[43]

The centrality of age as a category of difference at camps helps us to understand why festivities that subverted or parodied this order, such as "Campers' Day" or "Topsy-Turvy Day," had the resonance that they did. In 1938, "Campers' Day" at Camp Jeanne D'Arc, a private Adirondack camp for Catholic girls, began at breakfast. As the camp newsletter noted, the counselors who were pretending to be Kittens (the name given the youngest girls of six or seven) "came to breakfast all dressed up in pyjamas, balloons and dolls. They sucked their thumbs, refused to eat their food and generally gave a very uncomplimentary imitation of our youngest campers." While the young adults were playing at being babies, the oldest campers (the Parrots and the Bluebirds) took on many of the responsibilities of the staff.[44] Although this event officially allowed children to try out greater authority, in point of fact it did not always proceed smoothly. At some camps Topsy-Turvy Days degenerated into near-anarchy, as counselors playfully blew off steam by sneaking out of their bunks or showing poor table manners (inappropriate acts that humorously reinforced their "true" adult status while pointing out the difficulties of their work), and campers ran wild.[45] In such instances, activities that ostensibly gave campers insight into the workings of camp called attention to something else entirely: the everyday age-bound social hierarchies that circumscribed the community.

"Baby play" at Camp Severance, 1920s. (Courtesy Adirondack Museum)

Whereas Campers' Days advanced adolescents toward adulthood, baby parties and baby parades, other popular camp entertainments, returned campers (and the counselors who joined them) backward in time. Campers who played at being babies broke with convention while marking, through exaggerated performance, their own fundamental nonbabyness. In 1937, the Camp Andree girls initiated a "baby party" at dinner one night, when, sitting in their lounging pajamas, the campers spontaneously decided to put bows in their hair and to pick up dolls.[46] Boys also derived pleasure from baby parades in which they played at performing the "ugliest baby" or the "baby from Mars."[47]

The occasional subversion of age-bound norms was exciting precisely because it transgressed the regular social order within which camp culture reinforced age hierarchies. These special events also playfully expressed the nebulousness of age-bound social identities. The teenagers at Camp Andree could dress as little girls one evening and assert their independence the next; betwixt and between, they attended a camp for older Scouts to which they had brought dolls from home. Camp culture divided childhood into component parts, granting different rights to different age groups. It also playfully allowed campers to consider what they were leaving behind in growing older, the social space that they currently occupied, and the adults that they would soon become.

Campers at mixed-age camps experienced themselves variably as members of groups large and small: their closest friends, their age group, their skill group, and the camp as a whole. As the Kehonka girls moved from one activity to the next, they moved between variations on community. Across age differences, many campers grew close to certain older campers and to well-loved counselors. At Camp Pasquaney, camper Frederick Dawson was deeply attached to an older camper (and later, counselor), Fred Kneeland, whom he considered his best friend. When Kneeland had to leave early one summer, Dawson later recalled, "I felt my heart would break to see him pack his suitcase. In a flood of sorrow I threw myself into his arms; he held me like a little child— which I really was in those days."[48] However, the trend at camps, as in American children's culture more broadly, was toward the development of semiautonomous age cohorts. As individual camp communities grew larger, campers tended to move through social worlds demarcated more specifically by age. By 1916, Camp Mowglis counselor Alcott Farrar Elwell noted that activities at many larger camps were organized for specific groups of tentmates and their own leaders, a practice that would later be termed the "unit plan."[49] Even where camp activities were not formally divided by age, campers usually sat around the campfire, went from activity to activity, and ate their meals with their tent or cabin group, and their most intense personal relationships tended to emerge within their own age cohorts. At a time when few camps were coeducational and fewer still were interracial, age remained camps' single most important organizing distinction.

Camp Activities and the Work of Play

Children's entrance into camp community was a process, not a one-time event. Returning campers enjoyed a brief moment of social superiority, and older campers arrived at camp with greater cultural capital. But once children settled in, their place at camp was also decided through their own athletic and social achievements. To the degree that they acquired new skills or made better (or worse) reputations for themselves, their status changed over time. A child who learned to swim could move into deeper water; an improving baseball player might be selected to participate in a game against another camp; a popular and accomplished camper might be invited to join the camp honor society; a member of an extended canoe trip might receive a special badge or award commemorating the event; an aspiring actor might successfully entertain his or her peers on the camp stage; a shy camper might be unexpectedly popular at a dance with a neighboring camp. These stories of progress, consonant with popular American ideologies of self-improvement, reinforced camps' mandate: that leisure time should be productive and well-managed and should offer tangible results.

By the early twentieth century, the informality and relative experimentation characteristic of many late-nineteenth-century camps had given way to more clearly defined goals and programs. Mattoon's schedule was flexible, weather contingent, and allowed for camper input. Typically, however, the girls moved from one area of the campus to the next at predictable time intervals. They awoke to the sound of a bugle or bell and performed calisthenics or took a quick dip in the lake (both of which were held to be invigorating and toning activities) before filing into the dining hall for breakfast. Athletic activities filled the morning and afternoon, with a brief rest hour after lunch during which campers were supposed to nap or rest quietly. After dinner, campers generally attended some event, whether a campfire, bunk party, or play. This routine was slightly abridged on Sundays (or Saturdays, at religiously observant Jewish camps), when campers slept in, attended a religious or spiritual service, and enjoyed a few hours of unstructured free time in the afternoon.

At most camps swimming was the most important athletic activity of the day. Swimming lessons were one of camps' central draws: "No girl leaves camp without learning to swim," as a Kehonka brochure of the 1920s proclaimed.[50] In an era when many children arrived at camp unable to swim, and others rarely swam during the school year, this sport made the transformative promise of camp life particularly tangible.[51] Swimming displayed the unique opportunities available in the natural world, symbolizing the liberty and physicality of camp life. It attested to the special skills and supervision of waterfront staff. It also exemplified camps' promise of physical improvement. For girls, swimming suggested athletic emancipation. For muscular Christians, swimming offered "spiritual growth, being used to teach courage and altruism and thus assist in the highest type of character," as the YMCA's *Association Boys* magazine suggested in 1914.[52]

Camp Wehaha girls at the waterfront, circa 1920s–1930s. (Courtesy Hyman Bogen)

For campers, learning to swim or perfecting their technique was a central accomplishment of the season. Typically proud was the 1920 Camp Dudley boy who boasted enthusiastically in a letter to his mother that "Erd [a staff member] pushed me off the high dive and I swam like a fish while the rest of the camp looked on and cheered and cheered loudly."[53] Nonswimmers generally started at the "crib," a fenced-in pen in shallow water. The appellation suggested juvenile status. As camps of the 1920s began to adopt new Red Cross standards, nonswimmers were also increasingly restricted from boating or canoeing until they had demonstrated some competence in the water. "Lake swimmers," on the other hand, having proved themselves in the water, were free to swim farther from shore and to take out boats under supervision.

Camps' emphasis on swimming by no means represented a "natural" return to rural American tradition. In the 1880s, the farmers near Holderness, New Hampshire, few of whom knew how to swim, found Ernest Balch's emphasis on water sports bizarre and unappealing.[54] Rather, swimming introduced children to an important vacationing custom, and it was the starting point for other important leisure activities such as boating, water pageants, and aquatic competitions. By the 1920s, many camp waterfronts were quite elaborate. The Kehonka girls, as befitted members of an elite private camp, had the use of a camp water slide,

Boy Scouts from Camp Manhattan on a canoe trip, 1937. (Courtesy Ten Mile River Scout Museum)

a springboard for diving, row boats, and two "war canoes," each of which was big enough to fit eleven girls at once.

From the earliest camps onward, the other most important athletic event at boys' camps was baseball. "A baseball nine is an important adjunct to every well-regulated camp, and receives most loyal support," one observer of the camp scene wrote in 1900.[55] At many boys' camps, baseball was a near constant, pitting cabin against cabin, camp against neighboring camp, campers against the staff, and even campers against their own visiting parents. Any relatively flat grassy space could be fitted out as a baseball field at low cost, so even camps that had few special activities tended to offer baseball. Girls played competitively as well, at Kehonka and elsewhere, and baseball was one sign of their successful appropriation of a traditionally male athletic endeavor. The leaders of camps for ethnic and immigrant Americans, meanwhile, often saw their campers' ability to play the "American game" as a sign of successful acculturation into American life.[56] Other sports were on the schedule—tennis and riding were popular at private camps but less available elsewhere, shooting and boxing were among the offerings at certain boys' camps, and in the interwar years, basketball began to gain in popularity—but no other camp sport had baseball's wide appeal. Across a diverse range of boys' and girls' camps, baseball marked the season.

Although baseball was a modern sport, many other important camp activities referenced preindustrial and indigenous traditions. Archery and canoeing, for instance, were commonly taught at camps but rarely practiced elsewhere. Horseback riding, mostly the privilege of private campers due to its cost, suggested old-fashioned transportation. So, too, woodwork and crafts activities were held to be quintessentially "campy." At elite Camp Kehonka, the girls had opportunities to try many traditional crafts including weaving, spinning, chair caning, bookbinding, jewelry making, and woodworking.[57] On wet days, when the girls had to stay indoors, they built birdhouses and organized the nature

Camp Wehaha baseball team, 1926. (Courtesy Hyman Bogen and Betty Jablon)

specimens that they had gathered on hikes for display in their own natural history museum.[58]

All camp directors extolled the "improving" properties of nature, but Mattoon was unusual in the degree to which she emphasized "nature work" and lectured on ecological themes. Having taught science for many years, her training and interests were similar to those of some of the earliest nineteenth-century camp leaders who founded camps with natural history as their focus. But by the 1920s, "woodcraft" was in decline. Its champions chastised their peers for neglecting to make better use of the educational and spiritual opportunities offered by the woods and fields, but camp leaders more often used the landscape as a springboard for other outdoor activities, such as swimming or riding, than as an endpoint in and of itself. Charles Hendry, co-organizer of a series of influential Camp Institutes in Chicago in the 1930s, suggested one reason: campers themselves were much more enthusiastic about ping-pong and dramatics programs.[59]

Camp religious programing, however, made much of the beauty of the outdoors. At Camp Chocorua, the boys participated in Episcopal services at a "chapel" in a clearing in the woods. Seated on rustic wooden seats facing a white birch cross and a flower-bedecked rock that served as the altar, they could see an inspiring view of Mount Chocorua in the far distance.[60] Laura Mattoon co-authored a nondenominational Protestant guide to camp services, entitled *Services for the Open*, in 1923.[61] As her title suggested, the outdoors added a special dimension to religious contemplation.

Evening campfires, a near-ubiquitous part of camp life, conjoined the spiritual and the secular. At the earliest muscular Christian camps, adult leaders tried to inspire "conversions" by the romantic glow of the campfire. In later years, campfires were less explicitly religious, but they remained spaces of intimate soul-searching and discussions of community ideals as well as group singing and marshmallow toasting. Around the campfire, campers sat on logs or the grass, singing and watching the fire as their fellow campers' faces blurred in the growing darkness and smoky haze. For many, the effect was magical, appearing as it did to offer entry into a so-called primitive or premodern realm. Yet campfires, like the rest of camp, mediated between freedom and order. They were often at least partially scripted; the campfire was generally accorded a permanent outdoor spot, and songs, games, competitions of various kinds, and reenactments of Native American ceremonies were often planned in advance. Staff often lit these fires with matches rather than by rubbing sticks together, and in some instances they poured gasoline on the logs to achieve a more impressive flame.[62]

Following the lead of Ernest Balch, who instituted an annual "Long Walk" at Chocorua, most camp leaders planned at least one significant trip away from camp each summer. The Kehonka girls regularly hiked and canoed through the region in small groups, and they particularly looked forward to a three-day climb over New Hampshire's Presidential Range, including a hike up Mount Washington.[63] As camps grew more established, overnight hikes (or "tramps," as hikes were often called) and canoe trips took on growing importance as adventurous breaks from the ordinary routine. Many camp leaders came to believe that their own camps were too civilized to provide a full dose of outdoor adventure. By 1912, when the New York YMHA's Surprise Lake Camp was only ten years old, campers were already retreating to a "pioneer" spot for overnight camping, because, as the camp's leader suggested, "Camp is tending year by year to lose some of the old 'roughing it' spirit that so appeals to every boy."[64]

These trips could be both grueling and deeply satisfying. On Balch's "Long Walks," the heavy supplies traveled by oxen, and tired campers could ride in a wagon.[65] In the years to come, some camp directors sent off boys and girls (but more often boys, as part of the project of rugged masculinity) on hikes with heavy backpacks.[66] Because most camp leaders believed that it was unhealthy to drink much during hikes, many campers undoubtedly were quite thirsty by the time they reached their destinations. On wet days, they tramped soggily. On hot days, they broiled under the sun; after a 1907 hike to Santa Cruz by YMCA campers from San Jose, California, one of the adults who led the group noted that "nearly every boy received a dandy dose of sunburn" and that one boy had "blisters on his shoulders the size of goose eggs."[67] Even if (or perhaps especially if) it rained every day or the hiking was arduous, campers who completed such trips took pride in their accomplishments and felt closer to nature. One young Adirondack camper of 1942 wrote for many when he praised his camp's "over nyghts" and "hicks."[68]

Cooking out was a central element of these adventures. Back in 1885, the first Dudley cohort set their tents on rocky ground and cooked their own meals (with mixed results: as one member of the group later recalled of their first dinner, "we ate and ate, and if some boy did put his foot in the corn, and a very few other trivial accidents happened, I tell you we relished that dinner").[69] In later years, camp leaders became increasingly conscious of health considerations and oversaw larger groups with correspondingly more significant food requirements, so they delegated less and less of the daily cooking to children. On camping trips, however, small groups of children helped to set up tents, made their own campfires under adult supervision, and contributed significantly to the cooking and cleaning, bringing them temporarily closer in spirit to some of the earliest small camps. Even cook-outs at camp were novelties for campers used to eating at long tables; as the Kehonka newspaper, *Goose Quills,* described one such evening in 1917, "Hot dogs sizzled over the leaping flames; faces glowed with anticipation and heat; mosquitoes bit with great gusto; sandwiches, lemonade and olives disappeared with remarkable rapidity . . . chocolate cake and marshmallows were ravenously devoured."[70] The results were not always ideal—1920s Kehonka camper Hope Lord described "our rather sandy supper" on one overnight excursion—but most campers enjoyed their own efforts.[71]

At full-season camps, each week brought a new special event, whether a canoe trip, a national holiday like Independence Day, or a camp circus or pageant. Campers searched for stones painted gold at the "Gold Rush," dressed up as animals and performers for circuses and carnivals, watched humorous "mock trials," created elaborate floats for their water pageants, and participated in Indian pageants and blackface minstrel shows. The number of such events and their degree of elaborateness varied according to the length of the camp season (or session) and the type of camp, but their intensity peaked in the final weeks or days, when the routine might have begun to seem too predictable. Just before campers returned home, a series of particularly exciting events such as large-scale competitions, theatrical performances, award ceremonies, and final banquets raised the emotional pitch to its highest level. These events marked the passage of time, showcased skill, bravery, and community solidarity, and heightened the sense that camp space and time stood outside the ordinary mundane world.

From the 1920s onward, Color War held a place of honor as the single most important special event at many camps. Blending pageantry and athletics, this competition was possibly an elaboration of a war game, Capture the Flag, popular at many northeastern boys' camps by the 1910s, in which teams named after colors (often blue and gray for the Union and Confederate armies of the American Civil War) tried to enter one another's territory while remaining unseen.[72] By the mid-1910s, Color War had evolved into a large-scale competition comprising many smaller contests, held near the end of the camp season, when campers had tired of the ordinary routine. Schroon Lake Camp did not claim to have invented the event, but theirs was among the first. Beginning in 1916, the camp's "Red and Gray week" at the end of August involved several days of competition within each age division, including track and field events, checkers, swimming, and Indian leg wrestling.[73]

Temporarily reconfiguring camp community, Color War drew the youngest and the oldest campers together across lines of age difference while dividing individual tents or cabins into two. As such, the event dramatized camps' inevitable internal factions, while allowing every child to feel part of a team. Some might succeed at field sports; others helped their team by winning a crucial game of checkers, writing a popular camp song, or simply cheering especially loudly. At many camps, the entire community, including the camp doctor and nurse, participated. New campers looked forward with eagerness to the opening ceremonies, when they found out which team they would be on. The entire camp followed the score as the teams battled, day by day. For many campers, Color War represented a highlight of camp life. In 1924, a *New York Times* reporter overheard "sunburned children" returning to the city at the end of the summer tell their families "how the Blues had beaten the Grays, how the baseball game with the rival camps had been won and how the medals had been distributed."[74]

Theoretically these competitive divisions were only temporary, dissipating when the team hatchets were reburied in the ground and ending in reconciliation. But the festivities left some campers enervated and unable to let go of team rivalries. Starting in the 1930s, some camp leaders rejected the competitive fervor of Color War.[75] They deployed pageantry and intracamp competition in ways more suited to their own specific causes and political convictions: in the mid-1930s, for instance, campers at the Communist Camp Kinderland undertook biweekly thematic projects such as National Minorities, the Scottsboro Project (efforts to free a group of southern black adolescents who had been imprisoned on false rape charges), the Anti-War Project, and the Anti-Olympic Project.[76]

Children also worked toward individual glory. Those who completed difficult hikes, swam across the lake, took on lead roles in camp musicals, learned the names of a certain number of plants, or scored the pivotal goal in an intercamp baseball game were often rewarded with badges and plaques. At Camp Kehonka, girls who showed proficiency in swimming, diving, a ball game, field sports, a five-mile walk, and a long paddle by canoe won their camp "K," a badge of distinction that the girls sewed onto the front of their sweaters.[77] At the end of the season, camp award ceremonies and campers' inductions into honor societies provided grander and more public recognition for the "Best Boy" or "Peppiest Girl." These awards and attendant public acclaim motivated many campers. When Robert Holzworth attended Adirondack Woodcraft Camp in 1929 at the age of eleven, this slim boy only one year past a bout with polio eagerly seized on the camp's many opportunities to shine, and as he later recalled, "I studied one craft and one specialty after another and colored the totems on my totem leather with enthusiasm. I was a big hero when I finally swam to the raft and back. What a victory! Then I won my emblem."[78] Decades later, these achievements remained highlights of his camp experience.

Camps' emphasis on productive, goal-oriented leisure reflected distinctly modern American sensibilities. Camp activities were designed to improve campers as well as to bring them more deeply into the group: swimming lessons to introduce campers to a mainstay of modern vacation culture, teach children to overcome a fear of the water, introduce them to competition, and help them to master their bodies; baseball to teach children to work collaboratively with others while moving their bodies more precisely and powerfully; archery to teach focus, good posture, and premodern skill; boxing for boys and dancing for girls to reinforce gender roles. Even rest hour had a goal: to refresh campers for the afternoon activities to come. After days filled with such purposeful play, it is no wonder that campers were tired by the time evening taps was sounded. As Kehonka camper Marguerite De Buys concluded, "We stumble to bed, 'Lights out down the line,' / And settle our limbs for slumber sublime."[79]

Transformation Embodied

In 1916, the Camp Kehonka newspaper, *Goose Quills*, wryly described the enthusiasm with which campers were working toward the camp emblem, the "K": "One may see these ambitious geese trudging wearily to Wolfeboro and back, or see pairs of determined looking goslings paddling to town over a ruffled lake. The star-covered bulletins show the progress made in aquatic sports. Even now the goslings are mentally sewing K's on their sweaters."[80] Children's physical transformation was central to these projects. The process was disciplinary, in that adults worked to improve children's health and to influence their social and sexual development. For those campers who did not (or could not) conform to the rules of camp physicality, the process was stressful. For those who succeeded, the process was freeing; most campers were proud of their new skills and improved bodies, and they experienced the physical emphasis of camp as at once serious work and playful fun.

Children's inculcation into camps' body-focused culture began when they underwent precamp physicals. These exams were designed primarily to keep ill and potentially contagious children out of camps, where they might put others at risk. For the reformers who founded working-class children's camps, physical exams also represented early opportunities to influence campers and their families. Children who attended public clinics were more likely to suffer health problems than their middle-class peers were. They more rarely saw doctors, over a third was malnourished, and almost as many were in need of dental work.[81] At home, many lived in crowded and ill-ventilated housing. Unless their sponsoring organizations provided them with clothing and blankets, they were more susceptible to illness at camp, as they often arrived at camp poorly clothed and supplied.

For children attending low-cost and charitable camps, the exams were more public; at clinics run by medical staff affiliated with their camps' sponsoring organizations, these children began to become part of the larger group. They undressed in single-sex groups, wrapped themselves in sheets, and stood in line with many others until it was their turn to have their noses, throats, ears, teeth, chests, hearts, skin, and feet examined.[82] At some health clinics, prospective campers were also tested for venereal disease, often with little or no explanation of the exam or its relevance to camp.[83] Some children found the medical screenings intrusive, and some parents were defensive in the face of what they saw as unreasonable demands. As one mother told clinic staff in 1926, her son was not in need of dental care because "his father pulls his teeth."[84] In the end, reformers, not parents, had the final say. If parents did not comply, their child would not find a place at camp. In contrast, for middle- and upper-class children, who generally were screened by their own family doctors, the camp physical was a private and less stressful process.

Once children arrived at camp, they learned rules designed to preserve their health. In the early twentieth century, these rules generally
included reporting daily bowel movements or the lack thereof, changing
out of wet swimsuits after bathing, and staying out of the water directly
after meals. Girls were generally forbidden to swim while menstruating.
Left to their own devices, some campers had far looser ideas about
health and hygiene. One turn-of-the-century camp doctor recalled the
case of a boy who wore a single swim shirt night and day for six weeks
without washing either the garment or himself, subsequently developing
a strange skin rash.[85] In another case, a boy who arrived at a settlement-house camp in 1928 without a toothbrush explained to staff that
"I don't need to buy a tooth-brush; my brother has one."[86] For camp
staff, children's lack of caution justified their own oversight. A stomach-
ache could turn out to be life-threatening appendicitis, and fever and
fatigue sometimes presaged polio, a contagious disease that killed some
and permanently crippled others. When campers left camp stronger and
fitter, they provided compelling "evidence" of the season's success; when
they were sick, they threatened the community as well as their own
health.

From the turn of the century, when polio epidemics began to occur
regularly in American cities in the summer months, to the early 1950s,
when a protective vaccine was developed, urban outbreaks of the virus
were among the reasons why parents were eager to send their children
away to camps. However, polio sometimes surfaced in rural areas as
well. In these instances, camp staff tried to insulate their communities
by burning the wrappers around incoming packages, by barring parents
from visiting, and by forbidding campers and staff from leaving the
camp grounds. Fears of polio were instrumental in leading camp directors to create a single visiting weekend for parents, rather than allowing
parents to visit at will.[87]

Camp leaders' efforts to physically transform their young clients cen-
tered particularly on weight gains (and less frequently, weight losses). In
1926, the *New York Sun* explained that Henry Street Settlement had
reason to be proud of its recently concluded summer camp season: "The
average gain in weight of the children [at camp] . . . has been about
three and one-eighth pounds a child, [giving] to almost 300 mothers
about 800 additional pounds of happy healthy children."[88] Indeed, the
proof of the pudding (and of other good camp foods), as New York
City's Children's Aid Society proclaimed in 1921, was visible on chil-

dren's bodies: "pale faces become rosy . . . thin bodies fill out." Weekly weigh-ins at many camps, along with regular athletic competitions, drove home this ideal. After two weeks at the 92nd Street YMHA's Surprise Lake Camp, when one 1930 camper proclaimed that "I have a bigger chest, better lungs and a bigger breath than ever," he was responding to this culture of self-improvement.[89]

Under the influence of Progressive Era principles of organization, some early-twentieth-century camp leaders went further, sorting their campers by weight. Thinner children might eat at a special table where the portions of meat and milk were more bountiful, participate in "malted milk squads" for extra calories, or take part in longer rest periods, with sunbathing and graham-cracker snacks.[90] By the interwar years, camp leaders responded to a new concern, the overweight child, with "diet tables" where food consumption was limited.[91] At Camp Wohelo in Maine, Charlotte Gulick prohibited thinner girls from taking long trips or carrying their own packs while hiking, and she exhorted heavier campers to diet rigidly and to perform special exercises in order to lose weight.[92]

Children had varied reactions to these efforts. Many took satisfaction from what they understood to be their own improving physiques. One fourteen-year-old girl, who with her eleven-year-old sister attended a charitable camp in 1917, wrote from camp that "we have both taken on 5 lbs in weight since we came up here. Our eating is the best and plenty of it."[93] Not all campers felt so successful, and the very public nature of camp culture's relentless focus on the "normal" body made some campers anxious and uncomfortable. As a young girl, Lydia Stoopenkoff was embarrassed to be among those underweight campers at her settlement camp sent off at eleven o'clock each morning to drink a lumpy and unappealing glass of eggnog.[94] Other, heavier campers dreaded public weigh-ins, which took place even at some of the most self-consciously progressive camps.[95]

Children were already sensitive to the physical differences between them. In any tent or cabin group, campers were at varying stages of maturation. Because menstruating girls were generally forbidden to swim, campers were generally aware of which of their peers had passed through this sign of incipient womanhood. Writer Diana Trilling, who in the early 1920s was a Senior at Camp Lenore, a private camp for Jewish girls in Massachusetts, later recalled "how cruelly we teased the girl in the next Senior bunk because, unlike the rest of us, she had not begun to menstruate!"[96] Because boys swam naked at many camps, at least on occasion, they also had regular opportunities to compare their physical development to that of other boys and men.[97] Inevitably, some campers were more physically mature than others, just as some were temperamentally better suited to camp life. A camper who was shorter, thinner, or fatter than others—anything that set him or her apart—often faced some degree of teasing and name-calling. In 1938, when one Camp Lehman camper told his counselors that he wanted to lose weight, his desire was undoubtedly intensified by the ongoing harassment that he was experiencing at the hands of other campers who kept calling him fat.[98]

Camps' food regimens also served social ends. As part of their elite status, private camps generally offered more and better-quality meat and vegetables than did charitable camps. Camps run by members of religious minorities promised food that would reflect their clients' mores: kosher or kosher-style food for Orthodox Jews, fish on Friday at Catholic camps (although this practice was actually common at Protestant and Jewish camps as well). Reformers took a different approach: balancing their desire to keep costs low with their efforts to improve the health of working-class children and to introduce them to new, more middle-class habits and aspirations, these camp leaders saw food as a means to better acculturate their clients. Children's notorious pickiness made familiar foods a safer bet, but the leaders of many charitable and low-cost camps made a particular point of exposing their campers to "better," if unfamiliar, foods. White bread and lettuce and tomato salads were imagined to be agents of Americanization and social uplift.[99]

Camp leaders of all kinds vaunted the plainness of their fare, in the belief that simple foods were better for children. As a typical camp brochure of 1906 promised, "The cooking is both good and plain, and the fare abundant, nourishing and varied."[100] Spicy or otherwise unusual (and thus, by implication, un-American) foods rarely appeared on camp menus, even when the campers came from homes where such dishes were standard. Camp leaders relegated these "exotic" foods to special events such as luau roasts and international nights, which demarcated routine camp meals from "outside" food practices. However, what was standard in some homes was exotic in others. Jewish New Yorker Bess Wilkofsky, who attended a Christian settlement camp in the 1930s, later recalled that "the food was totally strange. It meant eating spinach (ugh!) beets (ugh!) bland meat—utterly tasteless. We were not accustomed to white bread—altho' I loved it."[101]

In camp industry magazines and books, camp leaders ascribed almost magical properties to appetizing meals and, by extension, to the power that children exerted as consumers and critics. Porter Sargent, whose primary focus was private camps, explained in 1932 that "many shrewd camp directors attain a large part of their success by appealing to the boy's stomach just as many wives do by appealing to their husbands'."[102] A traditional image of gendered kitchen hierarchy was here rewritten as adult deferentiality to the whims of a powerful child, usually a boy. In the competitive private camp marketplace, "good eats" represented a particularly important means of satisfying clients. However, the impulse to train youth remained strong. At mealtimes adults tried to insist on table manners, attempting, as Camp Mystic director Mary Jobe instructed her staff, to "not allow elbows on table or feet hooked around chairs or rapid mastication."[103]

Lessons in physical deportment extended well beyond the dining room. At camps that served immigrant families, reformers taught children to use their bodies in ways that would advance their assimilation into American culture. For instance, the interwar leaders of the New York City YMHA's Surprise Lake Camp, most of whom were native-born and fairly acculturated Jews, taught their first- and second-generation working-class Jewish campers, many of whom spoke Yiddish at home, to avoid slang and mispronunciation (such as the substitution of "goil" for "girl") and to practice "Correct American Posture" as opposed to "Foreign Posture." As the camp newspaper intoned, "Speak the English language, the language of America. Deliver it 100 per cent. correct in sounds, phonetically speaking, or not at all. Anything less sets you apart, marks you as a stranger, an alien, a 'gair,' a you-don't-belong."[104]

Boys and girls received somewhat different lessons about their bodies. Boys were frequently exhorted to be "men" or, in the words of a 1920 Camp Pok-O'-Moonshine newspaper, to "act the part of men all the way through."[105] Both boys and girls were encouraged to show courage, competitive enthusiasm, and good sportsmanship, but the pressures were greater on boys to participate in competitive sports and to avoid crying in front of others. On the other hand, boyhood had its privileges. Particularly in the early years of camping, these included the right to be naked, a sign of boys' emancipation from cultural constraints and female oversight. At New Hampshire's Camp Marienfeld, the boys remained undressed on land as well as in the water and slept naked wrapped in blankets.[106] Girls, especially adolescent girls, were far more physically restricted at camp, and swimming naked was at most a very occasional treat for all but the very youngest. The senior Che-Na-Wah girls were allowed, once a season, to swim "in nature's bathing suit" by moonlight. When the day arrived, they exclaimed, "I can hardly believe it," "May we?" and "Are you sure?" The girls spent their ten minutes in the water laughing, attesting to the strangeness and excitement of the event in their adolescent lives.[107]

The list of tasks incumbent on older girls at camp suggested that adolescent femininity entailed a rigorous process of self-regulation, even in the woods. In the 1930s, a decade of increased gender conservatism, proponents of camping for adolescent girls tacked particularly uneasily between the dictates of femininity and adventure. Camp rules confirmed this ambivalence. At the Girl Scouts' Camp Andree (where the girls never socialized with boys), each arriving camper received "Andree's Aids to Attractiveness," a list that mandated finger-nail care and the use of deodorant powder and that barred girls from swimming or chopping wood during their menstrual periods.[108] Counselors taught the campers adherence to a code of feminine conduct through lessons on makeup, hairstyles, proper clothing, and physical grace.[109]

Despite these limitations, camps represented for many girls the most freely physical spaces of their lives and a point of entry into traditionally male realms of adventure. Cross-gender play facilitated this process. Judging by the number of girls and women who took on gender-neutral or male nicknames while at camp, or who dressed up as male pirates, explorers, soldiers, and Robin Hood and his Merry Men, cross-gender play was evidently liberating and pleasurable for its participants. In 1929, for instance, one group of Camp Andree girls drew on the recent all-male Byrd and Shackleton expeditions to the South Pole to imagine themselves as a group of explorers. Each girl took up an area of scientific exploration or expertise: the "reporter" started the camp logge (the journal), the "photographer" documented the trip, the "surgeon" studied poison ivy and its treatment, the "meteorologist" looked at weather patterns. One night, the girls stayed up and completed a regular schedule as if they were living through an Antarctic winter day at Byrd's scientific camp.[110] Many girls came to Andree with romantic visions of primitive camping in the woods, and they were thrilled to learn skills that advanced these desires and gave them a sense of adventurous fulfillment. Using the conventions of frontier adventure to take social risks (albeit within enclosed, gender-segregated spaces), they drew on male models of pioneer adventure to imagine new forms of autonomous community. One 1929 "pioneer" group at Andree was especially excited to chop and to saw wood. "There are three things I want when I get home," one camper asserted, "a tent, an ax, and a wood pile."[111]

The social effects of this kind of playful transgression were limited. Girls still lived by gendered rules at camp and at home, and their cross-gendered play was semiautonomous rather than fully independent of adult control. Even as the Girl Scouts played at being knights and pirates, the national leadership frowned on "masculine" attire in daily camp life as "likely to cause adverse criticism of the organization."[112] In 1930, the Girl Scouts' national director, Jane Deeter Rippin, told the *New York Times* that at camp, "busy as the leaders are in making good woodsmen, good hikers, good swimmers and the like, they are even more interested in developing good homemakers."[113] Still, when female campers and staff took on male roles with serious intent, they had access to adventurous personae ordinarily denied to them. Rippin spoke of girls becoming "woodsmen," and indeed girls' models were often male.

Cross-gender play was itself gendered. When early-twentieth-century women and girls dressed in drag, their aim was sometimes comedic, but rarely did they seek to diminish men as a group. For instance, in a popular girls' camp prank, perhaps the female equivalent of the snipe hunt, women counselors told their campers to expect male visitors, and the girls excitedly prepared. At Camp Wanakena, a private Adirondack camp, the campers of 1919 donned "silk stockings, hair curlers, jewelry, powder and other beautifying articles." The joke was on them when their female counselors arrived for a dance dressed as army and navy men. Nevertheless, the girls and their "escorts" danced through the evening.[114] Girls risked little when they acted like men in play, and they often gained power by taking on gender-neutral or masculine nicknames.

At boys' camps, cross-gender play was also a regular part of the camp schedule, but drag was more explicitly satirical, a means of warning boys against the "feminine" realm that it portrayed.[115] Although boys and men sometimes played "serious" female roles in camp plays, cross-dressing was most often the prerogative of men whose masculinity appeared beyond reproach, entertaining their campers by exaggerating feminine characteristics. At Camp Dudley, "Chief" Herman Beckman, renowned for his leadership and his skill at hitting fly balls, regularly appeared on the Dudley stage in drag, as did many of the counselors.[116] In 1931, one group of Dudley leaders performed a parody of aesthetic dancing, poking fun at what was considered a girl's dance style; the "gay troupe of sylphs draped in lavender curtains" (as the camp newspaper described their scarves) also mocked what it coded as homosexual effeminacy. The act "brought down the house," as the *Dudley Doings* related, but it could hardly have reassured any camper or staff member questioning his own masculinity or sexuality.[117] Here, crossdressing reinforced the rules of appropriate gender performance and sexual identity even as it transgressed those rules.

Camps' focus on personal transformation and collective identity was not unique in children's experience. However, the culture of camp life was particularly intense in its insistence on the intimate transformation of campers' bodies. Camps emphasized change in ways that were visible to campers, staff, and outsiders alike, encouraging campers to monitor themselves as adults monitored them and teaching campers to perform new roles.

When campers returned home at the end of their vacations, they often understood themselves somewhat differently. For many, the past weeks had constituted their first break from family as well as an introduction to new social and athletic skills. The differences among them had never ceased to matter, but most had become insiders nonetheless. As they said goodbye to new friends, responded to nicknames, and laughed at shared jokes, their newfound familiarity proved their camp citizenship.

Whether or not children enjoyed the camp experience, and most did, at the end of a few weeks or months many felt as if they had been away from home for far longer: long enough, and far enough from their everyday lives, to look differently at themselves in some fundamental way. Numerous camp directors argued that although the camp season was short, it was actually equal in hours to a year at school.[118] This claim was somewhat disingenuous, in that it included the hours during which campers slept, yet it spoke to a fundamental truth: time at camp had its own rhythm and intensity. For unhappy campers, each hour could feel unending, while the busy days passed quickly for contented campers. "Is it possible that the summer is really over?" Ethel Rose Mandel wrote in late August 1914 as she prepared to leave the Pasquaney Nature Club in New Hampshire. "The days have been so short since we have all been so happy."[119] Children often experienced this transition as important, transformative, and unique. As Robert Steed Dunn, recalling his years at Camp Asquam from 1891 to 1895, explained, "We did not go to camp as we went to school. . . . School gave no key to the fjords of a new planet. Camp did."[120]

4

Between Generations
Tensions in the Camp "Family"

> It is not always necessary that a girl should be conscious of what
> is happening to her. She can be re-orienting her habits of thought
> around a new ideal; she can be discovering the meanings of reli-
> gious "idioms" in terms of everyday living; she can be awaking to
> the powers of personality in herself and others—and never discuss
> the changes in herself. Perhaps she calls it happiness!
> —Guide for YWCA camp organizers, 1926[1]

In the 1920s, some of the YWCA Girl Reserves from Clearwater, Florida, and the surrounding area attended week-long summer
camp sessions at Camp Bay-Lea in nearby Port Richey. The Girl Reserves, a patriotically named youth group, was founded in 1918 during
the First World War as a means of consolidating local YWCA chapters'
work for girls aged ten to eighteen under one national program. A late
entry in the field of national children's organizations, it proved popular.[2]
As at other Girl Reserves camps, the Bay-Lea staff emphasized the development of Christian fellowship as well as outdoor recreation. After
an early-morning swim and breakfast, the girls raised three flags to sig-
nal their allegiances: the U.S. flag, a "Christian" flag, and the Girl Reserves flag.[3] They spent their mornings attending Bible study and crafts
classes. In the midafternoon, when the temperature began to drop, they
undertook more energetic activities: boating, hiking, "surf-boarding"
(an early name for waterskiing on a wooden board), and swimming in
the shallow waters of a sandbar along the Bay of Mexico.

One 1925 camper attested to the emotional intensity of the week's
vacation she spent at Bay-Lea in religious as well as social terms: "Camp
has meant very much to me this year, more than it has meant in other
years. I am older this year and can appreciate the wonders of God's

world more. . . . In Bible class I have met a new Jesus, an out door Saviour who loved nature as much as we ourselves and who knew how to understand it to a greater extent. . . . I have had a wonderful time making friends."[4] This was precisely the response to camp that the staff most wished to elicit. But not all Bay-Lea campers were as enthusiastic. Some were homesick, others irritable. They might at times strive for personal achievement and at other times rally toward a common goal, identify with their counselors and then their peers, play up injuries or else downplay the significance of a scrape or a sprain. In practice, communal affiliation was a fluid process, not a fait accompli, and campers' attitudes shifted according to the social context at hand.[5]

Despite the immense effort that camp administrators put toward rituals of incorporation, camp "families" were not always cohesive or comfortable. In 1926, for instance, one Bay-Lea camper, Amy, longed for extra attention from the staff. When she arrived, she was assigned to sleep in a room with counselors because the group was short on space. That first night, when the counselors returned to their shared bedroom, Amy was breathing rapidly and complained of a sprained back. Two of the counselors attempted to treat the injury by massaging her with witch hazel until she said she felt better. The next night, Amy again appeared faint. The camp director, Miss Sumner, had told the counselors not to "baby" Amy, so they did not respond. But the night after that, when Amy complained, they massaged her.

Over the course of a few days, the Bay-Lea counselors' opinion of Amy shifted from enthusiasm to concern to distrust, and then to outright scorn. Susan, one of the two counselors who shared a room with Amy, initially perceived Amy to be "a fine girl, well built + athletic," in a letter she wrote to a friend back home. By the fourth night, Susan's patience had worn thin. As she told her friend, on Amy's fourth night at camp she whimpered in bed, first quietly and then more and more loudly. Finally, her voice carried so far that the other girls could hear her from their rooms. The counselors then got up to tend to her. Amy complained of a pain in her side. As Susan later wrote, "I said in a whisper to Hazel [the other counselor], 'Well, that's too high for appendicitis, anyway,' and would you believe it, the pain moved right down! . . . I finally told her brazenly that we didn't believe her and she rolled over with her back to me and went to sleep." In the morning, they decided that Amy should go home. The girl appeared too weak and unwell to pack her own bag or to walk down the stairs from the bedroom without help. But Susan later heard that Amy was able to carry her own suitcase when she arrived back home. Some of the campers who attended school with Amy then explained that the girl often feigned a "spell" when anything went wrong or she had a test to take. As Susan concluded, "She wanted attention, and we unsuspectingly gave it."[6] In complaining about her health, Amy had found a means of eliciting sympathy and consideration from her counselors (at least initially) and a relatively nonconfrontational way to leave camp once the social environment felt intolerable to her.

It is likely that Amy was homesick from her first moments at camp and that she desired more adult attention—including physical intimacy—than her counselors wished to spare. Perhaps the girls who knew her at home were unfriendly or impatient with her. Our understanding of the subtleties of these campers' peer interactions, which they shared only selectively with counselors, is necessarily incomplete. Although the counselors were young, often college students, they represented an intermediate generation in some ways like parents and in other ways like older peers. They cared about campers, but not in the same way as might campers' own parents; children admired the staff but held back information from them. The relatively informal mixing of generations created new opportunities for children to come to know adults not much older than themselves, but as Amy's camp experience suggests, the camp surrogate family was not always warm, welcoming, and comfortably intimate. Camp initiations offered up communal identity and allegiance at a variety of levels. But not all children recognized the camp "family" as loving and supportive, identified with the group, or met the expectations of their leaders and their peers.

Some degree of intergenerational and interpersonal tension was inevitable when children lived in close quarters with other campers. Camps shared some of the basic structure of other "total institutions" (to borrow sociologist Erving Goffman's term for social arrangements wherein every sphere of life is regulated at once).[7] Campers rose to the sound of a bell or bugle, ate together at regular intervals, and participated in a series of adult-led activities throughout the day. However, camps were far less coercive or disciplinary than many youth institutions, such as the adult-run detention centers where so-called deviant or delinquent youth were forcibly restrained.

Only rarely did camp staff resort to sending a camper home, or did campers desperately try to leave. Unhappiness was a feature of camp

Girl Reserves at Port Richey YWCA Camp, 1925. (Courtesy of the Tampa Bay YWCA. Sophia Smith Collection, Smith College)

life, but it was not the primary or overwhelming feature. If campers sometimes allowed their disaffection to be seen, or refused to play by some of the camp rules, they generally fulfilled their major obligations nonetheless. The industry was a success not only because it fulfilled adults' fantasies about children's socialization but also because the majority of campers enjoyed the camp experience and accepted their prescribed roles.

The ways in which camp communities navigated common forms of resistance to the camp "family," such as camper homesickness, rule-breaking, and sexual experimentation, speak to a new model of American childhood in which children exerted more power in their relations with adults. In the new child-centered marketplace, of which camps were an important site, campers were clients to be pleased as well as improved. Thus, camps were sites of intergenerational negotiation as well as regulation. The staff knew that there were limits to their own age-based power. Counselors such as Susan and Hazel were at times hard-pressed to secure campers' consent or to control their actions, let alone to determine what they took from camp life.

Homesickness and Camp "Family"

William Steckel's arrival at Adirondack Woodcraft Camp in 1939 was hardly propitious. "I was not the most enthusiastic 12-year old," he later recalled, and "the ride to camp was wet and gloomy for the 'new boys.'" In 1930, when ten-year-old Charlotte Goldstein, a resident of New York City's Hebrew Orphan Asylum (HOA) during the school year, lay in her Camp Wehaha bunk at night, she felt similarly melancholy. She missed her family and thought about her deceased mother. "I was a little lonely. You'd hear the trains at night. All in the big room there, ten of us girls." For some campers, the distress was simply overwhelming. One Girl Reserve from Phoenix, Arizona, who traveled to a New Mexico camp in 1939 was so homesick that she returned home after a single day.[8] Most other homesick campers tried to be brave. In 1921, when Dick D. arrived at Camp Dudley, "there was a slight drizzle making everything kind of gloomy in this new place and I was lonely, boy was I homesick." He knew, however, that his parents wanted him to benefit from camp, and so he "performed the first major prevarication that I can recall clearly and managed, through the tears, to produce my first letter home, which began (to use the idiom of the day): 'Dear Mother and Daddy, Camp Dudley is the berries, bush and all.'"[9]

The problem of homesickness offers a unique lens through which to consider the intergenerational production of children's culture and experience: that is, adults' attempts to create cohesive communities for their young charges and the processes through which children came to understand themselves as members of new communities. For children, camp life represented an important rite of passage, often a first experience of community and self-reliance beyond the physical boundaries of families and home neighborhoods. Their conversions from lonely newcomers to secure members of the camp family represented a central industry project. Yet as the foregoing stories suggest, this transition was not always effortless. Although camp activities were designed to foster communal identities, campers experienced rituals of incorporation in divergent ways. Camps may have been total institutions of sorts, but children attended them for limited periods of time, and they had outside experiences against which to measure, and sometimes to resist, camp worlds. Homesickness was emblematic of the difficulty that many experienced in moving from one mode of life to another, and of the limits of the "camp family" ideal.

Homesick children's feelings of loneliness and alienation tended to be most severe during the first few hours or days of camp, when everything seemed new and unsure, and at particularly quiet moments such as while lying in bed at night. These feelings were often most acute for younger campers and for those who had never before been away from home. Camp staff made a special point of welcoming and showing interest in those children who seemed bewildered by the transition. As William Steckel later noted, on the morning after his arrival at camp, "The man called 'Chief' stopped a skinny kid with steel-rimmed glasses and said 'Hi, Billy, how are you doing?' He actually knew my name on the first day."[10] Herman Beckman, director of Camp Dudley, was reputed for knowing his campers by number (each Dudley camper, from 1885 onward, was assigned his own number, in ascending order), as well as by name and hometown. For many "new boys," Beckman's personal interest "filled the gap which made you feel being away from home was not so bad and Camp Dudley was a good place to be," as one former camper recalled.[11]

Camp leaders acknowledged the difficulty of adjustment and addressed children as active partners in their own transformation. Although some directors questioned just how organized the day should be, all held in common the belief that homesick children needed to throw themselves into camp life. In July 1927, the Surprise Lake Camp newspaper gave the following advice to its campers: "If you find you are becoming homesick it means that you are not active enough and you are not a good mixer. The remedy is simple, play more games with other boys and mix with them and you will be just like the other campers." A decade later, at the end of the camp season, the paper publicly credited "Ned Weiss who made a sensational jump from a typical homesick case to splendid camper. Good work, Ned."[12] In the early 1930s, the girls of Camp Severance sang the following song of reassurance:

> I never heard of anybody dying
> From camping, did you?
> I've often heard of pretty maidens sighing
> For just a trip or two;
> So when you come to camp, don't you start to faint,
> You may think the camp is going to kill you, BUT IT AIN'T;
> For I never heard of anybody dying
> From camping, did you? NO!![13]

Getting over homesickness, camp staff argued, was part of growing up, and those who felt sad should simply keep busy until the feeling passed.

Most parents agreed with staff that homesickness was a temporary phase that campers would soon transcend. With this idea in mind, even those parents who were sympathetic to their children's misery usually kept them at camp, no matter how hard their children begged to come home. From the perspective of the most disconsolate campers, however, leaving camp was the only real solution. One boy at Camp Boiberik, a New York camp that emphasized Yiddish and Jewish culture, wrote a postcard to his mother in late July 1936 begging her to "please come for me as soon as you can. If by August 2, you are not here I think I will run home. If you come and stay here with me I'll stay. But please come as soon as you can." The situation did not improve, and a letter then followed:

> Please come for me because I'll get very sick for you. Mother I've changed my mind, if you do not come for me in 5 days I'll go alone home without my trunk. In this case I'll be home maybe August 20. I mean it mother. Please don't let everybody read this letter. When I come home I'll never again go to a camp.

Despite the piteous tone of these messages, the boy's parents did not relent. Instead, they turned to the camp director for professional advice, explaining that "we are just lost for words to express our sorrow and would like to know what you would advise."[14]

Others were less sympathetic to their children's unhappiness and tried to shame their sons and daughters to conform. In 1943, after a ten-year-old boy attending Camp Dudley wrote to his mother that he was homesick and wanted to come home, she replied that he would better enjoy camp when he came to know his cabinmates and participated in a greater number of camp activities. In the meantime, she explained, he must learn to hide his feelings:

> Don't let anybody know you are homesick and enter in as many things as you can and you won't have time to be homesick. Men never show their feelings like this and you would be a "SISSY" if you came home. Buck up and be a sport and the answer is YOU CAN NOT COME HOME, so you must make the best of it. If you don't enter in things, the boys will not like you and it will then be even harder for you.[15]

Boys were just as likely as girls to experience homesickness. Some parents decried it as unmanly in their sons; others were more sympathetic to their sons' distress. And like the counselors at Camp Bay-Lea, many parents vacillated between indulgence and impatience.

Harriet S. was unusual in persuading her parents to take her home. She attended Camp Ta-Go-La in New York for only three weeks, during which time her family was staying at an area resort: "I missed my mother and all the rest of the family especially since I knew they were nearby. The camp was beautiful but I found excuses to want to leave saying the food was bad and they make you clean the bunk." With the active support of her grandmother, Harriet left camp and joined her family at their hotel.[16] Most campers had less success. In 1939, Alan Lurie was six years old when he first attended summer camp. When his father came to visit him, the unhappy boy tearfully begged to leave. Despite this show of emotion, his father refused. The next year, however, when Alan asked to go to a different camp, his wishes were respected.[17] Because many camps charged parents by the month, some homesick children hoped that they could leave before their parents paid the next installment of the bill. One unhappy boy, upon hearing that his parents already had paid for the rest of the summer, cried bitterly in the realization that now he would have to stay on.[18]

To an important degree, children's homesickness diminished when caring adults nurtured them. In 1940, Surprise Lake counselor Bill wrote in his diary of several encounters with Eddie, a camper who, at the beginning of the summer, was clearly unhappy. The counselor "persuaded him to try licking his case of loneliness. He promised to tell same to his folks when they come up tomorrow." The next day, Eddie had decided to stay and, according to Bill, "seems happy."[19] On the other hand, those campers who had encounters with inexperienced or uncaring counselors were more likely to feel homesick. In the spring of 1941, many returning counselors broke their contracts with Surprise Lake Camp in order to take better-paying jobs in the wartime economy. The camp director speculated that the immaturity of the counselors whom he was finally able to recruit was to blame for a serious bout of homesickness among the boys that summer. As the counselors became more experienced, the boys' anxiety abated.[20]

Children who got along well with their peers at camp were also less likely to feel homesick. In July 1933, one boy wrote to his mother that the other boys were ruining his vacation at Camp Boiberik. "I wan't [*sic*] you to either take me home or send me to another camp at the end of the month," he pleaded, explaining that his fellow campers treated him as their inferior, had ripped up his bathing suit, and frequently used water pistols to wet his shirts. "I don't enjoy any of the meals because the boys are always goading me if you know what that means," he concluded.[21] That same summer, another Boiberik camper wandered around the camp by herself. Feeling alienated from her peers, she counted the days until she would be released from her misery. "Just 1 ½ weeks more and I'm going home," this lonely adolescent wrote to her parents. "It will be swell. . . . Mom, please let me come home a week before the camp." Camp had become a kind of torment, she explained, because "I'm not getting along well with the girls."[22]

While parents speculated about the events or personnel that had precipitated their children's unhappiness, staff tended to blame parents (an extrinsic factor) when campers were discontent or difficult. As one camp counselor bluntly put the case, "Most of the problem cases in a boys camp can be traced directly to the home, severe as that indictment may sound."[23] Boys' camp staff, who frequently posited their communities as alternatives to the overly feminized home, were particularly likely to blame mothers for overprotecting and overindulging their sons and to imagine that possessive mothers resisted sending their children away from home.[24] Joseph Lieberman, who in the 1920s directed the innovative coeducational Pioneer Youth Camp, wrote with disdain of the way one mother doted on her twelve-year-old son: "During her first visit she fawned on him, petting and hugging him, inquiring after all his needs, repacked his valise, remade his bed."[25] Such parents, Lieberman implied, would only have themselves to blame if their children subsequently became homesick.

Although it was convenient for staff to blame outsiders for children's discontent, parents did influence their children's relative happiness at camp. Some children correctly surmised that their parents were eager to get rid of them.[26] Others felt homesickness most acutely when their parents came to visit. These reunions, however eagerly awaited, sometimes culminated in tearful farewells that left children discontented. In 1924, one Surprise Lake Camp counselor reported in exasperation that "in all frankness, it may be said that if the parents had not visited the camp there would have been less homesickness. There was only a little homesickness but that little can be directly traced to parents who came to camp and asked their children if they would not like to go home with them."[27] Perhaps the parents in question were worried about their children's happiness or felt guilty or anxious about leaving their children behind. Whereas many parents saw in camps opportunities to advance their children's independence or their own freedom from child care, some were ambivalent about this short-term separation and their own lessened role in childrearing. After all, children's successful acclimatization to camp life signaled their growing independence, necessary and exciting but somewhat bittersweet for loving parents. Children were sensitive to competing adult claims for attachment and authority, and their homesickness was engendered both by their own anxieties and by those of the adults around them.

Because relatively few early-twentieth-century parents had themselves attended summer camps as children, most were as new to this ritualized separation as were their children. In an era in which parents derived increasing comfort from the companionate family ideal, enduring this separation was as difficult for some adults as it was for campers. In 1930, the mother of one boy attending Maine's Camp Waziyatah (then a coeducational Jewish camp, later a girls' camp) wrote to the director, "I certainly have missed my baby. I had no idea two months could possibly be so long," and another described herself and her husband as having been "two neurotic, lonesome parents" while their son attended the same camp in 1929.[28]

The ideal camp "family" that would somehow respect and restrict parents' access to their children was not easily achieved. Camp leaders often invited parents to attend Sports Days, pageants, and the final banquets that celebrated their children's achievements. For the owners of some full-season private camps, the practice of lodging parents or offering them meals, for a fee, represented an important secondary source of income.[29] Yet many camp leaders found such visitors distracting or even demoralizing to the project of camp "insiderness." Despite having selected the camps that their children attended, some parents chafed against camp authority, tested their child's loyalty, or tried to reassert the primacy of their own family bond. A few acted out on visits in dangerous or bothersome ways, such as taking boats out from the dock without permission or arriving at camp without prior notification. More frequently, the parental challenge operated on a subtler register. "I am sure," director Cornelia Amster of Camp Che-Na-Wah wrote to parents in 1930, "I can . . . regard the packages that have come simply as an oversight on your part, and not an attempt to undermine the morale of the camp."[30] Amster, like many of her peers, explicitly forbade parents from sending food packages to their children, but some parents simply could not resist this means of demonstrating their affection and asserting their parental rights. The situation was awkward for camp directors, especially at expensive private camps where parents exerted enormous authority and could, if they so desired, pull their children from camp.

To reassure these adult clients, camp leaders generally required that children write home regularly. One common camp rule required campers to produce a sealed envelope addressed to their parents before sitting down to Sunday dinner. Unsurprisingly, the contents of such letters were often uninspired. Frank Cheley, director of the coeducational Cheley-Colorado Camps in the Colorado Rockies, tried to reassure parents that "camp days and evenings are full of fine, vigorous fun with little or no time for long letters."[31] Most children were poor letter-writers to begin with. Their days at camp were busy and highly scheduled, and only a minority were driven to write long letters home, as much as they eagerly awaited the day's mail call. "I really think she is just too lazy to write more fully," wrote one Camp Waziyatah parent. "His letters are very sketchy and tell us little about himself," complained another.[32] In the absence of this tangible sign of their children's devotion, some parents felt lonesome and unhappy.

Other parents, however, were not particularly nurturing or involved in their children's lives. Some wealthier parents shuttled their children between boarding schools and full-season camps. Others were simply distant. For children from such families, camp life offered valuable opportunities to forge emotional ties with sympathetic adults. New Yorker George Welsh attended the elite Camp Pasquaney in 1895 with his brother Sam. At home the boys were raised primarily by governesses, and as George later recalled, "to say that it was a relief to get away from apron strings is beyond my ability to express."[33] The Welsh brothers returned for four more summers, where they found meaningful companionship.

Most campers who were homesick overcame their homesickness, a sign of their resiliency and determination. In 1934, on her first day at the Central Jewish Institute's Camp Cejwin, New Yorker Mitzi Brainin was miserable, but the feeling, she later recalled, passed swiftly: "I cried myself to sleep during rest hour and after that I don't recall being homesick for even 5 minutes."[34] Although intense while it lasted, loneliness was often fleeting; many campers came to see homesickness as a phase that they had undergone during the transition to camp life, and even as a kind of strengthening ordeal. By the age of eight Alan Lurie was a seasoned veteran of three summer camps. As he explained in the pages of the Surprise Lake Camp newspaper, "You Get Used to All Kinds of Things."[35] Most campers did exactly that. Generally speaking, camps were successful in soliciting new identities and allegiances. Having converted to camp membership, many of the same children who had cried on arrival would weep even harder on their departure.

Children's homesickness, precisely because it was so often transient, usefully highlights both the mutability of children's identities and the complexities of their relations with adults and with one another. Campers were able to integrate themselves into the camp ideal to different and changing degrees. Like Charlotte Goldstein, some were lonesome at night and happy during the day. Like Alan Lurie, others were homesick one year and perfectly content the next. As children explored new forms of independence and of interdependence with others, their perceptions of camp varied. Many were successfully incorporated into the camp community and came to see its rules and structures not only as natural and desirable but as their own.

"Acting Out"

At Camp Dudley in 1940, one eleven-year-old camper drove the counselors (known at Dudley as "leaders") to distraction. Since the boy had first come to camp two years earlier, his leaders had consistently described him as selfish and prone to temper tantrums. In his third summer, they tried moving him into a new cabin group, but he continued to act out. In August, camp director Herman Beckman considered what to do next. By 1940, "Chief" Beckman was himself a Dudley institution. He had attended Camp Dudley as a boy starting in 1897, when the camp was under the leadership of one of Sumner Dudley's original 1885 campers, had risen to the rank of leader in 1903, and had became the camp's director in 1908.[36] By 1940, he had come into contact with many thousands of campers. Now, faced with this latest disciplinary problem, Beckman wrote to the boy's father in New York City, telling him to meet his son at Grand Central Station in two days' time.[37]

Staff expelled children from the camp community only as a last resort, sending home some campers who broke major camp rules or who were persistently aggressive with their peers, as well as some children who presented less willful challenges: chronic bedwetters and, in at least one case, a persistent sleepwalker.[38] However, the majority of so-called disobedient or troublesome children remained at camp. One unpopular Camp Lehman boy's offenses were manifold: he struck other boys with ping-pong paddles, put toothpaste in their beds, did not stay with his "buddy" while swimming, pushed other swimmers under the water, and took his fellow campers' food.[39] Another boy was, according to his counselor, "expert at 'frenching' [short-sheeting] beds, picking crab apples, and breaking every rule."[40] Both boys remained at camp. In fact, children who wished to be sent home often had to work hard toward this end. Amy, the Bay-Lea camper described at the beginning of this chapter, dramatized a series of physical ailments before she was finally sent home. Other unhappy campers deliberately transgressed camp policies. A few tried to run away.[41] For most campers, however, the prospect of being sent home midseason was a threat rather than an aspiration. In 1924, the Camp Andree nurse told three campers who were, in her opinion, "hysterical," that anyone with such attacks was not fit for camp life and that they would be sent home if they continued. All three girls soon quieted down.[42]

From the industry's earliest days, camp directors boasted that they ruled by applying commonsensical regulations rather than by brute force. A Camp Chocorua brochure of the 1880s called for "prompt and cheerful obedience to orders," prohibited firearms, and warned that boys could be sent home at the leaders' discretion.[43] At early YMCA camps, leaders prohibited firearms, swimming without supervision, smoking, gambling, and swearing. As director Henry Gibson of the YMCA's Camp Becket in Massachusetts declared in 1906, the boys were "given much liberty, and yet are under control."[44]

What became of those children who did not conform to the rules? Corporal punishment was rare at nineteenth-century camps and rarer (but not unheard of) by the early twentieth century. At the beginning of the twentieth century at Maine's Camp Medomak, staff member Archer "Pa Nick" Nicherson brandished a boat paddle, known as "trusty no. 8," when boys had misbehaved. Sometimes he hit campers at this private Christian boys' camp, but he was more likely to threaten them or to wave the paddle around than to actually use it.[45] The practice diminished in frequency as professionals devised what they considered more subtle methods of control, better attuned to the ideology of children's preciousness: one-on-one talks, the removal of privileges, peer pressure, attempts to shame campers into acquiescence, and positive reinforcement for good behavior. In Camp Pasquaney's early days, a boy who ate sloppily had to wear a cowbell around his neck as punishment; at Dudley, such a boy would get a "sinker," a kind of demerit, three of which would condemn him to watch when the boys next ate ice cream.[46] Untidy campers also drew the wrath of their peers when they cost their group precious inspection points.

Camp leaders hoped to persuade through positive incentives and friendly competition. The camper who excelled might win an end-of-season award for Best Camper, or at least Most Improved. Prizes and awards for "camp spirit," neatness, and sportsmanship all helped to produce the kind of campers that adults wished them to be. At Camp Bay-Lea, the neatest and best-behaved campers had the honor of raising the three morning flags. At other camps, the tent with the best record over the summer would win its own private party.[47] Campers often took up these competitions with enthusiasm. In the early part of the 1917 season, some of the Camp Kehonka girls began to follow counselor Mary Hume around on her inspection rounds, pointing out problems with their rivals' tents and debating why one group got the "E plus" (the top mark for cleanliness at inspection) but another did not. Finally, Hume began to refuse to share the scores as she went along, and she was left to inspect the tents in peace.[48]

Despite these incentives, campers were sometimes unwilling or unable to live up to their leaders' expectations. Most children did not rebel openly against camp authority, but neither did they always conform to camp ideals. Many had occasional fits of temper or failed at times to do their chores well or with good cheer. Staff considered the social contexts of these troublesome actions and their persistence in evaluating any particular camper's character. They were also sympathetic to, if sometimes frustrated by, those campers who were homesick or who wet their beds. These were not bad citizens, according to camp logic, but merely imperfect ones, and theirs were among the milder forms of resistance to camp life: relatively involuntary and tending to affect younger children disproportionately.[49]

Many of the children who enjoyed their camps did at times evade adult rules. One Camp Dudley boy sometimes paddled off to a private island, off-limits to the boys, to read nature books in peace and quiet. Another boy, attending the left-wing Camp Wo-Chi-Ca, managed consistently to avoid swimming lessons; having noted that counselors lost track of individual campers during group activities, he headed off to the athletic field unnoticed when it was his turn at the waterfront.[50] It was only by happenstance that one camp director found out from a visiting mother that some of the boys were competing to see who could urinate furthest from one side of the cots to the other.[51]

Camp staff allowed for certain kinds of challenges while bracketing out others. For instance, children sometimes built secret huts in the woods or founded their own "secret societies." Some camp leaders responded by founding official secret societies under their own leadership and control, whereas others quietly monitored but did not officially interfere with campers' "private" activities. Camps were also rife with parodic activities such as Topsy-Turvy Day, "talent nights" at which campers satirized their counselors, and singing songs that bemoaned the prevalence of mosquitoes or a series of rainy days. These rituals, as long as they occurred within bounds, were not inherently challenging to the hierarchies and ideals on which camps were founded. Rather, they allowed for (while muting) the expression of dissent. Consider one of the more popular camp plays of the 1930s, "If Boys Were Councillors." Written by Albert Brown, co-director of Ohio's Camp Caravan, and published in 1933, the play concerns a group of campers who wish to sleep late and eat "green" (or unripe) apples, among other tabooed camp activities. The skit gives expression to these illicit desires but concludes conservatively with the boys' realization that there could be no replacement for rest hour and adult leadership.[52]

Campers who occasionally indulged in pranks, parody, or "secret clubs" may have imagined that they were challenging authority, but in point of fact many of these acts left the social contract intact, enhancing community life rather than undermining it. Pranks, many of which explored the transgression of the community's social boundaries, exemplified this middle ground. In 1935, some Camp Lehman boys soiled counselor "Uncle" Al's bed with toilet paper, stones, gravel, and unripe apples—the latter being a source of contention between the staff, who said that "green" apples should not be picked, and the campers, who picked and ate them anyway.[53] Beds were among the few private spaces at camp, so to dirty or mess with someone else's bed was metaphorically to soil that person. In this instance, the toilet paper only enhanced the scatological symbolism.[54] Although the prank was more than likely annoying to Al, the fact that it was recounted in the camp newspaper, the

Tatler, set it apart from truly abhorrent activities. In settings in which children's bodies were explicitly being "improved," campers took particular pleasure in bodies gone awry—as witnessed by the Dudley boys' pleasure in calling the State of Vermont, which they could see across Lake Champlain, "Vomit" or the practice at some camps of wrapping toilet bowls in plastic so that the unsuspecting campers who used them were dirtied.[55] Depending on the context of any prank, its frequency, and its intended target, it might register within the community as playful rather than as destructive.

The most beloved pranks, like other important camp events, often required elaborate preparation, ingenuity, and collaborative effort. Consider the "Devil's Fiddle," a stunt organized by a group of Camp Wakitan boys to punish a cabinmate who ate loudly in his bed at night. The boys sneaked out of their beds after lights-out, hung fishing cord from one wall across to the opposite wall, then ran a rusty nail dipped in kerosene across the cord, making their cabin into a kind of giant string instrument. The sound of the nail, huge and eerie, woke the offending camper and sent him running into the woods.[56] It took similar skill and solidarity to move a tired Dudley counselor, sleeping in after a late night out in the town of Westport, from his cabin into the lake, or for a group of Camp Che-Na-Wah girls to short-sheet the beds of another cabin group.[57] These projects were among many participants' happiest moments at camp, often securing campers' sense of "family" membership and entering into the folk culture passed down from one year's campers to the next.

At times, a playful peer culture shaded into bullying and harassment. Despite the many ways in which camp life was organized to create community, not every camper had the respect of his or her peers. Many camp groups had a "goat," the butt of practical jokes and hostile remarks, and many more campers were given unflattering nicknames: "Gabby" for a garrulous camper, "Fatty" for the one who was overweight, "Baby" for the boy discovered signing a letter home "Your loving baby."[58] Children arrived at camp with a range of prejudices, and many picked on differences of ethnicity, religion, and national origin at those camps where such differences existed: "Greaseball" and "Wop" for Italian Americans, "Jewey" for the lone Jewish child at a mostly Christian camp.[59] The child who had a difficult time adjusting to camp was more likely to become a "goat," as were children who were less physically or mentally adept than their peers.[60] Camper E. C. Johnson later recalled that he was desperately homesick during his first summer at Camp Pasquaney in 1910, and bullies made his experience that much worse: "A special instinct told them where weakness existed, and they went after it with a sure and unerring aim."[61]

Although both boys and girls participated in name-calling, the ways in which children battled for status differed somewhat by gender. Boys were more likely to fight physically with one another or to destroy one another's belongings. Girls' interpersonal aggression, often characterized by gossip and backbiting, was subtler but no less hurtful.[62] One girl who attended Camp Waziyatah in 1943 wrote to director Bertha Gruenberg early the next year to complain that "last year [J.] + I weren't a bit happy because of all those cabin fights. Everybody knows that [N.] was the cause of them, so J. + I whish we could be in another cabin. . . . Even at the reunion N. was wispering to [R.] + every once in-a-while give us a dirty look."[63] Such social gestures of exclusion—a glare, a whisper—were not always obvious to adults, but they could be crushing nonetheless. Perhaps similar interactions at Camp Bay-Lea, unnoticed by the counselors, contributed to camper Amy's distress in 1925.

Counselors were sometimes at a loss to control campers who seemed aggressive, who "smart-alecked" too much, or who talked incessantly.[64] At Camp Bay-Lea, for instance, counselor Susan described one girl as "a regular pest, always hanging on the councillors, talking a blue streak and boasting, continually and imperially boasting. We got so we all avoided her as much as possible, and I don't believe the girls liked her very well either." The Bay-Lea counselors talked privately with the girl, whose behavior, they felt, improved as a result.[65] In many other cases, staff relied on the campers to enforce normative codes of conduct. One girl returned from Waziyatah in 1944 so demoralized, her mother contended in a letter to camp director Gruenberg, that she would no longer call her friends. Gruenberg replied that the girl was "aggressive," uncoordinated and overweight, unable to keep up with camp activities, and liable to lash out at others so as not to be hurt herself. Only then did Gruenberg acknowledge that "adolescent girls are usually pretty cruel. . . . a new [camp] might be better."[66]

Had they tried, counselors could hardly have quelled all campers' expressions of cruelty and exclusion, some of which occurred privately when adults were not around. But counselors were also sometimes distracted by their own social lives. Most were young adults caught up in their own summer adventures. They enjoyed their camps' loosening of social conventions, and they did not aspire to become strict authority figures. At Camp Bay-Lea, Susan was surprised to befriend a fellow counselor named Alice, whom she knew only casually at home. Writing to a friend, Susan reported that Alice "got a habit of coming up quietly behind me, slapping me vigorously on the shoulders and shouting 'Yip!' at the top of her lungs. It's our mode of greeting now. She's surely capable of shedding all dignity at camp."[67]

As counselors' own youth culture grew more daring, they brought playful and sometimes risqué sensibilities to their work, especially after hours, when campers had gone to sleep. At 1930s-era Camp Severance, a private Adirondack Jewish girls' camp, women staff members circulated playful handmade invitations to evening "skin dipping," a "Hash party" for which admission was "One Handful of Grass," and a naked party at which, the invitation promised, "We'll all get *stewed!*"[68] Some counselors regularly stayed up (or went out) late at night and were too tired to pay close attention to their campers in the morning. Children took note of their counselors' priorities. One group of Camp Waziyatah girls complained of their counselor (a fourth-grade schoolteacher during the school year) that "she is always in too big a hurry to get out for her date."[69] Romance and sexual experimentation among counselors tended to occur after hours, reinforcing age divides and counselors' privacy. At Surprise Lake Camp, members of the kitchen staff invited their "sisters"—actually prostitutes—to camp on one visiting day during the late 1930s, and for a fee, some of the counselors "visited" with them.[70] Some young men actively sought out potential sexual partners: "With a lot of luck / We'll get some ———," wrote one hopeful (but ultimately unsuccessful) male counselor at Camp Lehman in 1940.[71] Although some women counselors were sexually active, the sexual stakes were higher for women than for men, and a woman who gained a reputation for being "easy" could lose her camp position.[72]

Occasionally counselors did involve children in their own "acting out." At turn-of-the-century Camp Algonquin in New Hampshire, one counselor, a Harvard student during the school year, took boys off on "mountain hikes" that were actually quiet games of poker. When another group of campers accidentally discovered them, the counselor threatened to beat any tattletales, and for the moment the secret was upheld.[73] At Vermont's Brown Ledge Camp in 1931, one young woman joined five of her girls in breaking into and ransacking a nearby summer home.[74] At coeducational camps, counselors sometimes visited girl-

friends' or boyfriends' cabins in full sight of the campers, making campers complicit in their rule-breaking.[75] These incidents were exceptional
and not the rule. Although counselors were playful, most kept a certain emotional and social distance from their campers. The majority of
counselors were at once invested in their own youth culture (within
which children generally were not welcome) and eager to prove themselves as adults. At Camp Bay-Lea, for example, counselor Susan felt
conscious that she was only learning how to lead. As she confessed to a
friend at home, some of her encounters with the girls were more successful than others. She was annoyed with Amy but felt herself to be inexperienced in the ways of campers.[76]

Camps flourished through intergenerational negotiation, a significant
degree of permissiveness, and attention to children's peer culture. Although adults worked to set limits on children's behavior and activities, children had substantial power. Even anxious and unhappy girls
like Amy found ways to get attention or to change their circumstances.
Indeed, most campers who "acted out" did not suffer draconian consequences, not even expulsion from camp. At camps, as in a growing
number of American homes, a considerable range of mischief either was
acceptable, slipped by unnoticed, or was quickly forgiven.

Sexuality and the Preservation of Childhood

At the coeducational Camp Wo-Chi-Ca in 1938, some of the girls expressed their interest in boys by posting a list of "WHO LOVES WHO" in
large letters on the girls' bathroom wall. The staff of this Communist-
affiliated New Jersey camp, founded by the International Workers Order in 1936, responded to the graffiti as an affront to the rules. "Those
who have no regard for the sweat of the working class and a lust for destruction do not belong in a camp like Wo-Chi-Ca," the camp newspaper, the *Wo-Chi-Can*, intoned.[77] But was it a lust for destruction, or was
it lust per se that so bothered the staff? Sexual maturation constituted
an important marker of children's physical and social development, but
for camp staff it also threatened the ideal of camp as a community of
innocents protected from modernity's accelerated pace. Like smoking
or running away, the Wo-Chi-Ca girls' desire appeared potentially too
adult and independent for camp life.[78]

Homesickness and rule-breaking were perennial camp problems across the generations. In contrast, the ways in which early-twentieth-century camp leaders and campers negotiated questions of sexuality suggested a generational shift. Early-twentieth-century American culture was becoming more open about sexual matters and more accepting of children's inherent sexual drives. At camps, staff increasingly acknowledged children's sexual curiosity as a natural developmental undertaking on the path to adulthood. At the same time, many camp leaders represented their camps as spaces for the preservation of childhood innocence. As the Camp Directors Association claimed in a typical 1926 editorial, camps were a throwback to an era before "lip sticks, cigarettes or bootleggers" brought bad taste and low standards to the nation.[79] Thus, camp staff often found children's sexual expressivity challenging. The Wo-Chi-Ca girls' graffiti upset their leaders' fantasies of childhood innocence because it indicated that the girls considered the camp to be sexually charged.

The earliest camp directors assumed that the gendered segregation of campers was natural and appropriate. The leaders of the first boys' camps praised masculine retreats from an overly feminized world; the directors of the first turn-of-the-century girls' camps argued mainly for parallel camping experiences, not coeducational ones. Through the 1930s, most coeducational camps specialized in preadolescent children, who in the minds of most camp leaders and parents were too young to create sexually charged environments.[80] An even smaller number of radical and progressive interwar camps, such as Wo-Chi-Ca, Kinderland, and Pioneer Youth, were exceptional in redrawing the boundaries of camp "family" to include adolescents of both sexes.

Although most interwar camps remained single-sex, the "separate spheres" assumptions that had long undergirded such camps were coming under attack. In an era marked by greater frankness about sexual matters and more experimentation outside marriage, some of the traditional divides between women and men were declining. Adults were more often socializing in mixed-sex groups. Even the YMCA, a traditional bastion of male leisure, began in the 1910s to promote gender-integrated programs.[81] Among middle-class youth, heterosexual dating had become the new standard; among adults, the ascendant companionate-marriage ideal represented husband and wives as best friends enjoying shared leisure pursuits.

Concurrent with the increasing valorization of heterosocial leisure was increasing scrutiny of same-sex intimacy. The shift from homosociality to heterosociality that served to redefine adult heterosexual relationships in more "companionate" terms stigmatized a growing range of same-sex relationships, serving to pathologize homosexuality more stringently.[82] New theories of childhood development suggested that camps could help or hinder the establishment of heterosexuality among children. Such early-twentieth-century luminaries as Sigmund Freud and G. Stanley Hall described the emergence of heterosexual attraction as a central project of adolescence. By implication, just as the single-sex "gang" served a critical function for boys in early adolescence, appropriate coeducational experiences fostered the wholesome emergence of heterosexuality a few years later.

These trends had important implications for the camp industry. Coeducational camping for adolescents was the subject of much discussion by the mid-1920s, as interwar camp leaders began in increasing numbers to question the appropriateness of single-sex camps. As an editorial in industry journal *Camp Life* asked in 1929, "are we going to establish camp monasteries and nunneries, or are we going to run camps as we do public schools . . . on a sane, normal co-ed basis?"[83] A certain degree of heterosocial mixing was healthier, the magazine concluded, particularly for adolescents. The owners of the coeducational Camp Kinacamps in Colorado put the case more boldly. Their 1931 brochure warned that "Boys and Girls who are afraid of themselves and afraid of each other are just the types that develop dangerous, unnatural crushes between members of the same sex and that need very badly the wholesome contacts under adequate chaperonage to be found at Kinacamps."[84]

Single-sex "crushes," expressions of special affection or desire, had long been a feature of camps, particularly at girls' camps, where for decades girls and women had long enjoyed openly close and loving ties. From the 1920s onward, as an older model of respectable female sexual purity gave way to a greater acknowledgment of respectable women's (and girls') sexual desires, female affection came under new scrutiny. By the 1920s, single-sex organizations such as the Girl Scouts and the YWCA warned women counselors about the possible pitfalls of all-girl environments. In 1926, Elizabeth Kemper Adams, educational secretary of the Girl Scouts, argued that girls' crushes might "stand later in a girl's way when the time comes for her to fall in love."[85] In a similar vein, Abbie Graham argued in her 1933 book *The Girls' Camp*, a study of YWCA camps, that "with only girls present . . . relationships easily become abnormal. . . . Just a few boys at dinner, or a man with a good hearty laugh, will do much to give girls perspective in their own relationships."[86]

In light of these anxieties, it is striking that more single-sex camps did not become coeducational. What is more, girls' camp crushes remained widely accepted and unashamed. The term's fluidity may have contributed to its continued public use. Some crushes were based on sexual desire, but others expressed campers' admiration for confident college women and talented older girls. Libby Raynes, who with her older sister Ruth attended Camp Greylock in the late 1920s and early 1930s, later recalled that "I was proud because of all the girls who had crushes on my sister Ruth—she was pretty, athletic, and had beautiful blond hair."[87] At some camps, crushes extended in many directions at once. When Helen Weisgal was a camper at Camp Carmelia in the mid-1930s, her camp shared facilities and a few joint activities with Camp Keeyuma for boys, and as she later reflected, "It was common practice at camp to have crushes—on the counsellors, the older girls, the boys."[88] Despite the ways in which "deviancy" was coming to be defined in early-twentieth-century American culture, girls at camp also continued to enjoy physical closeness with one another. At Camp Andree, the camper-run Court of Honor, which arbitrated many camp policies, stated tersely in 1923 that "girls are not to sleep with each other."[89] But this very decree provides evidence of the practice that it was designed to combat. Fourteen years later, an Andree camper known as "Van" mentioned quite casually, in an account of a 1937 canoe trip, that "this morning early Scotty [another girl] crawled into bed with me."[90] Whether the two adolescent girls lay under the covers together to stay warm or out of a special affection for each other, they were not embarrassed or furtive about their actions.

Boys' camp culture was never as publicly affectionate, but as in other institutional settings, open sexual experimentation among boys did occur.[91] The meaning that boys ascribed to such sex acts varied, but it is telling that their camp staff seemed inclined to read much of this activity, including boys' masturbating in front of one another, as more bothersome than deviant, examples of aggressiveness rather than of incipient homosexuality. In 1940, counselors at Camp Lehman made no more fuss about the boy criticized for "his own masterbation [sic] and inciting the other boys to do likewise" than the camper who was "too sex minded" or the one known for his "'nasty' talk—girls, bad jokes, rather filthy-minded."[92] When in 1929, Hedley S. Dimock and Charles E. Hendry published their widely read *Camping and Character: A Camp Experiment in Character Education,* they noted, without dwelling on the matter, that almost 7 percent of the boys in their study occasionally demonstrated unspecified "irregular sex behavior," suggesting that sexual play was fairly common.[93]

Counselors were far more concerned about so-called sissies, those boys who appeared weak or effeminate, most at risk of becoming homosexuals, and most in need of vigorous outdoor activity.[94] Girls' camp leaders described crushes as a byproduct of the single-sex circumstances of camp life, but boys' camp leaders described "sissies'" lack of virility as extrinsic to camp experiences: like homesickness, traceable to well-meaning but overprotective mothers. This willingness to blame mothers for their sons' supposed lack of masculinity was not simply misogyny or medical pathologization. It was also competitive in origin. Boys' camp staff, after all, often envisioned their communities as alternatives to the overly feminized home.[95] In blaming mothers, staff grudgingly acknowledged an alternate world in which women exerted tremendous influence. A number of boys' camp directors pointedly invited fathers, and fathers alone, to stay at camp or to partake in special activities with their boys, in order to shore up the masculine influence in their campers' lives.[96] Some went so far as to confront mothers who they felt were inhibiting their sons' development. In 1940, one Surprise Lake Camp counselor told a boy's visiting parents that their son "was developing into a 'sissy.' It was a shock to them but they took it nicely. . . . I convinced Mrs. M. . . . that a great deal of it was her fault, which is probably the best thing that ever happened to the kid."[97] Such efforts on the part of staff reflected concern that children remain on the path to normative gender and sexual roles.

By the beginning of the twentieth century, boys' camp leaders cautioned explicitly about the perils of adult gay men's sexuality, warning their peers not to hire (or to immediately fire) "effete or effeminate" men and those who appeared to have special favorites among the boys.[98] These writers tended to treat gay male sexuality and predatory pedophilia as one, implying that "crooked" counselors would seek out inappropriately intimate contact with boys under their care. Girls' camp advocates did not warn of lesbian predation, but by the 1920s some cautioned female counselors to consider their campers' affection with care and to avoid undue intimacy. "If girls have a 'crush' on a certain coun-sellor," the Girl Scouts' Adams argued in 1926, "let that counsellor ask herself if at the bottom of her heart she does not enjoy being the kind of person that girls are crushed on."[99]

It is likely that summer camps were attractive work environments for some gay men and lesbians. These communities provided a kind of fa-milial intimacy with others of the same sex, a degree of privacy from the outside world, and, for adults who might not raise sons and daugh-ters of their own, the chance to work closely with children. Although we know little of the affective lives of camping pioneers Ernest Balch, Sumner Dudley, Ned Wilson, and Laura Mattoon, for instance, they are among a significant number of early camp directors who never mar-ried, were not publicly partnered, and devoted their lives to working with children. Perhaps some of these directors had same-sex adult part-ners, at camp or at home. If so, they were undoubtedly discreet, like camp director Lillian Smith (later a bestselling novelist) and her longtime lover Paula Snelling, who worked together at early-twentieth-century Laurel Falls Camp, a girls' camp in Clayton, Georgia, while remaining closeted.[100]

Inasmuch as camps brought together many children in quasi-familial settings, they also drew a small number of adults who were sexually at-tracted to children or to older adolescents. The temporary intimacy of camp "family," which brought adults into close and unsupervised prox-imity to youth, lent itself to possible abuse. For example, at a number of boys' camps, it was considered an honor to be invited to spend a night as a guest in the camp director's cabin. One adolescent camper of the 1930s alleged that when he slept over, his camp director appeared in front of him naked and invited the boy to sleep with him in his bed. The boy refused, and the matter was dropped.[101]

The early-twentieth-century camping literature was officially silent on the related question of heterosexual desire across age differences. Few camps were entirely single-sex; boys' camps often had a "camp mother" (often the male director's wife) or nurse on staff, and girls' camp direc-tors often hired a few men as instructors. That these camp "families" were sometimes sexually charged across the generations is unsurpris-ing, given that many staff members were young adults only a few years older than the campers they supervised and that most of the adults and children had had no prior contact as a "family." A number of the Camp Wakitan boys, for instance, had what former camper George Greenberg later called "rather strong sexual feelings" for the "very beautiful" wife of director "Pop" Sprung.[102] At Camp Kehonka, staff members "Bally" Ballentine and John Moore were young adults when, as Bally later acknowledged, they "spent a little time rating the thirty or so girls!"[103] Perhaps some of the Kehonka girls speculated about the two young men in return. Fourteen-year-old camper Rena Kunis, who attended the coeducational Camp Sequoia in 1936, "fell madly in love with a boys' counselor, a handsome [twenty-two-year-old] medical student. I made no secret of my feelings, and taking pity on me the drama counselor gave me a duet to sing with him in the big play of the season. After the performance, my beloved kissed me (my first kiss, except for family) and I literally walked into a tree."[104]

In principle, most camp leaders supported coeducational camping. However, many were uncomfortable in the face of children's sexual expressivity and preferred the status quo to the challenges of managing children's sexuality in coeducational settings. Father Shelton Hale Bishop, for years the director of Camp Guilford Bower, one of the nation's few black-owned camps in the interwar period, wrote that during the camp's first season in 1928, "we almost had to go around and take boys' arms from around girls' waists at our evening meetings." Bishop claimed that in the following years there was not one single "boy-and-girl problem," but it is possible that he overstated the case to make a claim for his campers' (and by extension his community's) respectability.[105] Many adults were uneasy in the face of physical affection between boys and girls. One mother, after visiting her son at Camp Waziyatah (one of a number of girls' camps to accept some younger boys in its early years), wrote to director Bertha Gruenberg in 1929 to complain: "I was not pleased to see the older boys [of eleven or twelve] lying with their heads in the laps of the big girls, and to hear the type of conversation I heard amongst them."[106] Once Gruenberg decided to restrict her clientele to girls, such scenes did not recur. But where girls and boys shared land and facilities, even younger campers might participate in the realm of dating. By the age of ten, Helen Weisgal had a camp boyfriend of sorts. Although she liked a boy named Joey, he expressed no interest in girls, so on Friday nights, when the boys and girls were allowed to meet and mingle, Helen walked with Sammy, Joey's older brother, who was, she decided, "better than nothing." In subsequent years, Helen had what she considered her first "real" romances at camp.[107]

Especially for older campers, sexual and romantic exploration constituted a partially independent social space beyond adult control. At Camp Wo-Chi-Ca, campers of the late 1930s were outraged when the staff decided to curtail the practice of daytime "visiting privileges" between the boys' and girls' bunks. Drawing on the principles of collective struggle that the camp officially endorsed, a few of the campers put out a secret edition of the camp newspaper in protest. When their deed was uncovered, former camper Irwin Silber recalls, "We were told we had undermined the principles of Wochica, besmirched the good name and work of our martyred former director and jeopardized the camp itself. And indeed, we were told, if we didn't confess and apologize immediately, we would all be sent home." When, in 1940, fourteen-year-old Silber slipped out of his tent after lights-out to meet up with a girl, the counselors who found them kissing on the baseball outfield chastised them in similar terms. As Silber later recalled, "These 'adventures' became part of the camp's underground folklore and contributed to our sense of being a part of camp and still independent of it." Campers' desires discomforted adults, but for most of them, their sexual experiences at camp were fairly limited. At Wo-Chi-Ca, according to Silber, "Sex . . . was certainly on the minds of the older kids, but most of us were not only inexperienced, we were pretty innocent. Nevertheless, we often speculated on whether any of the oldest kids were 'doing it,' and maybe one or two actually were. But for most of us there wasn't much (in those prewar years anyway) beyond kissing and some clumsy groping."[108]

The Wo-Chi-Ca girls' bathroom graffiti may particularly have galled camp staff because it was written by girls. Although camp leaders did not ignore the possibility of boys' sexual corruption, girls' sexual purity carried far greater social weight. In American culture at large, girls signified both as innocent subjects in need of state and family protection and as possible threats to the social order if their sexuality went unchecked and undefended. Many camping leaders saw modern life, with its faster pace, higher hemlines, and lowbrow Hollywood films, as threatening to childhood innocence in general but as especially perilous for girls. Camps' relative seclusion, camp leaders often suggested, mitigated against the threat to girls' morality represented by commercial culture, the overheated pace of metropolitan life, and the promiscuous minglings of the sexes and ages typical of summer resorts and popular entertainments.

However much adults hoped that camps would shield girls from sexual maturity, many girls arrived at camp as self-acknowledged sexual beings. Watching a group of New York City Girl Scout girls heading off to camp in 1923, one of the organization's leaders reported her disapproval that they were wearing "about as little on as they could get away with."[109] Whereas so-called delinquent girls' attempts to assert social and sexual autonomy through similar acts sometimes landed them in reform schools, campers were chastised but rarely severely punished for such acts. They generally got away with breaking curfew, swearing, smoking, and dressing "immodestly," acts that many early-twentieth-century reformers associated with female sexual delinquency.[110]

A cohort of self-consciously progressive interwar camp leaders tried to guide children's pathway to sexual knowledge through sex education, arguing that frankness was preferable to allowing children to pick up ideas from popular culture or from one another. That increasing numbers of adults were willing to discuss sexual matters with children was one sign of an increasingly liberal sexual culture, although as Laura Garrett of Connecticut's Housatonic Camp cautioned, such instruction should take place "in the day time, outdoors, with a view of the mountains and the river and with good, brisk exercise after it" rather than as "a bedtime story at night."[111] When handled well, such conversations were meaningful for campers. At Echo Hill Farm, a camp serving girls from Henry Street Settlement, camp psychologist Elizabeth Caro gathered the older girls together one evening in 1941 to discuss the development of what she termed "the love impulse" from early infancy to heterosexual courtship. When she described "latency," a period of same-sex desires, the girls responded strongly, suggesting that they had "lived the period well with particular girl friends!" One girl asked to be told in detail how sperm reached the ova; another intervened, claiming that her cabinmate was just trying to be "mean" by putting Caro on the spot. Caro impressed the campers by drawing a simple diagram for them by the light of her flashlight. A number of the girls thanked her afterward for having been so receptive to their curiosity.[112]

Camp staff could never hope to fully control the process of children's sexual education, given that children arrived at camp with some degree of knowledge and that the living conditions themselves encouraged informal intimacies. Helen Weisgal, recalling her years at Camp Carmelia, explained that

> my first knowledge of menstruation came to me at camp at the age of
> ten or eleven. (My mother was completely closed on the subject until I

finally—at the age of twelve—got my first period . . .) One day I walked into the bathroom and a girl from the other bunk, a little older than I, started screaming at me to get out. This was not common practice. I asked her what the big deal was and her answer was: "You know goddamn well what I'm doing." So help me God, I didn't have a clue. But my curiosity was aroused and I found out something about the rudiments of adolescent sexual hygiene. What is interesting is that not long after, I had my first sexual dream, which I remember to this very day. I was feeling warm and moist and dreaming about slithering snakes and the feeling was wonderful![113]

Such moments, critical to individual children's development, were beyond adult oversight.

Recognizing that children had the right to some degree of autonomy and self-direction, increasing numbers of camp leaders organized occasional adult-supervised coeducational social events: a middle ground where adolescent boys and girls might mingle under adult supervision. The Florida girls of Camp Bay-Lea, who spent only a week at camp, did not meet with boys during their short camp stay. Nor did Dudley boys, or many Girl Scout campers. From the 1920s onward, however, organized coed dances and parties grew increasingly commonplace, as local camping networks grew, as more girls' camps were founded, and as camp leaders tried to foster children's heterosocial development.

Campers anticipated dances with pleasure and anxiety. As one camper reported in the Camp Jeanne D'Arc newsletter in 1941, after a successful dance, "We realized how foolish we had been, worrying ourselves that afternoon."[114] Children practiced dancing with their cabinmates, and they groomed themselves to look their best.[115] In 1939, one bemused YWCA staff member at the El Paso, Texas, Girl Reserves camp in southern New Mexico noted that the boys of a nearby YMCA camp brought out "heretofore, unused combs and brushes" when the Girl Reserves came to visit and that the girls "had their share of 'primping' for the 'get-acquainted' picnic" soon thereafter.[116]

Many camp owners ritualized social relationships with a particular "brother" or "sister" camp owned by the same family or run by a respected colleague whose clients came from the same ethnic and class backgrounds. "Brother" and "sister" camps were not always exclusive, but they formalized what had been more flexible arrangements in earlier years. The Catholic girls of Jeanne D'Arc, for example, participated in the social life of private camps around the Adirondacks' Chateaugay Lakes: as one girl noted in the camp log of 1922, "there was not much rest going on in camp [during rest hour], for the girls were 'curling' and 'primping up' for the expected visit of the boys from Mrs. Barrow's Camp."[117] Their efforts were in vain, as the boys did not come. Following camp director Ruth Israel's marriage (at camp, with her campers in attendance) to Charles McIntyre in 1925, the couple opened Camp Lafayette, for Catholic boys, nearby. They then inaugurated dances for older campers within the safe and relatively predictable social space of their own two camps.

Camp dances did not always live up to the excitement they had generated. The Che-Na-Wah Senior girls of 1926, preparing for a dance with the Camp Balfour boys down the hill, dreamed of wearing evening gowns, being fetched in fancy cars, and dancing all night under the rapt gaze of the captain of the Yale football team. But the truth of the matter, one camper claimed, was that "we go to Balfour in a truck. The stag line is composed of a few boys who are afraid to dance. The good dancers are dancing with our councillors. There ain't no justice! But—we love it!"[118] Che-Na-Wah girls vacillated between praising and criticizing these intercamp social events, especially the dances that, in 1925, one camp wag termed "Much Ado About Nothing." That August, when the Senior girls had the Balfour boys over as guests, the criticism was particularly pointed. After an imitation of one boy's dancing skill, "So well was George imitated, that our audience was hysterical, and the real George did not dance that night."[119] For the Che-Na-Wah girls, dates with boys were a perk of Senior life, and the girls who wrote about these events clearly took pleasure in recalling their own (mis)adventures and those of the boys. Anecdotally, it would appear that boys were more often reluctant to dance, perhaps because they had the additional burden of asking girls to dance. Counselors sometimes forcefully reminded boys of their gendered social obligations (and their masculine prerogative in choosing partners) so as to ensure the success of these social events. In 1909, for instance, when the boys of Camp Mowglis (a camp for preadolescent boys) met their counterparts among the girls of Camp Redcroft, a Mowglis counselor "grabbed some of the nearest boys and told them to ask some girl to dance," as the camp newspaper reported.[120]

Within a decade, many counselors and their former campers would become near peers, but for the moment the two groups viewed one another across a substantial cultural and age divide, vast differences separating the seven-year-olds from the fourteen-year-olds, and the fourteen-year-olds from the twenty-two-year-olds. Counselors often initiated children into the tropes of their own college-based youth culture, penning camp songs to the tunes of college songs and developing camp skits and entertainments in the style of college pageants. At the same time, camp leaders tried to preserve distinctions of age and appropriate childhood leisure—in effect, childhood itself—while guiding children to maturity. This project entailed teaching children (in small, controlled doses) the skills they would need to become normative sexual adults and sheltering them from too much sexual knowledge. Camp was supposed to be a protective barrier, but one flexible enough to allow for growth and learning. The rules of this project changed over time, however, as the adult culture to which children were being introduced itself underwent revision. In the context of an increasingly sexually frank culture, and growing discussion of heterosexual development, many camp leaders aspired to help children make the transition from innocence to romantic preparedness through such adult-monitored functions as camp dances. But the degree to which children had the right to be sexually exploratory was controversial, and the idea of children's sexual curiosity made many camp leaders deeply uncomfortable.

In general terms, camp leaders aspired to some version of the companionate family ideal, in which they would wield power over children but exercise that power very lightly. This project was often successful inasmuch as many campers grew to identify with their camp leaders. It was also inherently vexed, as many campers' adjustment to camp was slow or difficult. Even at the happiest camps there was some degree of disconnect between the aspirations of camp administrators, campers, and counselors. At Camp Bay-Lea, Amy's case was extreme in that she was sent home. Generally speaking, camp staffs made significant allowances for camper transgressions, tolerating "everyday" acting-out (when they found out about it). The adults at camp had little choice but to ignore some of the lesser transgressions that did not directly challenge their own leadership; a certain degree of "bad" behavior was ubiquitous, and campers were clients to be pleased. Adults' relatively permissive response to much of children's "acting out" was also a measure of staff recognition of children's peer culture. Camp staff tried to regulate the pace at which their campers "grew up": enough to master homesickness, not so much as to be "precociously" sexual. Offering up a small dose of transgressive play or supervised "dates" in their official programs, camp leaders guarded against more serious insurgency.

These scenarios acknowledged children's power as consumers in camp marketplaces. For the camp family to flourish, children had to become "good campers," but adults had to engage campers' interest and earn their respect. If camps were important adult-run institutions of social instruction, ideology, and indoctrination, where communal values were reinforced and new forms of association were nurtured, they were also, if imperfectly, spaces of children's own desires.

PART II

Modernity and Tradition in Children's Socialization

5

Is It Progress?

Modernity and Authenticity in Camp Life

The broad white track which led us on through woods and fields
    of green
Now flashes past beneath the wheels propelled by gasoline;
And twenty miles of countryside—a good day's walk, with luck,
Speeds by us in an hour, for we're hiking now by truck!
The friendly people we once met and talked with by the way
Now take the ditch and grab their hats as we dash by to-day.
The farmhouse where we used to rest and feast on milk and pie
Is hidden now in clouds of dust as we go rolling by.
For progress will not be denied, and with its steady gain
We'll soon be climbing Marcy by means of aeroplane.
But sometimes, just for old-time's sake, let's leave our modern
    mode,
And taste once more the pleasures of the friendly open road.
                    —Camp Dudley staff member, poem published in
                        Dudley Doings, the camp newspaper, 1922[1]

In 1885, Sumner Dudley's first campers slept on top of rubber ponchos to protect themselves against the damp and somewhat stony soil.[2] One of the boys, who found these conditions trying, muttered, "Oh, how I suffer," while trying to get to sleep on the bumpy surface. The others teased him, both at camp and for years afterward, for whining when he should have been stoic.[3] Perhaps they too suffered, if silently, on the day that the canvas awning under which they ate came crashing down in heavy rain and high winds. The sodden boys were pinned down, their heads pressed against the table, until Sumner Dudley and the cook were able to release them.[4]

Conditions at the camp grew more comfortable over the decades. At the turn of the century, the boys still slept on the ground on top of

Camp Dudley tents, circa 1887. (Courtesy Camp Dudley)

rubber blankets; groups of eight to fourteen campers slept side by side in tents of twelve by fourteen feet.[5] Over the next few years the tents were set on wooden boards to keep them dry. In 1908 the New York State YMCA purchased land for a campsite near Westport on Lake Champlain. Instead of moving from one rented field to another, the camp would now occupy a permanent site. More substantive building projects ensued, and within a few years Dudleyites had a new dining hall; a dark room for photographic work; a doctor's office; a store where boys could purchase necessary items and treats; a manual training (wood) shop; a boat house with a reading room, library, and study rooms; five tennis courts; a baseball diamond; a basketball court; a rifle range; and new waterfront equipment.[6] In 1911, the camp tents were also updated; for the next few decades, campers slept on canvas double-decker beds set on wooden platform floors.

The Dudley leadership and its alumni celebrated various improvements to the property as signs of their camp's success. Among some older alumni, however, the new tents were controversial, a sign of "softness" in camping.[7] In 1930, similar concerns were voiced when three cabins were built as a first step toward replacing the tents altogether. An article in the camp newspaper, *Dudley Doings,* contended that the cabins "are a distinct step forward in Dudley" but conceded that "many of the oldtimers are a bit skeptical," though "they are being convinced of the value of these additions."[8] Were the new cabins truly an illustration of the camp's rising quality of life? Or as many experienced Dudleyites fretted, were they a sign that the boys were no longer truly and authentically camping?

This turn was controversial within the interwar industry at large. Which changes to the camp landscape qualified as improvements, and which might actually weaken the next generation? To what degree should children be sheltered not only from the wind and the rain but from the culture from which they came? These questions were motivated in part by the industry's increasingly heterogeneous nature, but they also attested to a broader hesitation about the value of modern convenience and contemporary technology at what were supposed to be nostalgic "toughening" institutions. In an increasingly diverse industry, camp leaders used the term "campy," suggestive of "authentic" camping, to justify a widening range of enterprises. "Moss Lake Camp is a *Real Camp,* in the campiest way," boasted the 1931 brochure of an elite private Adirondack camp at which the girls lived in spacious

Camp Dudley cabins, circa 1930s. (Courtesy Camp Dudley)

cabins, took regular fencing lessons, and rode horses competitively in the region.[9]

Camp leaders balanced divergent ideals, inasmuch as they promised protected exposure, comfortable adventure, and modern pioneer living. As camps gestured simultaneously toward tradition and progress, they exemplified a broader societal ambivalence about which direction was healthiest and most beneficial. American cities were growing larger and more ethnically and racially diverse, and new technologies were reshaping modern life. At the same time, the early twentieth century was the period in which American folklore studies and Americana collecting began in earnest, when local historical pageants reached their largest audiences, and when tourist attractions such as Colonial Williamsburg and Henry Ford's Greenfield Village were built to celebrate a (sanitized) American past.[10]

The interwar Camp Directors Association (CDA) and its official magazine, *Camping,* lauded old-fashioned "campiness" as a necessary corrective to modern popular culture. The first issue of the *Camp Directors Bulletin,* precursor to *Camping,* offered direct opposition to modern leisure trends: "Someone is sitting up nights to originate new ideas in amusement, earrings, cosmetics, candies, cigarettes, jazz, and ragtime. Camp directors must sit up nights to compete. We have to increase the consumers of sensible dress, milk and vegetables, fresh air, healthy games, folk dances, and folk songs."[11] Were camps places of amusement or somehow above the fray? If camps were to achieve their true mission, these writers argued, such seductions as overly luxurious lodgings must be kept at bay.

This project was an impossible one. Camps were entwined with the outside world, and as that world changed, so did camps. At Camp Dudley's Westport location, for instance, campers originally walked to the trailheads of various Adirondack mountains. The process of getting to the mountains was itself a significant hike. By the early 1920s, however, automobile traffic in the area had become much heavier, due in part to the expansion of regional tourism. Groups of boys walking along the side of the road were now at greater risk of being injured by careless drivers. In 1922, the camp leadership decided that the boys would henceforth travel by truck to the mountains. The Dudley campers reached their destinations more quickly, but this was progress at a price. As one Dudley staff member suggested in the poem that begins this chapter, campers lost contact with the region's slower rhythms and with local people and places. However, the growing automobile traffic proved that rural regions were themselves undergoing change.

By its nature, innovation threatened camp tradition. Until the 1930s, for instance, Camp Dudley's main field quickly became muddy during rainstorms. The boys would strip naked and run and slide in the field until they were caked in mud and were sent to wash off in the lake.[12] In the 1930s, the field was regraded; it was never as muddy again, and the game came to an end.[13] Some traditions were mourned more than others. There is no record of anyone at Camp Dudley objecting to the introduction of flush toilets, for example, which replaced the malodorous latrines.[14]

New campers generally arrived unbound by their elders' concerns for authenticity and purity. Active agents of modernity, they were enthusiastic about the pleasures of the outside world and eager to integrate some of their more urban leisure experiences into camp life. As part of their socialization as campers, these children learned the terms of camp nostalgia from their elders. Many of them subsequently became firm partisans of certain camp traditions and, as alumni, retained strong ideas about what constituted true "campiness." But no camp was preserved just so, and every cohort of campers developed its own understanding of what authenticity entailed.

From Tents to Cabins

The material conditions of authentic camping have always been open to interpretation. In the 1880s, Camp Chocorua's Ernest Balch found nearby Camp Asquam overly civilized.[15] But Chocorua also became more comfortable over the years; when Balch closed the camp after the 1889 season, the staff and campers had constructed nine buildings of various kinds, including wooden dormitories for the boys.[16] Had the camp survived beyond 1889, it would likely have grown to accommodate more boys and facilities, changes that proved typical of later successful camps. Success over time entailed expansion, which the leaders of most established camps measured in part through the acquisition of more property and equipment.

Camp Dudley was typical in this regard. By the 1930s, it was the oldest extant summer camp in the country. Nationally renowned, it was one of the more expensive organizational camps in the nation; the 1931 fee of two hundred dollars for the summer was twice as high as that of the average local YMCA camp.[17] The camp also boasted an unusual number of dedicated alumni who supported the camp financially and made it possible for the camp to compete for clients with many high-priced private camps. The turn to cabins was part of this larger project.

In the name of progress, the majority of interwar camp directors nationwide either made the switch from tents to cabins or chose cabins from the start. Cabins were more healthful, they argued, because they were better ventilated and dry on the inside when it was wet outside; more fireproof given that campers commonly lit kerosene lanterns inside tents in the evenings; generally safer since the occasional tent did blow down in a storm; and more comfortable on rainy days and cool nights. From a practical perspective cabins promised much less trouble: they did not require constant repair and did not have to be carefully dried and put away at the end of the season. Although they cost more than tents, their durability made them more cost-efficient in the long term, making them attractive to organizational camps. And especially at private camps, attractive cabins replete with fireplaces and electric lights, hot and cold running water, and inside flush toilets helped to justify fees in the hundreds of dollars. It was with pride that the writers of the Camp Dudley 1935 brochure promised that "a locker for each boy, electric lights, comfortable beds, and open wood fireplaces offer a contrast to the tent with its familiar drawbacks."[18]

For many years the Camp Dudley tents, arrayed in a semicircle around the perimeter of the main field, had been a focal point of camp life. Made of strong canvas, each was large enough to accommodate several bunk beds along with a counselor's single bed. In good weather the boys opened the flaps to let in fresh air; during rainstorms they left the flaps closed. Ropes tied to tent pegs set into the ground secured the tent covers. "We never had the feeling that we were roughing it," a Dudley camper of the 1920s later recalled. "It was wonderful to feel the cool—sometimes cold—night air flowing over you when the tent flaps were up. We were snug as could be sleeping between the folds of a warm quilt kept tightly in place by a wool blanket stretched across us and tucked under the two by fours that held the canvas bottom of our two-decker bunks."[19] As greater numbers of boys came to Camp Dudley, more tents were added, each named consecutively after a letter of the alphabet; after the twenty-sixth tent, they were called Annexes.

Every night, "Chief" Herman Beckman would walk down the line, calling out to each tent group in turn and bidding them a good night. Warm under their covers, the boys would reply in kind.

These tents required near-continuous maintenance. The boys who served as tent Aides, along with the Junior Leaders, were responsible for repairing rips in the canvas; using a heavy needle, twine, and a special device to push the needle through the canvas, they repaired the tents by hand.[20] The boys also had to tighten the tent ropes on sunny days and loosen them on wet days. One camp alumnus recalled that "usually thunderstorms began during afternoon swim, just before supper, so dozens of naked boys rushed up from the point [where they swam] to lower sides, tie flaps, loosen ropes and then hang on, hoping it will all be over before the bell for supper."[21] The wooden floors, elevated to keep the tents dry, presented occasional hazards of their own, as small animals sometimes crawled underneath them, causing, as another former camper recalled, "a lot of turmoil and disaster" when skunks were prowling underfoot.[22] Campers stored their more precious possessions —best clothes, musical instruments, and tennis rackets—in the main lodge, where such items were safer.[23]

Dudley tents were vulnerable not only to the natural world but also to campers' pranks and high spirits. Campers commonly raided one another's tents, usually on rainy days or in the evening just before bedtime. Boys from one tent would rush to another, attempting to release its ropes and cause its collapse.[24] More surreptitiously, campers would sometimes sneak over to a neighboring tent and loosen the ropes, which had the effect of making the tent sink slowly down onto its occupants. Bolder campers sometimes tipped a sleeping counselor's cot over the side of the tent in the morning. A common hazing ritual, one ex-camper of the 1920s recalled, involved finding "some gullible new camper and assur[ing] him that the tent pegs required daily watering and that he had been selected for this honor. He would then be dispatched to find a watering can and could be seen dutifully watering each peg."[25]

At many established camps of the interwar years, tents were among the camp traditions that provided a context for group loyalty. In 1923, Henry Wellington Wack, having returned from a tour of northeastern camps, reported what camp directors around the region had told him: the campers "insist on having tents." Wack himself dismissed this desire as nothing more than "an odd camper's romantic flapdoodle," but boys and girls were generally thrilled to live in tents, which they saw as authentically adventurous.[26] Campers resisted cabins not out of eccentricity but because tents were central to their understanding of the camp experience.

If anything, however, Dudley's transition to cabins demonstrates the speed with which new traditions could be forged and old ones laid aside. Camp Dudley was venerable, but the average camper attended for only a few years. Camp "generations" turned over quickly, and what one group of campers imagined to be apostasy would appear familiar and traditional only a few years later. As older cohorts of children aged out of camps, and as new traditions connected to cabins emerged, rituals that had once been central to collective memory were rapidly displaced. Despite the initial grumblings of Dudley traditionalists, the fuss over cabins subsided as campers came to see their benefits. As one boy, whose tenure spanned the precabin and postcabin eras, recalled, "some of us resisted the idea of building cabins. That, we felt, would mean we were no longer camping, and in a sense that was true." He continued, "I'll have to admit, though, that the summer when the first three cabins were available, and my tent was one of the nine which each had three weeks in a cabin, and our turn coincided with three weeks of almost continuous rain, I weakened a bit."[27]

Not only did the Dudley leadership overcome many former campers' resistance to change, but they also successfully campaigned for alumni contributions to the cabin-building campaign during the worst years of the Depression. In 1932, the year that the Princeton, Yale, and Dartmouth cabins were constructed, Princeton alumni who had attended Dudley as boys received invitations to contribute to the "Princeton Lodge." This cabin would, the camp explained, "be truly representative of Princeton in every respect," down to walls festooned with photographs of the campus and the school banner.[28] The savvy marketing campaign evidently appealed to the joint loyalties of devoted alumni who credited camp as a first step on the way to Ivy League achievement. By the end of the decade, the camp had thirty-five cabins, enough for all the campers. Many of the cabins had stone fireplaces and outside balconies, and most were named for colleges and universities.

Camp Dudley's turn from tents to cabins was typical of the interwar industry at large. By 1940, one fairly comprehensive study of New York State summer camps found that only 40 percent of camps used tents. Broadly, the trend was toward greater convenience and comfort: over

60 percent of camps had flush toilets instead of pits or outhouses, and most relied on electricity rather than oil lanterns to provide light in the evening hours.[29] Organizations such as the Boy Scouts and Girl Scouts continued to endorse tents as "campier" and more authentic than cabins. But the leaders of most other organizational camps calculated that cabins represented a savings over the longer term. Within the private camp market, meanwhile, there was competitive pressure to make the switch to cabins, electricity, and flush toilets. An advertisement for flush toilets and sewage systems published in *Camping* in 1931 put the point bluntly, asking directors, "Will they come back to *your* camp? . . . the parents—who pay the bills—must be satisfied that your camp is absolutely sanitary. . . . Let the Sword of Sanitation Fight for You!"[30]

Increasing numbers of camp directors argued for cabins on ideological grounds as well. They praised cabins for invoking both a rough-hewn American pioneer tradition and their own adherence to modern health and safety standards. Camp leaders were proud of the ways that they had improved on nature: damming streams or piping in water to make ponds, engaging in reforestation efforts, or hauling in sand to cover over rocky shores.[31] Pioneer iconography further resonated with directors who saw their own hard work made manifest in "improved" landscapes. The turn to cabins represented one such effort to balance varied imperatives: tradition and progress, authenticity and modern comfort, purity and a competitive marketplace.

Self-proclaimed traditionalists, usually representing older and more self-consciously historical camps, expressed concern about a tendency toward ease in camping. As George Meylan, director of Maine's White Mountain Camp for boys, warned with dismay in 1922,

> Unfortunately, there is a tendency in some camps to rival with summer hotels in providing luxurious equipment, fancy food, a candy store, city entertainments, marble bathrooms, sun parlors and numerous attendants. The inevitable result of such a policy is that boys and girls continue the habits of physical indolence, self-indulgence, and dependence fostered by modern city life and fail to develop those rugged physical, and moral qualities characteristic of noble manhood and good citizenship.[32]

Meylan's account of marble bathrooms and sun parlors overstated the point. Still, this prominent director of one of Maine's oldest private camps, who in the mid-1910s had served as president of the Camp Directors Association, spoke for many who wished to keep alive the spirit of a simpler time in what seemed an increasingly decadent world.

This ideal remained powerful even as camps made the transition to cabins. Still, there was nothing inherently purer or more authentically "campy" about tents. Not all early camp leaders preferred them. And by the interwar years, tents reminded many observers of the fervor attending the First World War, when many summer camp leaders laid out rows of tents with military precision. The same canvas structures that symbolized rugged recreation could also connote militaristic excesses. By the interwar years, tents were fast becoming emblems of "old-fashioned" camping: traditional, yes, but not entirely up-to-date.

Motion Pictures and Commercial Culture

From his camp's inception in 1912 onward, director Frank Hackett proclaimed that Camp Riverdale stood for old-fashioned wilderness camping. Headmaster at the Riverdale Country Day School in the well-to-do Bronx suburb of Riverdale, Hackett extolled his elite Adirondack boys' camp's remove from modern urban life, ten miles from the nearest road and twenty minutes by motorboat to the village of Long Lake. The 1932 brochure began by quoting Romantic poet Percy Bysshe Shelley: "Away, away from men and towns / To the silent wilderness."[33] That same year, as president of the Camp Directors Association, Hackett called on his colleagues to eschew artificial and passive "city" pleasures in favor of simpler joys. "Without something of pioneer experience, a camp cannot satisfy," he argued.

> Campers long for this bread, and often we give them the stones of protection, of luxury, of imitation of the very city life they are fleeing. They may think they want movies, shows, highly organized sports, and other transferences from accustomed environment, but give them a chance really to camp out, to explore, to swim, to paddle, to sail, to fish, to hunt with a camera, to learn wild life and its haunts, and you will find tamer occupations falling into the background in which they belong.[34]

In 1940 Hackett declared a change in policy. In a front-page editorial in the camp newspaper, Hackett told his readership of campers and par-

Camp Riverdale tents, circa 1920s–1930s. (Courtesy Adirondack Museum)

ents that the boys had recently started to attend movies in Long Lake. "It may be," he reflected, "that on some small trips counselors and boys secretly had this experience, but one of the boasts of Camp was that from beginning to end, our life was wholly in the wilderness. If we touched the Village at all, it was merely to pass through, or to take part in Sport's Day." On one occasion, he recalled, a counselor had decided to bring some boys into the village to see a film, "and that raised heaven and earth! Now, we are deliberately planning trips to the movies, perhaps a half dozen or so in our eight weeks. What is the source of this change, and is it progress?"

Hackett justified a somewhat faint "yes" on two counts. He claimed that the new fireproof movie house in Long Lake made possible what would once have represented "an unjustifiable risk [in] the old fire-trap of a theater." But that was not all: "The change in Camp policy . . . rests upon the training of fellows to use and not abuse opportunities which will give them legitimate pleasure. If campers who have good sense are given much more freedom to do what they like, they will probably come to like better what they have to do."[35] Despite his own reservations, Hackett wished to please his campers. Perhaps, he proposed, campers who were permitted to enjoy popular culture in moderation would achieve a better balance between self-indulgence and self-control.

Like the debate over tents and cabins, the question of whether camps should enjoy or spurn motion pictures was an ongoing controversy of the interwar camp industry, bringing into high relief the debate among camp leaders about authenticity in camping. What did it mean that campers could go to the movies and participate in "old-fashioned" pleasures almost simultaneously, taking in a film as a break from an extended days-long hike or canoe trip or as the endpoint of a community hayride?

In truth, pastiche was a longstanding camp tradition. At turn-of-the-century Camp Dudley, for instance, campers and staff entertained themselves by putting on circuses, musicals, minstrel shows, and vaudeville routines; by the 1910s they enjoyed weekly slide shows on the camp's stereopticon machine. However, by the 1920s a growing number of camp leaders feared that "outside" cultural forces were exerting too great an influence on camps. American mass culture had expanded significantly after the First World War. Not only were children increasingly targeted by advertisers and businesses, so too the dissemination of popular culture in fairly remote locations was more widespread. Although Hackett defined his camp to a significant extent through its difference from contemporary urban life, films were available just across the lake.

The motion-picture industry actually had much in common with summer camps. Both appealed particularly to children and both were successful examples of the new commercial recreation, having begun as small-scale enterprises in the late nineteenth century and achieving national prominence by the 1920s.[36] As the *New York Times* noted in 1930, summer camps were "along with the movies . . . a dominant modern enthusiasm."[37] But from the perspective of the traditionalists (as they saw themselves) who dominated the CDA and who worked to define the camping agenda, the two industries represented very different approaches to modern leisure. Hackett typified the CDA leadership during its first few decades in describing movies as a contributing factor to that dread modern disease, "spectatoritis." Within this cohort, movies were a convenient shorthand for the perils of modernity. Camps must stand firm, proposed A. E. Hamilton, director of Maine's Camp Timanous (one of the Luther Gulick camps) and the author of an extensive interwar camping literature, "against the tidal wave of jazz and crowded hall and movie and cabaret."[38] If camp life was to be an antidote to modernity's cheap thrills, these traditionalists argued, movies should play no part in it. Urban children had become "pitiful sophisticates," Louis

Fleisher, director of Maine's Kennebec Camps, complained in 1941, through their exposure to sensational "sex exciting movies, radio thrillers, comic strip books."[39]

Outside of camping circles, others expressed similar reservations about the effects of film on children. A typical 1929 article in *Child Study* made the claim that movies posed "grave dangers—physical dangers of bad air and eye strain; psychological dangers to manners and ethical attitudes."[40] Numerous reformers called for the censorship of so-called racy or violent films on the grounds that these were of particular risk to children. Implicit in these arguments was the idea that cinema's heterogeneous, age-mixed audiences threatened the ideal of childhood as a space distinct from (and protected from) adult culture.[41] But children often rejected this ideal, choosing entertainments across what adults felt to be appropriate age divides.

Most interwar campers were enthusiastic about "movie nights." At Camp Dudley, the campers of the early 1920s were seasoned viewing professionals who knew a film genre when they saw one; when the hero of a Western first appeared on screen, they would immediately burst into their own special camp yell: "The hero on a white horse, alloy alloy alloy."[42] Children at other camps frequently talked to the screen, urging heroes on, applauding a successful adventure, or groaning when a reel ended at a particularly dramatic moment.[43] Their boisterousness was increasingly unacceptable at first-run urban movie theaters. At camps where films were shown, their behavior stood for "camp spirit."

Children were also partisans of other new forms of popular culture. In increasing numbers they packed comic books, records, and sensational "pulp" magazines such as *True Story* in their trunks and suitcases, often to their counselors' dismay.[44] Comic books enjoyed particular popularity among boys from the late 1930s onward and were the source of frequent confrontations between staff and campers. Some children used them to evade camp routines, reading "funny books" alone in their bunks when they were supposed to be at group activities.[45] Others stole comics from their peers, forcing counselors to intervene in interpersonal disputes. The camper who had comic books to barter or to loan enjoyed higher status among his peers; as one thirteen-year-old Surprise Lake Camp boy described the scene in 1942, rest hour was a flurry of boys offering to "trade ya Flash for Superman."[46] While many camp leaders fretted about the implications of modernity, their campers did not have the same concerns. If children were not entirely transformed by camp, they did not expect or wish to be. Possessing limited access to many institutions of public life, they found in popular culture an exciting, semiautonomous space for self-definition.

At Camp Riverdale in 1940, perhaps the greatest cultural crisis of the season concerned the great number of comic books owned and read by the "middlers," the campers aged twelve to fourteen. These periodicals did have an adult audience, and a number of parents willingly sent such literature to their children. Still, many camp directors and counselors saw children's fascination with comic books as an affront to camp ideals. "Comics having become a nuisance at camp," one Riverdale counselor reported, "left hither and yon, and used at every odd moment, we had pursued a course of confiscating and destroying them when they were discovered." But the Riverdale staff's idea of worthy leisure came up forcefully against the campers' own sense of entitlement. The boys registered their independence by continuing to read comic books on the sly. Campers watched only those films that the staff allowed them to see, but as one of the "middlers" explained, books were "easy to carry around and hide under mattresses." Finally, in August of that year "Chief" Frank Hackett and several staff members met with the "middlers" to discuss what should be done. Most of the boys rose to defend their pastime as "very good fun." Only a few dissented, calling comic books "trash" or "a lazy man's kind of amusement." The adults in the room attempted to cast comics in this less positive light. However, everyone agreed that the problem of "sneaking" was worse than the problem of comics themselves. In the end, the group adopted a camper's suggestion: that the boys be allowed to read comic books for a short period of time after the evening meal.[47] Because campers were clients, even their most lowbrow interests mandated some degree of intergenerational compromise; thus, adult attempts to tame the threat posed by a semiautonomous children's culture were only partially successful.

In a divided industry without a uniform philosophical mandate, let alone a recognized code of standards, camp leaders did not agree about how to shelter children from the wider world. Many thousands of interwar camp leaders chose to show films at camp on a weekly basis or regularly took their campers to see movies in town. While *Camping*, the CDA's official organ, generally disapproved of this practice, some competing industry journals were more accepting. In 1930, for example, *Camp Life* published an article by Henry Levy, a publicist at Universal Pictures and a veteran of eleven summers at eastern camps. Levy argued that films served an important purpose in the camp routine, as a physical respite from the often intense athleticism of the day. Like Hackett, he acknowledged that the pressure exerted by children themselves was perhaps even more compelling: "A judicious selection of films by the camp director will make his movie night a most popular camp feature and one that he will find of inestimable value as a sales talk when he makes the rounds the following winter to re-register his enrollment for the coming summer."[48]

Many camp directors were receptive to Levy's line of argument. Their work required that they provide a constant stream of enjoyable activities, day in and day out, rain or shine. Movies, they knew, were sure-fire evening hits, demanded relatively little preparation, and created pleasurable anticipation among campers eager to find out just what "Movie Night" held in store that week.[49] Not every camp director aspired to create a space protected from modern commercial culture. Some wished primarily to entertain children reliably. They turned to movies, as they turned to cabins, as part of an effort to build and retain their clienteles. A 1931 advertisement for Willoughbys, a New York City–based company that sold and rented films and viewing projectors, put the matter boldly, arguing in *Camp Life* that "Boys and Girls COME BACK . . . Summer After Summer . . . to the Camp That Shows MOTION PICTURES."[50]

Although traditionalists often framed the debate about the place of film at camps as a contest between "high" and "low" culture, camp movie nights cannot neatly be summed up as a litmus test of camp purity. Even critics of camp film showings conceded, for instance, that not all films had the same values. Selections varied widely from camp to camp and even from week to week: Hollywood films that included so-called bedroom scenes, educational documentaries, animated cartoons, even commercially produced shorts sponsored by companies selling safety glass or cigarettes.[51] At Camp Riverdale as elsewhere, trips to the Long Lake movie house remained a sporadic reminder of city life rather than a dominant force in the camp's entertainment schedule. As camper Walter "Sheepy" Simon wistfully pointed out at the conclusion of that summer, "The end of camp always conjures up visions of New York, cinemas, and steam heating."[52] For all the hubbub about film as a positive or negative factor in camp life, movies were at most a weekly treat.

The rise of camp movie nights suggests both the growth and limits of camps' participation in mass culture. By the 1920s, motion-picture technology was more readily available and more affordable to rural clients than ever before. As distribution networks became more advanced, camp directors were able to rent a greater range of products, including cartoons, comedies, nature films, and full-length commercial releases, and to have films shipped to their camps on a weekly basis.[53] But the actual exhibition of film at summer camps lagged behind the mass-cultural standards of the day. The films themselves were generally a year or two old, and sometimes older. Since amateurs usually ran the equipment, and the "screen" was often a wall or a curtain, viewing conditions tended toward the primitive. Film showings also depended on access to electricity or to portable (but noisy) generators, and in many rural areas, prior to the New Deal electrification projects of the mid-1930s, electric power was unavailable or unreliable.[54]

In effect, camps represented the end of the line for the commercial distribution networks through which films circulated. Large, luxurious, urban picture palaces, which constituted perhaps 5 percent of movie theaters, hosted the most recently released films. Less expensive neighborhood theaters serving ethnic, working-class audiences were the next link in the chain.[55] As these progressively less lucrative markets were tapped, movies finally became available for small-scale rental. Some of the campers likely already had seen these films before they saw them at camp. This lag time between films' first release and their appearance at camps increased after "talking pictures" such as *The Jazz Singer* (1927) were released in the late 1920s. Many camp leaders continued to show silent films well after the industry converted to sound. They had already purchased projectors capable of showing the earlier and more affordable movies, and the new technology was very expensive. Because campers clamored for sound, a number of private camp leaders began to hire traveling film operators, who traveled from camp to camp with generators, projectors, and talking pictures.[56] At less elite camps such as the YMHA's Surprise Lake Camp, it was not until 1940 that the boys saw their first "talkies" at camp, over a decade after sound first hit the commercial market.[57]

Even as camp leaders debated the merits of commercial films, many created their own "home movies" for recruitment purposes. They did so without worrying that shooting film to sell a vision of simple living was inherently contradictory. Rather, they differentiated between commercial movies, which brought the city into the woods, and their own efforts to bring the pleasures of the woods into the city. As early as 1915, the Camp Fire Girls' national leadership sponsored a film with scenes including a canoe full of girls speeding along a lake, which the youth organization then rented out to local branches to stimulate enrollment in the group.[58] From the 1920s onward, as the process of amateur filmmaking became increasingly affordable, greater numbers of individual camp directors began to shoot film.[59] Even camping "purists" like Hackett who anguished about where to draw the line between nature and modern recreation enthusiastically embraced "home movies." Hackett produced films for his own commercial purposes as early as the mid-1920s. Thereafter, Hackett regularly showed amateur footage of the past summer at his camp's annual winter reunions, held at the Riverdale school in the Bronx. By 1939, the Riverdale reunion footage reflected the latest in amateur film: a "remarkable display of camp colored pictures."[60]

Most camp "home movies" did not have high production values. Often, the camera remained motionless while campers filed past it, dove from platforms, or let arrows fly from their archery bows.[61] Former campers enjoyed seeing themselves on film nonetheless. More ambitious films used storylines to provide flow and cohesiveness to what would otherwise have been a motley assortment of scenes. One common device was the illustration of "a day in the life" from dawn to sunset, beginning with a shot of the bugler waking up the campers, followed by scenes of the morning swim, various craft classes, the construction of buildings or objects, lunch, the afternoon swim, life-saving class, and so on, culminating in an evening campfire.[62] Similar plot arcs included "a letter home," "the newcomer making his or her way, from first day to last day," and "father's visit to camp."[63] These were all parables of adventure, pleasure, skill, and personal transformation.

Of the more polished and ambitious promotional camp films, one of the first was *The Golden Eaglet: The Story of a Girl Scout,* filmed in 1918 under the aegis of Girl Scout National Headquarters to promote the organization.[64] American Girl Scouting had begun only six years earlier, in 1912. By 1918 the movement had grown to thirty-two thousand members across the country.[65] *The Golden Eaglet* tells the fictional story of one such member, Margaret Ferris, and her rise from bored town girl to fledgling Girl Scout to possessor of twenty-one badges and the organization's highest honor, the Golden Eaglet. Once Margaret becomes a Girl Scout, she attends "Central Valley Camp," where the girls are shown hiking, marching, swimming and diving, and practicing semaphore (a method of signaling with flags), among other occupations. Margaret puts all these skills to good use when, in the film's most dramatic sequence, camp director Caroline Lewis asks her to take a message from camp into the nearby town of Huntsville. The intrepid Girl Scout navigates all kinds of terrain, swims across a river in her clothes (under supervision by Lewis, who watches with binoculars), and climbs a tree to communicate by semaphore with her leader on the other shore.[66] When Margaret gets to town, she finds that the telegraph man has been attacked; using her Girl Scout first-aid skills, she tends to him and uses Morse Code to tap out a call for help. In the film's final sequence, founder Juliette Low pins the Golden Eaglet onto Margaret's khaki uniform.[67]

Unlike *The Golden Eaglet,* few camp films were made with a real budget, an artistic vision, or plans for national distribution. Few deployed continuity editing, in which each shot derived meaning in relation to the scenes that immediately preceded and followed it. *The Golden Eaglet,* like more commercial films of the classical era of cinema, included such stylistic innovations as crosscutting between actors and the use of intertitles. The girl who played Margaret was likely a professional actress, not a Girl Scout. Still, no one viewing *The Golden Eaglet* would have mistaken it for a Hollywood production. In *The Golden Eaglet,* as in more overtly amateur productions, some campers looked directly or sidelong at the camera or moved past it self-consciously, essentially disrupting the standards of classical-era film that *The Golden Eaglet* sought to emulate.

The "Central Valley" campers were actually Manhattan Girl Scouts (a close look at the shot of an envelope addressed to one Girl Scout at home reveals a Park Avenue address) attending Camp Calemaco, founded in 1917 at Upper Twin Lake in the Palisades Interstate Park. Calemaco was the first troop camp for New York City girls. Caroline Lewis, then director of both the Manhattan Girl Scout Council and the camp, appears in the film in her actual leadership role; national leader Juliette Low made a special trip to the camp to take part in the film. The Manhattan girls performed their daily routines under the gaze of the "movie man," who orchestrated every last detail: "Unroll your blankets quickly; be careful, don't stand in front of each other; keep doing something—anything, but don't stand still; two of you start out for firewood." The girls acting out one overnight-hike episode packed real food for their trip, but the scene in which they set out on the hike was filmed a number of times before they got it "right" (walking in a straight line while looking away from the camera). Once the scene was completed, the campers were bundled into an automobile and whisked off to the next location.[68]

The filming of *The Golden Eaglet* and of numerous other Girl Scout films in the decades that followed underscores the contradictions inherent in camp traditionalists' use of popular culture. Throughout the interwar years, Girl Scout leaders continually decried the supposed passivity of modern leisure. In 1931, for example, a New York City Girl Scout fundraising brochure asked its readers, "How are our city girls to find stimulus for creative impulse in an age when entertainment is theirs without effort at the movies or from radio?"[69] Yet the organization's leaders produced exactly such entertainment, emulating adventurous Hollywood heroines to sell their own institutional vision to girls. For camps with large enough film budgets, the sky was literally the limit. The leaders of the Massachusetts YMCA's Camp Becket went so far as to charter an airplane to film the camp from the air. As the camp photographer later explained, "the lake looked like a sparkling jewel in an emerald setting, and when the film was eventually shown on the screen it drew delighted 'Oh's' and 'Ah's' from the audience."[70] Even as traditionalist camp leaders feared the seductive power of popular culture, they eagerly employed the latest technology to sell their old-fashioned ideal. For campers, meanwhile, moviemaking represented a new kind of outdoor adventure.

The popularity of the summer camp industry reflected the resonance, in an era of rapid social transformation, of fantasies about pristine land, simple living, and close-knit community. But no matter how strenuously certain camp leaders professed their desire to disengage from the hurly-burly of modernity, their camps were zones of boundary crossing: between urban and rural, old-fashioned and up-to-date, the realm of artifice and the realm of nature. Many camp directors willingly embraced film's seductive power to entertain children. More of them turned to film, as one writer put it, to "unloose the purse-strings," as a good home movie could sway prospective clients (or, in the case of charitable camps, philanthropists) with greater immediacy than a traditional printed brochure.[71] Campers saw none of this as inherently contradictory. Summer camps were part of their participation in a wider children's culture. Their ideas of camp purity were learned at camp and could just as easily include movie nights as walks through the woods.

A Touristic Wilderness

William Abbott, a graduate of the New York State College of Forestry, a Boy Scout leader, and the founder of the Adirondack Woodcraft Camp in 1925, was proud of his camp's emphasis on camping trips. In the pages of his camp's 1927 brochure, Abbott promised that "the boys really learn how to camp by taking a great number of both short and long trips out from Camp, which is used as a base."[72] Around 1930, Walter and Smittie, two of the counselors on staff, took one group of ten-year-old boys on an overnight trip. They stopped for the evening in a grassy glade, cooked their dinner around an open fire, and settled down for an evening of stories and songs. The haunting sound of a loon close to their campsite inspired Walter to tell the boys a spooky tale about being trailed by timber wolves. Then Smittie told a story about the intelligence and treachery of bears. The boys seemed rattled, judging from their subsequent conversation. The counselors, worried that they had overemphasized the dangers of the wild, assured the campers of the docility of bears, especially black bears in the Adirondacks, and the boys slept well. In the morning the two men found two fresh bear tracks, each ten inches in diameter, a mere fifty feet from their fire. While none of the boys was watching, Walter and Smittie carefully stamped out the bear tracks with their feet.[73]

This story suggests the ambiguity of wilderness adventure at children's summer camps: good for a story or two, good for a scare before bedtime, but best at some remove from the unpredictability, even danger, of the natural world. Excursions into the "real" wilderness were special events, which campers experienced in relatively small and controlled doses before returning to the comforts of camp. The Adirondack Woodcraft Camp brochure explained that the camp was very close to "railroads, good roads, telephone lines" but that "to reach Camp it is necessary to go over our private road through the woods for nearly a mile from the nearest public road."[74] Privacy and convenience, ruggedness and civilization—camps promised them all.

The idea of wilderness was central to the summer camp project. Camp brochures often described camp properties as nearly undeveloped, known only to Native Americans and celebrated military expeditions before campers set foot on the land. At the same time, wilderness offered a blank slate for tales of personal and communal transformation: from underweight child to hearty camper, or from shabby tent to cozy log cabin. In fact, however, almost all camps were built on land that had already served other economic purposes, such as farming, mining, logging, and tourism, and most were located within a few miles of towns or villages. The majority of camps were located in rural neighborhoods that had already become or were in the process of becoming recreation centers. These more layered commercial histories were set aside in favor of mythic American wilderness and "virgin land."[75]

In most camping regions, children were more likely to run into other parties of vacationers on area hiking trails than to encounter bears.[76] In the 1880s, parents of Camp Chocorua boys often vacationed at resorts around Squam Lake, joining their sons on the island for Sunday-morning church services. By the early twentieth century, most campers spending nine weeks at a private northeastern camp could expect their parents to visit at least once during the season. Local business owners adapted to this rising tourist industry by cultivating new clienteles, through not only their proximity to nature but also their ability to offer a variety of "city" entertainments, from jazz bands to movies to dinner clubs.

Adirondack Woodcraft Camp, although somewhat isolated from its neighbors, was not alone in the woods. As a greater number of middle-class Americans took to the roads, recreation and tourism became major sources of income for the region. By the early 1920s, ten thousand vacationers came each year to Old Forge, a town of 750 year-round residents, with the majority of the vacationers coming in the summer months. Within a few miles of Old Forge there were at least two Boy Scout camps, two private Jewish camps, a private Protestant girls' camp, and Adirondack Woodcraft, as well as a variety of small hotels and country homes.

Camps' social networks were sometimes quite extensive. From the 1880s, when the boys of Chocorua occasionally participated in sports tournaments with the boys of Camp Asquam, competitions and pageants drew members of local camps together. In the 1910s, the Camp Kehonka girls mingled frequently with campers from several other private camps along the Winnipesaukee shore, attending a theater performance at a local girls' camp, a sports meet between two boys' camps, and dances with some of the boys, while the few younger boys in attendance played baseball against boys from a neighboring camp.[77] In later years, movie nights were vehicles of intercamp sociability between "brother" and "sister" camps. All of these activities reinforced networks of reciprocity while protecting children from chance encounters with strangers.[78]

Relations with local rural communities were more variable. Camps offered locals, often in depressed rural areas, some maintenance and construction opportunities. Camps were also ready markets for area farmers' milk, fruits, and vegetables. However, most campers and staff were outsiders in what were generally insular areas. From the perspective of full-time residents, some camp communities were annoying or disrespectful outsiders. Campers traveling through rural areas sometimes ate apples or berries without permission, left farm gates open as they passed through private property, or made a mess of carefully stacked hay.[79] In 1921, Laura Mattoon, in her role as secretary-treasurer of the Camp Directors Association, reminded her colleagues to treat their rural neighbors with respect. Perhaps she recalled the time a few years earlier when her camp's cow wandered over to a neighbor's property, eating his hay and treading on his garden.[80]

Jewish and black campers and their families often faced hostility from locals in the rural communities in which their camps were situated. In the late 1910s and early 1920s, members of the Ku Klux Klan from around Cold Spring, New York, burned crosses on the grounds of the YMHA's Surprise Lake Camp, and the organization's Camp Lehman experienced suspiciously regular vandalism in the off-season.[81] In the 1920s, on the way to her private Adirondack camp, camper Libby Raynes passed by numerous signs stating that Jews and dogs were not welcome. In other parts of the Northeast, Jewish parents could not find accommodations at hotels and resorts near their children's camps.[82] Black children faced similar forms of harassment, and a greater threat of violence. The black boys from the St. Louis, Missouri, YMCA who attended Camp Rivercliff, an interwar camp in the Ozark Mountains, were unnerved to see a burning cross and white-hooded men in the distance some evenings.[83]

Many minority camp communities worked to bridge the gap with local residents through their purchases in town, their fundraising on behalf of local institutions, and the invitations they extended to town residents to attend their theatrical and sports events. The management of Surprise Lake Camp was able to establish a more cordial relationship with the Cold Spring community over time, perhaps as a result of its contributions to such causes as the Cold Spring Fire Engine Fund.[84] Although Camp Rivercliff's leader also made a point of buying supplies from local merchants and farmers, he was told that he and his campers should stay on their own property at night. Only after a group of his campers helped local white residents find the body of a drowned white youth did the local community become more supportive.[85]

Overall, camp communities engaged often and significantly with outsiders and what they imagined to be "outside" culture. The degree to which camp leaders controlled this process varied. They might choose to ban movies or comic books, but they often had less control over their physical surroundings. Many leaders ran camps in busy recreational areas or shared a lake with other kinds of recreational users. In the interwar years, for instance, more than a dozen nonprofit organizations including the Bronx and Manhattan Girl Scouts, several New York City settlement houses, and the Hebrew Orphan Asylum rented low-cost campsites around Lake Cohasset, in the Palisades Interstate Park north of New York City. Campers often saw other groups of children canoeing out on the lake and fishermen who tied their boats to camp docks. In the summer of 1930, a series of rapes and physical assaults on campers and counselors around Lake Cohasset demonstrated area camps' vulnerability to outside predators. The perpetrator, when he was finally apprehended, turned out to be on the kitchen staff at a similar institutional camp on nearby Lake Stahahe. Because so many men fished on the lake with park approval, his presence on the lake had not appeared suspicious.[86] By contrast, Adirondack Woodcraft was indeed a "wilderness" camp. Yet even in the central Adirondacks, campers entertained and went sightseeing, attended local churches and movie theaters, had access to radios, and eagerly awaited the daily mail.

However culturally mediated this "wilderness," it represented for many children a revelatory and formative engagement with nature. Nathan Jaspen, an HOA camper of the 1930s who attended Camp Wakitan on Lake Cohasset, later recalled, "I loved the hiking, the swimming, the living in tents. Walking through the trees. It was just the highlight of my life."[87] For urban children like Jaspen, most of whom did not otherwise have access to quiet lakes and wooded forests, camp provided a formative experience of nature. The outdoors felt real even at the most modern, up-to-date camps. For some city children, nature was even scary. Some shuddered when they saw ants scurrying on the ground.[88] Others were extremely reluctant to venture beyond camp into the woods.[89]

To be truly out in the woods was to give up the conviviality and comfort of one's camp. This fact was not lost on some Camp Riverdale boys who were suddenly hit by a fierce rainstorm while climbing down a mountain in 1938. "The next few minutes will not soon be forgotten," one camper wrote in the camp newspaper, the *Stag and Eagle*. "With lightning striking all around us, with sparks jumping from the telephone wires, with hail and rain so heavy that at times visibility was reduced to about twenty feet, we ran through the forest clutching our cameras."[90] Such a scene was not what parents had in mind when they consulted camp brochures. Ironically, the greatest risk faced by the Riverdale boys was accidental contact with telephone wires, whose presence indicated that this landscape was not entirely "wild."

Camps gestured with ambivalence in two directions, toward a rose-tinted past and a modern, cutting-edge future. At camps, children became partisans of traditionally "campy" experiences and were inculcated into a culture of nostalgia. "I suppose," one 1910s-era member of Camp Pok-O'-Moonshine later recalled, "that every boy or master who has ever been at Pok-O is sure that the happy days he spent there really represent the camp's golden age."[91] Any camper who spent a few years at a particular camp, however, experienced the excitement of change as well as continuity. New buildings went up, kitchens were improved, and electric lights made possible new kinds of evening activities that were not thinkable by lantern. New songs became camp favorites, and old ones fell out of use. Rural neighborhoods were transformed by market forces and by other vacationers. The revision of tradition was a camp constant, as was nostalgia for camps' early days.

6

Tans, Tepees, and Minstrel Shows
Race, Primitivism, and Camp Community

We have a Camp and its name is Mystic
It's perched way up a hill;
The Indians used to find it jolly,
And we find it jolly still.

—song excerpt, Camp Mystic minstrel show
(circa 1916–1930)[1]

At Camp Mystic, the annual performance of "The Passing of the Pequots" was a highlight of the end of the season. The camp's director, Mary Jobe, wrote this "Indian Masque," as she called her historical pageant, in 1916, the year she opened her elite private Christian girls' camp near Mystic, Connecticut. Loosely based on the early-seventeenth-century demise of the Pequot tribe, the masque told of the pressures exerted by the competing Mohegan tribe and by white settlers, the 1637 treaty by which the land was ceded to the settlers, and finally, the ascendancy of Camp Mystic on the very hill where the Pequots had made their last stand.[2] For the occasion, Jobe, a white woman, dressed in an Indian costume, bound her hair in two long braids, wrapped a headband across her forehead, and placed a long, decorative feather in her hair. Her campers, according to the Camp Mystic brochure, dressed as "savage Indian warriors, beautiful Indian maidens, or stern Puritan pioneers."[3]

Jobe had already made a name for herself as an explorer, writer, and New York City teacher before founding her camp at age thirty-eight.[4] The Cree tepee that she pitched at Mystic was one reminder of the travels she had made hiking and visiting native communities in British Columbia, the Rocky Mountains, and the southwest United States.[5] The names that she bestowed on her campers' tents referred to places she

Carl and Mary Akeley
send Christmas Greetings
and the Best of Wishes for the New Year

AT HOME, MARCH TO OCTOBER 1926, NAIROBI, KENYA COLONY, AFRICA.

Holiday greeting card from Carl Akeley and Mary Jobe Akeley, mid-1920s. (From the Akeley Collection, reprinted courtesy of Mystic River Historical Society, Inc., Mystic, Connecticut)

had camped in the Western Rockies, where a mountain peak was named in her honor, and were thus another reminder of her travels.[6] Jobe achieved her greatest fame, however, through her 1924 marriage to explorer and naturalist Carl Akeley. She accompanied her new husband twice to Africa, touring the Kenya Colony and the Belgian Congo while Carl sought out specimens for the dioramas he was creating for the Hall of African Mammals at New York City's Museum of Natural History. On their second trip to Africa in 1926, Carl insisted that she should bring back at least one "natural history specimen" to her Camp Mystic girls. As she later told the story, she acquiesced to his wish, but with the restraint befitting a civilized woman, she was careful to avoid unnecessary carnage. "Two shots, the only ones I fired in Africa, secured for me a very large and beautiful old lion with an impressively dark mane."[7] The lion's pelt that she brought back to Mystic represented yet another memento of a well-traveled life.

Although Mary Jobe Akeley's experiences were unusual, her interest in collecting the "impressively dark" souvenirs of other races and regions was consistent with most of her camping peers. The foregrounding of authentic experience at camps, which industry proponents understood to be a cornerstone of the experience, often had racial overtones. Indeed, a degree of "primitive" cross-racial play, albeit temporary and contained, was at many white-only camps central to the community experience. Having effected a retreat from heterogeneous and increasingly multiracial urban centers, camp communities turned back with desire to images of darkness. Like the jokes, songs, nicknames and special colors that were central to camp life, racial "outsiders" helped to create a sense of being inside. The racial segregation that marked most camps often went hand in hand with an interest in those groups who were excluded from or marginal to the camp "family."

In the early twentieth century, racial play at camps shuttled primarily between two important loci of imagined primitivism: Native Americans and African Americans.[8] Indian play was more widespread, but in overlapping and yet distinctive ways, African Americans (and sometimes Africans) were also made to stand in for pleasurable sensuality, freedom from modern industrial labor, and an authentic and natural state of being, as contrasted to the "artificial" aspects of modernity. "Playing Indian," as Jobe and her campers did during their annual masque, was one expression of the possibilities of ritual transformation. Blackface was another; at Camp Mystic, among the annual highlights of the season was a minstrel show, a traditional entertainment genre that offered white performers the chance to black up, sing, and tell jokes against the backdrop of an imagined rural South.[9] These genres appeared to camp leaders to facilitate a regenerative foray into "primitive" life. Indian pageants and minstrel shows also represented a form of intergenerational cultural transmission, socializing white children into modern American citizenship. Racial play was designed to be transformative, but it was also a form of regimentation, its adult-organized rules serving to establish the parameters of racial difference and of "advanced" civilization.

In the early twentieth century, the meaning of race was increasingly contested by civil rights activists among racial minorities, by southern and eastern European immigrants, many of whom were Catholics and Jews (and who flocked into the nation's largest cities until, starting in the early 1920s, new restrictions made immigration into the United States more difficult), and by the many native-born white Americans who feared "racial degeneration." Against this backdrop, cross-racial play at camps catering to white children taught campers their place in a racial hierarchy while it initiated them into a specifically American

brand of racial nostalgia. "Old-time" entertainments, and their tempo-
ral displacements of darkness, implicitly located racial difference outside modern life. In so doing, they relegated so-called primitive people
to fanciful, long-gone pasts and imagined, generic locales: a pan-tribal
Native American life before or at the moment of first colonial contact,
and a homogeneous black culture in the plantation South (or, occasionally, tribal Africa). Minstrelsy and Indian play were thus doubly nostalgic cultural forms. Gesturing to imagined pasts, they elided the particular histories of colonial and racial oppression. In positioning people of
color at a historical remove, cross-racial play allowed white-only camp
communities to contain the threat that racial difference represented as a
constitutive agent in white children's subjectivity.

Yet the racial connotations of primitive play were not entirely pejora-
tive, inasmuch as they paid equivocal tribute to qualities deemed at risk
in modern children's busy lives: health, sincerity of feeling, simplicity,
play. Such play further implied that white Americans might in some essential way be deficient in emotional range and vigor. Often convoluted
and internally contradictory, the activities associated with racialized
primitivism were in the minds of many camp leaders a much-needed (if
necessarily temporary) loosening of civilized social strictures.

The culture of camping was indebted not only to representations of
Indianness and blackness but also, in many cases, to the actual labor of
adult Native Americans and African Americans. At Camp Mystic, Jobe
relied on two black women cooks, Abby and Anna, to keep the girls
well-fed.[10] In this and many other instances, and often in contradistinc-
tion to other adult staff who were addressed more formally, many black
cooks were known to the white camp communities for whom they
worked by their first names only. At numerous early-twentieth-century
camps for white children, Native Americans performed as visiting entertainers. From the interwar years onward, a number of American Indians
also served as camp counselors. Although most camps continued to represent racial difference in stereotypically demeaning ways, a small number of interwar camp leaders began to use their camps to foster interracial unity and exchange. Moving from symbolic to real interactions
across racial divides, racial minorities broached the borders of seemingly homogeneous camp communities: as imagined icons, as workers,
as ritual mediators of the American past, and occasionally as full and
equal members of the staff.

In the interwar years, a few urban-based organizations went further, offering integrated camping experiences to children. Their actions were propelled by the growing numbers of urban minorities seeking camp experiences, by concerns about the nature of American democracy, and by burgeoning civil rights activism, all of which put into question traditional representations of racial minorities and practices of segregation. However, even as mainstream organizational camps based in the northern states began to explore more inclusive policies of admission, they often did so grudgingly, suggesting the limits both of camp "family" and of national belonging.

White Children, "Native" Bodies

White children acquired ideas about race and racial difference long before they became campers. These impressions developed out of interactions with their parents and neighbors, friends, and members of their own and other races. Children also gathered information from their experiences of popular culture. In the late nineteenth and early twentieth centuries, a range of entertainments provided "colorful" comfort for white American audiences while reinforcing their sense of cultural superiority. In the late nineteenth century, these included blackface minstrel shows, world's fairs, where visitors viewed exhibitions of "primitive" tribes, and Wild West shows, where Native Americans simulated war dances, lived in "native" villages, and reenacted historical military battles. In the early twentieth century, new recording technologies that brought jazz music and Western films to American audiences perpetuated this tradition of racial exoticism and expanded its range.[11]

Although camps did not initiate white children into the iconography of darkness, these were distinctive institutions in that they encouraged children to enact in play, under adult supervision, what they had read about or had seen performed on stage or screen. Moreover, campers did not have to put on face paint to invoke racial difference. Many ordinary camp moments were imbued with racial meaning. White campers explored the world of supervised, corporeal darkness in casual ways including summer tans, Indian war-cries, and racial slurs, as well as in organized community performances.[12]

In everyday camp practice, summer tans exemplified both the healthful possibilities of "going native" and the promise of physical transformation. "The brownest body gives the toughest nerves," claimed

Winthrop T. Talbot of Camp Asquam in 1899.[13] Camp leaders regularly promised that campers under their care would become bigger, stronger, and darker. As George Matthew Adams, a visitor to Camp Dudley, declared in 1927, "Under the healthy Sun their brown bodies tell the story of their happy days."[14] Tans further attested to the power of parents and social organizations to provide outdoor recreational opportunities. Through much of the nineteenth century, tanned white skin generally signified rural manual labor. By the early twentieth century, the workplace was increasingly a factory or office, not a farm. With each passing decade, meanwhile, more and more children spent their days indoors at school. Tans expressed the privilege of temporarily escaping one's indoor responsibilities for more vigorous leisure pursuits. Camp brochures' claims to the contrary, the sun did not actually shine more brightly at camps than in urban settings, but it is fair to say that campers exposed more of their skin at camps than they did on city streets. When they returned home, their tans left the lingering imprint of their adventures on their bodies. "Brown arms and tanned faces bore witness where they had been," wrote one Missouri Camp Fire Girl after a week at camp in 1914.[15]

For children, acquiring a "coat of tan" was an important rite of passage, among the many rituals through which they became campers. At Camp Dudley, although the staff warned the boys to be careful about sun exposure when they first came to camp, some of the boys insisted that they "never get sunburnt, but tan right up"; a day later, they were heard asking, "What's good for sunburn?"[16] When given the choice, many children spent their afternoon rest hours sunbathing outdoors.[17]

At its limit, the tanned white body might appear playfully to cross racial lines. A 1933 poem entitled "The Dudley Bug" facetiously included blackness among its physical markers of a happy summer in the wilderness:

When Willie came from Camp last year, as happy as a lark
Folks took him for a negro, he was burned so very dark.
His parents were delighted, though 'twas hard to recognize
The skinny lad they'd sent away—he'd grown to such a size.
His old clothes wouldn't fit him, but his mother didn't care.
She said, "He'll look lots better when the barber cuts his hair."
They had him trimmed and tailored until Willie looked himself;
They put a collar on him, and his camp togs on the shelf.[18]

Camp Mystic girls performing morning calisthenics, circa 1920s. (From the Akeley Collection, reprinted courtesy of Mystic River Historical Society, Inc., Mystic, Connecticut)

This fanciful telling is worthy of note. Willie's creolized body—bigger, wilder, darker, almost unrecognizable to his own parents—might make him appear for a moment to be a "negro," but he would never truly pass as black. The ultimate sign of his privilege was that his whimsical hybridity could be reversed; its power to confound visual representations of whiteness, and its transgression of distinctions of high and low, light and dark, did not entail a permanent violation of racial boundaries. That the tan would fade was what made it so useful as a symbol of transgressive regeneration. Although Willie's psyche had been marked permanently by his camp experience—as the poem went on to suggest, for the rest of the year the boy would not stop talking about the camp, this passion being the Dudley "bug" of the poem's title—the exterior signs of blackness would lessen in the chill of fall and of modern urban life. The other markers of camp primitivism would be undone by mothers, barbers, and other agents of civilization.

The tanned female body, like its male counterpart, stood in direct contrast to the pallor of contemporary city life. It also represented a modern rejoinder to past idealizations of womanly paleness. Tans suggested activity, freedom of movement, and healthiness. As such, they represented the expanded opportunities available to emancipated women and girls. The New Girl, like the New Woman, was athletic and competent in the outdoors. As the fictional narrator of the Girl Scouts' 1924 annual report remarked, "Watch Betsy in camp with her Girl Scout patrol! Is this not a school for pioneers? See how muscular and wiry she is. Her skin is tanned, her cheeks glow like autumn-stained oak-leaves, her hair is pert, bobbed, and brown. It wasn't genteel in my day for a girl to be that robust."[19] Like Willie, whose brush with blackness visibly attested to the intensity of his experience, Betsy's tanned body identified her as adventurous and free.

Even as girls had increased access to "the primitive life," they had it on different terms. Boys' camping literature often depicted mothers, like that of the fictional Willie, as agents of civilization whom boys must evade for a few months in order to experience primitive life. Girls, however tanned and robust they might become, were not sent to camp to release "innate savagery." While their leaders promised what one Camp Mystic brochure called "a fund of health and buoyant spirits for the ensuing year," they vowed to put a rosy color in the girls' cheeks, not (even in humor) to return them home looking like wild and unkempt Others.[20] At Camp Mystic, Mary Jobe directed her counselors to "supervise personal appearance of the girls."[21] She wished her campers, like the fictional Betsy, to appear conventionally attractive, their glowing faces attesting to their modern, sporty appeal.

This is not to suggest that boys were free to choose bodily disarray. Camp Dudley boys left their traveling suits in a special locker for the summer, far from their tents or cabins, so that they could dress like gentlemen, albeit bigger and darker ones, for the return trip home. At all camps, the enormous responsibility inherent in caring for other people's children impelled staff to scrutinize both boys' and girls' bodies, often with intense or anxious interest. By weighing children frequently to ascertain their "improvement," insisting that underweight and overweight campers follow special diets, and requiring that each camper let his or her counselor know whether and when they moved their bowels, camps established important routines of physical constraint. The skills that children learned at camps called for increased self-mastery, and for social as well as bodily control. Swimming, for example, with its many rules to prevent drowning, provided physical freedom under continuous physical restraint. The same supervision held true for tans. Adults monitored children's skin for rashes and sunburns, allotted particular moments of the day to sunbathing, and warned children to be careful in the sun during their first few days at camp. Campers' tanned bodies reflected this culture of surveillance as well as the freedom to play outdoors.

The elaborate costumings of Indian pageantry and blackface minstrelsy were more choreographed variants on the theme of racial difference.[22] In applying special makeup to darken or blacken their skin, staff and campers took further the idea that camp was a space of physical transformation, while making more explicit the racialized possibilities of "primitive life." The "Indians" of Camp Mystic's annual masque painted their skins bronze to accentuate the transformative nature of Indian play; performers in minstrel shows generally applied greasepaint or burnt cork to darken their faces, and sometimes they added wigs.[23]

These special events, which allowed staff and campers temporarily to bypass ordinary social conventions, were part of camp's broader emphasis on bodily awareness and supervision. Campers were encouraged to express themselves in new ways, but mimicry required a knowledge of the protocols of impersonation. Campers had to learn how to dress and speak appropriately, whether as chanting Indians or eye-rolling "negroes." However liberating for their participants, such performances were, like other camp skills, confined by scripts, rules, and costumes. Spectatorship similarly required training. Audiences had to understand something of these genres in order to enjoy them. In one telling incident, most of the new Dudley campers of 1919 did not grasp the meaning of "some old stuff in a coon [blackface] dialogue" on the first Saturday-night show of the season.[24] Over the course of the season, campers would learn to distinguish between "funny" depictions of Otherness (such as blackface) and "serious" depictions (such as Indian pageants). A sign of their integration into the camp community was their ability to laugh at the appropriate moment.[25] If camps did not initiate campers into tropes of darkness, they nonetheless sharpened children's racial repertoires.

Recent histories of racial cross-dressing have highlighted its multiple and ambivalent politics. As scholars have noted, minstrelsy reassuringly articulated "real" racial identities beneath white performers' face paint. At the same time, the intensity of interest in dark bodies suggested not only antagonism to racial minorities but also cross-racial identification and longing. Participants in minstrelsy desired, however temporarily, to inhabit the body of the Other along with the attributes—excess, joy,

Camp Severance girls in blackface, 1937. (Courtesy Adirondack Museum)

authenticity, freedom from the industrial workplace—that they imagined these Others to typify.[26] The Camp Mystic masque exemplified this ambivalence. It represented native peoples as spiritual and full of feeling (among its narrative elements was what Jobe called "an Indian romance and tragedy," in which a doomed Pequot couple sang fatalistically of their love) and as the poignant historical losers in a story of progress culminating in the founding of summer camps. At the same time, it displayed them as bloodthirsty warriors avid for battle.

The antimodern anxiety that pervaded the camp industry made camps natural outposts of primitive play. At an individual level, those who became "brown" at white-only camps achieved insider status. At a community level, organized performances that more explicitly transgressed racial boundaries reinforced the group and served as tools of intergenerational social transmission. In both casual and organized ways, the positive, revitalizing effects of racial play were imaginatively imprinted onto campers' bodies as well as those of the staff. Tans faded over time, however, and makeup rubbed off. White campers' darkened bodies were meant to be temporarily dark, not fundamentally to challenge racial distinctions.

The Conventions of Racialized Entertainment

Every summer, the older children who lived at the Hebrew Orphan Asylum (HOA) in upper Manhattan got a brief taste of life outside their institution's walls. They traveled to HOA summer camps in the Palisades Interstate Park for a few weeks of vacation, Camp Wakitan for the boys and Camp Wehaha for the girls.[27] For many of these children, this sojourn was the highlight of the year, a release from the strict constraints of life in a large urban orphanage. When the boys stepped off the train, a few miles before the girls, they faced an immediate and, for the youngest boys of eight or nine, sometimes daunting challenge: the Indian Trail. This mile-and-a-half-long walk across rocky ridges was neither steep nor dangerous; moreover, adults came along to help the youngest boys carry their belongings. But as Hyman Bogen, a Wakitan camper of the 1930s, later recalled, the counselors played up the trail's exotic connotations. They told the newcomers that the half-hour hike was as dangerous as the infamous Khyber Pass on the Pakistan-Afghanistan border and that painted "savages" would ambush them before they emerged from the woods. Upon their safe arrival at Wakitan, the boys were then assigned to bunks named for Indian tribes.[28]

Native American ritual became a central element of the camp experience under the influence of Ernest Thompson Seton's Woodcraft movement. Before that time, the earliest camps made little of Indian iconography. By the 1910s, the majority of campers were "playing Indian" to some degree. Camp Dudley was typical in this respect: its annual Indian Pageant, to which visitors came by the hundreds, debuted in 1914, thirty years after the camp was founded, and its Woodcraft League was inaugurated in 1918.[29] Despite the lasting and impressive success of the Seton model, at only a few self-consciously Woodcraft camps was Indian ritual central to the daily routine. At many other camps, interest in Indian campfires and "villages" waxed and waned over the years, like other cultural elements in play.

Camp Dudley Indian Pageant, undated. (Courtesy Camp Dudley)

Indian iconography allowed camp communities to lay claim to exciting local histories. Many camps celebrated the Fourth of July, the first
festive holiday of the summer season, by reenacting the history of the
nation in pageantry, often beginning with a scene based on local Indian
legend before recounting the story of the Pilgrims, the Founding Fathers, and their own camp's success.[30] Whether or not the historical
record accorded with these claims was another matter. Mary Jobe, for
instance, had no evidence to back up her contention that Camp Mystic,
located only a short walk from Mystic Village, was built where the Pequot made their "last stand." Historical accuracy was often an after-
thought. "If history had been twisted a bit to suit the occasion," Elizabeth Knox, a Mystic camper of 1916, later recalled of the Indian
Masque, "nobody knew or cared."[31]

Throughout the summer, Indian pasts served a variety of goals.
Camp staff told Indian tales to set a reflective tone around the evening
campfire or to interest children in "nature study." Many camp owners
gave their camps and cabins Indian (or faux-Indian) names and divided
campers into "tribes." In 1937, eleven-year-old Irwin Silber of Brooklyn

assumed that his new left-wing camp's name, Wo-Chi-Ca, was adapted from an old Indian word. Although the name was in fact a contraction of a longer name, the Workers' Children's Camp, such Indian wordplay was common.[32] So too, at a significant number of boys' camps across the country, male directors took on the moniker "Chief" or "Big Chief." In all these ways, at a very wide range of camps, Indianness was an important element of "authentic" camp experience.

At boys' camps, G. Stanley Hall's vision of necessary boyhood savagery lived on long after its heyday in child-study circles. Boys were more likely than girls to play Indian, to live in Indian Villages, to belong to a camp "tribe," and to be led by a "Chief."[33] As the 1928 brochure for Camp Ticonderoga, an Adirondack boys' camp, reported, its Indian Village, complete with three "tribes" of boys, was a great success:

> This Indian Village gives the boy the much needed opportunity to express his inherent savagery. Just to be free, to run, to climb, to shout and yell like a wild Indian on a war-path! The historical background and picturesque setting not only stimulates the boy but it provides material for abundance of imagination which will help in an instructive way. The natural beauty and colorful background awakens the stagnant in all of us.[34]

This "colorful background" represented a masculine retreat from the "stagnant" conventions of everyday modern life that ordinarily hemmed in white urban boys in favor of qualities ascribed to Indian cultures: greater playfulness, physicality, and emotional expressivity.

At girls' camps, Indianness often took on a different, more domestic character. Many girls practiced artistic skills such as sewing, dyeing, and beadwork while making their own Indian dresses. But as the Mystic masque suggests, within the relatively homosocial spaces of summer camps, girls sometimes took on male warrior roles as well. The Mystic girls who played Indian fighters in the annual masque performed war dances and tied their "enemies" to trees, laying claim, for a moment, to the power of "wild savages." The most primitive primitivism, like the most rugged adventure, was gendered male, but in play girls, for a moment at least, could be men.[35]

If the project of learned femininity sometimes appeared to be at cross-purposes with primitive play, girls at camp did not have to cross racial or gender boundaries to create the space of a romantic prehistory.

Moss Lake Camp "Grecian dance," circa 1920s. (Courtesy Adirondack Museum)

On the same day that the Mystic girls presented the Indian Masque, they also participated in a "Grecian" dance performance. This Greco-Roman imagined past was what one could call a "Euro-primitive" past. Available only to female campers, it promised a sensuous, healthful antidote to the physically debilitating effects of civilization. Unlike Indian play, this nostalgic, feminine, and very popular performance genre was coded white.[36] In the style of modern dancer Isadora Duncan, girls frolicked outdoors as nymphs and fairies, dressed in loose tunics with garlands of leaves or flowers in their hair. As Sargent's guide to camp reported in 1932, "There are few girls [sic] camps that do not present photographs of barefooted girls in cheese cloth on the lawn."[37]

Campers were generally excited by the Indian content of camp life. Robert Pfaff, who attended "Indian ceremonies" at the Adirondack Woodcraft Camp from 1928 through 1935, enjoyed "especially hearing one's name called from the four points of the compass and then having to pull the blanket tight around you and with heart pounding walk out into the night."[38] By the light of the campfire, or in a canoe by moonlight, arriving at campfires dressed in their bathrobes or wrapped up in blankets, colorful stripes or even cocoa powder painted on their faces, campers often experienced wilderness adventure and Indian play as analogous.[39] For many campers, such play provided a sense of connection to their fellow campers, to American history, and to the spiritual possibilities of the outdoors.

Camps for white children never mobilized blackness to the degree that they drew on Indianness. Native American imagery resonated more centrally with camps' efforts to introduce children to a preindustrial, romantic landscape. But the frequency with which minstrel shows were produced at early-twentieth-century camps (long past the genre's heyday on the urban, professional stage) deserves greater attention, as does the general popularity of blackface in camp entertainment. The minstrel genre was, by the early twentieth century, a fading relic of an earlier era.[40] Like other "old-fashioned" cultural forms, it had not died but rather migrated from Broadway theaters to amateur stages, where it aimed to provide old-fashioned if admittedly hackneyed fun, and where youth leaders recommended the genre directly to children and to camp leaders.[41] Camps, with their promise of imaginative primitive play, were particularly receptive to amateur racialized entertainments. The recycling and enthusiastic perpetuation of minstrelsy spoke forcefully not only to white Americans' pleasure in racial crossing but also to the power of such play to secure camp community.

At Camp Mystic, "The Passing of the Pequots" was an end-of-season closer. Many other camps gave that place of honor to blackface minstrel shows. For example, the children who attended Georgia's Camp Dixie, with separate camps for Christian boys and girls, reunited at the end of the season at the Atlanta Theatre, where they performed a minstrel show in front of family and friends. The boys donned blackface; the girls sang without it.[42] As a season closer, the minstrel show reinforced the "old-timey" nature of camp, while it intensified community by humorously playing out what the group was not. Staff took the lead. At Camp Wakitan, camp director Murray "Pop" Sprung played the interlocutor, or master of ceremonies, on the last evening of each camp session. The college students who worked as Wakitan counselors played the minstrel show's end men, who sang, danced, and told jokes in blackface, brandishing tambourines. As camper Hyman Bogen later recalled, the production was always hastily thrown together, with off-key singing and less-than-clever repartee, but the Wakitan campers found it "immensely endearing."[43]

When the Playground and Recreation Association surveyed interwar camp directors about their dramatics programs, the organization found that "the minstrel show, in miniature, as produced in camps . . . never fail[s] in popularity."[44] There were practical reasons for this choice. Minstrel shows offered low-budget, predictable fun while asking relatively little in the way of talent or supplies. One interwar distributor of commercial minstrel-show sketches noted that minstrel-show scripts were "usually the first form of entertainment attempted by the Amateurs."[45] *The World's Best Book of Minstrelsy* promised in 1926 that

> blackface is the easiest make-up in the entire make-up box, and requires little or no experience to do acceptably. While any other character requires a great deal of thought, study and experimental work, the "nigger" make-up is most elemental, simple in application and anyone using the least care can achieve a satisfactory result, with little or no practice.[46]

This explanation implied that black people were so simple and thoughtless as to afford foolproof imitation. It also suggested that minstrel shows suited the limitations of amateur talent. Unlike full-length plays, minstrel shows were variety hours, collections of short skits and songs that did not require extensive memorization. At camps, the most difficult role was that of the interlocutor, who set the pace and played the "straight man." This role was generally played by a staff member. The "end men," who blacked up, bantered with the interlocutor, told jokes, and sang songs, were also often staff members or older campers who had some talent and could memorize various skits and jokes. The minstrel chorus, generally composed of children, had only to black up, sing, and laugh at the appropriate moments. The central pleasure of racial transgression—its humorously grotesque visual appeal—had already been achieved when the cast walked onto the stage in burnt cork or greasepaint.

The content of minstrel shows focused in part on black people's supposed lack of intelligence and culture. In one typical interchange from a Surprise Lake Camp minstrel show, two characters ironically named Speedy and Ambitious discuss the purpose of bridges. Ambitious triumphantly concludes, in racial dialect, "Wall, the purpuss of a bridge is to keep the fishes from gettin' sun-burnt, see, nigger?"[47] But other parts of the minstrel show bore little direct connection to race. Campers sang camp songs, and comedy routines included the "usual old jokes," as *Dudley Doings* termed them, including such wordplay as a pun about feeling great ("grate") like the bottom of a stove and feeling "Oil Right" like John D. Rockefeller.[48] The blacked-up cast helped to provide continuity to these disparate elements.

Adult camp leaders praised the minstrel show for its unifying effects. At Surprise Lake Camp in 1940, counselor I. K. Cohen later reported, the "Sioux Nation" boys' minstrel show was

> a boon, in spite of the fact that the actual production was poor, towards making the participants feel that they were partaking in a special camp activity. Such participation did necessarily leave the boy with a camping spirit which is invaluable. Many lessons of cooperation, group feeling and responsibility were thereby also learned.[49]

The quality of the performance was not of great importance, given that the event engendered that much-vaunted "camping spirit."

The ubiquity of nostalgic minstrel songs about physical displacement and longing for one's southern home may also have appealed particularly to camp communities. In song, this longing could take disparate forms; at Surprise Lake Camp, for instance, the 1922 minstrel show juxtaposed the well-known minstrel-show songs "Carry Me Back to Old Virginny" and "My Old Kentucky Home" with Yiddish songs that more closely evoked the Jewish campers' home lives.[50] In this context, minstrel shows allowed the boys safely to express homesickness and the cultural loss inherent in migration.

Minstrel shows were performed at all kinds of white-owned camps: private and organizational, Christian and Jewish, YMCA and YMHA, those for boys and those for girls, indeed at all but a few left-wing endeavors and camps for minority children. At numerous camps, these events were open to parents or the general public. In some cases, they were charitable fundraisers. For white Protestants, at a time when "provisional" whites were increasingly attaining full-fledged whiteness and when black Americans were beginning to leave the rural South for northern urban centers that promised greater opportunity, camp minstrelsy articulated the anxiety of a changing racial landscape. For camps that served ethnic communities working to achieve full recognition as "whites," these minstrel performances likely held an additional appeal: black bodies served not only as primitive icons but also as contrast figures against which camp members could foreground their own whiteness and modernity. Their minstrelsy could thus be understood as the recourse of a marginal group asserting its claims to whiteness, while acknowledging the precariousness of its racial status.

The 1910s and early 1920s, the heyday of Jewish camps' minstrel performances, corresponded to the height of national anxieties about "racial degeneration," the resurgence of the Ku Klux Klan, and the restrictions on eastern and southern European immigration that culminated in the Immigration Acts of the 1920s. At a time when Jewish Americans were among the anxious targets of American racial debates, blackface was part of the public presence of Jewish camps in gentile (and often anti-Semitic) rural areas. When camp communities like Surprise Lake Camp staged minstrel shows as charitable fundraisers, they not only proclaimed their own racial assimilation; they articulated a shared connection to the mostly Christian and white rural communities surrounding them.[51]

Camp minstrel shows also served to attenuate campers' anxiety about sharing space with blacks at home. The HOA inmates who attended Camp Wakitan lived during the school year in a multiracial neighborhood in upper Manhattan. Groups of Jewish and black boys jostled for power on the streets, and occasionally large-scale fights broke out.[52] For Hyman Bogen, the trip from the "H" down to the Lower East Side to visit his father was fraught with racial tension: "We had to go through a park. We were right on the edge of Harlem and we had trouble with black kids. We usually traveled and came back in groups."[53] The boys' anxiety about their safety may have added to the pleasure they took from their camp's annual minstrel show. Within the protected and secure space of Camp Wakitan, they could enjoy burlesque renditions of urban neighbors whom they found threatening in everyday life.

Minstrel shows and other camp performances sometimes poked fun at other ethnic groups. Ethnic jokes allowed camp communities safely to express anxiety about immigrants and an increasingly heterogeneous social order. At Camp Abnaki, the Vermont State YMCA camp, for example, one of the Abnaki counselors donned what the camp newspaper described as a "Jewish costume and nose" to perform "a Jew proprietor, Izzy Igottakoffsky," at the camp's 1918 minstrel show.[54] At the Jewish Schroon Lake Camp, camper Charles Basch, who attended from 1907 to 1911, served as chairman of the Entertainment Committee of the Sunday-night show. "We could not wait until the Sunday paper came," he later recalled, "to supply us with a Dutch, Italian or blackface dialogue so we could memorize it for the evening performance."[55] Yet ethnic put-downs never sparked full-length, large-scale camp productions on the order of Indian pageants or minstrel shows. In the minds of most white Americans, blacks and Native Americans were more intimately allied to primitive, premodern experience, and representations of these groups were thus more resonant at camps.

Both Indian play and blackface minstrelsy mobilized modern white identities while enjoyably transgressing them in play. There were, however, important differences between the two genres. The Indian body was the site of greater ambivalence, appearing both as classical (tragic, slow-moving, and contained) and grotesque (colorfully shouting and yelling). The black body, on the other hand, was almost invariably protuberant, excessive, and amusing.[56] Whereas Native American peoples were represented both as wild savages and as noble "people of nature," the minstrel figure, whether set in Africa or in the plantation South, was meant to be a humorous buffoon. Indians, in the summer camp tradition, had an authentically spiritual relation to nature. Black Americans, on the other hand, were depicted as unskilled agricultural laborers who, although close to the natural world, had little cultural authority to teach campers anything useful about it. Unlike Indian pageants, minstrel shows made little pretense of authenticity. They openly exaggerated bodily and cultural differences: huge lips, wild hair, coal-black skin, racial dialects. Whereas Indianness suggested a spiritual bond between the performer and the performed, blackface insisted on the disjunction between white performers and the objects of their attention, rejecting the possibility of respectable interracial communion. In the quest to mediate modernity and nostalgia, camp culture privileged certain kinds of darkness over others.

The Racial Politics of Nostalgia

Indian campfires and pageants were among the most public displays of camps' quest to recuperate authenticity in the modern age. Given that Native American cultures were held to have mostly "disappeared," Indianness was collectible, valued highly in proportion to its rarity. Historical accuracy was not, however, the genre's central concern. In the camp imaginary, Native American people were confined by tribal traditions, whereas modern camp communities were free to pick and choose among many options. Woodcraft practices drew from a heterogeneous mix of tribal customs, a mélange of North American native traditions: the Omaha Tribal Prayer, the totem poles of the Northwest, the Plains war bonnet and tepee, the Woodland wigwam, and dances of many regions.

The prevalence of Plains imagery at camps across the country was an important example of this selective collecting. By the early twentieth century, the imagined Indian of the Woods (the Hiawatha model) was being supplanted by the Plains warrior of Wild West shows and motion pictures. Even as organizations such as the Boy Scouts and Camp Fire Girls continued to celebrate the Woodland Indian, Plains Indians were representationally ascendant, as the last and most resilient enemies of colonization.[57] Camps across the country traded on Plains aesthetics, especially the feathered headdress and the tepee. Once the actual histories of particular regions had been erased, they became canvases for the production of a more generic Indianness.

Indianness represented less a serious attempt to recapture the past than a modern romance with an object of conquest. Bernard Mason, who would later author the widely read *Camping and Education,* suggested in 1926 that modern interpretations of Native American artifacts were far more relevant than Native American intentions: "Totem Poles may have meant many things to the savage mind [but they] are mighty strong medicine for boys and girls. Grotesquely carved and weirdly painted, these fantastic bits of the magic Northland add a touch of romance to the camp which can be obtained by no other medium."[58] Helen Ferris, editor of the Guardian Leaders' *Bulletin of the Camp Fire Girls,* similarly boasted that "the Indian legends are our American folklore. The romance of them is universally appealing." And, she pragmatically added, "More than this, most boys and girls love to dress up as Indians."[59]

As many camp leaders saw the matter, Indian play was particularly suited to children's culture because Native Americans represented a less advanced stage of civilization. The conventions of Indian play rendered Indians as simple and their vocabulary stilted and somewhat ungrammatical, like that of young children. Inevitably, when camp staff labeled one age group the "Indians," these were the youngest campers.[60] In an echo of G. Stanley Hall's recapitulation theory, as campers grew up and moved toward Senior ranks they left their Indian status behind. Historical pageants, which achieved widespread popularity in American communities of the 1910s and became staples of camp entertainment for decades to come, similarly conjoined childhood and Indians. Pageant vignettes generally began with scenes of Indian rule, but Native American peoples quickly stepped aside or were bested to make room for a succession of colonists, national heroes, and American icons. Whereas the urban pageant typically culminated in a celebration of the contemporary host town or city, the camp pageant often concluded in a salute to camp life. The final scene of "The Passing of the Pequots," for instance, depicted the Spirit of Camp Mystic awakening the fairies of Joy, Comradeship, Loyalty, and Open Air. Now the girls of Camp Mystic appeared in their own camp uniforms, rightful heirs to the land.[61]

In imagining "authentic" Native American cultures as special and yet yielding inevitably to a more "adult" modernity, early-twentieth-century camp culture resonated with the increasingly influential field of anthropology. Anthropologists such as Columbia University professor Franz Boas and his protégée Margaret Mead argued that non-Western cultures had their own intrinsic validity but posited that these primitive cultures would ultimately disappear, doomed to extinction as they were disrupted by the modern world. The Boasians worked assiduously to locate and study so-called primitive cultures, recording information about rituals, legends, songs, and other cultural artifacts that they felt would soon be lost. Still, their efforts ignored their own influence in the process of meaning-making and the possibility that traditional groups could adapt and survive nonetheless. Camp communities on quests for "real" experience similarly elided their own role in creating racial Others and the rigid contexts that they constructed for such Otherness.

A broader American fascination with "exotic" cultures made possible a wider range of camp borrowings. By 1929, at one New Hampshire camp whose leader had embraced the possibilities of international "primitivism," a group of boys lived in the "Malay village," dressed in Javanese head cloths and sandals, and built houses out of saplings. A second group, the "American Indians," slept in tepees and made arrowheads. A third became "Australian aborigines," complete with spears and body paint.[62] Even Porter Sargent's annual guide to camps, pitched primarily to parents and youth leaders, began to praise anthropological research, mentioning some of the more famous scholars by name.[63]

However, the iconography of continental American Indians held the greatest sway. For camps' purposes, no other "primitive" group could so satisfyingly meld American experience and nostalgia for a lost world.

When non–Native American racial minorities began to have camping opportunities, they too made use of Indian play to claim modern American identities, to explore a bygone American past, and to participate in a mainstay of camp culture. In the interwar years, boys affiliated with St. Philip's Church, an elite black church in Harlem, attended an Indian Village at their church's Camp Guilford Bower; black Boy Scouts affiliated with the same church staged an Indian pageant at their own camp.[64] The El Paso YWCA sent Mexican American Girl Reserves to Camp Rest-A-While in New Mexico, just south of the Mescalero Apache Indian Reservation, but for the campers Native Americans figured more as mythic historical icons than as contemporary neighbors.[65]

Blackface minstrelsy, as a nostalgic holdover from an earlier era, also suited many white camp leaders' ambition to provide children with "old-fashioned" American experiences. It was one of several kinds of performances, including Indian pageants, vaudeville, circuses, and Wild West and frontier reenactments, that had been standardized before the turn of the twentieth century. Precisely because it was old-fashioned, it seemed particularly appropriate for children's entertainment. Adults watching or performing in the "old-time minstrel show" returned in play to the entertainment of their own childhoods while training the next generation in racial tropes. As late as the Second World War, the U.S. Army's entertainment division justified amateur minstrel shows for the (implicitly white) troops on similar grounds: "Minstrelsy is the one form of entertainment which is purely our own. It delighted our great-grandfathers and has survived through the years because it offers an audience a full evening of amusement, complete with comedy, singing and various 'specialties.' "[66] In this interpretation, minstrelsy's venerable reputation across the generations proved the modern nation's claim to maturity.

The codification of minstrelsy and Indian play was critical to their persistence, but these were not embalmed forms. Each camp group tailored the basic genre to its own needs, adding camp songs and community-specific gags. Some camp minstrel shows drew inspiration from *Amos 'n' Andy*, the interwar radio show about (fictional and comical) black migrants to the North.[67] One year the sides of the pageant tepees facing away from the audience at Camp Dudley were decorated, presumably by counselors, with Greek fraternity letters.[68] These gestures trafficked between modern and primitive iconographies. Overall, however, the dramas that played out at early-twentieth-century camps tended to place both American Indians and African Americans at a sentimental, historical remove. In so doing, they elided the actual political conditions of the groups being performed and their contemporary struggles for racial equality.[69] Primitives of the past, after all, were hardly citizens of the present.

This distancing is striking in the context of increasing assertions of civil rights among early-twentieth-century African Americans and Native Americans. Black middle-class activists working with white allies founded the National Association for the Advancement of Colored People (NAACP) in 1909. The First World War inspired heightened expectations of citizenship rights among black soldiers and their families. The war also set into motion the Great Migration of hundreds of thousands of African Americans to northern cities from the rural South, seeking better employment in the war industry and freedom from the segregation and violence of the Jim Crow South. Although most black migrants moved to a few racially segregated and crowded neighborhoods and to blue-collar work, they continued to vote with their feet, emigrating to northeastern and midwestern cities until the Great Depression temporarily lessened their options. In New York City, for instance, the 1890 city census reported that one in seventy Manhattanites was a "negro"; by 1930, that ratio was one in nine.[70] Thus, in urban regions of the country where summer camps were most popular, more and more white Americans were coming into regular contact with black Americans.

In the early twentieth century, Native American communities were also resurgent, if still impoverished and mainly disenfranchised. In 1887, the federal Dawes Severalty Act had envisioned assimilating Indians into the white mainstream as small landowning farmers. In this imagined triumph of individualism, communally owned terrain was parceled off, and what was "left over" was made available for sale to non-Indians. This policy of allotment had disastrous effects; by 1934, when the U.S. government changed course, Indian landholdings had been reduced almost threefold to about fifty million acres, of which twenty million were useless for farming.[71] Yet after reaching a historic low of 250,000 in 1890, the Native American population was beginning to increase. Inspired in part by the NAACP, a new wave of Indian activism emerged; Native Americans ran the Society of American Indians from 1911 to

1923. The First World War was also a watershed for Native American soldiers and their communities, inspiring a younger generation who had been forcibly removed from their families and educated at boarding schools successfully to pursue citizenship rights. A decade later, the Indian Reorganization Act of 1934, officially known as the Wheeler-Howard Act, finally ended the government policy of allotment in favor of tribal organization on reservations.[72]

As the particularities of camps' racial play suggest, the migration and political ambitions of African Americans were more visible and threatening to white families. The early-twentieth-century minstrel show allowed communities at white-owned camps to refuse the social and political rights of those people whom they imitated. Minstrelsy was also a means to contain cultural elements of modern life that were deemed black in some way. Its nostalgia worked, for example, to tame the appeal of "black" jazz to white children by returning black people imaginatively to a rural, premodern South and by responding with grotesque humor to emerging black claims to respectability. At many other camps, children played "Hit the Nigger in the Eye" at camp carnivals and came to masquerades dressed as such commercial icons as Aunt Jemima, the imagined "mammy" enshrined by the eponymous pancake mix, or as the Gold Dust Twins of the then-popular powdered soap.[73]

Indian play, though sometimes quite derisive, did not respond directly to contemporary Native Americans' citizenship claims. Most white Americans in high-density camping regions felt entirely unthreatened by contemporary Indians. They had little knowledge of Native Americans' civil rights struggles, most of which occurred in relative rural invisibility. They understood Indians to have "stood in the way" of American empire and modernity but at present to have mostly "disappeared." The threat of racial difference thus contained, Indians could serve as noble protagonists in camp plays and even as inspirational figures who provided a vital metaphorical connection to American history.

While allowing white children (and adults) to tour an adventurous past, Indian play and minstrelsy both imaginatively returned racial Others to spaces where they enjoyed little power in their relations with white people. Participants in camp Indian pageants and minstrel shows asserted their right to transgress boundaries, while reserving the right to deny political and social rights to the objects of their fascination. Like other old-time entertainments, these genres highlighted tradition and the intergenerational transmission of ideas. At the same time, they reflected modern realities, including growing ethnic and racial diversity in urban areas.

Camps as Racial Crossroads

At Camp Mystic, as at many racially exclusionary camps, the chefs were black. As early as 1876, a black cook named Isaac Rollins served the boys at Dr. Rothrock's School of Physical Culture.[74] In 1894, a description of the campers' arrival at Camp Dudley mentioned "a big camp fire by which stand a couple of colored cooks, with white aprons and caps."[75] Some black cooks returned year after year to the same camp, becoming important members of the community. Edward Cameron Jr., a Camp Pok-O'-Moonshine camper from 1911 through 1921, later described the chef, known to the boys as James, as "always more than a chef. . . . His strength of character matched his powerful physique. Though he was a strict disciplinarian, he was admired and beloved by all."[76] Still, chefs' power was limited to their own kitchens; they generally lived in an area apart from counselors and campers, and they did

Chef Roberts and his assistant, at Camp Dudley, early 1900s. (Courtesy Camp Dudley)

not exert as intimate an authority as counselors. For black kitchen staff, the social contradictions of camp culture must at times have seemed acute. On the final evening of camp, the boys of Camp Wakitan saluted the black chef, Leroy McWright, in appreciation of food of higher quality than they were usually served at the "H." "We want the chef! We want the chef!" they yelled until McWright emerged from the kitchen, spatula in hand, to public acclaim. That same evening, the boys went on to enjoy their annual minstrel show.[77]

Although few Native American children attended early-twentieth-century camps, increasing numbers of adult Indians worked at camps, first as traveling entertainers and later as counselors. Dressed impressively in full regalia, entertainers performed traditional ceremonies, told Indian tales, and taught campers tribal rituals and Native American crafts. One Mohawk Indian who went by the name Manabozho (presumably a stage name, since it referenced Chippewa/Ojibway mythology rather than Mohawk culture) met Dan Beard, founder of the boys' group Sons of Daniel Boone, in 1925. Both men were participating in a summer camp show at Macy's department store in New York City, where parents and children enjoyed free entertainment and Macy's sold camp-related clothing and equipment. Two years later the Brooklyn-based entertainer wrote to Beard, proposing that he visit Beard's camp in Pennsylvania. He explained that renowned Sioux activist and doctor Charles Eastman "told me that you had thrown many jobs, such as entertaining in-to his hands," and then he made his own pitch: "I give a very interesting lecture on the Indian of yesterday and to-day, I next sing some true aboriginal Indian songs with my Tom-Tom, I finish with three War Dances. My costume is excellent, and one of the best in New York City." Beard did not hire him, but Manabozho found work as a riding instructor that summer at another camp.[78] Indianness, the urban-based Manabozho understood, was a marketable commodity.

Some white camp directors, Ernest Thompson Seton among them, sought to channel the premodern themselves, but by the late 1920s a significant minority of institutional camp leaders sought out Native Americans as full-time staff members. The Plume Trading and Sales Company of Brooklyn boasted in 1931 that it could procure not only "Indian Materials, Feathers and Beads" but also "genuine Indian counselors for your camp."[79] Numerous camp directors contacted Indian colleges and advocacy groups specifically to look for Indian counselors.

In 1929, a number of camp directors contacted the American Indian League (AIL), organized by white Americans in 1910 to preserve Indian arts and culture, to request help in securing Indian college students as counselors. The AIL was able to secure three men and two women from Bacone College in Oklahoma, a Christian junior college for Indians supported by the organization. According to Reverend William Brewster Humphrey, the AIL executive secretary, the experience was so successful that the school hoped to inaugurate a course for Indian counselors in the near future. The idea had the approval of such camping notables as Professor Elbert Fretwell of Teachers College and leaders of the national YMCA, the Boy Scouts, the Girl Scouts, the Camp Fire Girls, and numerous private camps.[80]

In the late 1930s, New Deal federal and state programs advanced these initiatives further. The National Youth Administration (NYA), launched in 1935 by President Franklin Delano Roosevelt, provided employment and training programs for youths aged sixteen to twenty-four across the country. In New York State, the NYA offered young adult Native Americans a one-week course on Indian stories and crafts, teaching them how to be "Indian counselors" and then sending them off to work.[81] In 1938, eighty-three youths were assigned to nonprofit organizational camps in New York State, including Surprise Lake Camp. Other young Native Americans found employment at private camps in Pennsylvania and the New England states.[82] The performance of camp Indianness did not come naturally to Native American counselors, many of whom were students at schools such as Syracuse University and Dartmouth College.[83] Despite their modern achievements, they were hired for their connection to Indian tradition.

Campers often perceived Indian counselors to be living embodiments of history. At Camp Wakitan, camper Hyman Bogen was thrilled, for example, when Seneca counselor Basil Williams found and boiled sassafras roots for the boys on an overnight hike, even though the camper found the taste unpleasant. Bogen was disappointed, however, when he found Williams reading up on Indian tales before leading evening campfires.[84] It is not surprising that some prospective counselors feared being treated with maudlin sentimentality.[85] Most campers held Native American counselors in high regard, but to an important degree they remained objects of camp curiosity, at once insiders and outsiders. According to Bogen, for instance, the Native American counselors at

Wakitan "received the most attention" and "remained the most distant and mystifying" to him.[86]

Indian counselors played varied roles at camp, some demeaning and some more empowering. They could use their authority, vested in a supposed connection to antimodern primitivism, to make money, but their power to alter racial stereotypes was limited.[87] Consider the position of Vernon Clute, a popular Seneca counselor at Surprise Lake Camp. In July 1938 at the camp's Indian Council fire, various staff members took on the roles of historical Indian chiefs. Clute played the role of the last chief of the Delawares. The performance required him to present the other chiefs with a birch-bark roll deeding the surrounding lands to the care of the white people, before leading some of his "braves" in "The Dance of the Happy Warriors." Here, Clute was expected to play the acquiescent Indian, ceding the land in a narrative of inevitable progress and colonial expansion.[88]

A few weeks later, Clute played a different role when the campers were participating in a water pageant. Organized around the theme of Columbus's discovery of America, the pageant included standard vignettes: startled Indians encountering white men, the establishment of good relations between the Spanish and the native peoples; Columbus's claim to the land on behalf of Spain; a peace-pipe ceremony and other entertainments; and finally Columbus's return to Spain, accompanied by the son of an Indian chief who was to be educated in the Old World. Like most camp historical pageants, this one emphasized the transfer of power from Indians to white colonists. The theme of romantic American conquest continued that same evening; it was Cowboy Night for some of the younger campers, and the boys sang songs like "Home on the Range" and heard the story of Jesse James. Then, as the camp paper related,

> a still silence fell over the campers: all eyes were glued to the entrance of the council ring. For there stood Vernon Clute in his ancestral robes. His face was stern and his eyes glittered as his voice rang out. He described the battles between the soldiers and the Indians. He said that a victory for the soldiers was called a battle whereas a victory for the Indians was called a massacre.[89]

For a moment, Clute was able to use his authority and the space of the council ring to encourage boys to rethink standard camp practices. But although he inspired respect, and had the right to supervise children intimately, he was never an ordinary member of the camp family.

Some children did arrive at camp with negative preconceptions of Indians. When camp director Raymond Jacoby hired a Cherokee woman (and Syracuse University undergraduate) from Oklahoma for his 1930 camp staff, her impending arrival caused a storm of debate. As he explained, some of the girls thought "an unintelligent Indian girl from the plains of Oklahoma" would add little to the camp."[90] Although the counselor became extremely popular and well-respected, she had to win over the campers. Acknowledging these problems, advocates of Indian counselor programs argued that intercultural exchange could help to alleviate white Americans' racial prejudice.[91]

The Native American who perhaps best made use of camp Indianness was Charles Eastman. Reared on the American Santee Sioux reservation and among Sioux in Canada, Eastman began his formal American education as a teenager. After graduating from Dartmouth College and Northwestern University's medical school, he became a reservation doctor, bureaucrat, original co-founder of the Society of American Indians, and the author of several bestsellers about Indian life, including *Indian Boyhood* (1902), *Indian Scout Talks: A Guide for Boy Scouts and Campfire Girls* (1914), and *From the Deep Woods to Civilization: Chapters in the Autobiography of an Indian* (1916). Socially active among both Indians and whites, Eastman was a selective acculturationist who used his Christian name interchangeably with his Indian name, Ohiyesa. For Woodcraft enthusiasts such as Ernest Thompson Seton, Eastman emblematized the modern Indian spokesman, equipped for inclusion in mainstream white culture.

In 1876, when Eastman was a young man at Beloit College, only a few years removed from the all-Indian world in which he had grown up, he was harassed by white children "playing Indian." As Eastman later wrote, "when I went into the town, I was followed on the streets by gangs of little white savages, giving imitation war whoops."[92] Eastman learned to channel that mimicry in his own interest by teaching "little white savages" a more positive variant of Indianness. His wide-ranging youth work included visits to a number of northeastern camps in the early 1910s.[93] The camp leaders who employed him exploited his Indianness to full effect, as visible proof of their own claims to offer genuine wilderness experiences. The Pine Island Camp brochure described a visit to this Maine boys' camp in glowing terms; Eastman is said to be the greatest Indian and better fitted than any living man to bring to us the glorious past of that vanishing race. No one thing at camp brought more interest and enthusiasm than Dr. Eastman's talks about the fire or in the tents. It was like living the old frontier days over to hear him tell of the battles between the whites and Indians.

The Pine Island brochure included a photograph of Eastman, symbol of "that vanishing race," outfitted in a Plains feather headdress and attire.[94]

From 1915 to 1921, Eastman and his white wife, Elaine Goodale, ran a New Hampshire summer camp, the School of the Woods. The camp, founded for privileged white girls, reflected Eastman's unique financial resources and prestige across racial lines. Like many other camps, this one was a family enterprise, within which the three eldest Eastman daughters served as camp counselors. Within a year, the popularity of what Eastman termed "The Summer Camp with a Difference" encouraged the Eastmans to expand, founding Camp Oahe for girls and Camp Ohiyesa for boys.[95] The end of the Eastman marriage later spelled the camps' demise.

Just as Native Americans traveled to camps to demonstrate traditional dances, African Americans were able to capitalize on the popularity of certain African American traditions. Camp Dudley's first evening show is said to have occurred at the turn of the twentieth century, when two campers teamed up with two black cooks to sing spirituals.[96] Many white campers, at a wide range of types of camps, learned gospel songs, which represented blackness as a respectable part of an American "folk" tradition consonant with European folk songs.[97] Here was a different variant on rural blackness: old-fashioned, yes, but also spiritual, Christian, and humble. This was the "high" mode of nostalgic imagined blackness, a counterpoint to the slickness of the modern age.

However, the degree to which gospel music challenged racial attitudes in all-white camp communities is debatable. By the late 1910s, singers from black southern schools such as Tuskegee and the Piney Woods boarding school traveled to northeastern summer camps on fundraising tours.[98] Campers could appreciate such performances and still refer to black walnuts as "nigger toe nuts," just as they could listen to a weekly chapel talk arguing against ignorant first impressions of blacks and then participate in minstrel shows.[99] And just as some Native Americans refused to join in camps' Indian play, some African Americans disputed the politics of gospel performances. During the mid-1920s, students at three black institutions of higher education, Fisk, Howard, and the Hampton Institute, protested the practice of singing spirituals for white philanthropists on fundraising occasions. The students claimed that spirituals were retrograde "darkey songs" that implied happy subservience.[100]

Far more radical were the small number of interwar camps that took up the project of integrated camping. Innovators in the field, such as Camp Wo-Chi-Ca and the Pioneer Youth Camp, were led by progressive northeastern activists, many of them union activists and some of them socialists or communists, who as a matter of policy made a point of recruiting black campers. The Camp Wo-Chi-Ca leadership, for instance, actively recruited campers and staff in Harlem, and by 1940, the membership was about 20 percent black. Members of Harlem's artistic elite taught dance and visual arts at the camp. Campers named their bunks for black leaders such as singer and actor Paul Robeson and antislavery activist Harriet Tubman, and during rest hour, counselors led discussions on topics such as racial discrimination. Blacks remained in the minority of campers and staff, but as former camper Irwin Silber later argued, "Perhaps the ideological point emphasized more than any other was that Wochica was an inter-racial camp. . . . For kids like myself, it was our first experience interacting and living with Blacks." When Robeson himself came to visit, Silber and his fellow campers "were all thrilled" to meet such a legendary actor, athlete, and activist.[101]

By the 1930s, mainstream organizations began ambivalently to open their camps to interracial groups. Youth groups such as the YMCA, the YWCA, and the Girl Scouts moved slowly. Most offered access to segregated camps before integrating campers of different races together. In El Paso, Texas, for instance, many of the native-born white women who were most active in the local YWCA were anxious about the growing and enthusiastic participation of Mexican American teenage girls in Girl Reserves programs affiliated with local settlement houses. As an official from the national office reported after a visit to El Paso, these girls "would swamp the Association if allowed and really present a problem."[102] By the late 1930s, the local YWCA created a special one-week camp session at Camp Rest-A-While, located in New Mexico, for a small number of Chicana Girl Reserves. The counselors were white but made efforts to recognize the girls' cultural heritage. One evening the girls performed Spanish dances and songs; another time, they helped to prepare enchiladas and tacos. Those who wished to attend Catholic Mass on Sunday were escorted to a nearby church.[103]

Segregated camping programs grew gradually throughout the nation, in numbers inadequate to meet minority communities' interest. In the South, a few segregated summer camps served black children. On the West Coast, the Seattle, Washington, YMCA ran segregated camps for Asian American and black boys up until the Second World War.[104] On the Plains and in the Southwest, the Girl Scouts began organizing separate summer camps for Native American girls living at government-run residential Indian schools in the late 1930s.[105] Defending their own poor record of camp integration, the Girl Scouts' national Camp Committee pointed out in 1941 that racist attitudes were not the only impediment to full integration. "There is not an influx of Negroes because of their limited income," this study, and many others like it, concluded.[106] It was true that fewer minority families could afford camp fees, and for this reason alone, many would-be campers could only attend day camps, troop camps, and weekend camps. However, most established overnight camps also had exclusionary policies designed to protect racial boundaries; day camps were less threatening to these boundaries because they were inherently less intimate than sleepaway camps, and small-scale troop and weekend camps were conducted separately.

The history of separate and integrated Girl Scout camps exemplifies the slow pace of change and the resistance such change engendered. The Girl Scouts had long been an interracial organization. However, in the North, individual troops generally were organized within the parameters of racially segregated neighborhoods, and in the South, local white-led councils regularly blocked the formation of black Girl Scout troops.[107] In 1927, the National Camp Committee recommended that "if it is not feasible to have colored girls in camp with the others, a camping period for them should be provided . . . or a separate camp should be conducted to take care of them."[108] By the late 1930s, in response to a new surge of civil rights activism, the national leadership began tentatively to explore interracial camping. On the eve of the Second World War, talk of democratic values suffused the American camping industry. The Girl Scouts' response to this progressive rhetoric was ambivalent. Nationally, the organization continued to defer to local interests in deciding whether "colored" Scouts should be admitted to camps alongside white girls. In effect, this policy served to maintain the status quo. By the early 1940s, more black Scouts attended day camps with white girls, but almost none attended integrated overnight camps anywhere in the nation.[109] Those councils that did allow a few black Girl Scouts to attend their camps did so cautiously and somewhat grudgingly, the Brooklyn, New York, council in 1937 reporting that they "planned to keep the registration as low as possible" and that the three black campers were housed separately.[110]

By the late 1930s, black parents, troop leaders, and campers began to protest exclusionary Girl Scout camping policies. In upstate New York, for example, one of the black troops of Schenectady refused to take part in the local council's cookie sale because proceeds supported the established camp, which they could not attend, and the Poughkeepsie council reported that two black parents who complained about camping policies and "who have caused most of our troubles are highly educated and quite proud. They are fighting for recognition of their race, and frown upon camps which are solely for colored children." However, white Girl Scouts and parents who objected to integrated camps were generally successful in discouraging their councils from trying similar experiments in the near future.[111]

Camp Andree, the showcase camp for teenage Girl Scouts, made token concessions to black girls and their families. The camp's leadership accepted one black girl in 1935, while sending twenty-four others as a group to a segregated YWCA camp.[112] Two years later, ninety-three underprivileged girls (of whom twenty-four were black) attended Camp Andree on scholarships at a special postseason session. The African American girls lived in their own encampment with their own wash house, and they were accompanied by what the camp's annual report condescendingly called "an unusually attractive and intelligent" Girl Scout field captain from Harlem as well as "regular" (white) counselors from the season. The African American unit was overwhelmingly described as the best and most courteous group of those that had participated that summer. Aside from their segregated living and washing quarters, the girls shared activities, "and not once was any objection made or unpleasant or unfortunate remark heard from a white or colored girl."[113] Reviewing the Andree experiment, one of the white counselors suggested that black girls should be admitted as regular campers, with a black staff person in attendance.[114]

Despite the experiment's apparent success, the Camp Andree Committee concluded by reiterating the common argument that black girls were simply not as "ready" to camp as were their white counterparts.[115]

Others within the organization came to similar conclusions. In 1938, for instance, the Special Committee on Camping argued that "Negro Girl Scouts are not yet prepared for a two-week camping experience, and . . . day, troop, and week-end camping would meet their needs more adequately."[116] Although it is true that campers from minority racial groups usually had little experience camping, many children, regardless of race, arrived at camp without prior camping experience. Some minority children may also have felt uncomfortable, at least initially, at camps run by all-white staffs or where they were among a few visible minorities. This unease may explain why one white staff member found the Mexican American girls who attended Camp Rest-A-While in 1939 "rather silent and awe-stricken" or why an Andree counselor of 1937 reported that the few black girls were more dependent on staff suggestions than the white girls.[117] Without camps to attend, these girls would not gain camping experience. Without significant numbers of peers and counselors of their own race, they were also less likely to feel fully comfortable at camp.

Integrated camps challenged the racial divisions of American life inasmuch as they reframed camp family along interracial lines. For many minority parents, however, the most important goal was to find camps where their children would feel welcomed, not camping opportunities per se or integrated camps more particularly. Many parents had reason to assume that their children would feel uncomfortable or be treated poorly in a majority-white environment. When Joshua Lieberman, director of the interracial Pioneer Youth Camp, experienced difficulty recruiting black children, he guessed that the problem stemmed from the fact that "Negro parents seemed very hesitant about sending children to a so-called 'white camp.'"[118] Segregated camps usually offered less well equipped facilities and programs, but they promised more congenial company.

In the 1930s, as Americans began to respond more strongly to the threat of fascism in Europe, the rhetoric of democratic citizenship compelled many mainstream organizations to rethink their exclusionary policies, if to a limited degree. Despite successful experiments in racial integration at northern summer camps, many national youth organizations only grudgingly supported more substantive changes, and only in the North. At Camp Andree, for instance, official Girl Scout policy held that black Girl Scouts could attend the camp only during the last two-week period and only if there were enough registrations to fill a unit of twenty-four girls, requirements that made the camp relatively inaccessible. The camp leadership, concerned about (white) "parental objection," informed prospective black campers that they would likely be the only African Americans in attendance. It is no wonder that not a single black girl attended Camp Andree at the end of the 1930s.[119]

Within white-only camp communities, racial outsiders played important symbolic roles. They served as nostalgic vehicles for camp comradeship. They allowed campers to imagine themselves temporarily transformed. They also provided camp communities a means to reinforce social norms and to express anxiety about their place in the modern world. But that world was changing. As the nation prepared to enter the Second World War, antifascist rhetoric made the idea of "democratic principles" more compelling, at least in theory. Camps traded on unchanging, seemingly "authentic" primitive pasts, but increasingly their representations of racial difference and their policies of segregation were up for debate. Camps were mythic spaces, but they were also real political playing fields. Interracial camps, though still experimental, were harbingers of changes to come.

Camp Indianness would long outlast the interwar years. But despite its persistence and codification, some non–Native American interwar observers began in the interwar years to criticize particular variants on the theme. In 1937, *Camping World* condemned Indian Council Rings that were just for show:

> The use of grease paints, the wearing of a "G" string, and the yelps of an injured crybaby do not add up to an Indian at one of his most serious ceremonies. If we are going to be Indians let us be good ones, as good as the best of their race. You know well what would happen if you took some sacred ceremonies of some of the other races or creeds and burlesqued them the way we do those of the Indians in camp today.[120]

This and other arguments acknowledged "bad" Indians as well as bad representations of Indians. Seemingly, only "the best of their race" were worthy of solemn representation. As the director of the YMHA's Camp Lehman explained in 1926, after an Indian Village was established at camp, "The Indian virtues were emphasized rather than the savage instincts."[121] Camp leaders who aimed to produce meaningful ceremonies felt that they had to prepare their campers accordingly. At Surprise Lake Camp in 1940, staff advised the boys that their "Indian Day" would not be a "farce day" but "a serious attempt to achieve the spirit and be-havior of real Indians."[122]

The 1930s saw the gradual decline but not the eradication of black-face minstrelsy at camps. Critics of the genre tended to sidestep the in-sulting nature of its representations, arguing instead that the entertain-ment whose very predictability had made it so comforting had become stale and insufficiently creative. This critique intervened less in racial politics than in a perennial camp question: how to provide alternatives to modern popular culture and yet remain pedagogically up-to-date. As Camp Andree's dramatics counselor argued in 1935, camps should avoid "minstrel show style. Develop a taste for worthwhile 'good' pro-ductions. You will find the girls grow to like, accept, and expect it."[123] Indianness could be tasteful, but minstrel shows were never "good" theater.[124] Still, some of the most influential national figures in camping continued to promote the genre. Henry Gibson, for instance, served terms as the national president of the CDA and as the organization's secretary-treasurer and spent a quarter century as director of the Mass-achusetts and Rhode Island State YMCA's Camp Becket. In 1931, af-ter he retired from Becket, he and his wife, Ina, founded nearby Camp Chimney Corners for preadolescent girls. At Chimney Corners, adult women played the blackened "end ladies" (Sisters Puffball, Goldenrod, Sassafras, and Peppermint) while the girls sang camp songs and south-ern melodies.[125]

The decline of camp minstrelsy did not occur evenly, nor did it mean the end of blackface. Sometimes the genre merely mutated into more subdued, less orchestrated forms, such as "Plantation" nights and pro-ductions of the musical *Showboat,* based on the 1926 Edna Ferber novel. During the first years of the twentieth century, when the Camp Dudley boys enjoyed minstrel shows at least once per summer, the camp leadership instructed the counselors to "bring any old stuff for cos-tumes, make-up, grease-paint and burnt cork."[126] From 1918 onward, an original musical replaced the minstrel show as the dramatic high-light of the season, but the camp continued to offer occasional minstrel shows and blackface vaudeville routines.[127] In 1940, for instance, the camp's "Big Show" was an original musical comedy entitled "Trader Corn," set in Africa, which included blackface numbers.[128] "Trader Corn" acknowledged the cultural power of a blackness that, though rel-egated to farthest Africa, was the source of much American popular cul-ture of the time. Some of the musical numbers reflected old minstrel traditions: "Shine Dem Shoes" and "Roll Dem Bones." However, in songs such as "We're Off for Jitterboog Land," the play turned toward more recent racial borrowings in entertainment, in this case the immense popularity of swing music in the late 1930s.

At a time when race relations were undergoing significant change, and when minority Americans were increasingly pressing for civil rights, camp communities explored the limits and possibilities of cross-racial identification through real and imagined relationships with Others. Just as camps promised to reconcile the contradictions of modernity by effecting a modern escape to the primitive, they offered a taste of Otherness within fairly homogeneous communities. Indianness was always the more privileged camp category. Reflecting the growing visibility of black urban communities, blackness was represented more negatively and bounded more closely in the "camp family." In both genres, white campers' power to "go native" for a day reflected their own racial privilege. In the safe spaces of these contradictions, camp communities desired, mobilized, incorporated, and rejected outsiders, sometimes all at once.

7

The Pioneer Ideal

Camp History, American History, Children's History

"P.Y.C." (to the tune of "Clementine")

In the foothills of the Catskills,
Is the camp that's dear to me,
And all the campers love it,
'Cause its [*sic*] good old P.Y.C.

Chorus:
Of the mem'ries of the good times,
That we had in P.Y.C.
They will surely live forever,
And loved they'll ever be.

—Pioneer Youth Camp song, 1930s[1]

The National Experimental Camp of the Pioneer Youth of America (PYC), founded in 1924 in Pawling, New York, by progressive education leaders and labor activists, was unusual in several respects. For one, it was coeducational and interracial. For another, most casual observers would have found it wildly disorganized. When the first group of campers arrived, their tents were not firmly pegged into the ground, there was no baseball field or tennis court, and the counselors had made no specific provision for the next day's activities. Aside from wake-up calls, bedtimes, meals, rest hour, and two optional swimming periods, the campers could pursue any activities of their choice.[2]

Much of what might appear the result of poor planning or an insufficient budget was actually part of a deliberate staff strategy: doing less in the hope that campers would take on more. The camp's first director, Joshua Lieberman, painted a rosy account of the results of this experi-

Pioneer Youth campers helping to build an Art House, 1929. (Courtesy Special Collections and University Archives, Rutgers University Libraries)

ment in *Creative Camping: A Coeducational Experiment in Personality Development and Social Living, Being the Record of Six Summers of the National Experimental Camp of Pioneer Youth of America* (1931). At the beginning of the first summer, he recalled, the campers wandered all over the camp, either pursuing their own projects or doing very little at all. As they adjusted to the program, they took on ever-greater degrees of initiative. Over the next few years, and from 1927 onward at a new site in Rifton, New York, the children helped to clear the grounds for a baseball field and tennis court, made up original plays to perform for their peers, and learned to enjoy taking responsibility for their own leisure because, as Lieberman explained, "the campers felt the camp was theirs."[3]

Although the Pioneer Youth Camp might seem a marginal experiment within an increasingly diverse interwar industry, the group's practices were at the vanguard of trends in camping and in children's education more broadly. In fact, *Creative Camping* was one of the most influential books in American camping circles of the 1930s and was required reading for counselors at many camps.[4] Lieberman, who led PYC until 1929 and went on to direct the private, coeducational Camp Robinson Crusoe in Massachusetts, received frequent invitations to speak to his peers about the Pioneer Youth experience. PYC pointed toward the postwar era, when coeducational and interracial camping became more common. But what sparked widespread enthusiasm among more mainstream camp directors was not the campers' earnest discussions of prejudice and labor activism. What made *Creative Camping* so broadly compelling was the way it appeared to reconcile longstanding industry impulses—nostalgia for the American past and the promise of professional child-management expertise—with a more companionate, "democratic" model of adult-child relations.

Lieberman penned *Creative Camping* at a time when an older model of camper regimentation was becoming increasingly controversial. The Pioneer Youth model explicitly downplayed order and obedience in favor of creative intergenerational collaboration. Other books published at about the same time, including Hedley Dimock and Charles Hendry's *Camping and Character* (1929), Bernard Mason's *Camping and Education* (1929), and Lloyd B. Sharp's *Education and the Summer Camp* (1930), similarly challenged what had become, by the 1920s, the most widespread model of camp management: careful hour-by-hour planning, an emphasis on competitive sports, and ribbons and awards doled out to the victorious and the best behaved.[5] Mainstream camps' traditions were comforting, these authors acknowledged, and the careful organization of time made it easier for staff to manage the days, but this very predictability denied children and adults what was actually most vital about the entire experience. Far better, Lieberman and others suggested, was to allow campers more autonomy even at the expense of learning new sports or specialized water skills.

Half a century after the first summer camps were founded, the camping movement continued to be the site of experimentation rather than a single-minded or cohesive culture. Some camps had lofty pedagogical aims; others had none. Some were models of Taylorist efficiency, miniature factories for the development of better bodies and better-socialized youth. Others, like the Pioneer Youth Camp, made a point of encouraging camper initiatives. Like educational practices and childrearing advice more generally, no single philosophy of camping fully held sway or was ever perfectly implemented. Because camp leaders lacked a unified philosophical core, aside from the idea that "country living" (however defined) was good for children, and because they enrolled very different kinds of clients, the industry's topography became increasingly difficult for observers of the time to map authoritatively. In 1932, David Pearlman, the educational director of the New Jersey YMHA's camps, explained that "camping education being, as it is, in the healthy experimental stage, has many faddists of fashion. Some camps are virtual barracks—military centers; others are replicas of Indian pioneer life, while a few are budding Bohemian colonies where Art with a capital A is exploited."[6]

The range of child-management philosophies governing summer camps of the early twentieth century spoke to the larger culture's lack of consensus about leisure and childrearing practices and, by extension, about childhood itself. In every generation, child-study experts, parents, and camp directors struggled among themselves to strike the right balance in their interactions with children. Some of the most popular childrearing manuals of the early twentieth century, including L. Emmett Holt's *The Care and Feeding of Children* (1894) and behavioralist John Watson's *Psychological Care of Infant and Child* (1928), advocated strict discipline even for babies. Watson, the bestselling American childcare author of the interwar years, represented young children as infinitely malleable and in need of firm, unsentimental guidance. This childrearing perspective accorded with that of many American parents of the period who expected their children to obey them unquestioningly, and it was replicated at those camps whose leaders promised to mold and reshape children through careful discipline. Yet a more companionate family ideal was gaining ground. The idea that parents should serve as friendly (if necessarily manipulative) guides rather than strict disciplinarians had become popular in some mid-nineteenth-century American middle-class families.[7] By the interwar years, as an ideological turn from self-control to self-gratification became more pronounced in adult culture, increasing numbers of parents (particularly but not exclusively those of the expanding middle classes) were inspired to adopt more permissive childrearing strategies and to allow their children greater say in family decision-making. Although even Lieberman's supporters sometimes found his ideas difficult to implement, *Creative Camping* resonated with a nation in which children's opinions and desires counted for more than ever before.

Lieberman's cohort rejected Progressive Era principles of child management in favor of what they called a "progressive education" or "child-centered" approach. These terms—"Progressive" and "progressive"—indicated different intentions. Progressive Era reformers stressed discipline and careful organization. Interwar progressives, who took their inspiration from "progressive education," owed a debt to Progressive Era ideals, but they advocated greater individual freedom of expression and self-determination for children, while rejecting what they perceived as overly rigid regimentation in camping.[8]

These differences can be overstated, in that camp leaders of every generation extolled the democratic possibilities of camp life and promised to mold better citizens without coercion. "We trust the boys, the boys trust us. They are given much liberty, and yet are under control," Henry Gibson, director of the YMCA's Camp Becket in Massachusetts, declared in 1906 of his highly organized camp.[9] Furthermore, each generation of camp leaders purposefully distanced itself from its immediate predecessors, perhaps making the differences between them appear more acute than they were.

Although all summer camps remained fundamentally hierarchical, in that adults continued to rule over children, many interwar camp leaders began explicitly to address children's right to determine more of their own camp experience. They posed this question not simply as a means of pleasing children as clients in a market economy but as a philosophical concern, one with implications for national citizenship. By the late 1930s, with the Second World War on the horizon, the question of democratic training for youth became more pressing, if still unresolved both at camps and in American culture more broadly.[10]

Young people's sensibilities were not always to adults' taste, their desires at times more conservative or experimental than their leaders would have hoped. The possibilities of intergenerational consensus were tested by certain aspects of children's experience that occurred in the realm of peer culture beyond their counselors' gaze. *Creative Camping* was one story: official, adult authored. Children's versions of camp emphasized somewhat different aspects of the experience. As camps became mainstays of children's culture, they also allowed increasing numbers of children to articulate their own place in history.

Trends in Camp Leadership

In 1889, Henry Gibson was a young man active in YMCA work when he directed his first YMCA camp near Lancaster, Pennsylvania. "Our knowledge of dietary rules, hygienic laws, nature study, and camp craft, was practically nil," he later recalled, but the two-week camp was a success nonetheless.[11] From 1903 to 1927, Gibson refined his craft as director of the Massachusetts and Rhode Island YMCA's Camp Becket in Massachusetts. In his widely read *Camping for Boys* (1911), Gibson advocated scheduling the days carefully, sometimes down to the quarter-hour, explaining that "if camping teaches a boy anything it teaches him the habit of being systematic. . . . From 'reveille' at 7 a.m. to 'taps' at 9 p.m. the day's program should be definitely planned."[12] In Camp Becket's early years, Gibson developed an elaborate system of points and honors to inspire good behavior. Boys working toward the camp's "Honor Emblem" had to demonstrate merit in such categories as "Discipline" (five points for "doing camp duty promptly, efficiently and cheerfully"), "Chivalry" (five points for the boy who could "control tongue and temper," two for the boy who could "secure the approval of the leaders"), and "Patriotism" (five points for showing "respect for the United States Flag at raising and colors").[13]

Twenty years later, Gibson had markedly amended his approach. In 1931, after his retirement from Becket, Gibson and his wife, Ina, founded nearby Camp Chimney Corners for preadolescent girls, including their own two daughters. Gibson's change of heart was reflected in the language of the first Chimney Corners promotional flyer, which promised that "all semblance of institutionalism is avoided. Directors, counselors and campers form one big family. . . . Exhaustive competition, the cause of over-strain among growing girls, is absent from the camp program."[14] There were of course important structural differences between the two camps: Becket, a large organizational camp, was inherently less intimate than a private camp planned for twenty-five girls; boys' camp leaders tended to extol competitive sports more than did leaders of girls' camps; and the girls at Chimney Corners were younger than most of the boys at Becket. But Gibson, like many camp leaders of his generation, had also come to believe that camps in general were overly regimented and that camp leaders must offer programs of greater intimacy and simplicity. He made this shift in attitude abundantly clear in his history of summer camps, published in installments in the magazine *Camping* in 1936, in which he wrote ruefully of "the danger of ultra-efficiency and super-scientific management."[15]

The highly structured model that Gibson himself had helped to promote reached its high-water mark in the 1910s and early 1920s, abetted by the practical needs of leaders whose camps were undergoing expansion. At Camp Dudley, for example, which by the beginning of the twentieth century hosted two hundred campers at a time, it was simpler to manage so many boys through structured, time-bound activities than through communal decision-making. It was less cumbersome to motivate the boys through awards, pennants, and "sinkers" (points off) for bad behavior than to rely on an amorphous notion of community spirit. And it was easier to organize activities if the daily program was carefully circumscribed.[16] While camping proponents continued to rail against "overcivilization," at many of the largest camps (most of which served boys) staff began to divide campers into increasing numbers of "tribes," moved them from activity to activity to the sound of bugles or bells, and inspired them through various prizes and awards.

Regimentation and carefully planned days were not new to Progressive Era camps. During the Civil War, the boys attending Frederick and Abigail Gunn's Gunnery Camp were, the Gunns' daughter later recalled, "eager to be soldiers, to march and especially to sleep out in tents."[17] In the decades that followed, campers often wore uniforms, slept in khaki tents, assembled to the sound of drums, and marched to their meals in military formation.[18] By the 1910s, the bugle's call had also become customary at many girls' camps at morning wake-up and at evening taps.[19] In the early years of the twentieth century, some observers criticized "overregulation" at camps. In 1905, G. Stanley Hall implored a group of camp directors, "Do not regulate too much."[20] Other camp leaders worried that campers were too focused on rewards, too apt to ask, "How many points do I get for that?"[21]

For many Progressive Era camp leaders, however, order and time-management were positive goods, providing children crucial lessons in discipline while proving their own competent, "scientific" leadership. Not only were such camps more efficient, their proponents argued, but routine was better for campers as well. These attitudes suggested a fundamental mistrust of what children might do if left to their own devices. Good American children were well-regulated, and so good camps must be orderly and fairly directive. Regimentation was also a point of pride for camp leaders committed to professionalism in a relatively unsupervised industry. As a spate of deaths, illnesses, and injuries proved, camp life could be dangerous. To safeguard children's well-being, camp staff devised more rules specifying what campers could do, where they could go, and when. Enforced teeth-brushing, afternoon rest hours, and more comprehensive safety standards at waterfronts provided Progressive Era camp leaders a sense of professionalism.

The entrance of the United States into the First World War in 1917 intensified this culture. At a time when fewer men were available to work as counselors, the ordering of daily life helped ease staffing problems, especially at boys' camps.[22] Furthermore, time-bound discipline fit well with the wartime emphasis on obedience to a higher cause. Boy "cadets" made wooden "guns" in the wood shop, dug "trenches," and marched in formation after dinner; marching taught "the lesson of obedience without question, and to think and act simultaneously," as Schroon Lake Camp's *Camp Chronicle* contended in 1918.[23] Girls took up some traditionally gendered modes of war support—knitting for soldiers, growing vegetables, raising money for European war orphans, and canning food for the war cause—but many also marched in their camp uniforms, "playing soldier," if to a lesser degree.[24] In all these ways, children practiced good citizenship at a time of heightened nationalism.

Postwar American culture was suffused by a backlash against militarism. Americans suffered relatively few war-related casualties as compared to other participant nations but were distressed by the war's shocking toll. Many camp leaders purged what now appeared to be excessive military regimentation in camping: the marching, the rows of tents, the careful time management, and the many awards. They retired the tents laid out around a central field in favor of "natural" clusters of cabins in the woods, and they substituted camp bells for buglers. In 1920, it was not unusual for a boys' camp brochure to promise that it was organized along "military lines."[25] By the end of the decade, however, the discourse of wartime self-sacrifice was long gone, and brochure claims that "there is no boresome routine, no semi-military disciplining, no wearisome schedule" were far more common.[26] Camp leaders had long expressed frustration about children who seemed overly focused on awards, but now more of them sought concrete alternatives to a points-centered system of governance. More camp leaders began to critique forms of camp management that had once seemed modern and efficient but now appeared overly militaristic and bureaucratic. In 1932, for instance, a typical *Camping* magazine editorial laid out the dangers of plotting out rational days at institutions envisioned as alternatives to the order and discipline of modernity:

Is organized camping in danger of losing its spontaneity, its freedom, its joy, its relief from too much civilization? Is undue emphasis being placed upon tests, measurements, values, interest areas, motivation, social control and the mechanics of organized camping? Are we in danger of making the organized camp so complex, so technical, so intricate, that only highly trained experts and specialists will be able to operate its machinery?[27]

In an increasingly complex world, the magazine editorialized, camps must resist the pressure to become as artificial and overorchestrated as the outside world.

Others claimed that camps already had succumbed to these pressures. As Julian Harris Salomon, author of *The Book of Indian Crafts and Indian Lore* (1928) and a recreational field coordinator for the National Park Service, argued in *Camping* in 1940,

> into our primitive Eden crept ideas, competition and regimentation. . . .
> With larger numbers the need for stricter organization and concentration of power is a necessity. So we turned to the schools for ideas on organization; and having successfully borrowed ideas on health and sanitation from the Army, we also accepted the Army's ideas on camp layout. To keep the campers' time fully occupied, competition was stimulated by systems of honors and awards.[28]

The early summer camps, as self-styled progressive camp directors told the tale, had been inventive, small-scale "primitive Edens" to which later generations were belatedly returning. These interwar leaders looked backward with enthusiasm to these earliest "pioneering" camps where necessity had dictated flexible scheduling and creativity in overcoming practical obstacles. Perhaps overstating their differences from their more immediate predecessors, they were often far more critical of the second, more regimented wave of the first two decades of the century. As Salomon and others contended, the industry had been seduced by the very trappings of civilization that it was meant to relieve.

The truth was more complicated, in that the industry represented varied and sometimes competing interests in every generation. Not all Progressive Era camps had been run along military lines, and many interwar camps remained highly scheduled, with little room for camper autonomy in choosing activities. The majority of camp leaders continued to award medals and badges for good behavior and special accomplishments. New health and safety safeguards made waterfronts more restrictive. Even at Pioneer Youth Camp, children underwent public weigh-ins.[29] Moreover, children's experiences of camp did not always reflect adult goals. Some campers felt free even at highly regimented camps. Others seized autonomy for themselves, "acting out" at the most carefully organized camps.

Still, the interwar industry was markedly different in certain respects. For one, camp directors and their clients now understood themselves to be part of a much broader and well-established movement, with an industry-specific literature, organizations such as the CDAA and the NADGC, and more colleagues and competitors. These points of connection gave interwar camp leaders more of a sense of themselves as a generation than ever before. Another difference was that the adults who planned interwar camps emphasized physical hardening to a lesser degree. Back in 1885, most of the boys who camped with Sumner Dudley understood physical discomfort to be noble and manly. A few generations later, campers expected greater comfort.

In addition, many interwar camp leaders were inspired by a changed cultural landscape within which older forces in social reform no longer exerted the power they once had. After the First World War, the Progressive Era idealism that had propelled so much of the industry's prewar expansion waned and became internally disputed. More specifically, the "muscular Christian" ideals that had inspired the founding of many early camps dramatically declined in influence as American culture grew increasing secular (particularly in the urban Northeast, where the greatest number of camps were in operation). Religion still mattered at camp, especially in social terms. Most camps remained segregated according to their Christian or Jewish clienteles, new religiously oriented camps were founded in the interwar years, and weekly religious services remained important camp events. Yet although camp leaders continued to praise the goal of "character" development, and saw recreation as critical to young Americans' proper socialization, most did so in far less explicitly religious terms than had their late-nineteenth- and early-twentieth-century predecessors, deemphasizing the link between muscles and morals.

For a new generation of youth leaders, secular goals, including children's burgeoning roles as consumers, were vital. In an expanding commercial market, these leaders claimed, young people must learn to choose among many leisure options rather than simply obeying their elders. As Jay Nash, professor of education at New York University and frequent contributor to summer camp magazines, wrote in *Spectatoritis* (1932), "The average man who has time on his hands turns out to be a spectator, a watcher of somebody else, merely because that is the easiest thing. He becomes a victim of spectatoritis."[30] If idleness remained a threat to good citizenship, so did the passive acquiescence of children to institutional leadership, mass culture, and even, for that matter, their own parents. Children schooled in the constructive pursuit of leisure, these experts promised, would grow up to become more appropriately self-directed.

Among those scholars who mandated a more "child-centered" approach to childrearing, the single most influential theorist in summer camp circles was philosopher and progressive educator John Dewey. Dewey had been a former student of G. Stanley Hall, whose theory of recapitulation represented to many turn-of-the-century camp directors the pinnacle of child-development theory. Dewey shared his teacher's nostalgia for an earlier, preindustrial era in which young Americans had purportedly been more meaningfully socialized within their communities. In widely read books such as *The School and Society* (1899) and *Democracy and Education* (1916), Dewey seconded Hall's argument that modern urban children's experiences were fundamentally different from those of their rural predecessors.[31] Like Hall, he saw children's play as deeply meaningful in developmental terms, and he argued for a system of education better fitted to the needs of the child. However, whereas Hall imagined that children involuntarily recapitulated the rise of civilizations, Dewey posited that children's development was shaped by greater individual choice. Dewey, and his progressive education peers, stressed both the importance of the external environment to children's socialization and, conversely, the ways in which children's socialization could effect broader social change.

The best education, Dewey argued, promoted the development both of individuals and of democratic communities. Schools were at the forefront of this mission. In a society in which old-fashioned agrarian training was less and less influential, Dewey argued, modern educators must better prepare children for a more complex world. Given the pace of transformation in American life, it was less important that students memorize specific information that might soon become irrelevant than that they learn to solve problems creatively and work with others harmoniously. As Dewey explained in *Democracy and Education,* "A democracy is more than a form of government; it is primarily a mode of associated living."[32] Within the miniature community of the classroom,

Dewey suggested, children could prepare for better citizenship, practicing on a small scale the social roles they would later assume as adults.

Dewey is well-known for his influence in the progressive education movement, but his ideas were perhaps even more influential in the summer camp field. He himself was not directly involved in any camp program, but after he joined the Philosophy Department at Columbia University in New York in 1906, his philosophy of education, foremost his emphasis on process and creative learning, exerted considerable influence. At Teachers College, Columbia's school of education, Dewey's foremost spokesman in the camping movement was William Heard Kilpatrick, chair of philosophy of education and one of the advisers to the Pioneer Youth Camp project. Kilpatrick wrote the introductions to *Camping and Character* and *Creative Camping*. Many camp leaders were also educators, and the growing popularity of the progressive education movement (the Progressive Education Association, founded in 1919, enjoyed its greatest success during the interwar years) gave this philosophy widespread visibility within camping circles. Dewey focused on formal schooling, but many progressive education enthusiasts saw camps as superior environments in which to put their ideas into practice. At schools, they argued, other pressures such as testing and the need to teach basic skills mitigated against creative play.[33] Because the educational stakes were lower at camps, self-described progressive camp leaders had more freedom to experiment. Drawing on Dewey, they portrayed their camps as miniature communities—"life in microcosm," as one camp director put it—within which children were socialized together.[34]

As a cohort, progressive camp leaders argued for less regimentation and more attention to children's individuality. In *Organized Camping and Progressive Education* (1935), for instance, southern YMCA leader Carlos Ward mentioned Gibson's early "Honor Emblem" requirements as an example of the "intellectualized" and ridiculous extremes to which past camp directors once had gone in their efforts rationally to chart out the camp day.[35] Gibson himself made the transition from a Progressive Era approach to one guided by precepts of progressive education. However, the apparent "freedom" of progressive camping can be misleading. Dewey was a strong proponent of scientific methodology, as were his camping disciples. Eager to prove that their work was successful, progressive camp leaders often outdid their Progressive Era predecessors in seeking measurable results that would measure campers' "adjustment to group living" more precisely than ever. In *Camping and Character,* Dimock and Hendry worked to quantify the conduct of the Camp Ahmek boys according to a complex, graphable "Behavior Observation Record." Bernard Mason's *Camping and Education* was replete with statistical charts quantifying children's testimony about their camp experiences. Sharp's *Education and the Summer Camp* included numerous flowcharts and tables calculating camper health.

In an era in which child-study experts had more prestige than ever, many interwar camp leaders were eager to align themselves with new "scientific" methodologies, sometimes without regard to their own programs' actual emphasis. In the 1930s, for instance, many private camp directors began to send parents regular reports on their children's "adjustment" to camp. Some organizational camp leaders went further, hiring specialty counselors with university training in psychology, or certified psychologists and psychiatrists, to more formally assess campers' psychological health. Many began requiring that counselors submit confidential "case files" on their campers.[36] At a few camps, staff administered Binet Intelligence Quotient (IQ) tests and Rorschach personality tests. Such "advanced" testing, camp leaders claimed, provided new insights into child betterment. As the 1931 brochure for the Colorado Kinacamps, run by New York City educators, claimed, "Kinacampers and their parents learn, often for the first time, the true development and cultural needs of the camper."[37]

Whereas muscular Christians had tried to develop their campers' souls, progressive camp leaders promised a more secular and scientific "social adjustment." Their brochures and messages to parents were peppered with "educational" and "psychological" rhetoric. As Eugene Moses noted in his introduction to the 1936 Schroon Lake Camp yearbook, "During an age of mental and social maladjustment we need to school a growing generation in the proper emotional balance as both mental and emotional instability reflect upon an individual's reactions and attitude toward society."[38] Countless brochures and industry articles quoted Charles W. Eliot, former president of Harvard University, who at a 1922 meeting of a group of girls' camp directors had reportedly claimed that "the organized summer camp is the most important step in education that America has given the world," thereby appearing to offer the industry the imprimatur of the nation's most prestigious university.[39]

Numerous interwar university scholars returned this interest, developing and sponsoring new leadership courses for camp staff. Perhaps the most influential and best-known nationwide was the course organized at Teachers College from 1920 onward.[40] At George Williams College in Chicago in the 1930s, Dimock led a series of Camp Institutes that attracted midwesterners and led to a series of influential publications. Campuses nationwide, including the University of Iowa, the University of Texas, and Mills College in California, offered similar programs on a smaller scale.[41] A number of social scientists affiliated with universities actually founded camps specifically to test new approaches to child guidance. In 1926, for instance, a number of children from Cleveland, Ohio, went on five-week vacations courtesy of the School of Applied Social Sciences at Western Reserve University. In return, the scholars gained a "laboratory" in which to observe the children's social interactions and to administer to them, in relatively controlled conditions, a range of psychological tests.[42]

At camps for low-income clients, the rising emphasis on psychological gains and "social adjustment" coincided with a diminishing emphasis on pounds gained. In 1933, the director of camping of New York's Association for the Improvement of the Condition of the Poor (AICP) informed his staff that "these camps are not to be thought of simply as places where boys and girls will gain so many pounds of flesh by reason of ample food regularly served and eaten, desirable as this may be, and which we hope will happen incidental to other things, where such gain is of health value."[43] After all, it was cheaper to feed children in the city than to remove them to the country to be fed. Nor could sending children to the countryside still be justified as an end in and of itself if the daily camp routines merely replicated the hustle and regimentation of urban life. During the interwar years, many charitable organizations expanded their camp activities and upgraded their facilities.[44] Sometimes these changes were dramatic, freed as these camps were from the constraints of the private camp marketplace. Under the guidance of Professor Sharp of Teachers College, for instance, the Life Fresh Air Camps in New Jersey and Connecticut were reorganized in 1925. As Sharp explained in *Education and the Summer Camp,* he hired a new staff, lengthened camper stays from fourteen to eighteen days, and designed a more consciously creative curriculum.[45]

Self-consciously progressive camp leaders tended to minimize competitive activities and offer campers more free time to themselves. One former camper, who had attended Maine's progressive Camp Waziya-tah, recalled in a letter to director Bertha Gruenberg in 1953 that "part of your wisdom lay in allowing us privacy + time alone, instead of hav-ing days constantly bristling with races, prizes, organized this and that, entertainments, teams, + all the rest."[46] At the same time, progressive camps enabled new forms of adult oversight. At Echo Hill Farm, a camp for girls run by the Henry Street Settlement in New York, the camp psychologist who ran Rorschach tests tried to give each girl whom she tested a basic interpretation of her personality, her strengths, and her anxieties, much to the amazement of the campers, who saw the test as a kind of magic, like "having [their] fortune told." On the last day of camp, those girls who had not been tested complained bitterly that they had missed out.[47]

Efforts to uncover children's "social adjustment," "personality," and "creativity" reflected the growing clout of professional child-study ex-perts, particularly in the fields of education, social work, and psychol-ogy, and camp leaders' eagerness to claim professional expertise in their own enterprises. Still, the new interwar social science rhetoric never completely overrode a more sentimental wilderness narrative. In the pages of interwar camp-industry books and magazines including *Camp-ing, Camp Life, Camping World,* and Sargent's *Handbook of Summer Camps,* and in their own individual brochures, camp leaders continued to reprint florid poems about the spiritual appeal of mountains, to praise the sublimity of sunsets over isolated lakes, and to quote Ernest Thomp-son Seton on the topic of Woodcraft. They also continued to vaunt the "character-building" work of camp life. Progressive camp leaders felt that they were building on the earliest summer camps, and their nostal-gia for so-called primitive Edens grounded very modern enterprises.

Pioneers in Action: "Child-Centered" Practices

Interwar summer camp directors, like Americans more generally, fre-quently asserted that national character was shaped by a distinctive out-doors tradition. In 1925, Henry Wellington Wack, associate director of *Red Book*'s camp department, breathlessly dedicated one of his books about summer camps to "A Courageous Spirit to Better the Race by a Rational Mode of Healthful Living and the Will to Practice those Rug-ged Virtues of a Simpler Life which Inspired the Founders of the Nation before the Genius of Man Carved his Cities from the Wilderness."[48] The Playground and Recreation Association of America claimed that "camping is the oldest of all ways of living. . . . In America, however, in addition to this remote heritage there is the comparatively modern heritage of a great people living for several generations in the open country."[49] Boy Scout executive Huber William Hurt noted likewise that "historically, we in America have always camped. The aborigines, the colonists, the armies, the frontiersmen and women on the Big Trails, the railroad builders, the highway makers—all camped. Washington, Lincoln, Roosevelt, Hoover—camped."[50] In these accounts, children's summer camps were the inheritors of a long tradition, one that had already socialized generations of American leaders.

Interwar summer camps were no longer experimental per se, having become part of the mainstream of American leisure. For progressive camp leaders, the pioneer continued to resonate as a kind of forward-thinking outlier, living where the ordinary rules of civilization did not fully apply. As educator Kilpatrick suggested in his introduction to *Creative Camping*, "educationally, the camp can be virgin soil."[51] These camp communities were not literal pioneers on the land, but they cast themselves as trailblazers at the cutting edge of political and social transformation.

The pioneer was well-suited to summer camps' simultaneous enactment of modernity and premodern Edens. Mediating imaginatively between the present and the past, pioneer iconography served a range of political and social goals.[52] In certain respects, for instance, pioneer nostalgia served conservative ends. Camps' historical pageantry justified the historical process by which Native American peoples lost their land to supposedly more energetic colonial newcomers; whereas pioneers had a firm foothold in the future, Indians generally figured as purely historical (and thus inherently limited) figures, quaint and racially unevolved. Many camp leaders also continued to imagine the pioneer as particularly male. When in 1939 the New York City Children's Aid Society planned "Pine Knoll," a frontier camp community that the boys themselves would help to make, they explained that if the program were successful, "perhaps even the girls will be allowed to 'rough it' in the old-fashioned way."[53]

Yet pioneer iconography also served experimental, politically progressive, and radical camp communities. The Pioneer Youth Camp, the Communists' Young Pioneers, and the Girl Scouts' "pioneer units," where girls made their own stoves and shelters, all deployed nostalgia for the American past in the service of departures from tradition. If pioneer history was used to reify a romantically colonial American past starring virile Euro-American men, the presence of increasing numbers of girls at camps was itself pioneering; at camps where girls learned to chop wood and make their own lean-tos, the pioneer ideal widened girls' gendered horizons. At camps serving ethnic Americans, camp pageants represented immigrants as pioneers, asserting their fully American status.[54] As the summer camp industry become more diverse, and its leaders' interests more varied, pioneer iconography helped to ground diverse camp constituencies' search for national identity and group loyalty.[55]

Varied pioneer possibilities emerged in *Creative Camping,* as Lieberman told the tale. Children (and adults) discovered new talents within themselves by surmounting the obstacles inherent to an old-fashioned "pioneer" setting. In building lean-tos and developing their own traditions, Pioneer Youth campers replicated in miniature the experience of American settlement. At the same time, the Pioneer Youth Camp, Lieberman claimed, was a veritable laboratory of modern childhood where staff worked to "cultivate dynamic, well-adjusted, creative personality; an inquiring social mindedness, and freedom from fear, dogma, and tradition."[56] To prove his point, Lieberman included in his book a range of quasi-sociological "case studies" of campers improved by (or, in a few cases, beyond the reach of) the camp experience. Here the pioneer symbolized the cutting edge of children's preparation for democratic citizenship.

Progressive camp leaders acknowledged that innovation and informality were difficult to maintain over time and that some degree of routinization at any established camp was therefore inevitable. For Joshua Lieberman, the first campers at the Pioneer Youth Camp were the true pioneers, those who had benefited most fully from the experience of fashioning a community; in later years, when certain routines had already become entrenched, new campers entered into the camp's established traditions, and "the opportunity to build on virgin land was not theirs."[57] Indeed, as Lieberman saw the matter, the Pioneer Youth Camp's very success (including its thriving system of camp governance and its population, which grew within a few years from thirty-five to over one hundred children) necessarily hampered campers' sense of proprietary interest in their camp. The truest Eden appeared to be the camp with the least actual history of its own, at the very moment when its own rules and system of communal living were being designed. Afterward, like the colonized frontier, the space itself ceased to exercise the same transformative power. The established camp, Lieberman seemed to imply, contained the seeds of its own creative demise.

Was it possible, then, to turn back the clock toward the originality of the earliest camps? In 1940, Salomon contended that camps of the preceding decade had in fact returned to a more creative model, characterized by greater democracy, relative informality, small-group work, and a rejection of intense competition and awards. However, progressive camping generally was piecemeal or sporadic in practice. The majority of American camp directors integrated the *Creative Camping* vision into practice only partially if at all, many of them vacillating over time between periods of greater and lesser camper self-rule.[58] Even the most enthusiastic camp directors found progressive ideals practical only insofar as their counselors were also skilled believers and their campers and parents were willing to go along with the changes. It took skill and talent to run a truly progressive camp program, and the period of adjustment that Lieberman described, during which both staff and children were often unsure how to proceed, was more than many camp leaders could bear.[59] Some camp directors found the whole idea impractical or undesirable, and others worried that parents would find fault with this approach. In 1931, when Lieberman presented his ideas to a group of northeastern YMCA camp directors attending a regional conference, one of the men present responded that if he ran a camp with the objectives and procedures of the Pioneer Youth Camp, he would be accused of running a sloppy enterprise. Lieberman acknowledged that the camp's first year was in fact sloppy. Parents, he acknowledged, had to be educated to appreciate the process of training young people to be self-reliant.[60]

Most camp directors could not afford to take the risk of alienating their constituencies. Therefore, few camp leaders radically reorganized camp life so as to make campers more accountable in planning camp programs. Instead, at increasing numbers of mainstream camps, children camped overnight at a more primitive "pioneer" site or enjoyed an occasional free afternoon to do as they pleased. Reflecting on the progressive impulse in camping a decade after the publication of *Creative Camping*, Lieberman acknowledged that the progressive ideal was difficult to implement. Some camp leaders who kept abreast of the latest educational initiatives, he explained, had tried to reshape their curricula to the latest trends—a free period each day for campers to choose an activity, new "creative" activities like jewelry making, fewer awards, and greater use of new educational terminologies—but they remained unsure how to replace competitive stimuli and adult-controlled programs. The result of this experimentation, Lieberman contended, had been confusion.[61]

Lieberman concluded that progressive camp leaders' acknowledgment of children's individuality, however imperfectly realized, had changed the industry for the better.[62] After all, progressive ideals did meaningfully reshape practices at a wide range of camps, not only those organized as "showcase" models for new ideas in camping. According to one early-twentieth-century YMCA administrator, for instance, YMCA camping changed substantially in the forty-five summers he spent at midwestern YMCA camps. Around 1910, he recalled, " 'Y' camps had made more use of the Bible, had more public prayer, magnified four-square tests [a YMCA invention], had given out many more awards to campers, had emphasized competition, had more military features, and had offered less personal choice in program planning and participation."[63] By the mid-1930s, some degree of freedom of choice and a decreased emphasis on badges and awards were standard at YMCA camps, even in what essentially remained a regimented system.

In 1924, when Lieberman founded the Pioneer Youth Camp, the camp's idealistic vision and its mostly trade-union clientele stood as a challenge to the era's social conservatism. By 1931, when *Creative Camping* was published, many Americans were becoming more open to the camp's ideals. The Great Depression was in large part responsible for this shift. Indeed, the Pioneer Youth Camp story was a perfect parable for a Depression-era readership, showing as it did what could be created with few resources but much good will. By the mid-1930s, Pioneer Youth's concern for the rights of the vulnerable and the dispossessed fit well with President Franklin D. Roosevelt's New Deal, which laid out a framework for new social programs and citizenship entitlements. Moreover, the book appeared to offer a particularly American model of political engagement. During the second half of the 1930s, as fascist regimes in Germany and Italy grew more militarily aggressive, American camp leaders highlighted the "democratic" character of their own camps as opposed to those sponsored by totalitarian governments.

By the beginning of the Second World War, the progressive model suggested by the Pioneer Youth Camp appeared deeply patriotic: a means of safeguarding the future of the American democratic system by fostering children's right to self-expression and choice of activity. Yet even as the ideal of camp "democracy" grew more compelling, most American camps remained deeply hierarchical, divided along lines of race, class, religion, gender, and age. The category of age was particularly vexed. After all, even the most progressive and "democratic" camp leaders had no intention of treating adults and children identically. What did democracy mean to communities premised on age hierarchy and adult socialization of youth?

However ambivalent its practice, the progressive camping movement attested to greater acceptance of children's peer culture and attention to children's rights in American culture at large. At the beginning of the twentieth century, Progressive Era activists had rallied around the figure of the needy child to call for the better regulation of food and drugs, education, health, and recreation. In the interwar years, a new cadre of experts claimed not only to speak for those too young to have their own political voice but also increasingly to listen and respond to children's own voices. *Creative Camping* was one popular expression of this legitimation of children's social power. Progressive camp leaders continued to exert oversight and to limit some of their campers' demands, but they also made greater allowances for a more self-directed youth culture, as that culture grew more visible and powerful over the course of the first decades of the twentieth century.

The history of Camp Andree Clark, a Girl Scout camp for adolescent girls founded in 1921 in Briarcliff Manor, New York, suggests both the idealism and the ambivalence undergirding progressive efforts. The experimental Camp Andree was founded under the sponsorship of former Montana senator and copper magnate William A. Clark and his wife, Anna. Their gift was a tribute to their daughter Andrée, who had died a few years earlier at the age of sixteen.[64] Educated mostly in France, Andrée had moved to the family's palatial Fifth Avenue mansion in New York City during the First World War. There she participated in the city's social whirl, joining a local New York City Girl Scout troop in which she remained active until shortly before her death. When her grieving parents read her diary, they found that Scouting had been among the highlights of her life: "It has changed me from a moody, thoughtless girl, and has shown me what life may be."[65] Moved by her daughter's enthusiasm, Anna Clark determined to fund a Girl Scout camp in Andrée's name. Camp Andree Clark, a showcase camp for older adolescent girls from many regions of the nation, was the result.[66]

Camp Andree girls on a hike, 1931. (Used by permission of Girl Scouts of the USA, National Historic Preservation Center, New York, N.Y.)

From the camp's inception, its leaders put into practice the kinds of innovations that would become emblematic of progressive camping, particularly rustic living and camper involvement in daily tasks. Camp Andree's emphasis on small-scale "group living" was exemplified by the deliberate absence of a central dining hall. This practice flew in the face of longstanding industry trends. Most large camps' leaders turned to paid cooks as soon as possible, in order to free campers for other pursuits. Campers, unless they were off on overnight trips, rarely did more than set tables, bus trays, or peel a few potatoes. At Camp Andree, however, each group of girls ate and lived separately from the others, making intimate community possible even at a camp serving 160 campers at once.[67] A few times per week the girls came together as a camp for shared meals, evening entertainments, and Scouts' Own Sunday services, and they sent elected representatives to the camper Court of Honor, where a variety of decisions about camp life were made.[68] Much of the girls' leisure and work occurred within their own small group and with their most proximate "neighbors." The Girl Scout leadership also regularly sought to assess their own efforts. In 1926, the Girl Scouts founded Camp Edith Macy, a leadership training "school" for adults, across the lake. At this "laboratory of the woods," participants took courses such as "Girls and Their Ways—Applied Psychology of Leadership," while conducting on-site fieldwork at Camp Andree. In this way, the camp exemplified the progressive effort to conjoin professional and practical expertise.[69]

Arriving at Camp Andree, campers of the 1920s and early 1930s were assigned to one of many "units" of eight, each with its own fireplace and cookstove, two large tents for the girls and a smaller tent for their counselor, an underground "cache" to keep food cool on hot days, a concrete dining table, and a washhouse with running water.[70] The pioneer units, founded in 1923, were even more rustic; here the girls built their own stone ovens and constructed lean-tos and other simple shelters.[71] Until the mid-1930s all Andree girls spent much of the day completing domestic chores: planning meals, "shopping" at the camp market, cooking on their stove, and cleaning up afterward. In their remaining free time, they had some degree of individual choice in selecting activities.

The organization of Camp Andree deliberately challenged what progressive leaders called the "mass" or "institutional" camp: what Camp Andree director Hazel Allen defined as "a place where everybody eats in the same dining room at the same time, where dormitories are provided for sleeping and where you have a regimented type of program which means that there is very little opportunity for choice in the program—everyone does everything at the same time."[72] As Allen defined it, the mass camp was the camping equivalent of mass culture, anonymous and mass-produced. Camp Andree showed that it was possible for a camp to be relatively large and yet remain rustic, intimate, and experimental. Yet some aspects of Andree life remained far more conventional. The girls wore khaki uniforms, worked toward Girl Scout badges and awards such as the Camp Letter (and, for the best camper, the Andree Silver Award), submitted to daily tent inspections, and gained or lost points for their patrol.[73] In 1937, to allow a broader range of camp activities, the staff decided to deemphasize campers' role in food preparation in favor of a communal dining hall.

As at Pioneer Youth Camp, the Andree staff engaged in significant reflection about their own leadership. Did Andree campers tend to fall automatically into routine patterns at the camp? Were the staff inhibiting the girls from developing leadership skills? In 1935, the camp leadership consulted with Joshua Lieberman, by then well-known as the author of *Creative Camping*, while planning their own experiment in camping.

To determine the degree to which their program freed the girls to take more initiative, the Andree leadership decided to allow one group of girls in the camp's "pioneer" wing, where campers lived in more "primitive" conditions, to design their own program. By all measures, the experiment was a happy success. The group's counselors learned to stop worrying so much about what they took to be the girls' carelessness and came to see that the campers were happier doing things their own way even if it took them eight days to put up a flagpole. The girls identified and solved many of their own community problems. To avoid creating a hierarchy of counselors "over them," they devised a system by which they took turns organizing their own activities. They also departed from the traditional Camp Andree unit system in favor of a "buddy system" in which they paired off by twos. As the report concluded, these campers enjoyed the program so much that they decided to continue with it throughout the full two weeks of their camp vacation, and they formed a more cohesive "family" than did campers in any of the other units that summer.[74]

This experiment did not propel the camp toward a radical shift in organization, for reasons that had as much to do with campers as with staff. Simply put, many campers enjoyed traditional systems of reward. Every year, the Camp Andree staff's efforts to minimize badgework ran up against the culture of the Girl Scout program more generally. During the school year, Girl Scouts worked to win merit badges proving their skill in a range of areas. Many such girls came to Andree eager to pursue specialized badgework in such categories as bird hunter, flower finder, and zoologist.[75] As one of the first groups promised Anna Clark, their benefactor, in 1921, "We all intend to return home with more merit badges than it is possible to sew on our arms."[76] The Andree staff struggled to reconcile girls' interest in badges with their own sense, as one 1927 counselor put it, that camp was not "the place for girls to work for badges that they can get in the winter."[77] Staff frequently fretted that the girls were "cramming" in order to gain as many honors as possible, thereby defeating the true value of their vacations in the search for points.[78] But the girls' interest in acquiring material rewards did not abate; as one frustrated counselor contended in 1938, many of the campers had come to Camp Andree purely for the badges.[79]

Indeed, conventional incentives were often very effective in motivating campers to strive toward adult-set goals. The quest for awards allowed children (and their parents at home) to measure progress over time. Most children were accustomed to the conventions of adult-run organizations, from schools to religious institutions to afterschool clubs, and at camp they expected similar systems of reward: honors for athletics, for bravery, for good manners, and for the "best all-around camper." Even at many self-consciously progressive camps, children eagerly took part in elaborate awards programs. At Camp Ahmek, the camp profiled in *Camping and Character,* campers could win "bars" that were mounted on personal "shields." The boys took to the project so intensely that many of them were willing to cancel canoe trips and hikes in order to work on their bar requirements.[80]

Progressive camp leaders who eliminated traditional incentives had to find other, more creative ways to elicit camper obedience and enthusiasm. How, for instance, should progressive leaders organize daily tent and cabin inspections? These inspections were at many camps a source of conflict between adults who expected clean bunks and children who were reluctant to do the work. During the first summer at the Pioneer Youth Camp, it became clear to the counselors that the children were not adequately cleaning their tents in the morning. The adults gathered the campers together to discuss possible solutions to the problem. One boy who had previously attended a more traditional camp suggested a daily system of points, with a banner to be awarded to the best tent each week. His suggestion was taken up enthusiastically by many of the other campers. This process might appear to exemplify "democratic" governance, but it was unsuccessful in practice. The plan was rescinded by popular protest after a week, when some children complained that other campers were deliberately sabotaging their own cleaning efforts in order to win the competition.[81] Only then did the campers begin to consider how to organize themselves in a new way. The results remained unpredictable. A few years later, the staff adopted a strict inspection plan for some particularly truculent campers, forcing them to stay in their tents in the morning until the tents were clean.[82] This was hardly the progressive ideal.

Experimental camp leaders also felt the weight of their own histories and of the traditions for which their campers returned. At Andree in 1928, a group of girls in the "Robin Hood" encampment arrived expecting to play out their traditional rituals, including a Knighting ceremony. Their counselor was convinced that the encampment was too rigid and insisted that the girls should let many of their old traditions die. Although the girls subsequently became interested in new ceremonies, "It was a hard blow for a few 'old Knights,'" the counselor reported.[83] Over time, the rituals and traditions out of which collective memory was forged could change, but in any given year the staff had to work to find a balance between pleasing campers and advancing what they felt to be more creative (or appropriate) activities.

Achieving this balance was a perennial problem since new camp traditions were so quickly formed. When Margaret Gibson took over the leadership of Camp Andree in midsummer 1921, the camp's very first year, she already felt hemmed in: "it was possible to go only so far in a condition that had become habit by the time I arrived."[84] The director of a private coeducational progressive camp put it more bluntly: children "abhor initiative."[85] By its nature, a truly radical camp broke with the stabilizing force of camp traditions. Not all campers desired new and unusual challenges, and those who remembered the "good old days" with pleasure were sometimes unhappy to let go of older rituals and routines. Even at consciously experimental camps, some campers (perhaps especially those who might have been happier at more traditional camps) actively resisted staff efforts to foster change, impeding their leaders' goals. In *Creative Camping*, Lieberman noted that although children came to embrace new opportunities for autonomy, they naturally gravitated to many traditions they knew; those who had attended camps in the past, he suggested, were particularly unsure how to proceed in new directions.[86]

The most successful progressive camps blended the innovative and the well-loved. Although campers were often partisans of tradition and expressed reluctance to depart from those customs, most did enjoy breaking new ground: climbing a mountain that no one from the camp had yet climbed, composing new songs, creating a camp emblem. These activities allowed children to achieve a greater degree of ownership of the camp experience. The desire for novelty was perhaps most intense among older campers such as the Camp Andree girls, many of whom had already attended camps before. "Girls are bored with coming back to camp year after year for the same experiences," one Camp Andree leader suggested.[87]

However, not all campers wished to be "pioneers." At Andree, for instance, some girls hated the pioneer wing, and others were disappointed by its difficulties. Poison ivy was endemic, and when continuous rain turned the soil into mud, the girls had a hard time even finding a campsite that met the requirements for "pioneer" work, let alone the skill to truly live like pioneers.[88] Many of the girls were partisans of activities that had grown familiar to them and of traditional modes of organization that helped them to find their place in the larger camp community. Still, those who took part in more self-directed camps often had powerfully transformative camp experiences.

Children's History of Camps

In 1938, fifteen-year-old New Jerseyite August "Augie" Meier, a five-year veteran of the Pioneer Youth Camp, served on a camper committee assigned to write a history of the camp for its fifteenth anniversary. Lieberman's tenure was by then only a distant memory: "As far as the directorship of Joshua Lieberman was concerned," Meier wrote, "almost no one had even so much as met him."[89] The committee relied on *Creative Camping* to tell this part of the story. After Lieberman, educator and anarchist Alexis Ferm had led PYC through 1932, after which point Walter Ludwig had assumed the directorship. When Meier and another camper contacted Ferm, the former director had little of substance to offer, describing his camp days as essentially unremarkable.[90]

The final document produced by the committee was factual and fairly straightforward. It was, Meier conceded, "a nice affair, consisting of sixteen glazed pages." That campers contributed to this (adult-supervised) publication made clear their active participation in camp culture. Yet privately, Meier found the official history rather tame. He began to write his own private account of his Pioneer Youth Camp experiences, which he completed the following year, and in which he observed that "it is very difficult to write interesting and yet objective history. It is against the rules to put in spicy side comments, to tell real scandal, and to give excellent color. . . . All we could do [in the official history] was to write generalizations."[91] Meier's far more colorful personal account, unpublished in his lifetime, ran to over seven hundred typewritten pages of "spicy side comments."

In many respects, Meier corroborated Lieberman's account of PYC. Meier enjoyed the relative freedom of the camp and felt a growing sense of responsibility to the group. "When I first came to the camp I wanted a good time," Meier concluded in 1939. "When I left at the end of my fifth season I respected Pioneer Youth for its ideals, and its principals [*sic*]."[92] However, Meier had little to say about the basic activities of the camp day, such as swimming, campfires, and group meals. Camp as he experienced it was governed by a playful and sometimes outrageous peer culture. What was most exciting and worthy of remembering, for Meier, was the friendly intimacy, the cliques and the couples, the teasing jokes, and the spirited debates that were too "spicy" for official publication.

Meier's own personal history focused on friendships and tensions within his peer group. He related scandalous incidents, such as the time that a Senior boy tied down another boy and cut off his pubic hair, an incident "discussed in dark whispers" among campers.[93] He wrote of boys raiding one another's bunks at night, tipping beds off the wooden tent platforms, and the ways in which he and his tentmates prepared defensively for such an attack. He described Senior boys crawling through the campus after lights-out, sneaking into girls' tents, and sometimes into their beds for petting sessions under the covers.[94] These kinds of stories, in which adults were only supporting characters, were a vital part of his peer underground.

Personally, Meier disapproved of some of these antics. He challenged the Senior girls' counselor, Lini, to explain why she let the girls stay up so late. According to Meier, she replied that in allowing the girls freedom, she would better command their respect and admiration, and they would be more inclined to follow her instructions when she asked them to. "I feel that Lini carried that too far," he wrote. "It was that whole attitude of 'Let the campers do what they want' in the Senior Division that well nigh spoiled the summer in some respects. Some control is necessary, especially when there was such a wild group of boys as there was that summer."[95]

Joshua Lieberman would likely have shared Meier's sentiment. As camp director from 1924 to 1929, his goal had not been anarchy but rather a balance between freedom and self-restraint. In *Creative Camping*, he had praised the possibilities of coeducational camping as a means of encouraging adolescents to develop healthy and sensible relations with the opposite sex. "As the children grew increasingly absorbed in activities, and the job of building up the camp," he had claimed, "their sex interest lessened and was replaced in a measure by friendly association. . . . Sex no longer played a dominant note. . . . There seemed to be no wish for petting."[96] Perhaps the PYC staff of the 1930s were far more lenient, but it is also possible either that Lieberman did not know what some of the campers were doing after hours or that he chose to soft-pedal this information for publication. After all, *Creative Camping* was meant to be celebratory, its few "problem cases" perhaps inevitable and even instructive but well outside the "norm."

Meier suggests that the staff's progressive approach was not always successful. For instance, director Walter Ludwig, having been alerted to the fact that boys were sneaking out of their tents at night to visit girls, tried ineffectually to lay down the law. "The discussion was long and arduous," Meier reported:

> the boys did not want to give up the visits. . . . Walter was calm, listened to their arguments in his unperturbed manner, and then tried to reason it out with the boys. He tried to convince them that the counsellors had some right to have fun, that they should not have to watch the boys. Of course Walter was starting on the assumption that the boys would not go on any more visits. . . . Maybe he really did not know the happenings, but then again possibly I may have drawn too wild an idea [of what had actually transpired between the boys and girls, based on the boys' possibly exaggerated boasts].

Ludwig's attempt to reason "progressively" with this sexually curious group of adolescents was ineffective. The boys vowed that they would not go on any more visits that season, but within a few days they had reneged on their promise.[97]

Meier noted this impasse wryly, but he remained loyal to progressive camping ideals nonetheless. In a verbal exchange with two other boys who were unhappy at camp because there were not enough sports or organized activities for their taste, he reminded them that "sports every day with a strongly competitive angle on the matter was not . . . good pettigogy [*sic*]."[98] And in his private writing, he frequently praised the camp for the effects it had had on his own development. "This may be the end of this book as far as the present time is concerned," he wrote in his 1939 installment, "but I sincerely hope that it will never end. I desire to be able to keep on adding to this account for many years to come, adding many rich experiences, as a camper, a graduate camper, and even a counsellor."[99]

To paraphrase Lieberman's argument in *Creative Camping,* Meier did feel that the camp was his. Undoubtedly, the boy learned some of his principles at home, as his mother, Clara, was on the board of directors of Pioneer Youth and he participated in the New York City Pioneer Youth club during the school year. In the significantly Jewish left-wing circles within which he traveled, he was used to debating communists (for whom, in the days of the Hitler-Stalin pact, he had nothing but scorn) and discussing the history of American labor radicalism. In the early 1940s, Meier would head off to the progressive and historically interracial Oberlin College in Ohio and then to a career as a scholar of African American history and a civil rights activist.[100]

Meier's tome was unusual in that few campers had the ambition to write at length about camp (or anything else). But campers had long memorialized their peer culture outside the purview of adults. At turn-of-the-century Camp Asquam, boys wrote their names (and the score of the 1899 Pasquaney-Asquam baseball game) in chalk, pencil, and pen-knife on dormitory walls and ceilings.[101] From the 1920s, some campers brought portable cameras with them to camp, and in addition to posing formally for official camp photographs, they posed far more exuberantly for one another. Others filled scrapbooks with camp memorabilia or collected ferns and flowers pressed under stones. Back at home, they recounted ephemeral stories of the moments that made camp "campy": the history of a prize watermelon, a running gag, special nicknames.

The official stories that appeared in camp newspapers and yearbooks, produced under adult control, were almost universally upbeat and positive. If unpleasant happenings were related, such as a hike through a rainstorm, then the description was humorous rather than grumpy. Many articles exhorted campers to show "pep" and to behave well and enlisted campers to write sermons on the perils of eating "green" apples or throwing stones.[102] At the Pioneer Youth Camp, the newspaper's "gossip column was very popular with the campers," August Meier noted, "and we overrode the saner elements amongst us and the staff in general in printing it."[103] This small act of rebelliousness aside, camp newspapers, as records of collective memory, were generally subject to adult mediation.

In its own way, Meier's more gossipy account of camp was also incomplete. His adolescent camp memoir focused gleefully on the various heterosexual couples that formed and dissolved each summer but revealed nothing of his own desires except that he consistently chose not to participate in the surreptitious evening "visits." The summer of

1938, when these "visits" between boys and girls began in Meier's circle of peers, was unhappy for Meier: "Somehow I did not fit in, I was lonely, without friends. None of the other boys were my type, I seemed to differ from them in almost everything."[104] He was embarrassed about being a poor swimmer, and he felt awkward about his self-imposed (but unexplained) refusal to pair off with any of the girls. This choice, duly noted by his peers, led some of them to compose a rhyme teasing him for his apparent lack of sexual libido: "Augy is a sexless guy, / Instead of girls he will take pie."[105] Later, as an adult, Meier would come out as a gay man. In a sexually charged peer culture, a boy unsure of his own sexuality or anxious about how to express it might well have preferred that adults exert a greater degree of control over his fellow campers' sexual escapades.

Every history of camp had its own biases and omissions. Five years at the same camp was a long time in the life of a fifteen-year-old boy; Meier's understanding of time, and of his place in (camp) history, was necessarily different from that of adults. Relatively few children attended individual camps for more than a few years, and only a minority witnessed major transformations of their camps over time. As compared to adults, children had fewer experiences against which to measure their camp vacations, and they experienced events that had transpired at camp a decade or more earlier as ancient history. Campers were often more conservative than their elders about change. They felt themselves to be the inheritors of tradition, and they sometimes fought for the preservation of older ways. Yet with less history of their own against which to consider camps, their nostalgia often focused on the past season, or even the events of a few weeks earlier in the season, and in many instances they were quickly diverted from their apprehensions about new plans.

Interwar progressives believed that camps should be molded by the wills of children as well as adults and that adults should help campers to begin to uncover their own desires. Under the influence of progressive education ideals, more camp leaders celebrated campers' right to some degree of self-determination, not only as practice for future citizenship but as a sign that children had rights (if limited rights) to make choices in the present.

The rising progressive style, which valued less regimentation and greater creative expression among children, was clearly ascendant in children's culture. *Creative Camping* and the Andree experiments both registered this shift in emphasis, justifying camp not through the tangible "proof" of swim competitions or weight gains but through the more nebulous outcome of children taking initiative for planning their own lives. In emphasizing individuality and self-expression, values that were manifest in American culture more broadly, these camps helped to make children's voices increasingly powerful, setting the stage for the greater permissiveness of postwar youth culture.

Conclusion

"I Had to Go On in Life": From Camp to Childhood Nostalgia

"Sing to Waziyatah!" (to the tune of "Auld Lang Syne")

Should Waziyatah be forgot
And our directors too?
We're sure before we leave this camp
We're coming back to you.
For Waziyatah 'neath the Pines
Will never be forgot
Let's sing a song to our dear camp
For we'll forget you not.

—Camp Waziyatah song, late 1940s[1]

In 1939, as another summer at Maine's Camp Waziyatah came to a close, camp director Bertha Gruenberg gave her final talk of the season. Twelve years after she had first become co-director of this private Jewish girls' camp, Gruenberg spoke to the campers gathered around her of the inherent impermanence of camp life. "Like history," she explained,

> we need the distance of time to feel and understand how much this summer is to mean to each of us thru all the days of our years. There's something mystical to me about the manner of a summer here. It can never be repeated. No will could gather us all together again in this place—it has been—it can never be again, and it will be cherished for its unique quality.[2]

At Wazi, as the camp was known to its members, each girl made a wish and then lit a small candle by the edge of the lake. Like campers across the nation, they set their candles into little paper rafts and watched carefully as the lights flickered in the evening calm and sailed off into the night. Those whose candles burned down completely before sinking, Gruenberg explained, would have their wishes granted.

The ephemeral nature of the camp experience was never clearer than at those moments when campers held one another tightly and promised to be friends forever. They could see the close-knit circle that had occupied weeks or even months of their time suddenly dissolving—never again, they were repeatedly reminded, to be reconstituted in exactly the same way. "Is it possible that the summer is really over? The days have been so short since we have all been so happy," wrote camper Ethel Rose Mandel in the Pasquaney Nature Club log of 1914.[3] For those who had invested their energy and enthusiasm into camp community, camp goodbyes were bittersweet. Many cried, as one teary New Jersey Girl Scout explained, because "we don't want to go home."[4]

In this book, I have represented camps as both signally modern and deeply nostalgic institutions. No time was more nostalgic than the last night of camp, a moment when the community gathered to recall the summer that was coming to an end. Goodbyes, like the initiations that came before them, took place through ritual events designed to secure camp community while acknowledging its endpoint. At New Hampshire's Camp Mowglis in 1907, a counselor held aloft a birch-bark megaphone over the final campfire. The megaphone had been used all summer, and as the counselor explained, "It has done its work, and it must go out with the camp." The boys reacted with a chorus of "Oh's!" and "give it to me," as the megaphone was consumed by flames in front of them.[5] At other camps, staff led rituals of continuity, saving a log from the final campfire to light the first campfire the following year. On the final evening of the season many camp organizers provided a particularly lavish final dinner in celebration of the life they had made together, a feast that returned campers, at least metaphorically, to civilization.[6]

End-of-season rites celebrated personal as well as collective transformation. Camp culture had helped to produce in children self-consciousness about the inevitable transitions they underwent as they moved from one stage of childhood to the next: acquiring new skills, growing bigger and stronger, and adopting new social roles. At many camps, children voted formally for the most spirited, the most courteous, the best athlete, or the most improved among them.[7] Those camps that had honor societies inducted new members. Staff gave out awards, badges, and cups to those campers they found most deserving. Both adults and children spoke movingly, humorously, and sometimes quite sentimentally about what they had learned or how much the camp experience had meant to them. As one New York City boy (whose letter of reference to a charitable camp had described him as "a rather tough lad who will bear watching") explained in 1926, "Every fellow here has had a square deal. Every fellow has been treated fair. I hope I've been fair to all the fellows here, too."[8]

Many campers took these ideals to heart. Those who had proved their worth to themselves and others—by making friends, winning athletic events, participating in long hikes, or learning the names of trees and flowers—had reason to feel that they had accomplished something of value. "Now, at the end of my stay I have a far stronger, healthier body than the one I took with me from New York," a Surprise Lake Camp camper noted.[9] Reflecting on how far she had come, one Wazi camper wrote to Gruenberg's co-director, Amy Faulkner, to say that "I guess you were right in the beginning of the year when you told me I would get over my homesickness. You certainly made me feel better because I loved camp and the kids. Be seeing you next summer."[10]

As children participated in these ceremonies, those who knew they were growing too old to attend camp as campers often felt wistful. By 1940, sixteen-year-old Estelle Silverman, a long-time resident of the Hebrew Orphan Asylum in upper Manhattan, had spent many happy summers at the institution's summer camp for girls, Camp Wehaha. Camp was always the highlight of Estelle's year, an interlude she looked forward to each spring with tremendous anticipation. At the end of what she knew would be her final season, she later recalled, "We had to row across [the lake] to get to our destination away from our camp. And I looked at it longingly and I knew that I had to go on in life, and yet I knew what I was leaving behind was something I could never replace and was something I'd miss and love all my life."[11] What Estelle left when she left Camp Wehaha for the last time was not just camp but childhood itself—and at sixteen, she knew it. So did the Wazi camper of 1942 who wrote to her parents to tell them about the wonderful summer she was having. Her pleasure was tinged with a kind of sadness, she explained, because "for some reason or other everything I do I sort of say goodbye to. And I have a feeling that I have completed my years in camp."[12]

Camp Waziyatah picnic, 1943. (Courtesy of Ellen McGeorge)

By the shores of quiet rural lakes, summer camps have come to serve as emotionally intense spaces of age-bound transition. Adult fantasies of an older American past provided much of the initial impetus for summer camps and were central to the socialization process. In eliciting from children a heightened awareness of change over time, camp life also taught children nostalgia for camp and for their own childhoods. Youth, the end of the season suggested, was itself transitory and impermanent. This triple nostalgia—for the American past, for camp community, and for individual childhood experience—is critical to understanding why camps have figured so influentially in American culture and in many former campers' lives.

Given the diverse range of life experiences and attitudes with which children came to camp, the camps they attended, and the home lives to which they were returning, it is difficult to generalize about how camps mattered to former campers. For the boys of Camp Wakitan, for instance, the end of the camp season appeared to constitute an end to pleasure. Like the Wehaha girls, they lived during the school year at Manhattan's Hebrew Orphan Asylum, a large institution where the food was less tasty than at camp and the staff far stricter. On the day of their return to New York City, some of the boys ran into the woods in an unsuccessful attempt to avoid being sent back to the "H."[13] Children who suffered at home, whether materially or emotionally, sometimes found in camp a world of possibilities that they were loath to leave behind. One working-class girl, the daughter of an abusive and alcoholic father, wrote plaintively in the log of a charitable camp that her stay had been the first pleasant experience of her entire life.[14] Others were relieved to be home. One young boy returning from a settlement camp proceeded to wail loudly as he ran along the street toward his New York City apartment. "I guess he's glad to be home," suggested his older sister as she watched him run. "I guess that's just the way he shows it."[15]

As one might expect, children who "grew up" at camp, and especially those who attended a single camp over the course of several years, often experienced camp and childhood as inextricably intertwined. "Camp for me was the defining experience," one former camper recalled from the distance of a half century. "It was the single most important thing that happened to me in the first 18 years of my life."[16] For many others, camp was the "going away" experience against which other rites of passage such as college, military service, and marriage would later be measured. A number of newlyweds went so far as to include their old camp on their honeymoon itineraries, in order to show their new spouse the place that had been so formative in their earlier development. "Our stopping in at Waziyatah was certainly a highlight in our honeymoon," one young bride of 1953 wrote to Gruenberg. "The meal and being with all my old friends again was very exciting to me and Ted enjoyed it as much as I."[17]

Camp life could be equally or even more important for those who enjoyed brief (but revelatory) camp vacations. "I can really remember EVERYTHING about those experiences," Lydia Stoopenkoff recalled of a few two-week trips to charitable camps that she made in the 1930s. "I was so thrilled to be in camp."[18] Conversely, Camp Waziyatah was no less special to the girls who attended it simply because they had such abundant year-round leisure opportunities.[19] As one former Wazi camper, who missed the 1935 season because she was on a family vacation to California, attested in a letter to Gruenberg, "You just can't imagine how I miss camp. . . . I try to avoid thinking about it but summer without camp isn't summer."[20]

Although campers came from diverse backgrounds and attended different types of camps, those who were happy at camp often looked back on their experiences in remarkably similar terms. Attending a camp, they reported, had provided them greater self-reliance, memorable adventures, important friendships, and a love and appreciation of the outdoors. One former Waziyatah camper, now a married mother living in the Midwest, recalled in a 1953 letter to Gruenberg that she cherished memories of "the rocks on the dip beach late at night, or walking up temple hill on one of those bright days that come at the end of August when the sky seems so huge."[21] Across variations in camping, generations, and ideological differences, most former campers recalled similar moments.

Camp continued to resonate in children's lives during the school year as they recalled happy moments, explained camp rituals to their family and friends, attended the occasional reunion, and prepared for the summer to come. Especially in the first days or weeks following their return home, former campers kept their experiences fresh by telling camp stories. "We kept hearing about camp for the first week, and there are still things to tell which Dotty regales us with, so we know Waziyatah was all we had hoped for in every way," wrote one parent.[22] Wrote a second, "Margery is still singing praise for a divine summer, and she's already begun anticipating another. You're liable to have a suit for 'alienation of affections' on your hands."[23] As happy campers recounted details of songs, special events, and counselors, they brought camp culture out of the woods and disseminated it throughout a wider children's culture. For this reason, many younger siblings and friends knew all about camp before they ever attended one. Those who had been unhappy at camp were often less talkative, but their summer experiences lingered as well. One adolescent Wazi camper who did not get along with the other girls in her bunk returned to her midwestern home so lacking in self-confidence that her anxious mother finally wrote to Gruenberg asking "what the matter was with [her]. . . . For since she is home this Fall she is even unwilling to call her friends to make dates with them."[24] Many hundreds of miles away from her camp antagonists, Waziyatah continued to matter.

After a few weeks at home, as former campers settled back into old routines, the intensity of the camp experience began somewhat to fade. Those who remained most connected during the school year tended to have found their camps through local networks of friends, neighbors, and youth organizations. Boy Scouts and Camp Fire Girls, for example, returned to year-round youth groups. Private camp alumni who lived in close proximity to one another also continued to socialize together without institutional oversight. Summers at Camp Allegro in Massachusetts provided Ellie Busman a network of year-round friendships ("friendships which exist to this day," she marveled fifty years later) with other middle-class Jewish girls from the greater New York City area.[25] Adult staff were better able to maintain friendships and romantic relationships, some of which led to marriage and several generations of loyal camp attendance. However much campers looked forward to winter camp reunions or to the following summer season, most were poor letter-writers and few spoke to long-distance camp friends by telephone, in those days a fairly expensive service. "I had [camp] friends," one former New York City camper recalled, but "we couldn't get together easily so I did not maintain friendships."[26]

Camp experiences were physically and temporally demarcated from ordinary life—few former campers practiced specialized canoeing skills during the school year—but they provided children a shared language with which to reflect on past achievements, to imagine new adventures, and to conjure up a larger world than the one in which they ordinarily lived. Campers were empowered by new athletic skills, important friendships forged at camp, adventures in the woods, quiet moments spent sunbathing at the lake, and opportunities to lead other campers. Coming back home again, they could not help but see their home lives a bit differently afterward, often with a greater sense of independence.

This period of familial separation also allowed parents to reassess their children with new eyes. Many were thrilled to find their children apparently transformed both physically and emotionally. "Our boy left home weighing 86 pounds," the parents of one Camp Pok-O'-Moonshine camper noted, "and when at the end of nine weeks he returned bright eyed, rosy cheeked, weighing 102 pounds, we hardly recognized him. But it was not only in flesh that he had gained, but in courtesy and general helpfulness."[27] The mother of a Camp Mystic girl wrote in similar terms: "It was not only the thrill of Elizabeth's accomplishments and the two imposing cups,—though I was so surprised and delighted all over that I nearly wept,—but we are particularly delighted with her splendid health and spirits."[28] Character development was harder to measure than weight, but parents often found what they took to be concrete evidence of social improvement. "When I saw my boy standing in that ring, taking it on the chin and giving back plenty, it was the happiest moment in my life," a man who watched his son box at Colorado's

Kinacamps exclaimed.[29] Sometimes, however, what parents noticed perturbed them. "It is a healthy thing, if not too encouraging," one Waziyatah mother wrote after visiting her daughter in camp,

> to see your child after a vacation from her and to see her in a different set-up from the accustomed one. She said a few things, particularly in connection with her worldly possessions that she seems to think are enough to knock out the eyes of her fellow bunk mates, that made me a bit ill in the middle. She gave evidence of having a peculiar set of values, or, what is equally significant, a lack of self confidence, and was out to impress the world.[30]

To what degree did these insights transform parenting practices? In 1934, to promote the camp industry, *Parents'* magazine devised an essay contest in which parents were asked to explain how their families had benefited from the camp experience. Winner Olive Burt confessed that she used to think that her daughter Eda was a difficult child. Watching her daughter at camp, Burt explained, taught her that her child was in fact well-loved and easy. Based on what she had seen at camp, Olive Burt decided to adjust her childrearing strategies. Now she called her daughter to dinner by ringing a gong, gave her a bed of her own instead of a shared double, and organized her daughter's day with more consistent routines.[31] Burt's story was atypical. Most parents did not expect to implement the camp model at home. They sent their children to camp to learn skills, like archery and canoeing, that had cultural cachet but that were impractical to pursue during the school year. They hoped their children would benefit from country air, expert guidance, and the experience of group life. But if their sons and daughters had learned to make their beds or tidy their desk drawers without complaint, gained weight, and made friends, most parents were satisfied.[32]

For former campers, camp provided a template for intimate community outside the immediate family, variations of which they would continue to encounter in adulthood. Some of them worked as camp counselors. Others joined college fraternities and sororities or immersed themselves in adult work communities or group residences where they reencountered some of the playful and sometimes transgressive conventions of camp life: gendered and racial cross-dressing, special songs, nicknames, and baby parties among friends.[33] More generally, camp experiences prepared young adults for living harmoniously with others. As one former camp girl of the 1910s reflected in her college years, "I have known college girls who wasted much of their freshmen [*sic*] year in learning the simple principles of community life—toleration, coöperation, and normal friendliness—which the camp girl has already been taught."[34] Many of the interwar campers who later served in the U.S. military during the Second World War had similar thoughts. One former member of Surprise Lake Camp noted patriotically in 1943 that "The life at S.L.C. has stood me in good stead. At present I am living in a barrack just as we lived in tents at S.L.C. Now as then, the ability to submerge your individual ambitions for the good of the service or camp is imperative."[35]

By the late 1930s, millions of mothers and an even greater number of fathers were camp alumni. That this summer world did not overtly permeate their everyday home lives did not make it any less revelatory or formative. Many adults held on to memories of their long-past camp adventures. And as the experience of attending a camp became an increasingly mainstream part of children's culture, many parents who once had been campers and who looked back with nostalgia on their vacation memories began to share this tradition with their own children. The eagerness with which they sent the next generation off to camps, as they themselves had been sent to camp, is perhaps the most eloquent testimony to the importance they accorded the camp experience in their own lives.

My study ends in the early 1940s, by which point the camp industry was well-established and highly regarded. Although the majority of early-twentieth-century children did not attend summer camps, the camp ideal saturated American culture. Educators and child-study experts feted camps, newspapers and magazines lauded them, urban (and in widening numbers, suburban) parents chose among a widening array of camp options, and children willingly (for the most part) attended them.

Frank Capra's celebrated 1939 film *Mr. Smith Goes to Washington* exemplifies this camping moment in American culture. *Mr. Smith* tells the story of Jefferson Smith, leader of a (fictional) youth group, the Boy Rangers. Through a series of political machinations about which he remains ignorant, Smith becomes a senator for his (unnamed) western state. Smith, a blend of the everyman and of Jeffersonian progress through agrarianism, turns out to be the camping industry's perfect spokesman. A man of high integrity, he arrives in the nation's capital full of naive enthusiasm and a single ambition: to start a national camp for boys in his home state. As it turns out, however, the site that Smith has staked out for his camp is the precise spot on which his corrupt fellow senator plans to locate a dam, the latest in a series of fraudulent, money-making schemes. The summer camp and political graft, the film appears to suggest, literally cannot coexist, for one is as pure a use of land as the other is impure. When Smith finally wins his battle against corruption, his victory is represented as a triumph for the nation as much as for his own Boy Rangers.

Mr. Smith, produced at the beginning of the Second World War, constituted a paean to patriotic American values at a time when the nation's ideals were perceived to be under imminent assault by fascism and totalitarian regimes. During the war years, as "democracy" took on greater urgency in the larger culture, summer camps appeared iconic of the possibilities of democratic American citizenship. In *Mr. Smith,* for instance, the boys' camp is represented as a uniquely American means of incorporating future (if, in this instance, only male) citizens into a symbolic national community, through which the intergenerational consolidation of democratic values can be achieved.

From 1941 through 1945, American adults integrated campers into patriotic activities reminiscent of those undertaken during the First World War.[36] At the beginning of the 1942 season, for instance, the Camp Waziyatah directors urged the campers to grow vegetables in the camp's Victory Garden, to help local farmers pick their crops, to volunteer with the local Red Cross, and to bale hay.[37] Campers across the country made money for the war effort by working on farms and by staging paid entertainments for visitors. Camp leaders argued that campers were becoming better citizens as they grew healthier and more skilled. For parents, wartime summer camps also appealed on practical grounds. These institutions represented one answer to the pressing problem of child care and to the fear that unattended "latchkey children" would become delinquents in the absence of adequate adult supervision.[38] Indeed, more parents were busy or away from home, as fathers left to serve in the military and more mothers entered the paid workforce. Furthermore, although family incomes rose sharply, gas rationing and housing shortages discouraged many parents from attempting family vacations.

Those children who attended wartime camps were only partially insulated from the war effort. They handed over their ration cards to camp staff upon arrival, heard the latest news from Europe and Asia while sitting around campfires, and worried about their parents and siblings overseas. Wartime camp communities were also generally more unstable from year to year, and even from month to month, as camp directors struggled to find and retain staff. Both men and women could find more lucrative summer employment elsewhere within the wartime economy, and many of the young men who formerly worked at boys' camps enlisted as soldiers. Boys' camp directors often had to make do with counselors in their forties or late teens, instead of the young adults they generally preferred.[39]

Then, in the immediate postwar era, the summer camp industry grew rapidly. Many young married couples chose to have larger families, so the number of potential clients grew dramatically. The economy was strong, and as more Americans achieved middle-class incomes, they used their relative prosperity to provide camp experiences to their children. At the industry's peak in the decade or two after the Second World War, perhaps one in six American children attended a camp. Over half of these camps were in the Northeast, but the industry was growing in tandem with urban areas nationwide.[40] The American Camping Association (ACA), surveying the industry in the early 1950s, found well over twelve thousand camps (of which perhaps a quarter were day camps), which it estimated served over four million children per year. As the ACA proclaimed, organized camping "has a good past record, a better present one, and a great future."[41]

Important challenges remained. Foremost among them was the question of the degree to which camps should be pluralistic spaces. At camps' late-nineteenth-century inception, children's segmentation into separate camps by class, race, religion, and gender reflected and even exaggerated divisions within American society. Back in the 1920s, only the most self-consciously radical camps attempted to make camp "family" more racially inclusive. In the 1930s, integration at camps was more widely discussed but rarely practiced. By the 1940s, propelled by civil rights activism and the wartime emphasis on "democracy," segregation was increasingly controversial in camping, as in American culture at large.[42] In Capra's *Mr. Smith Goes to Washington,* for instance, Senator Smith explains that his national camp will serve boys of all races and creeds; several shots visually indicate a few African Americans among the Boy Rangers from Smith's hometown. These sequences highlight as American the values of pluralism, inclusivity, and harmony across lines of difference, contrasting these values to the forces of corruption at home and, implicitly, to the totalitarianism and intolerance of the Axis powers. Racial integration at camps, these sequences suggested, was patriotically American.

In 1945, the American Camping Association officially promoted intercultural, interracial, interclass, and interfaith camps as a means to build democratic character, tolerance, and acceptance of difference.[43] However, the organization's official ideology was at odds with most camps' actual practices. In the 1940s and 1950s, some leaders of mainstream northern organization-run overnight camps did lead desegregation efforts, and a few organized new, explicitly interracial camps.[44] Even more northern organizations integrated day camps, less-intimate spaces where campers shared lunch but not a cabin. But in private camping, the color line continued to hold firm, with the exception of a very small number of self-consciously "progressive" camps.

The history of postwar YMCA camps typifies organizational camps' response to the civil rights movement. Like that of many other national organizations, the YMCA's national leadership continued to defer to "local custom" in regard to its membership policies. As a result, postwar camp desegregation was regionally inconsistent within the organization. Individual chapters' responses to the issue ranged from support to accommodation to outright resistance. At one end of the spectrum, the leaders of the New York City YMCA Camp Board founded Camp Custer in 1944 specifically to serve low-income families and an interracial clientele. That first year, about 20 percent of the Custer campers were black. The experiment's success inspired the board to admit black boys to Greenkill and Talcott, long-established and long-segregated New York YMCA camps, the following summer.[45] In the southern United States, YMCA camps were desegregated many years later, sometimes only under duress; the Baltimore YMCA, for instance, integrated its camp in 1960 under pressure from one of its sponsors, the philanthropic organization United Way. Other southern YMCA camps were desegregated in the mid-1960s, a full decade after the Supreme Court's ruling in *Brown v. Board of Education* stipulated an end to racial segregation in public schools.[46]

During this transitional period, organizational camp leaders who were sympathetic to integrated camping engaged in a delicate balancing act. They knew that the few black campers who integrated a mostly white camp community might feel uncomfortable or isolated. But when more than a few black children signed up for camp, some white parents began to disenroll their own children. In 1949, for instance, significant numbers of white clients of the Dayton, Ohio, YMCA kept their boys out of the town's recently desegregated summer camp, lowering enrollments overall and raising the possibility that the camps might become resegregated by default.[47] In Philadelphia, the YMCA camp was integrated in 1948. Five years later, local YMCA camp leaders decided to restrict black campers to 20 percent of the total enrollment because they accounted for over half the total number of campers at some of the 1953 sessions.[48] Urban black families were enthusiastic about camps, but they generally had few camp options. White families could vote with their feet.

Many youth groups were slow to change course. Some discontinued the minstrel shows, blackface performances, and dialect songs that had long appeared in their camp repertoires. Yet even where local policy favored the idea of interracial camping, few camp leaders actively solicited campers or staff from minority groups. Although the majority of postwar northern camps had some black campers, camp leaders often made the familiar case that many minority families could not afford the fees or were reluctant to send their children to integrated camps. In American cities with hybrid "North-South" identities, such as Cincinnati and Washington, D.C., local camping organizations were divided on the acceptability of camp segregation. A few southwestern camps aside, southern organizations' camp committees resisted integration.[49]

However, postwar American cities were changing in ways that made the racial integration of camps more pressing. Under the provisions of the 1944 Servicemen's Readjustment Act (popularly known as the G.I. Bill of Rights), returning soldiers and their families could draw on government aid to buy homes. In practice, white Americans benefited disproportionately from postwar government aid, and many settled in newly expanding suburbs with white-only admission policies (often an attractive feature for buyers concerned about cities' racial heterogeneity).[50] In the postwar years, these suburban communities constituted increasingly important camp clienteles. At the same time, increasing numbers of blacks and Latinos moved from rural areas to urban ones, leading more minority children to participate in activities sponsored by settlements and community centers. Traditional urban organizations that had once served mostly white ethnic communities now had more racially varied clients than ever. When urban ethnic whites threatened to remove their children from camps, they were expressing frustration with environments in which they felt themselves to be losing ground. By the same token, parents in minority communities were eagerly pursuing new leisure opportunities for their own children. This tension makes clear how radical the few "progressive" interwar interracial communities had been and how high the stakes remained.

However grudging and belated the process of integration in some parts of the country, and however symbolic at others, it did serve to redefine the parameters of intimate American social space. At integrated camps, observers noted some name-calling but fewer incidents of explicit racial antagonism than they expected. What racial tensions they found were often instigated by adults. For instance, when the Oklahoma YMCA's Camp Classen was desegregated in 1959, the boys in one integrated living group got along well on the first day of camp. Their eighteen-year-old counselor, however, confessed to another staff member that "I could hardly stand eating at the same table" with the black camper under his care. For the boy's own protection, he was moved to another cabin on an invented pretext, but not before his white bunkmates protested the switch.[51] In Seattle, nine-year-old Emory Bundy learned how to swim in 1947 under the tutelage of Jack Blount, the swimming director of the Seattle YMCA's Camp Orkila. "He was the first black man I ever met," Bundy later recalled, "and by his example, he offset the seeds of prejudice forming in my young mind—living, as I did, in a segregated, all-white neighborhood. In the Seattle of my youth a black person could not get a job even as a sales clerk in any downtown establishment—and yet here was Jack Blount, teaching us swimming, an exquisite role model and a person we greatly admired."[52]

In the 1960s and 1970s, as leaders of organizational camps across the country began to admit more "inner-city" minority children into formerly all-white camps, the language they used to describe their new clients bore a remarkable similarity to that employed by those early-twentieth-century youth leaders who had worked to Americanize recent immigrants' children. The experience of urban poverty in the 1960s was not entirely different from that of the 1900s. Restricted by the prejudices of the larger society and by their own families' poverty, few inner-city children had much experience of rural vacations; camp life was as foreign to them as it was to turn-of-the-century immigrants. The leader of a group of Baltimore girls attending a Camp Fire Girls camp mused in 1967 that "these children faced a new and often fearful world when they climbed off the bus."[53] Like generations of working-class urban children before them, many of these children had parents who could not afford medical exams, special camp clothing, or camp fees.

Separate camping networks constituted a second strain of civil rights activism. Following in the tradition of early-twentieth-century camps established by Jews, Catholics, and a small number of African Americans for their own children, some postwar activist youth leaders founded separate organizational camps. Camp Leslie Marrowbone, for instance, was the brainchild of Sioux organizers affiliated with South Dakota reservation YMCAs, who in 1970 began to offer overnight camping to Sioux children. These YMCA leaders aimed to reinforce Native American culture, not to assimilate the children into majority-white YMCA camp communities or to showcase American pluralism.[54]

In the postwar years, whereas racial integration in camping was controversial, the expansion of coeducational camping was far less so. The 1950s was a time of relatively conservative gender expectations, but boys and girls already led fairly parallel camp lives. Camps had helped to facilitate new opportunities for early-twentieth-century girls. Now, though the majority of established camp directors kept to their single-sex roots, perhaps one in five went "coed" by the early 1950s, often by adding a new section to an extant camp.[55] Here, private camp owners took the lead. As many traditional youth organizations served either boys or girls but not both, they were far less likely to offer coeducational camping than were individual owners (who stood to make a profit on their expanded camp facilities). Coed camps also responded to adult concerns about children's heterosexual development, which resonated among postwar American parents and youth leaders at a time when the heterosexual family was imagined to be a bulwark against communism.[56]

During this period, boys still attended camps in greater numbers than did girls. Members of racial minorities still had far fewer camping options than did white children, particularly but not exclusively in the southern states. Separate Jewish and Catholic camp networks continued to thrive. However, the degree to which camps sorted out children along lines of difference declined as traditional American social hierarchies came under attack and as many camp communities became less exclusive.

Interwar "progressive" and radical organizational camps were harbingers of this more democratic postwar camping landscape. However, such camps often fared poorly in the political climate of the Cold War. In the 1950s, at the height of fears that Communists might infiltrate American society, a number of left-leaning camps were "red-baited" and pressed to shut down on charges that they promoted subversive values. In mid-1950s New York, the State Committee on Charitable and Philanthropic Agencies and Organizations investigated accusations that Communists had, in their words, "moved in on a particularly American institution—the summer vacation camps—which gives them a direct path into the minds of the children." The committee concluded that ordinary parents might inadvertently send their children to a camp where "these children may well be completely enmeshed in the Communist conspiracy."[57] Although this was possible, it was unlikely; some Communist-led camps did indeed romanticize the Soviet experience, but the parents whose children they recruited were generally Communists or else sympathetic to the cause—that is, parents who wished, like other American parents, to choose camps that reflected their own values.

Some radical camps did not survive the uproar. For instance, Camp Wo-Chi-Ca served many "red-diaper babies," and it was interracial. For both of these reasons, the camp was a target of postwar anticommunist activism. In the late 1940s, the local branch of the American Legion protested when black activist, singer, and actor Paul Robeson, a frequent Wo-Chi-Ca visitor, gave concerts in the town. In 1949, a rock-throwing mob attacked concertgoers, including campers and their parents. In 1951, the camp's name was changed to Wyandot, but its leaders were not able to revive its fortunes. The camp closed in 1954.[58]

More mainstream camp directors also felt political pressure. Frederick Lewis, executive director of the Herald Tribune Fresh Air Fund, told his fellow camp directors in the pages of *Camping* in 1954 that a camp director who found concrete evidence that a Communist was on his staff should try to win the person over to American values. But he conceded that his own advice was impractical. "There is too much pressure on the average director in just serving his campers to make way for this attempt at re-education," Lewis noted. "As a camp director I would dismiss him, explain the situation to my staff, and turn the evidence over to the F.B.I."[59] Before the 1955 summer season began, New York governor Thomas E. Dewey required all camp owners across the state to swear that their camps were free of "subversive" influences.

Despite these pressures, the progressive strain in camping continued to enable a more critical appraisal of American modernity. In 1962,

Kenneth Webb, director of the progressive and interracial private Farm and Wilderness Camps in Plymouth, Vermont, argued for creative camping in the face of longstanding industry concerns: urban density, adult overprotectiveness, a scramble for status intensified by greater prosperity, the lessening of moral and spiritual values, and pressure to conform. To this list, Webb added new concerns: an increasingly mobile population, the disintegration of traditional family life, and world tensions in an atomic age.[60] Camp leaders such as Webb remained influential in the national organization, even if their camps were unusual.

From the 1960s onward, the camp industry as a whole faced new concerns. First, in the late nineteenth and early twentieth centuries, many prospective camp owners had been able to afford desirable rural properties. Rising land values placed such land beyond the reach of most newcomers. Second, the "baby-boom" generation aged out of camps in the 1960s, and there were fewer children in the following generation. In the wake of this generational shift, even some very old and venerable camps struggled to find clients. Third, in the early 1970s the economic recession and high inflation discouraged parents from enrolling their children. Both private and organizational camping suffered.[61] In Maine, for instance, long a bastion of private camping, almost a third of all registered camps closed over the course of the decade.[62] Nationally, perhaps half of all YMCA camps closed.[63] Even after the economy brightened, the camp industry remained shaky at best. As many as twenty-five hundred camps nationwide, or about one in five, went out of business from the 1970s through the 1990s.

Most successful camps of the 1970s and beyond were either well-established institutions with longstanding reputations or new "specialty" camps. The latter emphasized particular sports, like basketball, or opportunities such as travel, weight-loss, or computer programing, in shorter sessions than the traditional private eight-week camp. The success of short-term private camps inspired many private camp owners to reconsider their own eight-week seasons. In an era of rising divorce rates, short-term camps were practical for parents who shared custody in the summertime, more affordable because the sessions were shorter, and more flexible for the increasing numbers of middle- and upper-class children who had other vacation plans.

The rise of "specialty" camps, with their focus on concrete activities and results, is indicative of the importance of specialized achievement in modern children's culture. However, this trend was not new to the

1970s. Camps have long highlighted American adults' suspicion of "unproductive" leisure and their eagerness to provide their children the tools to succeed in the modern era. Some of the earliest summer camps were tutoring camps, at which campers spent a few hours each morning studying to pass college entrance exams. At numerous early-twentieth-century camps, staff made thinner campers eat extra meals and pushed heavier ones to exercise. Jazz music, comic books, and motion pictures were common at camps long before go-carts and model rockets made their appearance.

What was new was the era's more overtly rebellious youth culture. Many young counselors and older campers became disillusioned with American involvement in the Vietnam War and with their elders' values, were franker about sexuality, more accepting of recreational drug use, and more likely to object on principle to adult-controlled organized leisure and discipline. This attitudinal shift was most pronounced among counselors, many of whom spent the school year on college campuses roiled by antiwar activism and countercultural experimentation. In 1968, the New York City–based director of one organizational camp, Anne Fried, tried to explain the changes:

> Today's young counselors are different. Many of them come with a strong tendency to use camp for expression of their social convictions and desires for social change. . . . They object to what they consider a "sick society" and such of its manifestations as the war in Vietnam.[64]

Camp directors appealed to their counselors to remember, as the director of Maine's venerable Pine Island Camp told the incoming staff before the 1974 season, that camp was supposed to be "square."[65]

In early-twentieth-century popular culture, camps appeared to be virtuous and sheltering spaces far from the larger world's moral ambiguities. In 1939, for instance, the audience for *Mr. Smith Goes to Washington* was assumed to understand that camps were worthy moral spaces producing virtuous citizens-in-the-making. By the late decades of the century, camps had lost some of the moral high ground they had formerly occupied. In 1977, the *New York Times* described one summer camp in satirical terms: "The starry-eyed young couple walks hand in hand in the moonlight and the clean country air of Camp Monroe, 50 miles upstate in the rolling Hudson Highlands," wrote the reporter.

"The crickets chirp. The pines rustle. The owls hoot. And the bass guitar thunders. These young lovers are 11 years old, and they are going to the camp's disco." As this reporter implied, the purity of the summer camp experience was under attack, sullied by its prematurely sophisticated young lovers and by the popular music that polluted the "clean country air."[66] The eleven-year-old "lovers," as the *New York Times* described them, appeared to exemplify a more adult childhood of which camps were a part, even if the camp "disco" was likely the dining hall.

The idea that camps are not such pure spaces reflects the rise of a more jaundiced view of childhood, in which adults cannot and do not fully protect children from sexual pressures and interpersonal cruelty.[67] Consider *Meatballs* (1979) and *Little Darlings* (1980), films that depict adolescents engaged in practical jokes and hijinks or entering into sexual relationships while at camp. The plot of *Little Darlings* concerns a competition between two fourteen-year-old campers to see who can be the first to lose her virginity. Their coming-of-age at camp is represented in explicitly sexual terms. The girls, each of whom feels enormous pressure from her peers to prove herself sexually, pursue their male targets with little intervention or oversight from adult authority figures.

This more cynical appraisal of children's culture may have reached its apogee in the 1992 Kamp Krusty episode of the popular animated television show *The Simpsons*. The elder Simpson children, Bart and Lisa, attend Kamp Krusty, named for the most prominent television clown from their hometown, Springfield. Krusty is not in attendance, the food is terrible, and the counselors who run the place are Springfield's neighborhood bullies, who leave camp at night in search of sexual partners while the children shiver in their dilapidated bunks. As Lisa tells her parents in a letter home, "I no longer fear Hell because I've been to Kamp Krusty."[68]

In every modern generation American adults have claimed that their own era posed new dangers for young people, and camp leaders more specifically have decried negative "outside" influences. This "crisis of childhood" is notable for its longevity, as is the idea that children's exposure to "adult" culture threatens their innocence. However, a more skeptical popular representation of camps in recent decades does reflect real cultural shifts. Children of the 1970s and beyond did grow up amid franker discussions of sexuality, more open youthful sexual experimentation and drug use, more families fractured by divorce, and increasing permissiveness in childrearing. The definition of child normalcy had grown to encompass a broader range of behaviors, even as children had more leisure and were better educated than were earlier generations.

If camps' image is less pristine, the industry as a whole has continued to attract clients. At the beginning of the twenty-first century, camp enrollments have been steady, even rising somewhat in recent years. Currently, about seven million American children attend residential camps every summer.[69] The camp model designed by late-nineteenth-century innovators, with its emphasis on swimming, boating, mountain hikes, morning chores, athletic competitions, and special songs, continues to exert broad appeal. Even as the camp ideal has become ripe for parody, many parents have continued to endorse camps' "old-fashioned" promise of special opportunities and protection from the "outside" world. Indeed, the aspects of camp life that now appear most clichéd—old bunks, faux–Native American rituals, and art and crafts activities—have continued to appeal precisely because they are traditional and predictable. In 1997, when the first season of the Disney TV series *Bug Juice,* a multipart documentary about summer camp, was filmed at Camp Waziyatah, it highlighted many near-universal aspects of the camp experience across generations: incoming campers' swim tests, cabin dynamics, sports competitions and talent shows, the excitement and heartache of camp romances, canoe trips away from camp, and closing campfires.[70] This story, and the promise of a necessary break from convention, has remained resonant for children as for adults.

Camp traditions may tend to disguise the ways in which openness to innovation is itself fundamental to the camp experience. Over the past century, American society has become ever more urban, heterogeneous, and distanced from its preindustrial roots. Camps continue to make modernity more manageable by channeling it in new directions, even as they connect children to older traditions of community and nature appreciation. The specific details have changed. Whereas an earlier generation of camp leaders fretted about camp movie nights, today's camp directors consider whether to allow campers to bring cellphones to camp or to stay in touch with the outside world via email on camp computers.

Nostalgia for the imagined "good old days" when camps were somehow more authentic, and childhood better protected, is a longstanding camp tradition. But camps are fundamentally modern, hybrid communities, and their power as spaces of children's socialization lies precisely in their flexibility. The decisions taken by camp leaders (and sometimes their campers) about what to maintain and what to let go exemplify Americans' continued ambivalent negotiation of modernity.

Of the many camps that I have discussed in this book, Camp Dudley has undoubtedly been the most successful. Among organizational camps, this YMCA camp has had unusual advantages. Deep-pocketed and deeply loyal alumni have worked ceaselessly for over a century to improve the land and to maintain the "Dudley experience." Camp Waziyatah has also thrived, under various directors' management. In the 1920s, its original directors enrolled a few younger boys before choosing to make the camp girls-only. Today, the camp is again coeducational. Whereas once all campers attended for the entire two-month season, the camp's current owners offer sessions of two to four weeks in length. At both Dudley and Waziyatah, campers can take advantage of "specialty" offerings such as climbing walls, in addition to more traditional camp offerings. Other long-established camps include Adirondack Woodcraft, Che-Na-Wah, Kinderland, Kinder Ring, Mowglis, Pasquaney, Pok-O'-Moonshine, Wohelo, and Wyonegonic.

Most of the other camps discussed in this book have closed. A few Chocorua camp alumni purchased the camp island from Ernest Balch after the final 1889 season and maintained the outdoor chapel. Today, couples can rent the outdoor chapel for weddings in the summer months. The Clearwater YWCA shut down Camp Bay-Lea in 1930, unable to support the camp due to the economic downturn.[71] Mary Jobe Akeley shut down Camp Mystic the following year, also unable to keep her expensive girls' camp afloat during the Depression.[72] Camp Lehman was shut down during the Second World War. The Pioneer Youth Camp closed in 1960, but the property was purchased by a like-minded group, the New York City Goddard-Riverside Community Center, and continued to serve a diverse clientele. Camp Kehonka went the way of many private camps. Upon Laura Mattoon's death in 1945, long-time staff member A. Cooper "Bally" Ballentine and his wife, Althea, assumed ownership of the camp. After their deaths, when the Ballentine children did not take over the camp, the Kehonka property was sold to real-estate developers.[73]

Camp Andree was still a successful camp when the Girl Scout leadership decided to shut it down at the end of the 1941 season, declaring that it had accomplished its purpose as an experimental camp for older girls. The property was handed over to the New York City Girl Scout Council.[74] The fact that Andree was located in Westchester, an increasingly busy suburb of New York City, likely contributed to its demise as a showcase camp.[75] Local development also adversely affected Schroon Lake Camp. When Rabbi Moses purchased the property, it lay on either side of an unpaved dirt road that led into town. After the road was paved in 1915, campers traveled between the cabins and the lakefront through an underground tunnel.[76] In 1958, road work forced Eugene Moses to close the tunnel, which kept the entire camp closed for the summer. When the camp reopened in 1959, many of his former clients had developed new loyalties elsewhere.[77] Most of the Jewish camps around Schroon Lake eventually closed, and in recent decades the lake has become the summer leisure headquarters of Word of Life, an evangelical Christian organization.

From the late nineteenth century onward, camps have served as important staging grounds for the development and expression of modern childhood. These institutions emerged at a time when children were beginning to exert more cultural clout. Reformers worked to protect and improve them, retailers increasingly saw them as an important market for their goods and services, and in an age of greater child "preciousness" and decreasing child labor, many parents sought to forge more intimate and less coercive bonds with them. These three projects have been central to American adults' approach to childhood over the past century. Equally consistent over time is the idea that camps foster better health, community life, personal development, and skill building, while providing children some degree of protection from the problems, dangers, and differences of the outside world.

To a significant degree, camps have succeeded in providing unique experiences that resonate in former campers' lives. As Alfred Balch, brother of Chocorua founder Ernest Balch, wrote in 1893, Chocorua alumni

> can sail, row, and swim, and at night, sitting before the "camp fire," they can bring back the days when they were boys; they can tell their stories of the contracts and the trials, the sports and the cruises; they can laugh over half-forgotten jokes, or speak in lower tones of the boys who are now dead. For although Camp Chocorua has ceased to be, Camp Chocorua lives in the memories of the camp boys.[78]

Abbreviations of Archives

AB	Camp Kehonka Collection, Althea Ballentine, Alton, New Hampshire (*Note*: Ballentine died in 2004, and her collection has been dispersed.)
ACA	American Camp Association, Martinsville, Indiana
AJA	The Jacob Rader Marcus Center of the American Jewish Archives, Cincinnati, Ohio
AM	Adirondack Museum, Blue Mountain Lake, New York
AWC	Adirondack Woodcraft Camps, Old Forge, New York
BLC	Brant Lake Camp, Brant Lake, New York
CAS	Children's Aid Society, New York, New York
CD	Camp Dudley, Westport, New York
CNW	Camp Che-Na-Wah, Minerva, New York
CU	Columbia University Rare Book and Manuscript Collection, New York, New York
ESH	East Side House Collection
CSSC	Community Service Society Collection
LMHC	Laguardia Memorial House Collection
LW	Lillian Wald Papers
GSUSA	Girl Scouts of the USA, New York, New York
HGA	Camp Atwater Collection, Howard Gotlieb Archival Research Center, Boston University, Boston, Massachusetts
HHS	Holderness Historical Society, Holderness, New Hampshire
HSS	Henry Street Settlement, New York, New York
IHS	Indiana Historical Society, Indianapolis, Indiana
IUPUI	Ruth Lily Special Collections and Archives, Indiana University, Purdue University, Indianapolis
JDA	Camp Jeanne D'Arc, Chateaugay, New York
LOC	Library of Congress, Washington, D.C.
DBSC	Daniel Beard Special Correspondence, Manuscript Division

MRHS   Mary L. Jobe Akeley Collection, Mystic River Historical Society, Mystic, Connecticut

NCC   North Country Camps, Keeseville, New York

NHHS   New Hampshire Historical Society, Concord, New Hampshire

NHSL   New Hampshire State Library, Concord, New Hampshire

NYPL   New York Public Library Research Division, New York, New York

  DOR   Dorot Jewish Division

  MAD   Manuscripts and Archives Division

  SCH   Schomberg Center for Research in Black Culture

  UNP   uncatalogued pamphlets on camping, Research Division

NYSL   Manuscripts and Special Collections, New York State Library, Albany, New York

POM   Camp Pok-O'-Moonshine, Willsboro, New York

SL   Bertha Gruenberg Collection, Schlesinger Library, Radcliffe Institute, Harvard University, Cambridge, Massachusetts

SLHM   Schroon–North Hudson Historical Museum, Schroon Lake, New York

SWHA   Social Welfare History Archives, University of Minnesota, Minneapolis, Minnesota

TM   Tamiment Library, New York University, New York, New York

TT   Camp Treetops, Lake Placid, New York

UMO   Camp Collection, University of Maine, Orono

WCA   Wellesley College Archives, Wellesley, Massachusetts

YIVO   YIVO Institute for Jewish Research, Center for Jewish History, New York City

YMCA   Kautz Family Young Men's Christian Association Archives, Special Collections, University of Minnesota, Minneapolis, Minnesota

YMHA   92nd Street Young Men's Hebrew Association, New York, New York

YWCA   Young Women's Christian Association records, Sophia Smith Library, Smith College, Northampton, Massachusetts

Notes

NOTES TO THE INTRODUCTION

1. A. to Mr. Nadel, undated (1939), in Correspondence, 1939, box 1, Camp Lehman files, YMHA.

2. Jerome Hyman, Camp Director's Report, 1927, box 1, Camp Lehman files, YMHA. On the history of Camp Lehman, see Camp Lehman finding aid, YMHA.

3. H. to Mr. Nadel, undated (1940), in Correspondence, 1940, box 1, Camp Lehman files, YMHA.

4. "Camp Ticonderoga" (1928), Camp Ticonderoga, AM.

5. Christopher Lasch calls this process "the socialization of reproduction." See Lasch, *Haven in a Heartless World: The Family Besieged* (New York: Basic Books, 1977), xxii.

6. G. to Mr. Nadel, 8 May 1939, folder "Camp Lehman: Application 1939," YMHA.

7. E. to Mr. Kastenbaum, September 1941, in Correspondence, box 1, Camp Lehman files, YMHA.

8. In the late 1920s, when the camp fee was nine dollars per week, some boys came on full or partial scholarships. By the mid-1930s all the campers had full scholarships. See "Report, Jewish Vacation Association, 1936," "Jewish Vacation Assn," YMHA.

9. *Tatler*, 8 July 1923, in Newsletters, box 4, Camp Lehman files, YMHA.

10. Joseph Kett, *Rites of Passage: Adolescence in America, 1790 to the Present* (New York: Basic Books, 1977), 5–6.

11. The historical literature on late-nineteenth-century and early-twentieth-century childhood, child rearing, and child protection is now fairly extensive. The more general overviews and readers include Kett, *Rites of Passage*; N. Ray Hiner and Joseph M. Hawes, eds., *Growing Up in America: Children in Historical Perspective* (Urbana: University of Illinois Press, 1985); Viviana A. Zelizer, *Pricing the Priceless Child: The Changing Social Value of Children* (New York: Basic Books, 1985); John Modell, *Into One's Own: From Youth to Adulthood in the United States, 1920–1975* (Berkeley: University of California Press, 1989); Elliott West and Paula Petrik, eds., *Small Worlds: Children and Adolescents in*

America, 1850–1950 (Lawrence: University Press of Kansas, 1992); Harvey J. Graff, *Conflicting Paths: Growing Up in America* (Cambridge, Mass.: Harvard University Press, 1995); Grace Palladino, *Teenagers: An American History* (New York: Basic Books, 1996); Elliott West, *Growing Up in Twentieth-Century America: A History and Reference Guide* (Westport, Conn.: Greenwood, 1996); Joseph M. Hawes, *Children Between the Wars: American Childhood, 1920–1940* (New York: Twayne, 1997); Priscilla Ferguson Clement, *Growing Pains: Children in the Industrial Age, 1850–1890* (New York: Twayne, 1997); Joe Austin and Michael Nevin Willard, eds., *Generations of Youth: Youth Cultures and History in Twentieth-Century America* (New York: NYU Press, 1998); Julia Grant, *Raising Baby by the Book: The Education of American Mothers* (New Haven, Conn.: Yale University Press, 1998); David I. Macleod, *The Age of the Child: Children in America, 1890–1920* (New York: Twayne, 1998); Henry Jenkins, ed., *The Children's Culture Reader* (New York: NYU Press, 1998); Paula S. Fass and Mary Ann Mason, eds., *Childhood in America* (New York: NYU Press, 2000); Joseph Illick, *American Childhoods* (Philadelphia: University of Pennsylvania Press, 2002); Steven Mintz, *Huck's Raft: A History of American Childhood* (Cambridge, Mass.: Belknap Press of Harvard University Press, 2004). For a recent historiographical overview of the field, see Hugh Cunningham, "Histories of Childhood," *American Historical Review* 103, no. 4 (1998): 1195–1208.

12. Historians have traced the European Enlightenment roots of this more companionate philosophy to philosophers John Locke and Jean-Jacques Rousseau, both of whom emphasized sheltered childhood and parental oversight in childhood development. Locke's *Essay Concerning Human Understanding* (1690) argued that children's minds were blank slates best filled by competent parental discipline and good education, and Rousseau's *Emile* (1762) represented childhood more sentimentally as a time of innocence and unspoiled simplicity.

13. Such labor was documented by activist and photographer Lewis W. Hine, an investigator for the National Child Labor Committee from 1908 through 1916; see, for example, Vicki Goldberg, *Lewis W. Hine: Children at Work* (Munich: Prestel, 1999).

14. Zelizer, *Pricing the Priceless Child*, 3.

15. "Report, Jewish Vacation Association, 1936," YMHA.

16. Those working-class American adults who enjoyed paid vacations remained in the minority in the first few decades of the twentieth century. Cindy S. Aron, *Working at Play: A History of Vacations in the United States* (New York: Oxford University Press, 1999), 194–205.

17. Incoming students were asked to complete a survey about their past summer experiences. Out of the 275 who responded (out of 291 incoming students),

170 had attended a summer camp. Zita Thornbury, "Camp Directors as Seen Thru the Eyes of Counselors," *Camping* 3, no. 3 (December 1930): 5.

18. Owen R. Lovejoy, *The Negro Children of New York* (New York: Children's Aid Society, 1932), 5, 44; "Fresh Air Number, Seventy-Eighth Annual Report," CAS. By 1935, Harlem was the most densely populated neighborhood in the city, with 222 people per acre, as compared with 133 per acre in the borough of Manhattan and 36 per acre in the city as a whole. Nettie Pauline McGill and Ellen Nathalie Matthews, *The Youth of New York City* (New York: Macmillan, 1940), 25. In 1920s New York, the Negro Fresh Air Committee ran Camp Emetowa at Iona Island for mothers, boys, and girls; the YMCA's Camp Carlton in Staatsburg served boys; and the YWCA's Fern Rock Camp on Iona Island served girls, all at rates of ten dollars or less per week. Charity Organization Society of the City of New York, *Convalescent Homes and Vacation Camps* (New York: Charity Organization Society, 1927). On rural midwestern summer activities, see Orpha McPherson, *Summer Vacation Activities of One Hundred Farm Boys and Girls in a Selected Area* (New York: Teachers College, Columbia University, 1939), 52.

19. West, *Growing Up in Twentieth-Century America*, xii.

20. L. to YMHA, 28 June 1940, in Correspondence, 1940, box 1, Camp Lehman files, YMHA; and D. to Camp Director, YMHA, 10 June 1937, in Correspondence, 1937, box 1, Camp Lehman files, YMHA.

21. Numerous historians have traced the ways in which urban amusement parks, department stores, and motion picture theaters fostered a shared commercial culture among white Americans across ethnic and class lines even as they consolidated ethnic and racial communities. See, for example, John Kasson, *Amusing the Million: Coney Island at the Turn of the Century* (New York: Hill and Wang, 1978); Kathy Peiss, *Cheap Amusements: Working Women and Leisure in Turn-of-the-Century New York* (Philadelphia: Temple University Press, 1986); and David Nasaw, *Going Out: The Rise and Fall of Public Amusements* (New York: Basic Books, 1993). Rural vacationing, however, tended to reinforce rather than to diminish social distinctions. See, for instance, John F. Sears, *Sacred Places: American Tourist Attractions in the Nineteenth Century* (New York: Oxford University Press, 1989); Dona Brown, *Inventing New England: Regional Tourism in the Nineteenth Century* (Washington, D.C.: Smithsonian Institution Press, 1995); Aron, *Working at Play*.

22. Eunice Fuller Barnard, "We Turn Again to a Life in the Open," *New York Times*, 8 July 1934, 6. The first Chicago skyscraper was completed in 1885, within a few years of the founding of the first summer camps.

23. Porter E. Sargent, *Handbook of Summer Camps* (Boston: P. Sargent, 1924), 22 (published annually; hereafter cited by date only).

24. Ibid., 19.

25. On modern nostalgia for preindustrial pasts, see, for example, Peter J. Schmitt, *Back to Nature: The Arcadian Myth in Urban America* (New York: Oxford University Press, 1969), xvi; T. J. Jackson Lears, *No Place of Grace: Antimodernism and the Transformation of American Culture, 1880–1920* (New York: Pantheon, 1981); and Michael Kammen, *Mystic Chords of Memory: The Transformation of Tradition in American Culture* (New York: Vintage Books, 1991).

26. For example, in 1921 the national office of the Girl Scouts estimated that about fifty Girl Scout camps were operating, but they had good information on only five of them. Annual Report 1921, GSUSA.

27. The most extensive early histories include Sargent, *Handbook of Summer Camps* (1924), 24–29; and Henry W. Gibson's series, "The History of Organized Camping," *Camping* 8 (January-December 1936). Eleanor Eells, *Eleanor Eells' History of Organized Camping: The First 100 Years* (Martinsville, Ind.: American Camping Association, 1986), offers the insight of a camp insider but contains numerous factual inaccuracies. On early boys' camps, I found useful David I. Macleod, *Building Character in the American Boy: The Boy Scouts, YMCA, and Their Forerunners, 1870–1920* (Madison: University of Wisconsin Press, 1983); Robert H. MacDonald, *Sons of the Empire: The Frontier and the Boy Scout Movement, 1890–1918* (Toronto: University of Toronto Press, 1993); W. Barksdale Maynard, "'An Ideal Life in the Woods for Boys': Architecture and Culture in the Earliest Summer Camps," *Winterthur Portfolio* 34, no. 1 (1999): 3–29; and Clifford Putney, *Muscular Christianity: Manhood and Sports in Protestant America, 1880–1920* (Cambridge, Mass.: Harvard University Press, 2001), ch. 4. Daniel Cohen, "For Happy Campers, Nothing Beats the Old Rites of Passage," *Smithsonian* 21, no. 5 (August 1990): 86–94; Jenna Weissman Joselit with Karen S. Mittelman, *A Worthy Use of Summer: Jewish Summer Camping in America* (Philadelphia: National Museum of American Jewish History, 1993); and Philip J. Deloria, *Playing Indian* (New Haven, Conn.: Yale University Press, 1998), ch. 4, all were useful in shaping my thinking before I completed my own doctoral dissertation, Leslie Paris, "Children's Nature: Summer Camps in New York State, 1919–1941" (University of Michigan, 2000). From my dissertation emerged several articles: "The Adventures of Peanut and Bo: Summer Camps and Early-Twentieth-Century American Girlhood," *Journal of Women's History* 12, no. 4 (winter 2001): 47–76; "'A Home Though Away from Home': Brooklyn Jews and Interwar Children's Summer Camps," in Ilana Abramovitch and Séan Galvin, eds., *Jews of Brooklyn* (Boston: University Press of New England/Brandeis University Press, 2001), 242–249; "'Please Let Me Come Home': Homesickness and Family Ties at Early-Twentieth-Century Summer Camps," in Caroline F. Levander and Carol Singley, eds., *The American Child: A Cultural Studies Reader* (New Brunswick, N.J.: Rutgers University Press, 2003), 246–261; and "Tradition and Transition at

Adirondack Summer Camps," in Hallie Bond, Joan Jacobs Brumberg, and Leslie Paris, *A Paradise for Boys and Girls: Adirondack Summer Camps* (Syracuse and Blue Mountain Lake, N.Y.: Syracuse University Press, 2006), 1–12. A number of recent articles and dissertations have appeared on similar themes: Phyllis Palmer, "Recognizing Racial Privilege: White Girls and Boys at National Conference of Christians and Jews Summer Camps, 1957–1974," *Oral History Review* 27, no. 2 (2000): 129–155; Susan A. Miller, "Girls in Nature/the Nature of Girls: Transforming Female Adolescence at Summer Camp, 1900–1939" (Ph.D. diss., University of Pennsylvania, 2001); Michael Bruce Smith, "And They Say We'll Have Some Fun When It Stops Raining: A History of Summer Camp in America" (Ph.D. diss., Indiana University, 2002); Dale W. Johnson, "Camp Woodland: Progressive Education and Folklore in the Catskill Mountains of New York," *Voices: The Journal of New York Folklore* 28, nos. 1–2 (2002): 6–9, 11–12; Abigail A. Van Slyck, "Kitchen Technologies and Mealtime Rituals: Interpreting the Food Axis at American Summer Camps, 1890–1950," *Technology and Culture* 43, no. 4 (2002): 668–692; Abigail A. Van Slyck, "Housing the Happy Camper," *Minnesota History* 58, no. 2 (2002): 68–83; Sharon Wall, "Totem Poles, Teepees, and Token Traditions: 'Playing Indian' at Ontario Summer Camps, 1920–1955," *Canadian Historical Review* 86, no. 3 (September 2005): 513–544.

28. L. Noel Booth, "The World Fair Beckons You," *Camping World* 4, no. 7 (December 1938): 15. The claim that "50% of *all* children going to 'paid' camps, come from New York City" was likely overstated, but it reflects the centrality of camp clients from the New York City area.

29. Here as elsewhere, I use the modern spelling "counselor." The term was often spelled "councilor" or "councillor" in the late nineteenth and early twentieth centuries.

NOTES TO CHAPTER 1

1. Charles Platt 3rd, "Asquam—Pasquaney's Parent Camp: Winthrop Talbot's Brilliant Creation Experimentation and Failure" (self-published, Concord, New Hampshire, 1994), 9, HHS.

2. Ernest Berkeley Balch, "The First Camp—Camp Chocorua, 1881," in Porter E. Sargent, *A Handbook of Summer Camps* (Boston: P. Sargent, 1924), 30 (published annually; hereafter cited by date only). My description of the camp is based on Ernest Balch, "The First Camp," 30–41; Elizabeth Balch, "The Boys' Paradise," *St. Nicholas* (June 1886): 604–612; General S. C. Armstrong, "Summer Camps for Boys," *Southern Workman and Hampton School Record* 17, no. 9 (October 1888): 99; Alfred Balch, "A Boy's Republic," *McClure's* 1 (August 1893): 242–254; "A Sketch of Camp Chocorua," *The White Birch* 1, no. 1 (1899), Camp Pasquaney collection, NHHS; Porter E. Sargent,

"Beginnings of the Movement," in *Handbook of Summer Camps* (1924), 24; Chocorua Chapel Association, *Reflections: Chocorua Island Chapel* (Trustees of the Chocorua Chapel Association, 1993), 6–13; and W. Barksdale Maynard, "'An Ideal Life in the Woods for Boys': Architecture and Culture in the Earliest Summer Camps," *Winterthur Portfolio* 34, no. 1 (1999): 3–29. Balch referred to the lake as Asquam Lake, an earlier appellation, but by the late nineteenth century it was already called Squam Lake. On the late-nineteenth-century hotels and resort communities surrounding the lake, see Bruce D. Heald, *Around Squam Lake* (Charleston, S.C.: Arcadia, 2002).

3. On American "wilderness" nostalgia and the historical erasures that this nostalgia has engendered, see, for example, William Cronon, "The Trouble with Wilderness; or, Getting Back to the Wrong Nature," in William Cronon, ed., *Uncommon Ground: Rethinking the Human Place in Nature* (New York: Norton, 1996), 69–90.

4. On the distinction between agrarian and wilderness ideals, see Peter J. Schmitt, *Back to Nature: The Arcadian Myth in Urban America* (New York: Oxford University Press, 1969), xvi–xvii.

5. Ernest Balch, "The First Camp," 31.

6. Groton School Camp, 1897 circular, www.mayhew.org. The camp, founded by the Missionary Society of the elite Groton School, moved from Squam Lake to nearby Newfound Lake in 1920.

7. On Camp Hale, see Camp Hale Alumni Association, "Camp Hale: A Century of Camping, 1900–2000" (Boston: United South End Settlements, 2000), 5–14; "The Camp Conference," *How to Help Boys* 3, no. 3 (July 1903): 9, 160–163; and "The Camp Conference, Secretary's Report, 1905–6," 9, in "Early Years," Boys' Work, box 7, YMCA. The camp was established elsewhere for several years; the boys began to camp on the Squam Lake site in 1901, and the girls by 1904 if not earlier.

8. Porter E. Sargent, "Development of the Summer Camp," in *Handbook of Summer Camps* (1924), 47. Camp Asquam was nearby; the first mention of Pinelands, with which Asquam members were on visiting terms, appears in the 1902 *Asquam Record*, 9, HHS.

9. Ernest Balch, *Amateur Circus Life: A New Method of Physical Development for Boys and Girls* (1916; repr., New York: Macmillan, 1924), 153.

10. On the New Woman of the late nineteenth century, see Helen Lefkowitz Horowitz, *Alma Mater: Design and Experience in the Women's Colleges from Their Nineteenth-Century Beginnings to the 1930s* (New York: Knopf, 1984); Nancy Cott, *The Grounding of Modern Feminism* (New Haven, Conn.: Yale University Press, 1987); Rosalind Rosenberg, *Divided Lives: American Women in the Twentieth Century* (New York: Hill and Wang, 1992).

11. Randal K. Tillery makes this point in regard to modern summer camps, in "Touring Arcadia: Elements of Discursive Simulation and Cultural Struggle

at a Children's Summer Camp," *Cultural Anthropology* 7, no. 3 (August 1992): 374–388.

12. Ernest Balch, "The First Camp," 30–31.

13. Ibid., 37, 40.

14. Henry David Thoreau, *Walden; or, Life in the Woods* (1854; repr., Mineola, N.Y.: Dover, 1995), 59.

15. Frederick Jackson Turner, "The Significance of the Frontier in American History," *Annual Report of the American Historical Association for the Year 1893* (Washington, D.C.: Government Printing Office, 1894), 199–227.

16. Further underlying Balch's call for boyhood virility was what some historians of the late nineteenth century have termed a "crisis of masculinity." This literature includes Richard Slotkin, *Gunfighter Nation: The Myth of the Frontier in Twentieth-Century America* (New York: Atheneum, 1992); T. J. Jackson Lears, *No Place of Grace: Antimodernism and the Transformation of American Culture, 1880–1920* (New York: Pantheon, 1981); Mark C. Carnes and Clyde Griffen, eds., *Meanings for Manhood: Constructions of Masculinity in Victorian America* (Chicago: University of Chicago Press, 1990); E. Anthony Rotundo, *American Manhood: Transformations in Masculinity from the Revolution to the Modern Era* (New York: Basic Books, 1993); Gail Bederman, *Manliness and Civilization: A Cultural History of Gender and Race in the United States, 1880–1917* (Chicago: University of Chicago Press, 1995). Bederman argues persuasively that it is better to call this debate an obsession than a "crisis," since in every era masculinity has been discussed as if it were in crisis.

17. Cindy S. Aron, *Working at Play: A History of Vacations in the United States* (New York: Oxford University Press, 1999), 32–34.

18. Ibid., 5; Dona Brown, *Inventing New England: Regional Tourism in the Nineteenth Century* (Washington, D.C.: Smithsonian Institution Press, 1995), 7.

19. On the rise of the summer school vacation, see Kenneth M. Gold, *School's In: The History of Summer Education in American Public Schools* (New York: Peter Lang, 2002).

20. Brown, *Inventing New England*, 49.

21. Ernest Balch, "The First Camp," 37.

22. William H. H. Murray, *Adventures in the Wilderness; or, Camp-Life in the Adirondacks* (Boston: Fields, Osgood and Co., 1869). On Adirondack Murray and the rise of the Adirondack tourist industry, see David Strauss, "Toward a Consumer Culture: 'Adirondack Murray' and the Wilderness Vacation," *American Quarterly* 39, no. 2 (summer 1987): 270–286; and Philip Terrie, *Contested Terrain: A New History of Nature and People in the Adirondacks* (Blue Mountain Lake and Syracuse, N.Y.: Adirondack Museum and Syracuse University Press, 1997).

23. See, for example, Glenn Uminowicz, "Recreation in a Christian America: Ocean Park and Asbury Park, New Jersey, 1869–1914," in Kathryn Grover,

ed., *Hard at Play: Leisure in America, 1840–1940* (Rochester, N.Y.: Strong Museum, 1992), 8–38.

24. On muscular Christianity, see David I. Macleod, *Building Character in the American Boy: The Boy Scouts, YMCA, and Their Forerunners, 1870–1920* (Madison: University of Wisconsin Press, 1983); and Clifford Putney, *Muscular Christianity: Manhood and Sports in Protestant America, 1880–1920* (Cambridge, Mass.: Harvard University Press, 2001).

25. On the history of the YMCA, see C. Howard Hopkins, *History of the YMCA in North America* (New York: Association Press, 1951).

26. Theodore Roosevelt, "The Strenuous Life," in *The Strenuous Life: Essays and Addresses* (New York: Century, 1905), 1–21.

27. A broader elaboration of this argument appears in Bederman, *Manliness and Civilization.*

28. On the emergence of middle-class domesticity and family life, see, for example, Mary P. Ryan, *Cradle of the Middle Class: The Family in Oneida County, New York, 1790–1865* (New York: Cambridge University Press, 1981). On middle-class fatherhood and the emergence of a more companionate (rather than disciplinary) fatherly ideal, see Robert L. Griswold, *Fatherhood in America: A History* (New York: Basic Books, 1993); Ralph LaRossa, *The Modernization of Fatherhood: A Social and Political History* (Chicago: University of Chicago Press, 1997); and Shawn Johansen, *Family Men: Middle-Class Fatherhood in Industrializing America* (New York: Routledge, 2001).

29. G. Stanley Hall, *Adolescence, Its Psychology and Its Relation to Physiology, Anthropology, Sociology, Sex, Crime, Religion, and Education* (New York: D. Appleton, 1904).

30. William Byron Forbush, *The Boy Problem: A Study in Social Pedagogy* (Boston: Pilgrim, 1901), 44–45.

31. Macleod, *Building Character,* 50–51; Anne Scott MacLeod, "The Caddie Woodlawn Syndrome: American Girlhood in the Nineteenth Century," in Mary Lynn Stevens Heininger, Karin Calvert, Barbara Finkelstein, Kathy Vandell, Anne Scott MacLeod and Harvey Green, eds., *A Century of Childhood 1820–1920* (Rochester, N.Y.: Margaret Woodbury Strong Museum, 1984), 97–119.

32. Amy Susan Green makes a similar argument in "Savage Childhood: The Scientific Construction of Girlhood and Boyhood in the Progressive Era" (Ph.D. diss., Yale University, 1995), 114.

33. Macleod, *Building Character,* 51.

34. See Bederman's discussion in *Manliness and Civilization,* 77–120.

35. "The Camp Conference, Secretary's Report, 1905–6," 35–36.

36. On the history of the Gunnery Camp, see Eugene H. Lehman, "When and by Whom Was the First Camp Founded?" in Spalding's Athletic Library (Eugene H. Lehman et al.), *Camps and Camping, for the Information and Guidance of*

Campers, Parents, Directors and Counsellors (New York: American Sports Publishing, 1929), 39–41 (published annually; hereafter cited by date only); Henry W. Gibson, "The History of Organized Camping (Part I)," *Camping* 8, no. 1 (January 1936): 14–15; Daniel Cohen, "For Happy Campers, Nothing Beats the Old Rites of Passage," *Smithsonian* 21, no. 5 (August 1990): 86–94. A. S. Gregg Clarke attended the Gunnery Camp as a boy and later founded the pioneering Camp Keewaydin on Lake Temagami, in northern Ontario (1893), and Camp Keewaydin in Salisbury, Vermont (1910).

37. On the history of the North Mountain School of Physical Culture, see David S. Keiser, "The First Cultural Camp," *Camper and Hiker* 2, no. 4 (April 1929): 4–5, 17–18. On Rothrock, who went on to become Pennsylvania's first commissioner of forestry in 1901, see Lester A. DeCoster, *The Legacy of Penn's Woods, 1895 to 1995: A History of the Pennsylvania Bureau of Forestry* (Commonwealth of Pennsylvania: Pennsylvania Historical and Museum Commission and the Pennsylvania Department of Conservation and Natural Resources, 1995).

38. George W. Hinckley, *The Story of Good Will Farm* (1902; repr., self-published, 1903), 12–14.

39. "Hinckley and Not Balch Started the First Summer Camp," *Camping* 4, no. 8 (August 1929): 11.

40. Elizabeth Balch, "The Boys' Paradise"; Alfred Balch, "A Boy's Republic." Frank Roberts of New York City planned (and likely held, though its success is unknown) another 1881 summer camp at Croton-on-Hudson, New York, where boys were to attend lectures and to learn "practical teaching in the field and forest." "Summer School of Science for Boys and Young Gentlemen" (1881), n.c. 12, NYPL-UNP.

41. Ernest Balch, "The First Camp," 34–35.

42. "A Sketch of Camp Chocorua," 1–2; Ernest Balch, "The First Camp," 32.

43. Ernest Balch, "The First Camp," 35–36; "A Sketch of Camp Chocorua," 1.

44. Alfred Balch, "A Boy's Republic," 245.

45. Ernest Balch, "The First Camp," 34.

46. Alfred Balch, "A Boy's Republic," 248.

47. Ernest Balch, "The First Camp," 34.

48. For an anonymous camper's account of Camp Harvard, see "A Boys' Camp," *St. Nicholas* (June 1886): 607–612. Porter Sargent stated that the camp originated in Stow, Massachusetts, in 1882 and that the date of the move was 1884. However, the Camp Asquam newspaper, the *Asquam Record*, stated in 1902 that the name was changed when the camp moved from Rindge, New Hampshire, in 1887, after two years on another site, and a later *Asquam Record*, circa 1906, dates the original camp to 1883. Sargent, *Handbook of Summer*

Camps (1924), 24; *Asquam Record,* July-August 1902, 4, and circa 1906, 1, HHS.

49. Edwin DeMerritte, "The Future of Camping," *Camping* 4, no. 6 (June 1929): 12.

50. Sargent, *Handbook of Summer Camps* (1935), 33.

51. On Camp Asquam, see Louis D. Bement, "Recollections of Camp Asquam, 1889," in Sargent, *Handbook of Summer Camps* (1924), 42–43; and W. Barksdale Maynard, "Chocorua, Asquam, Pasquaney: Where Summer Camps Began" (master's thesis, University of Delaware, 1994), 10. On Camp Pasquaney, see C. Mifflin Frothingham, ed., *The Story of Pasquaney, 1895–1960* (n.p.: Murphy and Snyder, 1960); and Charles F. Stanwood, *Portrait of Pasquaney* (Bristol, N.H.: Pasquaney Trust, 1985).

52. Platt, "Asquam," 142.

53. "The Camp Conference, Secretary's Report, 1905–6," 11.

54. At Pasquaney, for instance, Wilson tried the "contract" system in 1899. *The White Birch* 1, no. 4 (26 July 1899): 27, NHHS.

55. Platt, "Asquam," 10.

56. Teddy Jackson, cited in Frothingham, *Story of Pasquaney,* 34–36; *The White Birch* 1, no. 6 (9 August 1899): 41, NHHS.

57. C. Hanford Henderson, "The Boy's Summer," in Sargent, *Handbook of Summer Camps* (1924), 45. On Camp Marienfeld, see also C. Hanford Henderson, *What Is It to Be Educated?* (Boston: Houghton Mifflin, 1914).

58. Platt, "Asquam," 142.

59. Early boys' work was dominated by men of similar backgrounds. The great majority of the first American Scoutmasters, for instance, were Protestant, college-educated, and native-born. Allan Richard Whitmore, "Beard, Boys, and Buckskins: Daniel Carter Beard and the Preservation of the American Pioneer Tradition" (Ph.D. diss., Northwestern University, 1970), 239–240.

60. Frothingham, *Story of Pasquaney,* 30.

61. David S. Keiser, "An 1876 Summer Camp," in Sargent, *Handbook of Summer Camps* (1929), 14–18.

62. Platt, "Asquam," 153–155. Talbot ran the camp until 1907, and a colleague of his led a final season in 1908.

63. Maynard, "Chocorua, Asquam, Pasquaney," 83; Platt, "Asquam," 9.

64. Frothingham, *Story of Pasquaney,* 11.

65. Ibid., 20–21.

66. Quoted in Maynard, "Chocorua, Asquam, Pasquaney," 16. Maynard had access to Wilson's diaries, which were subsequently destroyed.

67. Across social classes, over 40 percent of American adult males were bachelors in 1890, according to the U.S. Census Bureau. Howard P. Chudacoff, *The Age of the Bachelor: Creating an American Subculture* (Princeton, N.J.: Princeton University Press, 1999), 48. Late-nineteenth-century and turn-of-the-century

college-educated women were less likely to marry than were less-educated women. Horowitz, *Alma Mater,* 280–281.

68. Hinckley, *Story of Good Will Farm,* 14, 19, 146.

69. Platt, "Asquam," 158.

70. Ibid., 10; Chocorua Chapel Association, *Reflections,* 13.

71. Ernest Balch, *Amateur Circus Life.*

72. "Ernest B. Balch" (obituary), *New York Times,* 30 April 1938, 15; Chocorua Chapel Association, *Reflections,* 14.

73. Henderson, "The Boy's Summer," 44–45.

74. Quoted in Alcott Farrar Elwell, "The American Private Summer Camp for Boys, and Its Place in a Real Education" (Division of Education, Harvard University, 1916), 47, NHHS.

75. Two Pennsylvania camps were established in 1896: Camp Choconut in Friendsville and Camp Marienfeld along the Upper Delaware. In the South, both Camp Greenbrier in Alderson, West Virginia, and Camp Webb in Walling, Tennessee, were founded in 1899. In the Midwest, the Culver School's summer naval program was founded in 1902 in Culver, Indiana. In Wisconsin, both Camp Highlands, in Sayner, and Camp Minocqua, in Minocqua, were established in 1904. On the West Coast, Twin Oaks Ranch School began operations in San Marcos, California, in 1905. Sargent, *Handbook of Summer Camps* (1924), 26–29.

76. Porter E. Sargent, *A Handbook of the Best Private Schools of the United States and Canada* (Boston: P. Sargent, 1915), 225; "Geographical Distribution," in Sargent, *Handbook of Summer Camps* (1924), 49.

77. "Natural History Camp. Summer Camp for Boys" (1892), 30–31, n.c. 8, NYPL-UNP.

78. Ibid., 25.

79. All figures remain estimates since few generalizable records were kept. In 1905, Winthrop Talbot estimated that there were about five hundred camps nationwide, of which three hundred were YMCA camps. Winthrop T. Talbot, "Summer Camps for Boys," *World's Work* 10 (May 1905): 61–67. Charles F. W. Cunningham, "The Young Men's Christian Association Summer Camp for Boys" (graduating thesis, International YMCA Training School, Springfield, Massachusetts, 1904, unpaginated), estimates that in 1903 over seven thousand boys attended 250 YMCA camps. Camp Mowglis counselor Alcott Farrar Elwell estimated that approximately fifteen to twenty private camps operated in 1900, serving one thousand boys. Elwell, "The American Private Summer Camp," 1.

80. Louis Rouillion, "Summer Camps for Boys," in Albert Shaw, ed., *The American Monthly Review of Reviews* 21 (June 1900): 703.

81. The question of exactly what constituted "middle-class" income is difficult to establish with precision, nor was income the only marker of class status. On middle-class wages at the turn of the twentieth century, see Elaine S. Abel-

son, *When Ladies Go A-Thieving: Middle-Class Shoplifters in the Victorian Department Store* (New York: Oxford University Press, 1989), 17–18.

82. On the early history of YMCA camping, see George Sanford, "Camp Dudley: The First of the Camps," *American Youth* 19, no. 4 (April 1920): 2; Samuel E. Abbott, "Young Men's Christian Association Summer Camps for Boys" (graduating thesis, International YMCA Training School, Springfield, Massachusetts, 1904); Cunningham, "The Young Men's Christian Association Summer Camp"; Clarence Philip Hammerstein, "The State Boys' Camps of the Young Men's Christian Association of North America (Treating the Origin, Development and Growth)" (graduating thesis, International YMCA College, Springfield, Massachusetts, 1917); Minott A. Osborn, ed., *Camp Dudley: The Story of the First Fifty Years* (New York: Huntington, 1934); Eugene A. Turner Jr., *100 Years of YMCA Camping* (Chicago: YMCA of the USA, 1985); Macleod, *Building Character.*

83. One of the boys came from Warwick, New York, under the care of George Sanford, and it would appear that Sanford was present at the camp, although most records make no mention of him. Hammerstein, "State Boys' Camps," 73–74.

84. Cunningham, "The Young Men's Christian Association Summer Camp"; Abbott, "Young Men's Christian Association Summer Camps for Boys," 3.

85. Dudley is cited in George A. Stanford, "Camp Dudley—The First of the Camps," *American Youth* 19, no. 4 (April 1920): 2, YMCA.

86. Hammerstein, "State Boys' Camps," 74.

87. See, for example, Henry William Gibson, *Twenty-Five Years of Organized Boys Work in Massachusetts and Rhode Island, 1891–1915* (Cambridge, Mass.: Murray and Emery/State Executive Committee Young Men's Christian Associations Massachusetts and Rhode Island, 1915), 38.

88. Turner, *100 Years,* 45.

89. Henry William Gibson, "Camps Durrell and Becket," *Association Boys* 5, no. 3 (June 1906): 127.

90. Henry William Gibson, "The History of Organized Camping (Part III)," *Camping* 8, no. 3 (March 1936): 18–19.

91. "Photos," Boys' Work, box 7, YMCA.

92. Talbot, "Summer Camps for Boys," 61–67.

93. Ernest Thompson Seton, *Two Little Savages, Being the Adventures of Two Boys Who Lived as Indians and What They Learned* (New York: Doubleday Page, 1903).

94. Macleod, *Building Character,* 130–131.

95. Philip J. Deloria, *Playing Indian* (New Haven, Conn.: Yale University Press, 1998), 95–127.

96. "What Are You Going to Do with Your Boy?" (1918), CD.

97. Beard found the weather too hot and the landscape too flat in Culver. See

letter, Beard to William Edwards, 23 December 1915, "Dan Beard School, 1915," box 151, LOC-DBSC.

98. Letter, B. E. to DCB, 23 September 1915, "Dan Beard School, 1915," box 151, LOC-DBSC. Beard passed the daily management of his camp to his son, D. Bartlett Beard, in the 1930s. W. L. Saunders to William Davis, 6 November 1934, "Dan Beard School, Board of Directors and Stockholders," box 203, LOC-DBSC.

99. On the history of the Boy Scout movement in the United States, see William D. Murray, *The History of the Boy Scouts of America* (New York: Boy Scouts of America, 1937); Macleod, *Building Character*; Robert MacDonald, *Sons of the Empire: The Frontier and the Boy Scout Movement, 1890–1918* (Toronto: University of Toronto Press, 1993); Jay Mechling, *On My Honor: Boy Scouts and the Making of American Youth* (Chicago: University of Chicago Press, 2001).

100. Murray, *History of the Boy Scouts*, 2.

101. MacDonald, *Sons of the Empire*, 118.

102. Ibid., 153.

103. The original manual was by Seton, *How to Play Indian: Directions for Organizing a Tribe of Boy Indians and Making Their Teepees in True Indian Style* (Philadelphia: Curtis, 1903). The later version that B-P used was known as the "Birch Bark Roll of the Woodcraft Indians."

104. Murray, *History of the Boy Scouts*, 422–423.

105. Ibid., 32–33.

106. On 1911 camps, see Gibson, "The History of Organized Camping (Part III)," *Camping* 8, no. 3 (March 1936): 26. Boy Scouts from Chicago, Philadelphia, Boston, and New York City, as well as Montclair, New Jersey, and Columbus, Ohio, all attended camps that summer.

107. As Howard Utter, a Montclair camper from 1911 to 1915, later recalled, "my reason for joining the Scouts was to go to that 1911 camp." Quoted in Luther Edmunds Price, *Thirty Years of Scout Camping: History of Glen Gray and other Camps in Northern New Jersey, with Memoirs of Frank F. Gray* (Glen Ridge, N.J.: Monclair Arts and Crafts Press, 1941), 26.

108. Macleod, *Building Character*, 242.

109. George Peck, undated statement, in Camp Dudley file, Boys' Work, box 7, YMCA.

110. *The Wellesley Magazine,* April 1947, WCA.

111. The French Recreation Class for Girls was planned, if not already operating, by 1896. Camp Redwing was founded in 1900. In 1922, Eugene Lehman mentioned two girls' camps dating from 1892 and two from 1893, but he may have been using the term "girl's camp" loosely. Spalding's Athletic Library, *Camps and Camping* (1922), 28.

112. On Mattoon and Kehonka, see Spalding's Athletic Library, *Camps and*

Camping (1925), 8; Bea Lewis, "Laura Mattoon—Pioneer in Educational-Recreational Camping," *The Union Leader* (Manchester, N.H.), 29 January 1981, 16A, NHHS; and Sargent, *Handbook of Summer Camps* (1924), 47.

113. On Hall's understanding of female adolescence, see Crista DeLuzio, "The 'Budding Girl': G. Stanley Hall's Psychology of Female—and 'Feminized' —Adolescence," paper presented at the June 2003 conference of the Society of the History of Children and Youth, Baltimore, Maryland.

114. Henderson, *What Is It to Be Educated?* 101.

115. Roosevelt, "The Strenuous Life," 4.

116. On "new women" and reform, see Robyn Muncy, *Creating a Female Dominion in American Reform, 1890–1935* (New York: Oxford University Press, 1991); and Linda Gordon, "Putting Children First: Women, Maternalism, and Welfare in the Early Twentieth Century," in Linda K. Kerber, Alice Kessler-Harris, and Kathryn Kish Sklar, eds., *U.S. History as Women's History: New Feminist Essays* (Chapel Hill: University of North Carolina Press, 1995), 63–86.

117. This term was coined by Ellen K. S. Key, *The Century of the Child* (New York: G. P. Putnam's Sons, 1909).

118. Jean Elizabeth Garvin, "Women Pioneers: A History and Selected Biographies of Women Leaders in the Organized Camping Movement in the United States through 1924" (master's thesis, San Francisco State University, 1983), 94, ACA.

119. In 1890, Albert Fontaine of the Rochester Free Academy recruited forty boys to camp on nearby Canandaigua Lake before founding a separate girls' camp the following year. The other New York State camp, Professor Arey's Natural Science Camp (1890), accepted girls in 1892; renamed Camp Arey, it began to serve girls exclusively in 1902. See Rouillion, "Summer Camps for Boys," 698; and Gibson, "The History of Organized Camping (Part IV)," *Camping* 8, no. 4 (April 1936): 18.

120. For a discussion of Barrows's camp and ideals, see Isabel C. Barrows, "Summer Camping in the Woodlands," *New England Magazine* 24, no. 6 (August 1898): 732–739. On Redcroft, see Gibson, "The History of Organized Camping (Part V)," *Camping* 8, no. 5 (May 1936): 18–19; and the *Mowglis Howl*, 1909, NHHS, which mentions the Redcroft girls. Gibson claims that Elizabeth Holt disbanded her girls' camp after founding Mowglis, but Redcroft was operational at least through 1909.

121. "The Camp Conference" (1903), 156.

122. "Camp Idlewood, Lake Oscawana, New York" (1904), n.c. 1, NYPL-UNP.

123. Elwell, "The American Private Summer Camp," 23; and Sargent, *Handbook of Summer Camps* (1924), 29.

124. Sargent, *Handbook of the Best Private Schools,* 380–403.

125. Eugene Lehman, "Some Facts and Figures upon Which to Base Camp Policies," in Spalding's Athletic Library, *Camps and Camping*, 28.

126. "Chinqueka Camp" (1915), n.c. 8, NYPL-UNP.

127. Such camps were expensive: "For Tuition, Books, Stationary, use of Piano, Chaperonage, Board, Laundry and Traveling expenses to Lake Placid and return to New York, from $225 to $300 according to studies pursued for the fourteen weeks, beginning June 17th, 1896." See "French Recreation Class for Girls" (1896), AM.

128. "Camp Idlewood, Lake Oscawana, New York."

129. Helen Buckler, Mary F. Fiedler, and Martha F. Allen, *Wo-He-Lo: The Story of the Camp Fire Girls, 1910–1960* (New York: Holt, Rinehart and Winston, 1961), 9–10.

130. Buckler, Fiedler, and Allen, *Wo-He-Lo*, 83.

131. Ethel Rogers, with an introduction by Mrs. Luther Halsey Gulick, *Sebago-Wohelo Camp Fire Girls* (Battle Creek, Mich.: Good Health Publishing, 1915), 13–16.

132. Luther Gulick, quoted in Buckler, Fiedler, and Allen, *Wo-He-Lo*, 22.

133. Macleod, *Building Character*, 184; Cathy Shulkin, "The Girl Scout Movement on the Rise," *Nostalgia* (undated), GSUSA.

134. Macleod, *Building Character*, 50–51.

135. Juliette Gordon Low, *How Girls Can Help Their Country* (Savannah, Ga.: Press of M. S. and D. A. Byck, 1917), 48–49.

136. "Camping with Girl Scouts," *Rally*, July 1918, 2, GSUSA.

137. "Try Camping This Summer," *Rally*, July 1918, 4, GSUSA.

138. *Goose Quills*, 31 July 1916, AB.

139. David Nasaw, *Children of the City: At Work and at Play* (Garden City, N.Y.: Anchor/Doubleday, 1985).

140. For instance, *Life* magazine's Fresh Air Fund underwrote children's holidays at private homes, farms, and a remodeled village until 1894, when the organization gave up private home placements to concentrate on camps. Lloyd Burgess Sharp, *Education and the Summer Camp: An Experiment* (New York: Teachers College, Columbia University, 1930), 9–10.

141. William R. George, *The Junior Republic: Its History and Ideals* (1909; repr., New York: D. Appleton, 1912), 15.

142. Ibid., 64.

143. On child-centered Progressive activism, see, for example, Kriste Lindenmeyer, *"A Right to Childhood": The U.S. Children's Bureau and Child Welfare, 1912–1946* (Urbana: University of Illinois Press, 1997); and Michael McGerr, *A Fierce Discontent: The Rise and Fall of the Progressive Movement in America, 1870–1920* (New York: Simon and Schuster, 2003), 107–117.

144. Ernest Thompson Seton, "Organized Boyhood: The Boy Scout Movement; Its Purposes and Its Laws," *Success Magazine* 13 (December 1910): 804,

as cited in Betty Keller, *Black Wolf: The Life of Ernest Thompson Seton* (Vancouver: Douglas and McIntyre, 1984), 161.

145. Lillian Wald, *The House on Henry Street* (New York: Holt, 1915), 91. The first Henry Street boys' camp was founded in 1906.

146. "The Camp Conference" (1903), 175.

147. Ibid., 161–163.

148. "Summer Camps to Open," *Washington Post,* 20 June 1915, E12.

149. "Children's Aid Society, Sixty-Ninth Annual Report," 1921, 11, CAS.

150. The question of whether reformers' interest in immigrants and working-class Americans was ultimately oppressive has occasioned much debate. Cary Goodman, *Choosing Sides: Playground and Street Life on the Lower East Side* (New York: Schocken Books, 1979), for instance, argues that the playground movement represented an intentional effort to repress immigrant street culture. More recent scholarship has tended to emphasize working-class leisure as an expression of ethnic and class pride; see, for example, Roy Rosenzweig, *Eight Hours for What We Will: Workers and Leisure in an Industrial City* (New York: Cambridge University Press, 1983).

151. City Worker's Bulletin, the Tribune Fresh Air Fund, *New York Herald Tribune,* 1925, in "Fresh Air Camp-Sites, 1924–25," box 5, Series I—Administration, CU-LMHC.

152. Untitled report of 1919, "Fresh Air Home," box 126, CU-CSSC.

153. George Michaelis to Bailey Burritt, 14 May 1914, and letter, Harry Hopkins to George Michaelis, 18 May 1914, folder 76 (Fresh Air folder), box 26, CU-CSSC.

154. Sargent, *Handbook of Summer Camps* (1924), 25.

155. See Andrew Heinze's discussion of Jewish vacation resorts in *Adapting to Abundance* (New York: Columbia University Press, 1991). A small number of Jewish children did attend majority-Christian camps at the turn of the century. For one such account, see Robert Goldman to Dr. Jacob R. Marcus, 13 October 1975, MS Collection 31, Jacob Rader Marcus, AJA. The early Jewish camps, many of them in Maine, included Camp Cobbossee (1902), Camp Kennebec (1906), Camp Kohut (1907), and Camp Wigwam (1910) for boys; and Camp Accomac and Tripp Lake Camp (1911), Songo (1912), and Highland Nature Camp (1913) for girls. See Sargent, *Handbook of Summer Camps* (1932), 88.

156. "The Camp Conference," 162.

157. One young orphan whom Hinckley was helping to support said that if the "heathen Chinese" went, then he would not go. In the end the boy relented, and all the boys got along, but this experiment in interracial and intercultural community was not soon repeated. Looking back, Hinckley remembered the Chinese boys as models of decorum, recollecting that when a boy asked Woo, one of the three Hartford teens, to "chuck me a biscuit, will you," the boy re-

plied, "I will *pass* you a biscuit; we need not live like heathen if we are in the woods." *Camping* 4, no. 8 (August 1929): 11.

158. "The boys of the District" to "Dear Madam," 7 August 1910, in "Fresh Air Home," box 126, CU-CSSC.

159. M. and A. to Miss Struble, 28 June 1917, folder 269.1, box 42, CU-CSSC.

160. Ernest Balch, "The First Camp," 41.

161. *Asquam Record*, 1902, 9, HHS; Camp Hale Alumni Association, *Camp Hale: A Century of Camping, 1900–2000* (Boston: United South End Settlements, 2000), 9.

162. Quoted in "The Camp Conference, Secretary's Report, 1905–6," 83–84.

NOTES TO CHAPTER 2

1. "What Parents Say" (1926), SLHM.

2. Mike Hessberg, quoted in "A new camper's impressions of S.L.C.," "The Chronicle," Schroon Lake Camp, 1923, 33, SLHM.

3. Isaac Moses (1847–1926) was one of the charter members of the Central Conference of American Rabbis and was well-known in Reform circles. The Conference's Union Prayer Book of 1894 was based on his self-published 1892 manuscript. See the memoriam in *The Reform Advocate* 73, no. 23 (9 July 1927), SLHM.

4. "The Chronicle," Schroon Lake Camp, 1925, SLHM; and "Schroon Lake Camp for Boys," 1923, SLHM.

5. In 1924 there were, by one estimate, about 160 well-established private camps for girls and another 200 newly established camps. For boys, there were 300 well-established camps and another 300 that were not established. Porter E. Sargent, "Development of the Summer Camp," in *Handbook of Summer Camps* (Boston: P. Sargent, 1924), 48 (published annually; hereafter cited by date only).

6. A more conservative estimate of private camps appears in Sargent, *Handbook of Summer Camps* (1932), 82, and a more liberal one in "Children First," *Camp Life* 4, no. 6 (November 1932): 1. On overall figures, see Ben Solomon, "Camping as a National Movement," *Camp Life* 2, no. 2 (March 1930): 15. On mid-1930s attendance, see editorial, *Camping World* 3, no. 5 (May 1937): 5.

7. Research Bureau, Welfare Council of New York City, *A Survey of Work for Boys in Brooklyn,* study no. 7 (New York: Welfare Council of New York City, 1931), 31. The study surveyed 3,192 children.

8. On the range of magazines that advertised camps or offered camp services, see, for example, George Bird Grinnell and Eugene L. Swan, eds., *Harper's Camping and Scouting: An Outdoor Guide for American Boys* (New York: Harper and Bros., 1911), 185; "Camp Advertising Mediums," in Sargent, *Handbook of Summer Camps* (1924), 460–462; *Where to Buy Everything for Sum-*

mer Camps: A Select List of Firms Specializing in Supplying and Serving Summer Camps (1931), 747–752, NYPL.

9. *Camping* 2, no. 6 (June 1927): 3.

10. On the relative unimportance of paid advertising, see *Camping* 4, no. 12 (December 1929): 1; Charles E. Glendening, "Does Camp Magazine Advertising Pay?" *Camping* 12, no. 2 (February 1940): 6; William Abbott, "Advertising, Solicitation and Enrollment," *Camping* 12, no. 7 (October 1940): 7.

11. "Schroon Lake Camp for Boys."

12. Scholars have shown that mass culture was experienced in local ways. See, for instance, Lizabeth Cohen, *Making a New Deal: Industrial Workers in Chicago, 1919–1939* (Cambridge, Mass.: Harvard University Press, 1990); George Sanchez, *Becoming Mexican American: Ethnicity, Culture, and Identity in Chicano Los Angeles, 1900–1945* (New York: Oxford University Press, 1993); Ted Ownby, *American Dreams in Mississippi: Consumers, Poverty, and Culture, 1830–1998* (Chapel Hill: University of North Carolina Press, 1999).

13. Eugene Moses notebook, in "Schroon Lake Camp for Boys."

14. "The Chronicle," Schroon Lake Camp, 1923; and "What Parents Say."

15. For example, Amy Faulkner invited Bertha Gruenberg to join her as co-director at Camp Waziyatah because Gruenberg, a teacher, already had a client base of her own. Bertha Gruenberg Collection, carton 2, folder "Corres. 1926–39," SL.

16. When prices and salaries were at their highest in the late 1920s, the average new counselor without experience earned $50 to $75 per season at a boys' camp and $35 to $50 at a girls' camp. A head counselor could earn from $250 to over $600 per season at a boys' camp and $200 to $500 at a girls' camp. As in other workplaces, men generally earned more than women. See Spalding's Athletic Library (Eugene Lehman et al.), *Camps and Camping, for Information and Guidance of Campers, Parents, Directors and Counsellors* (New York: American Sports Publishing, 1928), 114–116 (published annually; hereafter cited by date only); L. Noel Booth, "Camp Profits—What Should They Be?" *Camping World* 3, no. 7 (November-December 1937): 14.

17. Abbott, "Advertising, Solicitation and Enrollment," 6.

18. See, for example, Schroon Lake Camp advertisement, *New York Times,* 7 June 1917, 13.

19. Porter E. Sargent, *Handbook of the Best Private Schools* (Boston: P. Sargent, 1916).

20. *Camp Life* 4, no. 6 (November 1932): 1.

21. Good Housekeeping, *Register of Endorsed Schools and Summer Camps,* 5th ed. (New York: Good Housekeeping Magazine, 1916), NYPL.

22. For example, in 1928 the fee at Adirondack Woodcraft was $290; for a set of brothers, parents paid $550. "Adirondack Woodcraft Camps, 1928," Adirondack Woodcraft Camp, AM.

23. Observers of the time sometimes suggested that Jewish camps were more expensive than their Christian counterparts. See, for instance, *Camping* 4, no. 12 (December 1929): 1. My own research did not find this to be the case. This notion may have reflected assumptions (even within Jewish camp circles) about Jews' willingness to spend on their children or to engage in conspicuous consumption.

24. F. F. C. Rippon, *A Survey of New York City Boys* (New York: Kiwanis Club of New York City, 1926), 14.

25. Sargent, *Handbook of Summer Camps* (1924), 302.

26. Spalding's Athletic Library, *Camps and Camping* (1923), 24.

27. Eugene Swan to Philip Cates, 3 June 1922, folder 20, box 794, Pine Island Camp, UMO.

28. In this manner, numerous camps were "related" to one another. When Goldwater, formerly on the Schroon Lake Camp staff, founded Camp Paradox, he brought along many former Schroon Lake campers. Then, in 1917, he lost Paradox campers and counselors to the new Brant Lake Camp, in nearby Horicon. See Porter E. Sargent, *Handbook of the Best Private Schools* (Boston: P. Sargent, 1915), 248; "A Brief History of BLC," Brant Lake Camp, AM.

29. Even in the bleakest Depression years, there remained an elite capable of paying high fees. Beth S. Wenger, *New York Jews and the Great Depression: Uncertain Promise* (New Haven, Conn.: Yale University Press, 1996), 89.

30. According to *Camp Life,* 75,000 children attended 1,500 private camps in 1932, as compared to 132,000 children attending 2,200 private camps back in 1929. *Camp Life* 4, no. 6 (November 1932): 1.

31. "The Chronicle," Schroon Lake Camp, 1930 through 1935 yearbooks, SLHM.

32. Orrell A. York, "A Study of Educational and Recreational Advantages of Boys' Summer Camps" (master's thesis, New York State College for Teachers, 1939). His study of fourteen boys' camps on and near Schroon Lake found a range of fees from $120 to $325, with many camps asking about $300.

33. Welfare Council, *A Survey of Work,* 30.

34. Ben Solomon, "Camping as a National Movement," *Camp Life* 2, no. 2 (March 1930): 15.

35. "Quannacut Camps," undated (circa 1936), n.c. 12, NYPL.

36. Sargent, *Handbook of Summer Camps* (1932), 13.

37. *Camp Life* 4, no. 6 (November 1932): 1–2.

38. On the difficulty of finding full-season campers at Camp Dudley, for example, see Herman Beckman, "A Letter to the Older Leaders," May 1939, "1939 Season," CD.

39. See, for example, Washington State Planning Council, *Organized Camping in the State of Washington* (Olympia, Wash.: Works Progress Administration, 1939), 11, NYPL.

40. Folder, B. B., E. G., box 287, CU-CSSC.

41. Lloyd Burgess Sharp, *Education and the Summer Camp: An Experiment* (New York: Teachers College, Columbia University, 1930), 2.

42. Children's Welfare Federation of N.Y.C.—Committee on Convalescent and Fresh Air Care, *Report of Survey of Fresh Air Homes and Camps, Summer 1925–26*, NYPL.

43. Parental complaints are recounted, for example, in Karl Hesley to Clementine DeRocco, 7 July 1929, reel 62, box 52, CU-LW.

44. Lydia Stoopenkoff to author, 16 February 1998.

45. "Camp Emanuel, Camp Registration 1936," 4, in *Jewish Vacation Association, Report 1935–40*, NYPL-DOR.

46. See, for example, "Report of the Jewish Vacation Association, Summer 1935," 5, in *Jewish Vacation Association, Report 1935–40*.

47. Robert S. Lynd and Helen Merrell Lynd, *Middletown: A Study in American Culture* (1929; repr., New York: Harcourt, Brace and World, 1956), 261–262.

48. Chaim Potok, "A Worthy Use of Summer," introduction to Jenna Weissman Joselit with Karen S. Mittelman, ed., *A Worthy Use of Summer: Jewish Summer Camping in America* (Philadelphia: National Museum of American Jewish History, 1993), 5.

49. For example, in 1935, fifteen hundred children registered with Laguardia Memorial House, but only nine hundred went to camp. Robert Neilson to Mr. Haines, July 1936, "Fundraising, 1918–39," box 5, Series I—Administration, CU-LMHC.

50. "Director's Report, Camp Guilford Bower, Season 1931," 226, book of minutes "1928–1932," box 37, St. Philip's Church manuscript collection, NYPL-SCH.

51. "Camp Lehman, Applications, 1938," YMHA.

52. On the paucity of girls' clubs, and girls' lack of spare time, see "The Children's Aid Society, Seventy-Sixth Annual Report" (1928), 20, CAS.

53. Folder, B., box 287, CU-CSSC.

54. Welfare Council, *A Survey of Work*, 31, 306–309.

55. Ibid., 31, 308.

56. Dorothy Reed, "Leisure Time of Girls in a 'Little Italy'" (Ph.D. diss., Columbia University, 1932), 52.

57. "Adirondack Camp for Boys" (1906), AM.

58. "Adirondack Woodcraft Camps, 1937," AM.

59. "Camp Pok-O'-Moonshine in the Adirondacks" (1936), POM.

60. "Camp Mystic—List of Campers 1916–1930," folder 6, box 11, MRHS.

61. See, for example, Elisabeth Israels Perry, "'The Very Best Influence': Josephine Holloway and Girl Scouting in Nashville's African-American Community," *Tennessee Historical Quarterly* 52, no. 2 (1993): 73–85.

62. State Planning Board, "Report on Organized Camping in Georgia, February 1940" (Georgia State Planning Board, 1940), 19, NYPL.

63. On Camp Atwater, see "St. John's Institutional Activities" (1926) and "Camp Atwater for Boys and Girls" (1940), HGA. Atwater campers spent several hours each day doing chores around the camp. On Camp Guilford Bower, see *The Anniversary Book of Saint Philip's Church* (New York, 1943), 53, and Shelton Hale Bishop, report of 1930 season, book of minutes, 1928–1932, box 37, St. Philip's Church manuscript collection, 150, NYPL-SCH. Guilford Bower was purchased by the Children's Aid Society in the mid-1930s and renamed Camp Wallkill River. "The Children's Aid Society, Eighty-Fifth Annual Report" (1937), CAS.

64. Henry Wellington Wack, *More about Summer Camps, Training for Leisure* (New York: Red Book Magazine, 1926), 41–42.

65. By 1929, New York State had forty-six Boy Scout camps, forty-four Girl Scout camps, eight Camp Fire Girl camps, and fifty-one YMCA camps. Sargent, *Handbook of Summer Camps* (1929), 46–47.

66. On camping in New York State at the end of the interwar years, see Arthur T. Wilcox, "Organized Camping in New York State: A Study of Attendance, Facilities and Finance, Together with Suggestions for Meeting the Camping Needs of the State" (master's thesis, New York State College of Forestry, Syracuse University, 1941).

67. On middle-class culture among white migrants to Los Angeles, see, for example, Victoria Bissell Brown, "Golden Girls: Female Socialization among the Middle Class of Los Angeles, 1880–1910," in Elliot West and Paula Petrik, eds., *Small Worlds: Children and Adolescents in America, 1850–1950* (Lawrence: University of Kansas, 1992).

68. Rosalind Cassidy, "Celebrating a Birthday," *Camping* 2, no. 8 (May 1930): 4.

69. Washington State Planning Council, *Organized Camping in the State of Washington*, 3, 4–7, 23.

70. Eunice Fuller Barnard, "Young America Is Off to Summer Camp," *New York Times*, 29 June 1930, sec. 5, p. 14.

71. E.L. to author, 27 November 1997.

72. Sargent, *Handbook of Summer Camps* (1924), 53.

73. Harriet Gulick, "What Camp Offers Your Child," *Parents* 10, no. 4 (April 1935): 50.

74. Chocorua brochures, cited in Henry W. Gibson, "The History of Organized Camping (Part II)," *Camping* 8, no. 2 (February 1936): 19–20; and Chocorua Chapel Association, *Reflections: Chocorua Island Chapel* (Trustees of the Chocorua Chapel Association, 1993), 8.

75. "The Chronicle," Schroon Lake Camp, 1934, SLHM.

76. See, for instance, the brochures in "Youth Summer Camp" box, LOC.

77. "What Parents Say."

78. Camp Andree Report 1931, GSUSA.

79. Eugene Lehman, letter to the editor, *Camp Life* 4, no. 7 (December 1932): 5.

80. Gertrude Middleditch Platt, "How We Chose Our Children's Camp," *Parents* 7, no. 5 (May 1932): 28.

81. "Camp Winnahkee" (1920), n.c. 1, NYPL-UNP.

82. "Camp Wonposet" (1919), n.c. 7, NYPL-UNP.

83. On this argument, see, for instance, Lois Hayden Meek, "Camping for Children," in Beulah Clark Van Wagenen, ed., *Summer Camps: A Guide for Parents* (New York: Child Development Institute, Teachers College, Columbia University, 1933), 4, NYPL. As *Outlook* magazine suggested in 1915, camp "does both the child and the parents good, and reunites them again even more closely." Mary Harrod Northend, "How to Choose a Summer Camp for Boys or Girls," *Outlook* 28 (April 1915): 1007.

84. C. Mifflin Frothingham, ed., *The Story of Pasquaney, 1895–1960* (n.p.: Murphy and Snyder, 1960), 103–104.

85. C. to Chief, 23 June 1939, Camper Reports, CD.

86. B. to Chief, 26 June 1940, Camper Reports, CD.

87. Mrs. L. to Mr. Beard (Bartlett), August 1932, "Dan Beard School, 1932," box 192, LOC-DBSC.

88. Camp Andree Reports 1934, 14–15, GSUSA.

89. See Paula Fass, *The Damned and the Beautiful: American Youth in the 1920s* (New York: Oxford University Press, 1978).

90. Cindy S. Aron, *Working at Play: A History of Vacations in the United States* (New York: Oxford University Press, 1999), 256–257.

91. "Summer Camps Boon to Parents," *New York Times,* 15 July 1923, sec. 2, p. 5. In the mid-1910s, the Schroon Lake Camp brochure was unusual in urging parents to consider camp for a "perhaps more selfish reason . . . that you may have your own summer vacation untrammeled by the care of a growing boy." When Moses next revised the brochure, this section was omitted, downplaying any hint of parental "selfishness." "Schroon Lake Camp for Boys," undated brochure (circa 1916), SLHM.

92. Numerous children were sent to camp when their mothers were pregnant or soon after the birth of a sibling, to ease child care at home. Rena Kunis, letter to author, 23 November 1997.

93. Bertha Gruenberg to Fred Gruenberg, undated (1928), carton 2, folder "Corres. 1926–39," SL.

94. On the rise of child-directed consumerism, see, for example, Roland Marchand, *Advertising the American Dream: Making Way for Modernity, 1920–1940* (Berkeley: University of California Press, 1985), 228–232; Miriam Formanek-Brunell, *Made to Play House: Dolls and the Commercialization of Amer-*

ican Girlhood, 1830–1930 (New Haven, Conn.: Yale University Press, 1993); William Leach, *Land of Desire: Merchants, Power, and the Rise of a New American Culture* (New York: Pantheon Books, 1993), 328–332; Gary Cross, *Kids' Stuff: Toys and the Changing World of American Childhood* (Cambridge, Mass.: Harvard University Press, 1997); Lisa Jacobson, *Raising Consumers: Children and the American Mass Market in the Early Twentieth Century* (New York: Columbia University Press, 2004).

95. Libby Adelman (nee Raynes), interview by author, 28 June 1997.

96. Frothingham, *Story of Pasquaney,* 22.

97. Mildred Sheppard to Mr. Matthews and Miss Randall, 26 September 1931, "Overhill Cottage, 1930–1928 [*sic*]," box 43, CU-CSSC; Camp Overhill case report, H. M. Webster to Mr. Burritt, 2 September 1932, folder 269.1, box 42, CU-CSSC.

98. *Blue Sparks* 10, no. 4 (December 1931), JDA.

99. Bob Noto, interview by author, 1 April 1999.

100. "Report of Work Involved in Camp Placements Made for Jewish Social Service Association 1935," 5–6, in *Jewish Vacation Association, Report 1935–40.*

101. Jewish Social Service Association, "Camp Registration 1936," 6, in *Jewish Vacation Association, Report 1935–40.*

102. Alcott Farrar Elwell, *The American Private Summer Camp for Boys, and Its Place in a Real Education* (Division of Education, Harvard University, 1916), 7, NHHS.

103. Paul Samson, "Modern Trends in Camping," *Camping* 11, no. 7 (October 1939): 14.

104. Hedley S. Dimock, ed., *Putting Standards into the Summer Camp* (New York: Association Press, 1936), 6.

105. Libby Adelman (nee Raynes), interview by author, 28 June 1997.

106. Wack, *More about Summer Camps,* 78–79.

107. David S. Keiser, "The First Cultural Camp," *Camper and Hiker* 2, no. 4 (April 1929): 18.

108. Charles Platt 3rd, "Asquam—Pasquaney's Parent Camp: Winthrop Talbot's Brilliant Creation Experimentation and Failure" (self-published, Concord, New Hampshire, 1994), 70, HHS; Will Twombly, phone interview by author, 8 July 2004; "Groton Pupil Drowns," *Washington Post,* 6 July 1906, 1.

109. J. Edward Sanders, *Safety and Health in Organized Camps* (New York: National Bureau of Casualty and Surety Underwriters, 1931), 56–57, 119.

110. *Camping* 4, no. 10 (October 1929): 5, 9–10. In one 1933 survey, of a sample of 617 camps, only 19 percent required a medical examination for food handlers. *Camping* 5, no. 3 (January 1933): 23.

111. Sanders, *Safety and Health,* 77, 108.

112. Platt, "Asquam," 153.

113. *Asquam Record,* July-August 1902, 26, HHS.

114. A fairly full account of the conference appears in "The Camp Conference," *How to Help Boys* 3, no. 3 (Boston: General Alliance of Workers with Boys, 1903). See also Henry W. Gibson, "The History of Organized Camping (Part V)," *Camping* 8, no. 5 (May 1936): 18–19.

115. "The Camp Conference, Secretary's Report, 1905–6," 33, in "Early Years," Boys' Work, box 7, YMCA. Hall argued that the summer months were not a time of physical growth for children, but the camp leaders present disagreed, based on their own observations.

116. Allen S. Williams, "Birth of the Camp Directors Association," in Spalding's Athletic Library, *Camps and Camping* (1921), 11–12; Gibson, "The History of Organized Camping (Part V)," 20.

117. Jean Elizabeth Garvin, "Women Pioneers: A History and Selected Biographies of Women Leaders in the Organized Camping Movement in the United States through 1924" (master's thesis, San Francisco State University, 1983), 94–95, ACA.

118. Williams, "Birth of the Camp Directors Association," 12. On the first leaders of the CDAA and the NADGC, see Spalding's Athletic Library, *Camps and Camping* (1921), 7–10.

119. On the early history of Camp Wawayanda, see "Charles R. Scott—Pioneer," in "Trail Blazers B," Boys' Work, box 7, YMCA.

120. Eleanor Eells, *Eleanor Eells' History of Organized Camping: The First 100 Years* (Martinsville, Ind.: American Camping Association, 1986), 87.

121. On the later beginnings of midwestern camps, see Timothy Bawden, "Reinventing the Frontier: Tourism, Nature, and Environmental Change in Northern Wisconsin, 1880–1930" (Ph.D. diss., University of Wisconsin–Madison, 2001), 262–271.

122. On the various internal and sectional conflicts that plagued these interwar organizations, see Sargent, *Handbook of Summer Camps* (1935), 104–105; and Eells, *Eleanor Eells' History,* 106. Some camp directors chose to affiliate with their regional group but not the national association.

123. In New York State, for instance, the State Department of Health, upon inspecting 241 children's camps in 1934, reported that the great majority were in need of some sanitary improvement. Thomas Parran Jr., "Camp Health Supervision, What Shall It Be?" *Camping World* 1, no. 1 (May 1935): 19. Inadequate hygienic standards were endemic at interwar vacation hotels and resorts as well. Aron, *Working at Play,* 224–225.

124. Edwin DeMerritte, "The Future of Camping," *Camping* 4, no. 6 (June 1929): 12.

125. On Jewish vacationing, see Andrew Heinze, *Adapting to Abundance: Jewish Immigrants, Mass Consumption, and the Search for American Identity*

(New York: Columbia University Press, 1990), ch. 7; and Samuel P. Abelow, *History of Brooklyn Jewry* (Brooklyn: Scheba, 1937), 330–331.

126. In the words of a typical interwar brochure, "Only campers who come from Christian homes of background and culture are accepted at Silver Lake." "Silver Lake Camp for Girls in the Adirondacks" (1934), n.c. 8, NYPL-UNP.

127. Welfare Council, *A Survey of Work,* 20. As Abelow noted in his *History of Brooklyn Jewry,* 332, "many Jews are indifferent, and some are antagonistic to the entire question" of the laws of kashrut. On assimilation and Jews of the second generation, see, for example, Deborah Dash Moore, *At Home in America: Second Generation New York Jews* (New York: Columbia University Press, 1981).

128. In 1930, the membership of the Flatbush Boys' Club, for example, was about 41.8 percent Jewish, 36.2 percent Catholic, and 8.1 percent Protestant (with an additional 13.9 percent of unknown religious or ethnic heritage). Welfare Council, *Survey of Work,* 240.

129. J. I., letter to YMHA, in "Surprise Lake Camp 1930–33 (4 files)," YMHA. On the ethnic permeability of urban neighborhoods, see Deborah Dash Moore, "The Construction of Community: Jewish Migration and Ethnicity in the United States," in Moses Rischin, ed., *The Jews of North America* (Detroit: Wayne State University Press, 1987), ch. 6; and Paula Fass, "Creating New Identities: Youth and Ethnicity in New York City High Schools in the 1930s and 1940s," in Joe Austin and Michael Nevin Willard, eds., *Generations of Youth: Youth Cultures and History in Twentieth-Century America* (New York: NYU Press, 1998).

130. On Jewish childhood and consumerism, see Jenna Weissman Joselit, *The Wonders of America: Reinventing Jewish Culture, 1880–1950* (New York: Hill and Wang, 1994), ch. 2.

131. "The Chronicle," Schroon Lake Camp, 1936–1937 (1936 season), SLHM.

132. Jenna Weissman Joselit, "The Jewish Way of Play," in Joselit, *A Worthy Use,* 15–28.

133. "Eugene F. Moses 1926 Diary," SLHM.

134. See, for instance, *Dudley Doings,* 2 September 1920, CD.

135. Bess Wilkofsky to author, 4 March 1998.

136. Gerald Sorin, *The Nurturing Neighborhood: The Brownsville Boys' Club and Jewish Community in Urban America, 1940–1990* (New York: NYU Press, 1990), 48.

137. Rippon, *A Survey,* 42. In a 1927–28 study, about 6 percent of Brooklyn boys surveyed had attended a Boy Scout camp within the past two years. See ibid., 13, 30.

138. Welfare Council, *A Survey of Work,* 13, 30. This is not to say that all

boys endorsed the Boy Scouts. At Surprise Lake Camp in 1926, the Scouting leader complained that "some find pleasure in making fun of the scouts and ridiculing their ideals." Camp report for 1 October 1925 through summer 1926, in "S.L.C., Reports Summer Camp 1905–1938," YMHA.

139. *Brooklyn Jewish Chronicle,* 11 July 1924, 1.

140. See Arnold M. Sleutelberg, *A Critical History of Organized Jewish Involvement in the Boy Scouts of America, 1926–1987: Based on Unpublished Archival Materials* (rabbinic thesis, Hebrew Union College—Jewish Institute of Religion, New York, 1988), 1.

141. *Brooklyn Jewish Chronicle,* 11 July 1924, 1.

142. *Scout Menorah* 2, no. 5 (May 1929): 3, NYPL.

143. Sleutelberg, *A Critical History,* 46.

144. *Scout Menorah* 1, no. 3 (May 1928): 3.

145. Alice Conway Carney to Sibyl Gordon Newell, 15 December 1937, in Council Materials, Council—Greater NYGSC—Outdoor/Camping materials 1936–1951, GSUSA.

146. On early-twentieth-century radical summer camps, see Paul C. Mishler, *Raising Reds: The Young Pioneers, Radical Summer Camps, and Communist Political Culture in the United States* (New York: Columbia University Press, 1999), 83–108. On Camp Wo-Chi-Ca, see also June Levine and Gene Gordon, *Tales of Wo-Chi-Ca: Blacks, Whites and Reds at Camp* (San Rafael, Calif.: Avon Springs, 2002). On Camp Boiberik, see Saul Goodman, ed., *Our First Fifty Years: The Sholem Aleichem Folk Institute* (New York: Sholem Aleichem Folk Institute, 1972).

147. Esther Wallace (nee Israeloff), interview by author, 4 February 1999. Kinder Ring was founded in 1927.

148. Don Poyourow, interview by author, 12 May 1999.

149. Pinelands brochure (1908), 12–14, collection of author.

150. "Camp Dixie for Girls" (1921), LOC.

151. "Camp Brosius" (1935) and "Camp Brosius" (1937), "Promotional Brochures," box 8, School of Physical Education Records, 1877–2000, IUPUI.

152. "A New Camper's Impressions of S.L.C.," "The Chronicle," Schroon Lake Camp, 1923, SLHM.

153. "What Parents Say."

154. "The Chronicle," Schroon Lake Camp, 1924, 1926, and 1927, SLHM.

NOTES TO CHAPTER 3

1. *Goose Quills,* 20 July 1916, AB.

2. "The Arrival," *Goose Quills,* 22 June 1917, AB. A description and photographs of the landscape appear in Kehonka camp catalogue, circa 1920–24, AB.

3. Spalding's Athletic Library (Eugene Lehman et al.), *Camps and Camping,*

for Information and Guidance of Campers, Parents, Directors and Counsellors (New York: American Sports Publishing, 1925), 8 (published annually; hereafter cited by date only).

4. Laura Mattoon, "The Evolution of Organized Camping for Boys and Girls," reprinted in *Granite State News*, 13 January 1933, AB.

5. See, for example, Anna Worthington Coale, *Summer in the Girls' Camp* (New York: Century, 1919), 10–11.

6. Helen Amir (nee Weisgal) to author, 20 January 1998.

7. "Report, Jewish Vacation Association, 1936," in folder, Jewish Vacation Assn, YMHA.

8. Hy Kampel, interview by author, 16 September 1998.

9. "American Citizens in the Making," in "Bagdad on the Subway" (circa 1917–1918), folder 269.1, box 42, CU-CSSC.

10. A. E. Hamilton, *Trailwise* (Columbus, Ohio: Outing Press, 1924), n.c. 5, NYPL-UNP.

11. Wouk's novel *The City Boy* was at least partly autobiographical. Herman Wouk, *The City Boy* (Garden City, N.Y.: Doubleday, 1952), 128–129.

12. "5,000 Milling Children Start for Camps; Freed From School, Begin Summer Exodus," *New York Times*, 1 July 1926, 1.

13. Bess Wilkofsky (nee Satz) to author, 4 March 1998.

14. "5,000 Milling Children," 1.

15. Libby Adelman (nee Raynes), interview by author, 17 July 1997.

16. "Idylwold Leaf" (1941), collection of George and Bea Adelman.

17. *The White Birch* 1, no. 7 (17 August 1899), NHHS.

18. *Goose Quills* 3, no. 2 (15 July 1916), AB.

19. See, for instance, "Lincoln House Bulletin for 1897," Lincoln House Annual Reports, box 1, United South End Settlements, SWHA.

20. Lydia Stoopenkoff to author, 16 February 1998.

21. "The Camp Log, AWC, 1930," 4 July 1930, AWC.

22. *Camp Riverdale Stag and Eagle* 4, no. 3 (28 August 1940), file 19, box 2, Camp Riverdale MS 70-12, AM.

23. "Canoe Trip—1937," Camp Andree Reports 1937, GSUSA.

24. "Summary of Questionnaires Filled Out by Campers," 74, Camp Andree Reports 1932, GSUSA.

25. Pasquaney Nature Club Diaries, vol. 2, 3 July 1909, NHHS.

26. "Report of Robin Hood Troop 1927," in Report of Camp Andree 1927, GSUSA.

27. Kehonka brochure, early 1920s, AB.

28. These examples are from Brant Lake Camp, Camp Che-Na-Wah, and Camp Jeanne D'Arc, respectively.

29. *Goose Quills*, 20 July 1916, AB.

30. See, for example, Lloyd Burgess Sharp, *Education and the Summer Camp:*

An Experiment (New York: Teachers College, Columbia University, 1930), 56–57.

31. As Balch confessed in his book *Amateur Circus Life* in 1916, "the term twelve–sixteen is used for convenience. All people in touch with boys and girls observe that the period I write about begins and ends, at times, earlier or later." Ernest Balch, *Amateur Circus Life: A New Method of Physical Development for Boys and Girls* (1916; repr., New York: Macmillan, 1924), 162.

32. Alfred Balch, "A Boy's Republic," *McClure's* 1 (August 1893): 247. One former camper described the boys at Camp Harvard, 1880s precursor to Camp Asquam, as "from ten to fourteen." Cited in Charles Platt 3rd, "Asquam—Pasquaney's Parent Camp: Winthrop Talbot's Brilliant Creation Experimentation and Failure" (self-published, Concord, New Hampshire, 1994), 20, HHS.

33. "A Sketch of Camp Chocorua," *The White Birch* 1, no. 1 (1899): 2, Camp Pasquaney Collection, NHHS.

34. See, for example, Welfare Council of New York City, *Preprint of Summary and Conclusions of a Survey of Work for Boys in Brooklyn* (New York: Welfare Council of New York City, 1931), 29, NYPL.

35. Undated Kehonka brochure (circa 1920s), AB; Porter E. Sargent, *Handbook of Summer Camps* (Boston: P. Sargent, 1924), 194 (published annually; hereafter cited by date only).

36. Ruth Saslov, "Midget Marshmallow Roast," *Che-Na-Wah Chat,* 1923, 30, in untitled scrapbook (1920s), CNW.

37. By the interwar years, few organizations accepted adolescents over the age of sixteen, and few private camps enrolled them. On typical age ranges, see Arthur T. Wilcox, "Organized Camping in New York State: A Study of Attendance, Facilities and Finance, Together with Suggestions for Meeting the Camping Needs of the State" (master's thesis, New York State College of Forestry, Syracuse University, 1941), 55.

38. From 1900 to 1920, the percentage of American children aged fourteen to seventeen who attended high schools rose from 8 percent to 32 percent. The percentage rose far more sharply during the Depression of the 1930s due to new child-protection laws that extended mandatory schooling to age sixteen in many regions and to new restrictions on adolescent employment. Elliott West, *Growing Up in Twentieth-Century America: A History and Reference Guide* (Westport, Conn.: Greenwood, 1996), 42–44.

39. "Andree Experiments, 1935," 13, GSUSA.

40. Camp Dudley 1915 brochure, "1915 Season—Camp Dudley," CD.

41. Kelly Schrum, *Some Wore Bobby Sox: The Emergence of Teenage Girls' Culture, 1920–1945* (New York: Palgrave Macmillan, 2004), and Ilana Nash, *American Sweethearts: Teenage Girls in Twentieth-Century Popular Culture* (Bloomington: Indiana University Press, 2006), both similarly explore the emergence of "teens" in the interwar period, focusing specifically on girls.

42. Sheldon Flory to author, 2 February 1998.

43. Lydia Stoopenkoff to author, 26 November 1997 and 16 February 1998.

44. *Blue Sparks,* August 1938, 5, JDA.

45. "Surprise Lake Echoes, 1938–1940," 31 August 1939, YMHA; Bill Schwartz, "Day Book, Permanents, 1940," entry dated 14 August, in "Daily Programs 1940," YMHA.

46. Camp Andree Reports 1937, GSUSA.

47. Phil Confer, interview by author, 31 July 1997, Camp Forest Lake, Warrensburg, New York.

48. C. Mifflin Frothingham, ed., *The Story of Pasquaney, 1895–1960* (n.p.: Murphy and Snyder, 1960); Charles F. Stanwood, *Portrait of Pasquaney* (Bristol, N.H.: Pasquaney Trust, 1985), 61.

49. Alcott Farrar Elwell, *The American Private Summer Camp for Boys, and Its Place in a Real Education* (Division of Education, Harvard University, 1916), 53–55.

50. Undated Kehonka brochure (circa 1920s), AB.

51. Anecdotal evidence suggests that by the 1930s, more middle- and upper-class children learned to swim before attending camps, whether at urban recreation centers or on family vacations. The 1935 brochure for the Luther Gulick camps contended that "twenty years ago two-thirds of the girls entering the older camp could not swim, while at the present time the non-swimmers are few and far between." "The Luther Gulick camps" (1935), box 501, Camping in Maine collection, UMO.

52. W. H. Ball, "Swimming for Camps," *Association Boys* 10, no. 3 (1914): 130. On the cultural history of swimming, see Thomas A. P. van Leeuwen, *The Springboard in the Pond: An Intimate History of the Swimming Pool* (Chicago: Graham Foundation/MIT Press, 1998).

53. W. E. to his mother, 22 August 1920, "1920 Season," CD.

54. Ernest Balch, "The First Camp—Camp Chocorua, 1881," in Sargent, *Handbook of Summer Camps* (1924), 37.

55. Louis Rouillion, "Summer Camps for Boys," in Albert Shaw, ed., *The American Monthly Review of Reviews* 21 (June 1900): 701. Abigail Van Slyck, in "Kitchen Technologies and Mealtime Rituals: Interpreting the Food Axis at American Summer Camps, 1890–1950," *Technology and Culture* (2002): 686, writes that baseball did not achieve popularity at camps until the 1930s, but archival records of individual camps unequivocally indicate otherwise. See, for instance, *The White Birch* 1, no. 5 (2 August 1899): 34–35, Camp Pasquaney file, NHHS.

56. The term "American game" was used at many camps, both Christian and Jewish. See, for example, *The Chieftain of Camp Oneida* 8 (1927): 19, AM.

57. Sargent, *Handbook of Summer Camps* (1924), 194.

58. Undated Kehonka brochure (circa early 1920s), AB.

59. Charles E. Hendry, "A Case Study of a Long-Term Private Camp," in Hedley S. Dimock, ed., *Putting Standards into the Summer Camp* (New York: Association Press, 1936), 42.

60. *The White Birch* 1, no. 1 (5 July 1899): 2, Camp Pasquaney file, NHHS.

61. Laura I. Mattoon and Helen D. Bragdon, *Services for the Open* (New York: Century, 1923).

62. J. Edward Sanders, *Safety and Health in Organized Camps* (New York: National Bureau of Casualty and Surety Underwriters, 1931), 57.

63. Undated Kehonka brochure (circa 1920s), AB.

64. "Report of Superintendent of Junior Section, Alliance-YMHA Camp, Aug. 23, 1912," YMHA. On the early history of Surprise Lake Camp, see Jack Holman, *History of Surprise Lake Camp* (New York: Surprise Lake Camp, 1972); "SLC—History—by Goldwasser," YMHA.

65. "A Sketch of Camp Chocorua," *The White Birch* 1, no. 1 (5 July 1899): 2, Camp Pasquaney file, NHHS.

66. For instance, one Camp Riverdale counselor complained that the boys under his care had departed on hikes carrying loads of as much as forty-five pounds. "Camp Riverdale Trip Reports I" (1941), box 4, Camp Riverdale, AM.

67. "Camp Campbell, the Camping History of the Santa Clara Valley YMCA," in Camp Campbell, box 7, Boys' Work, YMCA.

68. Camper comments, file 29, box 2, Camp Riverdale, AM.

69. Unnamed 1885 camper, quoted in Clarence Philip Hammerstein, "The State Boys' Camps of the Young Men's Christian Association of North America (Treating the Origin, Development and Growth)" (graduating thesis, International YMCA College, Springfield, Massachusetts, 1917), appendix B.

70. "H.G.," *Goose Quills* 4, no. 4 (22 July 1917): 2, AB.

71. Hope Lord, Kehonka camp log (circa 1920s), AB.

72. Eugene L. Swan, in George Bird Grinnell and Eugene L. Swan, eds., *Harper's Camping and Scouting: An Outdoor Guide for American Boys* (New York: Harper and Bros., 1911), 266. There were earlier camp war games by the turn of the century, but nothing as elaborate or extensive. See, for example, "War" as played by the Milwaukee, Wisconsin, YMCA boys' camp. M. C. Otto, "A Boys' Game," *Association Men* 25, no. 8 (May 1900): 265.

73. See "The Chronicle," Schroon Lake Camp, 1920, 35–36, SLHM.

74. *New York Times*, 3 September 1926, 7.

75. In 1936, the Surprise Lake Camp CITs were told that the "modern" trend was away from "color weeks." "Surprise Lake Camp, Cold Spring, N.Y., Camp Counselors Training Course 1936," 25 July 1936, YMHA.

76. "Surprise Lake Camp, Cold Spring, N.Y., Camp Counselors Training Course 1935," 8 August 1935, YHMA.

77. *Kehonka*, 18 July 1911, AB.

78. Elizabeth Chisholm Abbott, *Remembering Woodcraft, by Campers and*

Councilors over 50 Years (Old Forge, N.Y.: Adirondack Woodcraft Camps, 1975), 26, AM.

79. *Goose Quills,* 20 July 1916, AB.

80. Ibid.

81. These figures are based on doctors' estimates of the physical ailments that they saw while screening for Fresh Air camps in the 1920s. Lloyd Burgess Sharp, *Education and the Summer Camp: An Experiment* (New York: Teachers College, 1930), 91.

82. "Report of Registration for Emanuel Sisterhood Summer Home 1935," in *Jewish Vacation Association, Report 1935–40,* 3, NYPL-DOR.

83. Lydia Stoopenkoff to author, 16 February 1998.

84. *New York Sun,* 17 July 1926, in Tapawingo/Wald materials, HSS.

85. Eugene L. Swan, "Organized Camp," in Grinnell and Swan, *Harper's Camping and Scouting,* 232.

86. *The Echo* 2 (July 1928), Echo Hill Farm, HSS.

87. On precautions against polio in the case of Schroon Lake, see Thomas Williford, "Tourism in the Adirondacks: Schroon Lake and the Jews" (unpublished manuscript, 1985), SLHM.

88. *New York Sun,* 17 July 1926, HSS.

89. L. W., quoted in Max Oppenheimer, "Report of the Work Done at Surprise Lake Camp during the Summer of 1930," in "S.L.C., Reports Summer Camp 1905–1938," YMHA.

90. Muriel Freeman to author, undated; "The Joys of Jeanne d'Arc," undated (1920s), JDA.

91. Schroon Lake Camp, for example, had a diet table as early as 1920. "Camp Chronicle," December 1920, SLHM. In 1936, a group of Rondack counselors sang, to the tune of "Shortnin' Bread," "All the Senior Campers Are Dietin'." "Rondacts 1936," SLHM.

92. Charlotte Gulick, quoted in Spalding's Athletic Library, *Camps and Camping* (1921), 47.

93. M. and A. to Miss Struble, 28 June 1917, folder 269.1, box 42, CU-CSSC.

94. Mitzi Alper (nee Brainin) to author, 23 July 1999; Lydia Stoopenkoff to author, 16 February 1998.

95. E.L. to author, 8 May 1998.

96. Diana Trilling, "The Girls of Camp Lenore," *New Yorker* 72 (12 August 1996): 61. On the history of girls and menstruation, see, for example, Joan J. Brumberg, *The Body Project: An Intimate History of American Girls* (New York: Random House, 1997), chs. 1 and 2.

97. Dick Bliss, transcript of recording made 3 August 1987, 7, TT.

98. "Campers Reports, 1938," Camp Lehman, YMHA.

99. "Surprise Lake Camp, Cold Spring, N.Y., Camp Counselors Training Course 1936," 12 July 1936, YMHA.

100. Adirondack Camp for Boys, 1906 camp brochure, Adirondack Camp for Boys, AM.

101. Bess Wilkofsky to author, 13 April 1998.

102. Sargent, *Handbook of Summer Camps* (1932), 25.

103. "Private Directions for Councillors," circa 1920s, folder 1, box 13, MRHS.

104. "Surprise Lake Camp Echoes, 1914–1934," 17 July 1921, 29 August 1923, and 12 July 1936, and "Surprise Lake Camp, Cold Spring, N.Y., Camp Counselors Training Course 1936," YMHA.

105. *Moonshiner,* 1 July 1920, POM.

106. Elwell, *The American Private Summer Camp,* 19–20.

107. *Che-Na-Wah Chat,* 1923, 15, in untitled scrapbook (1920s), CNW.

108. "Andree's Aids to Attractiveness," Camp Andree Reports 1935, GSUSA.

109. "Report of Dramatics Activities at Camp Andree—1935," GSUSA.

110. Camp Andree Reports 1929, GSUSA.

111. Ibid.

112. Girl Scouts' National Camp Committee in 1927, cited in "Then and Now, Comments by Madeline Murphy at National Camping Committee Luncheon, October 25, 1966," Camp and Camping—General, GSUSA.

113. As Rippin explained, of the ninety thousand proficiency badges awarded over the past year almost 40 percent had been awarded for homemaking. "Girl Scouts Continue to Win New Members," *New York Times,* 30 September 1928, in "Camp and Camping—General," GSUSA.

114. "Wanakena Camp at Pilot Knob Opens for the Season," *Lake George Mirror* 36, no. 3 (12 July 1919): 1. In the interwar years, when girls and boys met more regularly for camp dances, this prank (as well as all-girl dances) became less popular.

115. S. Sylvan Simon, author of *Camp Theatricals* (1934), specifically argued that boys should only play comic female roles, while describing girls as adept at playing boys and men. S. Sylvan Simon, *Camp Theatricals: Making Your Camp Entertainments More Effective* (New York: Samuel French, 1934), 68–69.

116. In 1940, for example, "Chief" Beckman dressed up as Madame Lazonga, "beautifully gowned in a flowing and diaphanous job." *Dudley Doings,* 24 July 1940, CD.

117. *Dudley Doings,* 15 July 1931, CD.

118. See, for example, Wilcox, "Organized Camping in New York State," 8.

119. Pasquaney Nature Club Diaries, Camp Pasquaney, Bristol, N.H., 1906–1915, vol. 3, 27 August 1914, NHHS. This camp was also known as Mrs. Hassan's Camp, after its founder, Laura Hassan.

120. Cited in Platt, "Asquam," 39–40.

NOTES TO CHAPTER 4

1. Marian Dudley, *Explorers: A Camp Project* (New York: Woman's Press, 1926), 3.

2. For early perspectives on YWCA camps of the 1920s, see Dudley, *Explorers*; Ruth Perkins, *Magic Casements: The Chronicle of the Development of a New Kind of Camp Program* (New York: Woman's Press, 1927); and Mary S. Sims, *The Natural History of a Social Institution—The Young Women's Christian Association* (New York: Woman's Press, 1936). According to Sims, there were 20,000 Girl Reserves in 1918, almost 80,000 in 1920, and 325,000 by 1934. Sims, *Natural History*, 65.

3. The Christian flag was likely a flag with a cross on it, like the "church" flag pictured in Henry W. Gibson, *Camp Management: A Manual on Organized Camping* (1923; rev. ed., New York: Greenberg, 1939), 206.

4. Essay in scrapbook, "Pinellas County, Girl Reserve Camp 1925 at Port Richey, Florida," box 219, YWCA.

5. On the interpersonal cues and social structures that define the parameters of any event's significance, see, for instance, Erving Goffman, *The Presentation of Self in Everyday Life* (Garden City, N.Y.: Doubleday/Anchor, 1959); Stuart Hall, *Resistance through Rituals: Youth Subculture in Post-War Britain* (London: Hutchinson, 1976); Pierre Bourdieu, *Outline of a Theory of Practice* (Cambridge: Cambridge University Press, 1977); and Pierre Bourdieu, *Distinction: A Social Critique of the Judgement of Taste* (Cambridge, Mass.: Harvard University Press, 1984).

6. "Pinellas County," YWCA. The names Amy, Susan, and Hazel are pseudonyms.

7. Erving Goffman, *Asylums: Essays on the Social Situation of Mental Patients and Other Inmates* (Garden City, N.Y.: Anchor Books, 1961). See also Jay Mechling, "Children's Folklore in Residential Institutions: Summer Camps, Boarding Schools, Hospitals, and Custodial Facilities," in Brian Sutton-Smith, Jay Mechling, Thomas W. Johnson, and Felicia R. McMahon, eds., *Children's Folklore: A Source Book* (New York: Garland, 1995), 273–291. Camps were far less coercive than the institutions discussed in Goffman's study.

8. William Steckel, quoted in Elizabeth Chisholm Abbott, ed., *Remembering Woodcraft, by Campers and Councilors over 50 Years* (Old Forge, N.Y.: Adirondack Woodcraft Camps, 1975), 49, AM; Charlotte Cohn (nee Goldstein), interview by author, 13 May 1999; camp log, 25 June 1939, "CAMP LOG, Rest-A-While Cottage, Cloudcroft, New Mexico, 1939," box 219, YWCA.

9. Dick D. to Willie, 10 March 1977, in "Memories: Tents to Cabins," CD.

10. Steckel, quoted in Abbott, *Remembering Woodcraft*, 49, AM.

11. E. C. to W. J. Schmidt, 19 January 1976, CD.

12. "Surprise Lake Camp Echoes, 1914–1934," 16 July 1927; "Surprise Lake Camp, Echoes, Oct. 1936, Sept. 1938," 1 September 1937, YMHA.

13. Songbook, Camp Severance scrapbook, AM.

14. Postcard, G. to R., postmarked 24 July 1936; letter, G. to Mother, undated; R. to Director, 25 July 1936, folder 78, YIVO.

15. C. to her son, July 1943, in Camper Reports, CD.

16. Harriet Silver to author, 10 July 1999.

17. "Surprise Lake Echoes, 1940–1942," 10 July 1941, YMHA.

18. L. to Mr. Kneff, 28 July 1941, folder 116, YIVO. The YIVO collection contains a good number of letters from homesick campers forwarded from parents to the camp director and subsequently retained, but the percentage of unhappy campers at Camp Boiberik was likely no higher than any other.

19. "Day Book, Permanents, 1940," in "Daily Programs 1940," YMHA.

20. "Surprise Lake Camp, 41st Season, Report, 1941," 2, 11, in Surprise Lake Reports, 1939–1943, YMHA.

21. J. to Mom, 19 July 1933, folder 65, YIVO.

22. Letter to Mr. Lehrer, 24 August 1933, folder 65, YIVO.

23. Orrell A. York, "A Study of Educational and Recreational Advantages of Boys' Summer Camps" (master's thesis, New York State College for Teachers, 1939), 31.

24. On mother blaming, see, for example, Nat Holman, "What I Think of Camping," *Camping World* 1, no. 1 (May 1935): 9.

25. Joseph Lieberman, *Creative Camping: A Coeducational Experiment in Personality Development and Social Living, Being the Record of Six Summers of the National Experimental Camp of Pioneer Youth of America* (New York: Association Press, 1931), 181.

26. Ibid., 189.

27. "Report—Season 1924 Permanent Division," in "Report of the Temporary Junior Division, Season of 1924," YMHA.

28. Letters to Bertha Gruenberg, 21 August 1930 and September 1929, in "CW: letters of appreciation, 1926–36," carton 2, SL. Numerous parents turned for guidance to *Parents* magazine, which instructed its mainly middle-class readership in the arts of this adjustment: making a graceful goodbye to one's children at home, writing often during the first week, staying away for at least two weeks (advice that assumed a full-season camp), and keeping one's children in camp when visiting. See "A Parent's Part in Camping," *Parents* 11, no. 6 (June 1936): 7.

29. Belle Lowenstein, *Camper and Hiker* 1, no. 3 (February 1928): 27, NYPL.

30. Cornelia Amster to parents, 14 July 1930, CNW.

31. Frank H. Cheley, "The Other Horn of the Dilemma," *Camping* 13, no. 3 (March 1941): 24.

32. M. to Gruenberg, 10 July 1942, and Z. to Gruenberg, 9 July 1934, in "CW: letters of appreciation, 1926–36," SL.

33. Cited in C. Mifflin Frothingham, ed., *The Story of Pasquaney, 1895–1960* (n.p.: Murphy and Snyder, 1960), 59.

34. Mitzi Alper (nee Brainin) to author, 23 June 1999.

35. "Surprise Lake Echoes, 1940–1942," 10 July 1941, YMHA.

36. *Camp Dudley, In Memoriam, no. 310, Herman C. "Chief" Beckman,* box "N," CD.

37. H. file, Camper Reports, CD.

38. "Day Book, Permanents, 1940," YMHA.

39. "Campers Reports, 1938," Camp Lehman, YMHA.

40. "Reports—First Period, 1939," Camp Lehman, YMHA.

41. Accounts of would-be runaways are numerous, particularly at camps serving working-class boys or those sent by the (well-intentioned) court system. "Surprise Lake Camp, Cold Spring, N.Y., Camp Counselors Training Course 1935," 8 August 1935, YMHA.

42. See "Health Report, Camp Andree, 1924," in Camp Andree Reports 1924, and "Health Report," Camp Andree Reports 1925, GSUSA.

43. Chocorua Chapel Association, *Reflections: Chocorua Island Chapel* (Trustees of the Chocorua Chapel Association, 1993), 8.

44. Henry W. Gibson, "Camps Durrell and Becket," *Association Boys* 5, no. 3 (June 1906): 116.

45. Arthur Walworth, *The Medomak Way: The Story of the First Fifty Years of an American Summer Camp for Boys* (Lancaster, N.H.: Bisbee, 1953), 22–23.

46. York, "Study of Educational," 16; Charlie Stanwood, quoted in Frothingham, *The Story of Pasquaney,* 108; "1920 Season," CD.

47. *Goose Quills,* 27 July 1916, AB.

48. *Goose Quills,* 22 July 1917, AB.

49. Camps' bedwetting policies varied. At some camps, children were required to hang their own wet sheets to dry in the morning. At others, counselors woke bedwetters (or, as some staff jokingly termed them, "marines") during the night and sent them outside to use the latrines. A few chronic bedwetters were sent home. At a laissez-faire camp, bedwetting could be ignored despite the smell of urine-stained sheets. Lydia Stoopenkoff to author, 26 November 1997 and 16 February 1998; "Taps Patrol Card—1940" and "1940 Reports Period III," Camp Lehman, YMHA; Don Poyourow, interview by author, 12 May 1999.

50. Sheldon Flory to author, 24 November 1997; Don Poyourow, interview by author, 12 May 1999.

51. Ruth Heller Steiner, interview by Dorothy Horowitz, 1981, 5, William E. Wiener Oral History Library of the American Jewish Committee, NYPL-DOR.

52. Albert M. Brown, *A Collection of Boys' Plays* (Boston: Walter H. Baker,

1933), 89–95. On the skit's presentation, see, for instance, "Surprise Lake Camp, Echoes, Oct. 1936, Sept. 1938," 31 August 1938, no. 4, YMHA.

53. "Tatler, 1935, Camp Lehman," September 1935, YMHA.

54. A more contemporary exploration of campers' interest in "taboo" bodily functions appears in Jay Mechling, *On My Honor: Boy Scouts and the Making of American Youth* (Chicago: University of Chicago Press, 2001). See also Randal Tillary, "Touring Arcadia: Elements of Discursive Simulation and Cultural Struggle at a Children's Summer Camp," *Cultural Anthropology* 7, no. 3 (August 1992): 374–388. In my own interviews of former campers, I often noted the enthusiasm with which pranks were recalled even sixty years later.

55. "Reflections on Chief Beckman: Dudleyites Reminisce," in "Reflections on Chief Beckman and background correspondence—1976," CD; Esther Wallace (nee Israeloff), interview by author, 4 February 1999.

56. Arnold Wagner, interview by author, 16 September 1998.

57. Letter from Marty to Willie, undated, in "Memories: Tents to Cabins," CD; "Che-Na-Wit 1929," 2 August 1929, in untitled scrapbook (1920s), CNW.

58. "Bee Ell See, August, 1918," 19, and "Bee Ell See, Mid-Winter Issue 1918–1919," 10, BLC.

59. Bob Noto, interview by author, 1 April 1999; L. M. to "Dad, Ma and Inez," 21 July 1926, folder "Dan Beard School, 1926," box 180, LOC-DBSC.

60. See, for example, the case study described in Charles Carson and Carl Rogers, "Intelligence as a Factor in a Camp Program," *Camping* 3, no. 3 (December 1930): 10.

61. E. C. Johnson, quoted in Frothingham, *Story of Pasquaney,* 75.

62. Bernard Mason, *Camping and Education* (New York: McCall, 1930), 33. On girls' social aggression, see, for example, Marion K. Underwood, *Social Aggression among Girls* (New York: Guilford, 2003).

63. C. to "Mrs. G.," 17 January 1944, folder 90, carton 2, SL. I have substituted initials for full names but retained original spelling and grammatical inconsistencies.

64. At Camp Dudley, for instance, one boy "smart-alecked" so much that the other boys in his cabin threatened to speak to "Chief" about removing him from the cabin. Another boy drew his campmates' scorn for his "incessant" and "inane" talking and his lack of athletic skill. P. and K., Dudley Camper Records, CD.

65. "Pinellas County," YWCA.

66. Letter, 17 October 1944, in "CW: Corresp. 1940–53," carton 2, SL.

67. "Pinellas County," YWCA.

68. Camp Severance Scrapbook, MS 86-8, AM.

69. "July 1943," in "1940, 1941, 1942 activities," carton 3, SL.

70. Eugene Agler to author, 25 November 1998.

71. "Taps Patrol Card—1940," 13 July 1940, YMHA.

72. See, for example, the case of a nurse fired for being "very submissive" with male staff, in Robert Rubin to Mr. Hesley, 1931, reel 61, box 52, CU-LW.

73. Edwin DeMerritte, cited in "The Camp Conference, Secretary's Report, 1905–6," 20–21, in "Early Years," Boys' Work, box 7, YMCA.

74. "Six Girls Fined for Breaking into Summer Camp Near Burlington, Vt.," *Camping* 4, no. 1 (October 1931): 4, reprint of *Boston Herald* article, 13 August 1931.

75. Esther Wallace (nee Israeloff), interview by author, 4 February 1999. At the coeducational Camp Treetops, camper Dick Bliss later recalled, "we boys all felt that there were all kinds of libidinous things going on at Treetops underground, between counselors and maybe there was at the time." Dick Bliss, transcript of recording made 3 August 1987, 5–6, TT.

76. "Pinellas County," YWCA.

77. Faye Feinstein, editorial, *Wo-Chi-Can*, 14 July 1938, in "Daily Wo-Chi-Can 1938," TM.

78. There is a significant literature on young women's and adolescent girls' sexual and social autonomy (and the limits of such autonomy) in late-nineteenth- and early-twentieth-century commercial culture. See, for instance, Paula S. Fass, *The Damned and the Beautiful: American Youth in the 1920s* (New York: Oxford University Press, 1977); Kathy Peiss, *Cheap Amusements: Working Women and Leisure in New York City, 1880–1920* (Philadelphia: Temple University Press, 1986); Joanne J. Meyerowitz, *Women Adrift: Independent Wage Earners in Chicago, 1880–1930* (Chicago: University of Chicago Press, 1988); Mary E. Odem, *Delinquent Daughters: Protecting and Policing Adolescent Female Sexuality in the United States, 1885–1920* (Chapel Hill: University of North Carolina Press, 1995); Ruth Alexander, *The "Girl Problem": Female Sexual Delinquency in New York, 1900–1930* (Ithaca, N.Y.: Cornell University Press, 1995).

79. *The Camp Directors Bulletin* l, no. 1 (February 1926): 3.

80. Some girls' camp leaders experimentally accepted a few younger boys, who had their own separate programs, then later decided on a strictly single-sex clientele. Directors of boys' camp never enrolled a few girls on the side. Some organizational camps served boys and girls, but often at different periods of the summer.

81. John Donald Gustav-Wrathall, *Take the Young Stranger by the Hand: Same-Sex Relations and the YMCA* (Chicago: University of Chicago Press, 1998), 130–139.

82. See, for example, John D'Emilio and Estelle B. Freedman, *Intimate Matters: A History of Sexuality in America* (New York: Harper and Row, 1988); Lillian Faderman, *Odd Girls and Twilight Lovers: A History of Lesbian Life in Twentieth-Century America* (New York: Columbia University Press, 1991); Pamela Haag, "In Search of 'the Real Thing': Ideologies of Love, Modern Romance

and Women's Sexual Subjectivity in the United States, 1920–1940," in John Fout and Maura Shaw Tantillo, eds., *American Sexual Politics: Sex, Gender, and Race since the Civil War* (Chicago: University of Chicago Press, 1993); Lisa Duggan, "The Trials of Alice Mitchell: Sensationalism, Sexology, and the Lesbian Subject in Turn-of-the-Century America," *Signs* 18 (summer 1993): 791–814; George Chauncey, *Gay New York: Gender, Urban Culture, and the Makings of the Gay Male World, 1890–1940* (New York: Basic Books, 1994).

83. "How Do Your Camp Girls Look?" *Camp Life* 1, no. 12 (1929): 27.

84. "Rosenfield's Kinacamps in the Colorado Rockies" (1931), 4, n.c. 10, NYPL-UNP.

85. Elizabeth Kemper Adams, "What Counsellors Should Know about the Tendencies and Attitudes of Girls in Camp," Spalding's Athletic Library (Eugene Lehman et al.), *Camps and Camping, for Information and Guidance of Campers, Parents, Directors and Counsellors* (New York: American Sports Publishing, 1926), 111.

86. Abbie Graham, *The Girls' Camp: Program-Making for Summer Leisure* (New York: Woman's Press, 1933), 70.

87. Libby Adelman (nee Raynes), interview by author, Camp Greylock, 28 June 1997.

88. Helen Amir (nee Weisgal) to author, 8 February 1998.

89. Court of Honor log, 4 July 1923, Camp Andree Reports 1923, GSUSA.

90. "Canoe Trip—1937," Camp Andree Reports 1937, GSUSA.

91. On boys' explorations of sexuality in other institutional contexts, see, for example, Sam Arcus, "Sex at and in HNOH," in Ira A. Greenberg, with Richard G. Safran and Sam George Arcus, eds., *The Hebrew National Orphan Home: Memories of Orphanage Life* (Westport, Conn.: Bergin and Garvey, 2001), 156–161.

92. "1st Period Reports, 1940," and "2nd Period Reports, 1940," Camp Lehman, YMHA. It is difficult to know whether boys' masturbatory culture became more public among early-twentieth-century campers or whether the practice was simply reported more often once counselors started keeping official records on each of the boys. Girls' sexual practices were probably more discreet, inasmuch as counselor records do not mention them.

93. Hedley S. Dimock and Charles E. Hendry, *Camping and Character: A Camp Experiment in Character Education* (1929; repr., New York: Association Press, 1947), 161.

94. In 1923, for example, the director of New York's Camp Lehman introduced boxing to camp in order to bring out "qualities which are dormant in a great many boys, but which are essential to the normal boy." "Normal" boys were heterosexual. "Camp Director's Report, 1923, Camp Lehman," Camp Lehman, YMHA.

95. Mothers sometimes appeared in boys' camp plays as overbearing and

overprotective shrews. Elmer Way, "When Mother Came to Camp," undated, "Plays and Entertainment," NCC.

96. See, for example, "Remembering summers on the lake at Camp Kanuka," ADE 10-1-94, general camp file, AM.

97. "Day Book, Permanents, 1940," in "Daily Programs 1940," YMHA.

98. Samuel E. Abbott, "Young Men's Christian Association Summer Camps for Boys" (graduating thesis, International YMCA Training School, Springfield, Massachusetts, 1904), 17. Henry Gibson argued similarly that "the alert director can spot a 'crooked' man." Henry W. Gibson, *Camp Management: A Manual on Organized Camping* (1923; rev. ed., New York: Greenberg, 1939), 8.

99. Adams, "What Counsellors Should Know," 111.

100. Margaret Rose Gladney, "Personalizing the Political, Politicizing the Personal: Reflections on Editing the Letters of Lillian Smith," in John Howard, ed., *Carryin' On in the Lesbian and Gay South* (New York: NYU Press, 1997), 93–103.

101. Letter to author, name withheld, 1997.

102. George Greenberg, interviewed by Muriel Cadel, 15 June 1987, side 2, 30–31, Wiener Oral History, NYPL-DOR. The boys' desire for Mrs. Sprung was not usually foremost on their minds: "Mostly we were talking about the hike that was going to go on tomorrow."

103. Almyr Ballentine, "Bally's Kehonka Beginnings," AB.

104. Rena Kunis to author, 23 November 1997 and 23 January 1998.

105. "Camp Guilford Bower, Director's Report, Season 1932," 304, and "Director's Report, Camp Guilford Bower, 1929," 88, both in book of minutes, 1928–1932, St. Philip's Church manuscript collection, box 37, NYPL-SCH.

106. D. L. to BG, 19 December 1929, folder "CW: letters of appreciation, 1926–36," SL. Camp Waziyatah was primarily a girls' camp, but the co-directors accepted some younger boys in the 1920s.

107. Helen Amir to author, 12 February 1998.

108. Irwin Silber to author, 31 January 1998.

109. "Report on Camps Visited during the Summer of 1923 by Louise M. Price, Secretary Camp Department," in folder "Camp and Camping, Advisory Staff, Visits to Camps Reports," in "Camps and Camping—General," GSUSA.

110. Smoking, an activity with adult and sexual connotations, was generally prohibited at girls' camps, but here again the repercussions were often benign, especially at private camps. Rose Schwartz, on the other hand, was asked to leave the institutional Camp Wehaha—and the HOA, which sponsored her camp—soon after she was found smoking. Her action marked her as old enough and rebellious enough to be out on her own, but perhaps more important, she did not possess the clout of girls whose parents had paid for their camp experiences. Libby Adelman, interview; Rose Schwartz, interviewed by Rose Miller, 18 January 1987, Wiener Oral History, NYPL-DOR, 22.

111. Laura Garrett, cited in *Camping* 1, no. 3 (September 1926): 3. On the twentieth-century history of sex education, see, for example, Jeffrey P. Moran, *Teaching Sex: The Shaping of Adolescence in the 20th Century* (Cambridge, Mass.: Harvard University Press, 2000); Julian B. Carter, "Birds, Bees, and Venereal Disease: Toward an Intellectual History of Sex Education," *Journal of the History of Sexuality* 10, no. 2 (2001): 213–249.

112. "Supplemental Report (A Contact with Wendy Girls)" and "Little Miss Echo," 7–20 August 1941, in "Echo Hill Farm Activities, Reports 1941 SWHA," HSS.

113. Helen Amir (nee Weisgal) to author, 8 February 1998.

114. *Blue Sparks,* August 1941, 2, JDA. The Senior Jeanne D'Arc girls were older than the oldest campers at the boys' camp, Camp Lafayette, and had thus been paired with the Lafayette counselors.

115. "The Chronicle," Schroon Lake Camp, 1934, SLHM.

116. "CAMP LOG, Rest-A-While Cottage."

117. Camp log, 1922, JDA.

118. "Che-Na-Wit," 7 August 1926, in untitled scrapbook (1920s), CNW.

119. "Che-Na-Wit," 31 August 1925, CNW.

120. *Mowglis Howl* 3 (1909): 27, NHHS.

NOTES TO CHAPTER 5

1. Cited in Minott A. Osborn, ed., *Camp Dudley: The Story of the First Fifty Years* (New York: Huntington, 1934), 117.

2. "A Brief History of Camp Dudley," in "Varied Histories," CD.

3. Eugene A. Turner Jr., *100 Years of YMCA Camping* (Chicago: YMCA of the USA, 1985), 181.

4. *Dudley Doings,* "Spring Number 1931," CD.

5. Louis Rouillion, "Summer Camps for Boys," in Albert Shaw, ed., *American Monthly Review of Reviews* 21 (January-June 1900): 700. Some early YMCA campers slept on cots, others on mattresses made of straw or grass. "Report of the Camp Conference," in "The Camp Conference," *How to Help Boys* 3, no. 3 (July 1903): 204–218.

6. "Camp Dudley 1913," Camp Dudley file, AM.

7. Dianne DeGroff, "Milk Train," *Adirondack Bits 'n Pieces* 1, no. 3 (Spring-Summer 1984), Camp Dudley, AM.

8. *Dudley Doings,* 2 July 1930, CD.

9. "Moss Lake Camp for Girls" (1931), NYSL.

10. Michael Kammen calls this symbiotic relationship "nostalgic modernism," arguing that modernism did not simply supplant an older traditionalist ethos; each informed the other, in a symbiotic relationship. Kammen, *Mystic Chords of Memory: The Transformation of Tradition in American Culture*

(New York: Knopf, 1991). On progress and nostalgia in the interwar years, see also Lawrence Levine, ed., *The Unpredictable Past: Explorations in American Cultural History* (New York: Oxford University Press, 1993), ch. 10.

11. *The Camp Directors Bulletin* 1, no. 1 (February 1926): 3.

12. Marty to Willie, in "Memories: Tents to Cabins," CD.

13. *Dudley Doings,* "Spring 1940," CD.

14. The first Camp Dudley cabins had no interior bathrooms or showers. G. to Willie, 16 February 1977, in "Memories: Tents to Cabins," CD.

15. Ernest B. Balch, "The First Camp—Camp Chocorua, 1881," in Porter E. Sargent, *A Handbook of Summer Camps* (Boston: P. Sargent, 1924), 40.

16. Henry W. Gibson, "The History of Organized Camping (Part II)," *Camping* 8, no. 2 (February 1936): 25–26.

17. "1931 Season," CD. Some campers were enrolled at a reduced fee.

18. "1935 Season," CD.

19. J. R. to Willie, 14 February 1977, in "Memories: Tents to Cabins," CD.

20. P. to Willie, 13 February 1977, "Memories: Tents to Cabins," CD.

21. M. to Willie, in "Memories: Tents to Cabins," CD.

22. P. to Willie, 13 February 1977, in "Memories: Tents to Cabins," CD.

23. M. to Willie, in "Memories: Tents to Cabins," CD.

24. Ibid.

25. P. to Willie, 13 February 1977, in "Memories: Tents to Cabins," CD.

26. Henry Wellington Wack, *Summer Camps, Boys and Girls* (New York: Red Book Magazine, 1923), 39.

27. M. to Willie, in "Memories: Tents to Cabins," CD.

28. "To Princeton–Camp Dudley Alumni, Parents and Friends," "1932 Season," CD.

29. Arthur T. Wilcox, "Organized Camping in New York State: A Study of Attendance, Facilities and Finance, Together with Suggestions for Meeting the Camping Needs of the State" (master's thesis, New York State College of Forestry, Syracuse University, 1941), 7, 88, 92.

30. Kaustine Company advertisement, *Camping* 3, no. 5 (February 1931): 17.

31. On the water problems particular to southern camps, see Henry Wellington Wack, *More about Summer Camps, Training for Leisure* (New York: Red Book Magazine, 1926), 47. Northern camps also made substantial alterations to the landscape, dredging lakes and importing sand for their beaches. See, for example, "A Girl Scouts' Eden at Camp Andree Clark," *The World Magazine,* 17 July 1921, in Camp and Camping—Camp Andree Clark—Magazine/Newspaper articles, GSUSA.

32. George L. Meylan, "Luxuries in a Boy's Camp," in Spalding's Athletic Library (Eugene Lehman et al.), *Camps and Camping, for Information and Guidance of Campers, Parents, Directors and Counsellors* (New York: American Sports Publishing, 1922), 111 (published annually; hereafter cited by date only).

33. "Camp Riverdale in the Adirondacks" (1932), Camp Riverdale, AM.

34. Hackett, cited in *Camping* 4, no. 4 (January 1932): 10–11.

35. *Camp Riverdale Stag and Eagle* 4, no. 1 (24 July 1940), file 19, box 2, Camp Riverdale MS 70-12, AM.

36. On the history of early cinema and its audiences, see, for instance, Robert Sklar, *Movie-Made America: A Cultural History of American Movies* (New York: Vintage Books, 1976); Lary May, *Screening Out the Past: The Birth of Mass Culture and the Motion Picture Industry* (New York: Oxford University Press, 1980); Miriam Hansen, *Babel and Babylon: Spectatorship in American Silent Film* (Cambridge, Mass.: Harvard University Press, 1991); Lizabeth Cohen, *Making a New Deal: Industrial Workers in Chicago, 1919–1939* (New York: Cambridge University Press, 1990), ch. 3.

37. Eunice Fuller Barnard, "Young America Is Off to Summer Camp," *New York Times,* 29 June 1930, sec. 5, p. 14.

38. A. E. Hamilton, *Trailwise* (Columbus, Ohio: Outing Press, 1924), n.c. 5, NYPL-UNP.

39. Louis Fleisher, "Soft and Undisciplined," *Camping World* 7, no. 5 (May 1941): 10.

40. Bernard J. Fagan, "Safeguarding Children's Leisure," *Child Study* 7, no. 3 (December 1929): 70.

41. Reformers' anxieties were directed particularly toward immigrant and working-class children. For a perspective on the topic from the time, see Alice Miller Mitchell, *Children and Movies* (Chicago: University of Chicago Press, 1929). See also Lea Jacobs, "Reformers and Spectators: The Film Education Movement in the Thirties," *Camera Obscura* 22 (January 1990): 28–49; and Richard deCordova, "Ethnography and Exhibition: The Child Audience, the Hays Office and Saturday Matinees," *Camera Obscura* 23 (May 1991): 90–107.

42. John Lodge, interview by author, Camp Dudley, 24 August 1997.

43. For examples of audience responsiveness, see *Che-Na-Wah Chat,* 1923, 16, CNW; Dudley *Doings,* 4 August 1926, CD; *Idlewood Leaf* 12, no. 9 (14 July 1930), Camp Idylwood, AM.

44. "All Councillors' Meeting, Aug. 3, 1928," in Camp Andree Reports 1928, and Camp Andree Reports 1938, GSUSA.

45. See Camper Reports, CD.

46. "Surprise Lake Echoes, 1940–1942," 3 September 1942, YMHA.

47. "Memorandum of conference with Middlers about funnies," 14 August 1940, file 29, box 2, Camp Riverdale, AM.

48. Henry Levy, "Movies at Camp," *Camp Life* 2, no. 6 (June 1930).

49. "The Idylwold Leaf" (1937), 45, SLHM.

50. *Camp Life* 1, no. 2 (February 1931): 23.

51. See, for example, "Camp America for Girls" (1922), n.c. 1, NYPL-UNP;

"Camp Mystic," 1930, n.c. 10, NYPL-UNP; "Daily Programs 1940," 17 July 1940, Surprise Lake Camp, YMHA.

52. *Camp Riverdale Stag and Eagle* 4, no. 3 (28 August 1940), box 2, file 19, Camp Riverdale, AM.

53. For an example of a film-rental program, see advertisement for Willoughbys, *Camp Life* 4, no. 7 (December 1932): 24.

54. On electricity at Camp Dudley, see *Dudley Doings,* 21 July 1926, and *Dudley Doings,* 2 August 1933, CD.

55. Hansen, *Babel and Babylon,* 100.

56. "The Idylwold Leaf" (1937), 45, SLHM; Alan Hewitt to his parents, 6 July 1933, "Theater 1917–1940s," BLC.

57. "Surprise Lake Echoes, 1938–1940," 25 July 1940, YMHA.

58. *WoHeLo, A Magazine for Girls* 2, no. 11 (May 1915): 15.

59. See Arthur Gale, "Amateur Camp Movies," *Camp Life* 4, no. 4 (May 1932): 34; and "Movies," *Camping World* 1, no. 1 (May 1935): 14, 31.

60. Camp Riverdale reunion brochure, 1927, file 5, box 1, and "Camp Riverdale Bulletin, February 28, 1939," file 14, box 1, Camp Riverdale, AM.

61. See, for example, Moss Lake and Cedar Lake films, AM.

62. By 1932, Arthur Gale called this genre "rather overdone in all types of movies, and it is perhaps better to select some other approach." Gale, "Amateur Camp Movies," 5.

63. For example, see "Golden Jubilee Banquet, Camp Dudley," in "1935 Season," and "The Camp Dudley Movies, Edition 1937–1938," in "1938 Season," CD.

64. "A Gift from the Girl Scouts to Our Boys in Service," *Rally,* November 1918, 8, GSUSA. By October 1926, footage of Camp Calemaco, the Manhattan Girl Scout camp, had been shown in twenty-four states to over fifty thousand viewers. "Minutes of the Hendrick Hudson Regional Conference, Newark, New Jersey, October 15–17, 1926," Regions—Region II (Hendrick Hudson)—Conferences 1924–1934, GSUSA. On Camp Calemaco, see "Camping with Girl Scouts," *Rally,* July 1918, 2, 12, GSUSA.

65. Elin Lindberg, "Bloomer Girls to Blue Jeans," *American Girl,* March 1954, 58, GSUSA.

66. Lewis's role in this scene served to reinforce the organization's policy of adventure under adult supervision. Many amateur camp filmmakers made sure that counselors appeared, since parents liked to see them there. Alfred Kamm, "Camp Movies for Publicity," *Camping World* 7, no. 4 (April 1941): 13.

67. In the second half of the film, Margaret and her friends are shown back in their hometown, demonstrating a more domestic side of Scouting by coming to the aid of a family whose father is a soldier and whose mother must work. The film ends when Margaret, having won twenty-one merit badges, is awarded

the Golden Eaglet by Low. The only extant version of *The Golden Eaglet* has been adapted from the forty-minute, two-reel original length to its present length of twenty minutes. All scenes featuring the African American cook, Fannie, described in 1918 as "one of the most popular members of the Camp," have been eliminated; most likely, Fannie's portrayal, however "glowing" it appeared to its writer at the time, later came to seem offensive and inappropriate for an interracial girls' organization. See "A Gift from the Girl Scouts," 9.

68. "A Gift from the Girl Scouts," 8–9.

69. "New York Needs More Like Her" (1931), Council History—New York —Greater New York Scout Council, GSUSA.

70. Harold Le Maistre, "Movie Photography in Camp Promotion," *Camping* 12, no. 10 (October 1940): 20.

71. Gale, "Amateur Camp Movies," 3–4. See also "Movies" (*Camping World*), 14, 31; William Abbott, "Advertising, Solicitation and Enrollment," *Camping* 12, no. 7 (October 1940): 7; and Kamm, "Camp Movies for Publicity," 12. For examples of settlement-house and charitable camp films, see S. S. Keyser to Mrs. Frederick Vanderbilt, 23 February 1923, folder 269.5b, box 42, CU-CSSC; Karl Hesley to Mr. Rubin, 29 August 1932, reel 61, box 52, CU-LW.

72. "Adirondack Woodcraft Camps, A Summer Camp for Boys" (1927), AWC.

73. Walter Buehler, in Elizabeth Chisholm Abbott, ed., *Remembering Woodcraft, by Campers and Councilors over 50 Years* (Old Forge, N.Y.: Adirondack Woodcraft Camps, 1975), 50, AM.

74. "Adirondack Woodcraft Camps, A Summer Camp for Boys."

75. On "virgin land" in American myth, see, for example, the three generations of scholarship represented by Frederick Jackson Turner, "The Significance of the Frontier in American History," in *Annual Report of the American Historical Association for the Year 1893* (Washington, D.C.: Government Printing Office, 1894), 199–227; Henry Nash Smith, *Virgin Land: The American West as Symbol and Myth* (Cambridge, Mass.: Harvard University Press, 1950); and Richard Slotkin, *The Fatal Environment: The Myth of the Frontier in the Age of Industrialization, 1800–1890* (New York: Atheneum, 1985).

76. See, for instance, Kehonka camp log, 12 August 1926, AB.

77. *Goose Quills,* 7 August 1911, and 15 July 1916, AB. Camp Winnipesaukee was also known as Pierson's, after its owner.

78. See for instance, "The Bee-Ell-See 1925," 71, BLC; and "Che-Na-Wit," 30 August 1928, CNW.

79. For example, P. B. to Daniel Beard, 23 July 1921, box 166, LOC-DBSC.

80. Laura I. Mattoon, "Campers' Ethics," in Spalding's Athletic Library, *Camps and Camping* (1921), 25; letter from Burt Leon Yorke to Laura Mattoon, AB.

81. Lenore Hershey, interview by Women's Volunteer Corps, 1 March 1982,

1–9/10, William E. Wiener Oral History Library of the American Jewish Committee, NYPL-DOR; "Camp Director's Report, 1927, Camp Lehman," and "Camp Lehman—data—1935 (2 of 2)," YMHA.

82. See, for example, State Planning and Development Commission, "Resort Business in the Lakes Region, Part I—Boys' and Girls' Camps" (Concord, N.H.: State Planning and Development Commission, 1945), 12, 14, NHSL.

83. Turner, *100 Years*, 85.

84. Hershey interview; and "SLC—History—by Goldwasser," YMHA.

85. Turner, *100 Years*, 197–198.

86. "Petition to the Commissioners of the Palisades Interstate Park, Thursday, Sept. 4, 1930," Jacob Riis Settlement House collection, box 12, folder 3, "Summer Camps, 1915–36," NYPL-MAD.

87. Nathan Jaspen, interview by Muriel Meyers, 20 September 1988, William E. Wiener Oral History Library, NYPL-DOR.

88. "Hudson District Report for the Summer of 1910," in "Fresh Air Fund," box 126, CU-CSSC.

89. "The Camp Conference, Secretary's Report, 1905–6," 43–44, in "Early Years," Boys' Work, box 7, YMCA.

90. *Camp Riverdale Stag and Eagle* 2, no. 4 (25 August 1938), file 20, box 2, Camp Riverdale, AM.

91. Edward M. Cameron, quoted in *Those Elysian Fields: Camp Pok-O'-Moonshine's First Fifty Years*, 10, POM.

NOTES TO CHAPTER 6

1. "Song from the Minstrel Show," undated, box 14, folder 3, MRHS.

2. "Camp Mystic" (1921), n.c. 1, NYPL-UNP.

3. "Camp Mystic" (1920) and "Camp Mystic, a Summer Training Camp for Girls on the Sound at Mystic, Connecticut" (1922), box 11, MRHS.

4. Jobe, an Ohio native, graduated from Scio College and Bryn Mawr before completing a master's degree in history and English at Columbia University. She mapped previously uncharted regions of British Columbia, visited remote Inuit and aboriginal tribes of the Northwest and Southwest, and was elected to the Royal Geographical Society in 1915, two years after the organization first opened its doors to women. On her trips to Africa, see Mary Jobe Akeley, "My Experiences in Africa," *Camping* 2, no. 7 (April 1930): 13–15, 24; and Mary Jobe Akeley, *Carl Akeley's Africa* (New York: Dodd, Mead, 1929). Jobe is mentioned in passing by Donna Haraway in *Primate Visions: Gender, Race, and Nature in the World of Modern Science* (New York: Routledge, 1989), 26–58, and in some detail in Dorcas S. Miller, *Adventurous Women: The Inspiring Lives of Nine Early Outdoorswomen* (Boulder, Colo.: Pruett, 2000), 134–141.

5. Miller, *Adventurous Women*, 140.

6. "Recollections of a councillor at Camp Mystic 19—Ruth Newcomb," box 12, folder 8, MRHS.

7. Akeley, "My Experiences in Africa," 14. It is unclear whether the lion was entirely preserved through taxidermy or whether its pelt alone was displayed at camp.

8. When it comes to summer camps, scholars have long acknowledged an Indian fetish but have yet to excavate the uses of blackness at camps patronized by white campers; meanwhile, most scholarship on racial minstrelsy has focused exclusively on blackness. On the centrality of Indian minstrelsy to American self-definition, see, for example, Robert F. Berkhofer Jr., *The White Man's Indian: Images of the American Indian from Columbus to the Present* (New York: Vintage Books, 1979); S. Elizabeth Bird, ed., *Dressing in Feathers: The Construction of the Indian in American Popular Culture* (Boulder, Colo.: Westview, 1996); and Philip J. Deloria, *Playing Indian* (New Haven, Conn.: Yale University Press, 1998). The term "playing Indian" was first popularized by Ernest Thompson Seton in *The Red Book; or, How to Play Indian* (self-published, 1904). Scholars who have explored the term include Jay Mechling, " 'Playing Indian' and the Search for Authenticity in Modern White America," *Prospects* 5 (1980): 17–33; and Rayna Green, "The Tribe Called Wannabee: Playing Indian in America and Europe," *Folklore* 99, no. 1 (1988): 30–55.

9. "Camp Mystic" (1930), n.c. 10, NYPL-UNP.

10. "Camp Mystic" (1921), n.c. 1, NYPL-UNP.

11. On world's fairs, see Robert W. Rydell, *All the World's a Fair: Visions of Empire at American International Expositions, 1876–1916* (Chicago: University of Chicago Press, 1984). On Wild West shows of the late nineteenth and early twentieth centuries, see Richard Slotkin, *The Fatal Environment: The Myth of the Frontier in the Age of Industrialization, 1800–1890* (Middletown, Conn.: Wesleyan University Press, 1986); Richard Slotkin, *Gunfighter Nation: The Myth of the Frontier in Twentieth-Century America* (New York: Atheneum, 1992); and Jonathan Martin, " 'The Grandest and Most Cosmopolitan Object Teacher': *Buffalo Bill's Wild West* and the Politics of American Identity, 1883–1899," *Radical History Review* 66 (1996): 92–123.

12. There are numerous recorded instances of white campers calling other white campers "nigger," whether in play, as a nickname, or as a form of harassment. See, for example, *Dudley Doings*, 1 September 1925, CD.

13. Winthrop T. Talbot, "Summer Camping for Boys," *American Physical Education Review* 4 (March 1899): 33.

14. George Matthew Adams, "Today's Talk," 1927 season file, CD.

15. "The Camping Trip of 1914" (anon.), in "Lowello 1913," "Meeting Record Book, 1913," Camp Fire Girls of Central Indiana Records, 1913–1988, IHS.

16. *Dudley Doings*, 8 July 1920, CD.

17. See, for example, letter to Col. Ned Arden Flood, 10 August 1932, folder 269.1, box 42, CU-CSSC.

18. *Dudley Doings,* "Spring Number 1933," CD.

19. "Annual Report, 1924," in "Publications—A's, Annual Reports 1915–1935," GSUSA.

20. "Camp Mystic" (1930), n.c. 10, NYPL-UNP.

21. "Private directions for councillors" (circa 1920), folder 1, box 13, MRHS.

22. Boys' camps appear to have been somewhat more likely than girls' camps to put on minstrel shows, although the genre was popular at camps for both sexes.

23. *The Mystifier* 1, no. 1 (January 1919): 5, folder 4, box 14, MRHS. One performer is described as having appeared "under her heavy disguise of brown paint and feathers."

24. "Coon" was a common derogatory term used to describe black Americans. *Dudley Doings,* 3 July 1919, CD.

25. "Camp Chronicle," 11, no. 3 (December 1918): 13, SLHM.

26. Eric Lott makes this argument in *Love and Theft: Blackface Minstrelsy and the American Working Class* (New York: Oxford University Press, 1993). Other important sources on blackface minstrelsy include David Roediger, *The Wages of Whiteness: Race and the Making of the American Working Class* (London: Verso, 1991); Mel Watkins, *On the Real Side: Laughing, Lying, and Signifying—The Underground Tradition of African-American Humor That Transformed American Culture, from Slavery to Richard Pryor* (New York: Simon and Schuster, 1994); Michael Rogin, *Blackface, White Noise: Jewish Immigrants in the Hollywood Melting Pot* (Berkeley: University of California Press, 1996).

27. Estelle Nemeth, interview by author, 31 October 1998. On the history of the Hebrew Orphan Asylum, see Hyman Bogen, *The Luckiest Orphans: A History of the Hebrew Orphan Asylum of New York* (Urbana: University of Illinois Press, 1992). A brief description of the HOA camps appears in Lionel T. Simmonds, "Wakitan and Wehaha," *Camp News* 2, no. 2 (August 1927): 14–15.

28. Hyman Bogen, "Chapter Nine: The Place without Gates" (unpublished manuscript), 5. As Bogen relates, the infamous Indian Trail near Camp Wakitan was not a relic of old tribal pathways; it had been cleared by park rangers as a shortcut to Lake Stahahe in order to make the park more accessible to groups of campers. The boys quickly "became" Indians by association: Iroquois, Pequots, Sioux, Mohawks, Mohicans, Algonquins, Senecas, and Tuscaroras (this last group was nicknamed the Husky Snorers).

29. Minott A. Osborn, ed., *Camp Dudley: The Story of the First Fifty Years* (New York: Huntington, 1934), 90.

30. On the history of American historical pageants, see David Glassberg, *American Historical Pageantry: The Uses of Tradition in the Early Twentieth Century* (Chapel Hill: University of North Carolina Press, 1990); Naima Prevots,

328 | Notes to Chapter 6

American Pageantry: A Movement for Art and Democracy (Ann Arbor, Mich.: UMI Research Press, 1990); Ilana Abromovitch, "America's Making Exposition and Festival (New York, 1921): Immigrant Gifts on the Altar of America" (Ph.D. diss., New York University, 1996). Pageants were popular from the 1910s through the 1930s. Prevots, *American Pageantry*, 9, argues that pageants' decline in the 1920s corresponded to the moment that they became a staple of elementary school programing. At camp, the genre had a much longer life.

31. Elizabeth Knox, "Dear Old Camp Mystic," *Good Old Days* (August 1976), 30, folder 8, box 12, MRHS.

32. Irwin Silber to author, 31 January 1998.

33. For example, boys at the East Side House camps "played Indian" while the girls played croquet and participated in dramatics. "Thirty-fourth Annual Report of the East Side House, 76th Street and East River, New York City, for the Year Ending December 31, 1925," in "Annual Reports 1925–26," box 13, Series III—Board of Managers, CU-ESH.

34. Camp Ticonderoga brochure (1928), Camp Ticonderoga file, AM.

35. Philip Deloria argues that girls' organizations naturally drew more extensively on Indian imagery than did those for boys; Indians and women, after all, had long been symbolically intertwined as lesser citizens. Deloria, *Playing Indian*, 111. My research suggests that this pattern was not true of camps.

36. The "Fairy Program" put on by the Camp Andree girls in 1930 was typical of the genre. Blending dances, music, and the spoken word, it posited not a cross-racial adventure but rather a passive, explicitly white prettiness: "Men call me Birch Tree, yet I know / In other days it was not so. / I am a Dryad slim and white / Who danced too long one summer night / And the Dawn found and imprisoned me! / Captive I moan my liberty." "Reports of Special Activities at Camp Andree for 1930 by the Camp Staff," 70, in Camp and Camping—Camp Andree Clark—Reports—1921–1933, GSUSA.

37. Porter E. Sargent, *Handbook of Summer Camps* (Boston: P. Sargent, 1932), 56 (published annually; hereafter cited by date only).

38. Robert Pfaff, cited in Elizabeth Chisholm Abbott, ed., *Remembering Woodcraft, by Campers and Councilors over 50 Years* (Old Forge, N.Y.: Adirondack Woodcraft Camps, 1975), 30, AM.

39. On "cocoa-dipped" campers, see *Dudley Doings,* 25 July 1924, CD.

40. As amateur performance spaces, camps are distinct from the commercial venues that have captured most scholarly attention and that have led most historians of minstrelsy to maintain that the genre declined in the interwar years (while noting that blackface persisted in theater, film, and music even as its debasing stereotypes came under attack). However, Mel Watkins notes that in the mainstream popular culture of the 1920s, minstrel joke books abounded, Sambo routines and gags were extremely popular, and popular magazines commonly printed racial humor. Watkins, *On the Real Side,* 206–207. Summer re-

sorts continued to showcase amateur minstrel shows and cross-racial masquerades. See, for example, *Lake George Mirror* 36, no. 7 (9 August 1919): 9, AM.

41. Ernest Balch, former director of Camp Chocorua, enthusiastically endorsed the minstrel show in *Amateur Circus Life: A New Method of Physical Development for Boys and Girls* (1916; repr., New York: Macmillan, 1924), describing it as "a delightful entertainment. . . . the combination of lovely music and good old time-tested jokes made many people happy" (107). It is unclear whether he put on minstrel shows with the boys of Chocorua. Other mainstream interwar endorsements of minstrelsy include "Turn Pennies into Dollars," *American Girl* 13, no. 1 (January 1930): 29, GSUSA; Mari Ruef Hofer, *Camp Recreations and Pageants* (New York: Association Press, 1927); and Henry W. Gibson, *Recreational Programs for Summer Camps* (New York: Greenberg, 1938), 272–279.

42. See *Dixie Echoes* 1, no. 1 (3 July 1920), in "Camp Dixie for Girls," 36, and "Camp Dixie for Boys," 25, both in "Youth Summer Camp" box, LOC.

43. Bogen, "Chapter Nine," 24.

44. Playground and Recreation Association of America's Community Service, "Dramatics in Camp," undated (interwar years), in "Plays and Entertainment," NCC.

45. "Guide to Tams-Witmark Service" (circa late 1920s), in "Plays and Entertainment," NCC.

46. Herbert Preston Powell, *The World's Best Book of Minstrelsy* (Philadelphia: Penn Publishing, 1926), 55.

47. "Surprise Lake Camp Echoes, 1914–1934," 4 August 1922, YMHA.

48. *Dudley Doings,* 28 July 1921, CD.

49. "Surprise Lake Camp, 40th Season, Report, 1940," in "Surprise Lake Reports, 1939–1943," YMHA.

50. "Surprise Lake Camp Echoes, 1914–1934," 18 August 1922, YMHA.

51. In 1923, for instance, the Surprise Lake boys put on a minstrel show in the town of Cold Spring to benefit the local Fire Engine Fund. "SLC—History —by Goldwasser," YMHA.

52. The HOA stood at 138th Street and Amsterdam Avenue. On racial tensions for HOA boys, see George Greenberg, interview by Muriel Cadel, 15 June 1987, 56, Wiener Oral History, NYPL-DOR.

53. Hyman Bogen, interview by Mildred Finger, 1 April 1986, 14, Wiener Oral History, NYPL-DOR.

54. *Abnaki Herald,* 26 August 1918, NYPL. Similar sketches were performed at Camp Dudley. *Dudley Doings,* 2 September 1920, CD. On the public performance of Jewishness by non-Jews, see Harley Erdman, *Staging the Jew: The Performance of an American Ethnicity, 1860–1920* (New Brunswick, N.J.: Rutgers University Press, 1997).

55. "The Chronicle," 1926, 42, SLHM. Commercial versions of this material

included the 1930 Playcrafters' Guide, whose "stunts, short acts and novelties for the school and camp" included the Jewish-themed "Oi, Vhat a Bargain" and the Italian "Just-a Lak-a Dat." Playcrafters' Guide, 1930, "Plays and Entertainment," NCC; S. Sylvan Simon, *Camp Theatricals: Making Your Camp Entertainments More Effective* (New York: Samuel French, 1934).

56. On the grotesque Other, see Peter Stallybrass and Allon White, *The Politics and Poetics of Transgression* (Ithaca, N.Y.: Cornell University Press, 1986), ch. 1.

57. In the mid-nineteenth century, Henry Wadsworth Longfellow's epic 1855 poem "Hiawatha" inspired a cult of Iroquoian/Algonquian (northeastern and Great Lakes) nostalgia among white Americans. The fictional Hiawatha, raised among the Ojibway on Lake Superior, was a champion of his people who prophesized the coming of the Europeans and encouraged his people to heed the new religion. He represented spiritual leadership but was no threat to white dominance. Rayna Green, "The Tribe Called Wannabee," 38, argues that later white interest in the Sioux reflected fascination with a more confrontational style of Indianness. As Raymond Wilson notes, the reputation of Native American activist and writer Charles Eastman also foregrounded Sioux iconography. Raymond Wilson, *Ohiyeha: Charles Eastman, Santee Sioux* (Urbana: University of Illinois Press, 1983).

58. Bernard Mason, "Totem Poles—Big Medicine for Summer Camps," in Spalding's Athletic Library (Eugene Lehman et al.), *Camps and Camping, for the Information and Guidance of Campers, Parents, Directors and Counsellors* (New York: American Sports Publishing, 1926), 25 (published annually; hereafter cited by date only).

59. Spalding's Athletic Library, *Camps and Camping* (1923), 161.

60. See "Adirondack Woodcraft Camps" (1937), Adirondack Woodcraft Camp, AM; and "Brant Lake Camp" (1934), BLC.

61. On the Camp Mystic Indian Masque, see "Camp Mystic 1916," folder 2, box 14, and *The Mystifier* 1, no. 1 (January 1919): 5, folder 4, box 14, MRHS.

62. Sargent, *Handbook of Summer Camps* (1930), 27–28.

63. Sargent, *Handbook of Summer Camps* (1935), 37.

64. *The Anniversary Book of Saint Philip's Church* (New York, 1943), 47–48, NYPL-SCH.

65. "The Burning Logue," June 24–July 15 (circa 1941–42), in scrapbook, "YWCA GR," box 219, YWCA.

66. Introduction, the Writers and Material Committee of Camp Shows, Inc., *Minstrel Shows with Music, Being* "AT EASE" *Volume II.* (USO—Camp Shows, Inc., 1942).

67. See, for example, "The Chronicle," Schroon Lake Camp, 1930, SLHM.

68. *Dudley Doings*, 25 July 1934, CD.

69. Michael Rogin makes this point in "Making America Home: Racial Mas-

querade and Ethnic Assimilation in the Transition to Talking Pictures," *Journal of American History* 79, no. 3 (December 1992): 105–153.

70. Ann Douglas, *Terrible Honesty: Mongrel Manhattan in the 1920s* (New York: Farrar, Straus, and Giroux, 1995), 73. Not all of these migrants came from the South; a smaller number arrived from the Caribbean as well.

71. See Frederick E. Hoxie, *A Final Promise: The Campaign to Assimilate the Indians, 1880–1920* (Lincoln: University of Nebraska Press, 1984).

72. On the political activism of the Society of American Indians (SAI), see Frederick E. Hoxie, "Exploring a Cultural Borderland: Native American Journeys of Discovery in the Early Twentieth Century," *Journal of American History* 79, no. 3 (December 1992): 969–995. In 1924, Congress passed the Indian Citizenship Act, which gave many Indians the right to vote while still excluding those who were living on untaxed reservations or who were not deemed legally competent to manage their own land.

73. Bess Wilkofsky (nee Satz) to author, 4 March 1998.

74. David S. Keiser, "An 1876 Summer Camp," in Sargent, *Handbook of Summer Camps* (1929), 15.

75. *Camp Dudley Records* 1, no. 2 (April 1894), CD.

76. *Those Elysian Fields: Camp Pok-O'-Moonshine's First Fifty Years,* 12, POM.

77. Bogen, "Chapter Nine," 24.

78. Manabozho of Brooklyn to DCB, National Scout Commissioner, 7 March 1927, and Manabozho of Brooklyn to DCB, 23 October 1927, folder—"Dan Beard School, 1927," box 181, LOC-DBSC.

79. *Where to Buy Everything for Summer Camps: A Select List of Firms Specializing in Supplying and Serving Summer Camps* (1931), 775, NYPL.

80. Rev. William Brewster Humphrey, "American Indians as Counselors in Summer Camps," *Camping* 3, no. 1 (October 1930): 12–14.

81. On NYA counselor training, see Ellsworth Jaeger, *The Indian Counselor Handbook* (Buffalo: National Youth Administration, State of New York, 1938).

82. *Camping World* 5, no. 3 (March 1939): 15–16.

83. Vernon Clute, the popular Seneca counselor in charge of Indian lore at Surprise Lake Camp in 1937 and 1938, attended the School of Forestry at Syracuse University. See *Surprise Lake Camp Echoes,* 14 July 1938, no. 1, in "Surprise Lake Camp, Echoes, Oct. 1936, Sept. 1938," YMHA. Camp Henry's "full-blooded Seneca," Roland Sundown, was a Dartmouth College student. Letter, Karl Hesley to Robert Howard, 3 March 1932, reel 61, box 51, CU-LW.

84. Bogen, "Chapter Nine," 13–14. Wakitan camp director "Pop" Sprung had friends within the Onandaga community; most of Wakitan's Indian counselors came from upstate reservations, although a few came from western states.

85. Humphrey, "American Indians as Counselors," 14.

86. Bogen, "Chapter Nine," 13.

87. Deloria, *Playing Indian*, 125.

88. "Surprise Lake Camp, Echoes, Oct. 1936, Sept. 1938," 28 July 1938, YMHA.

89. "Surprise Lake Camp, Echoes, Oct. 1936, Sept. 1938," 11 August 1938, YMHA.

90. Tellingly, Jacoby included Indians in a larger discussion of the impact of "foreign" students in his camp. Raymond I. Jacoby, "Foreign Students as Guests in Summer Camps," *Camping* 5, no. 3 (January 1933): 5.

91. Humphrey, "American Indians as Counselors," 14.

92. Wilson, *Ohiyeha*, 24.

93. The Adirondack Camp, for example, hosted Seton in 1910, Daniel Beard in 1911, and Ohiyesa in 1912. "Adirondack Camp for Boys" (1913), 20, n.c. 2, NYPL-UNP.

94. "Pine Island Camp" (1916), n.c. 4, NYPL-UNP.

95. At the end of the 1918 camp season, several members of the camp, including Eastman's daughter Irene, sickened and died during a virulent influenza epidemic. After this misfortune, few campers returned for the 1919 season. The camp's fate was sealed when Eastman left his marriage, and his camp, in the summer of 1921. Wilson, *Ohiyesa*, 151, 163; and Karin Luisa Badt, *Charles Eastman: Sioux Physician and Author* (New York: Chelsea House, 1995), 109.

96. *Dudley Doings*, 16 August 1933, CD.

97. See, for example, Long Lake Sports and Band Concert, 3 August 1929, in "binder—1929, 1930," box 5, Camp Riverdale, MS 70-12, AM.

98. The tours included Camp Dudley. *Dudley Doings*, 7 August 1919, and "1937 Season," CD.

99. *Dudley Doings*, 2 August 1933.

100. Raymond Wolters, *The New Negro on Campus: Black College Rebellions of the 1920s* (Princeton, N.J.: Princeton University Press, 1975).

101. Irwin Silber to author, 31 January 1998 and 4 February 1998.

102. Visitation report to El Paso by Bertha Eckert, September 1935, reel 215.6, YWCA.

103. "CAMP LOG, Rest-A-While Cottage, Cloudcroft, New Mexico, 1939," box 219, YWCA.

104. "Young Men's Christian Association (YMCA) of Greater Seattle—Part 3: Readjustment, 1930–1980," essay 3100, HistoryLink.org website, http://www.historylink.org/essays/output.cfm?file_id=3100.

105. Of the twelve hundred Indian Girl Scouts nationwide, most lived at residential schools in Arizona, New Mexico, and Oklahoma. See "Minutes of Meeting, Field Division Special Committee on Camping, Monday, September 21, 1936, 10:30 a.m.," in Camp Committee, 1935–1936, and "Field Division Special Committee on Camping, Monday, January 25, 1937, 10:30 a.m.," in Camp Committee, 1937–1938, GSUSA.

106. Camp Committee Minutes, 9 April 1941, GSUSA.

107. On southern whites' effort to keep black girls out of camping, see Elisabeth Israels Perry, " 'The Very Best Influence': Josephine Holloway and Girl Scouting in Nashville's African-American Community," *Tennessee Historical Quarterly* 52 (1993): 73–85.

108. Camp Committee Minutes, 8 February 1927, GSUSA.

109. Camp Committee Minutes, 3 February 1943 and 14 April 1943, GSUSA.

110. "Questionnaire on Policies for the Admission of Negro Girl Scouts into Camps, Region II," Camp Committee Minutes, January 1938, GSUSA.

111. Ibid.

112. "Minutes of Meeting, Field Division Special Committee on Camping, Monday, November 18, 1935, 10:30 a.m.," in Camp Committee, 1935–1936, Meetings/Conferences—Camp Andree Clark to Camp Committee 1934, GSUSA.

113. "Report of Director of Program," Camp Andree Reports 1937, GSUSA.

114. Ibid.

115. "Camp Andree Advisory Committee Meeting, Tuesday, May 21, 1940, 7:45 p.m.," in Camp Andree Clark Committee, 1937–46, Meetings/Conferences—Camp Andree Clark to Camp Committee 1934, GSUSA.

116. "Field Division Special Committee on Camping, Wednesday, January 12, 1938, 10:30 a.m.," in Camp Committee, 1937–1938, Meetings/Conferences—Camp Andree Clark to Camp Committee 1934, GSUSA.

117. "CAMP LOG, Rest-A-While Cottage"; "Report of Director of Program," Camp Andree Reports 1937, GSUSA.

118. Joshua Lieberman, *Creative Camping: A Coeducational Experiment in Personality Development and Social Living, Being the Record of Six Summers of the National Experimental Camp of Pioneer Youth of America* (New York: Association Press, 1931), 210.

119. "Camp Andree Advisory Committee Meeting, Tuesday, May 21, 1940, 7:45 p.m."

120. Robert Marshall, "Hitch Hiking in Camping," *Camping World* 3, no. 5 (May 1937): 7.

121. "Camp Director's Report, 1926, Camp Lehman," YMHA.

122. "Day Book, Permanents, 1940," in "Daily Programs 1940," YMHA.

123. Report of Dramatics Activities at Camp Andree—1935, GSUSA.

124. A. E. Hamilton, "What Can Camps Do to Make Democracy Safe for America?" *Camping World* 5, no. 2 (February 1939): 6.

125. *The Fire Fly* ("Season of 1934"), Camp Chimney Corners file, Boys' Work, box 7, YMCA.

126. "Camp Dudley" (1906) and "Instructions for Leaders at Camp Dudley 1911," in "1910–1913," CD.

127. Erd Harris, "Chief," in "Memories: Tents to Cabins," CD.

128. The play concerned a broken-down orchestra leader and his mechanic, who had crashed in what the play's promotional flyer called "the black and unexplored reaches of the Dark Continent" of the Belgian Congo. The men are captured by the Jitterboogei tribe, the original colony of swing, who are distressed at American appropriations of the genre. "Trader Corn (1940)" and "Trader Corn, A Musical Comedy" (1940), "Big Show Programs," in "Big Show Stuff from Willie's Office," CD.

NOTES TO CHAPTER 7

1. *P.Y. Clarion* 3, no. 3 (16 August 1939), folder 23, box 3, August Meier Papers, NYPL-SCH.

2. Joshua Lieberman, *Creative Camping: A Coeducational Experiment in Personality Development and Social Living, Being the Record of Six Summers of the National Experimental Camp of Pioneer Youth of America* (New York: Association Press, 1931), 5. The camp is not to be confused (as it sometimes was) with the Communists' Young Pioneers, an organization that also ran youth clubs and summer camps. The Pioneer Youth subsequently founded several other interwar camps: one for Philadelphia-area Pioneer Youth and two for southern workers' children, including Camp Larry in North Carolina. A brief discussion of the Pioneer Youth's southern programs appears in John Beck, "Highlander Folk School's Junior Union Camps, 1940–1944," *Labor's Heritage* 5, no. 1 (spring 1993): 28–41.

3. Lieberman, *Creative Camping*, 24.

4. For example, in the mid-1930s the YMHA's Surprise Lake Camp counselors read the book as part of their training. "Surprise Lake Camp, Cold Spring, N.Y., Camp Counselors Training Course 1936," 27 June 1936, YMHA.

5. A list of the most important progressive camping books of the period would necessarily include Hedley Dimock and Charles E. Hendry (foreword by William H. Kilpatrick), *Camping and Character: A Camp Experiment in Character Education* (New York: Association Press, 1929); Bernard S. Mason, *Camping and Education* (New York: McCall, 1930); Lloyd Burgess Sharp, *Education and the Summer Camp: An Experiment* (New York: Teachers College, Columbia University, 1930); Hazel K. Allen, *Camps and Their Modern Administration* (New York: Woman's Press, 1930); Beulah Clark Van Wagenen, ed., *Summer Camps: A Guide for Parents* (New York: Child Development Institute, Teachers College, Columbia University, 1933); Roland W. Ure, with foreword by Charles E. Hendry, *Fifty Cases for Camp Counselors* (New York: Association Press, 1935); Carlos Edgar Ward, *Organized Camping and Progressive Education* (Galax, Va.: self-published, 1935); Hedley S. Dimock, ed., *Putting Standards into the Summer Camp* (New York: Association Press, 1936); Louis H. Blumenthal, *Group Work in Camping* (New York: Association Press, 1937);

Hedley S. Dimock and Taylor Statten, *Talks to Counselors, as Given to Counselors at Camps Ahmek for Boys and Wapomeo for Girls* (New York: Association Press, 1939); J. Kenneth Doherty, *Solving Camp Behavior Problems: Individual Guidance in Group Work* (New York: Association Press, 1940); Bernard S. Mason, *Democracy in the Summer Camp* (Washington, D.C.: U.S. Government Printing Office, 1941); and the nine monographs published in the series Institute on Character Education in the Summer Camp, drawn from the sessions at George Williams College in Chicago from 1930 through 1947.

6. David Pearlman, *Camping* 4, no. 5 (February 1932): 9.

7. L. Emmett Holt, *The Care and Feeding of Children: A Catechism for the Use of Mothers and Children's Nurses* (New York: D. Appleton, 1894); and John B. Watson, *Psychological Care of Infant and Child* (New York: Norton, 1928). Recent scholarship on prescriptive childrearing literature demonstrates that modern American childrearing theories have long oscillated between stricter and more permissive approaches. See Julia Grant, *Raising Baby by the Book: The Education of American Mothers* (New Haven, Conn.: Yale University Press, 1998); Peter N. Stearns, *Anxious Parents: A History of Modern Childrearing in America* (New York: NYU Press, 2003); and Ann Hulbert, *Raising America: Experts, Parents, and a Century of Advice about Children* (New York: Knopf, 2003).

8. The term "progressive education" was in common use by the 1910s. See Lawrence A. Cremin, *The Transformation of the School: Progressivism in American Education, 1876–1957* (New York: Knopf, 1961), 88.

9. Henry W. Gibson, "Camps Durrell and Becket," *Association Boys* 5, no. 3 (June 1906): 116.

10. Over the course of the 1930s, democracy became a more central theme of industry literature, increasingly juxtaposed to fascism abroad. See, for example, Hedley Dimock, "The Contributions of the Camp to Democracy," *Camping* 11, no. 4 (April 1939): 3–5, 23–25.

11. Henry W. Gibson, "Camp as a Social Adjuster," *Camping* 2, no. 2 (February 1927): 1.

12. Henry W. Gibson, *Camping for Boys* (New York: Association Press, 1911), 75–76.

13. Henry W. Gibson, "Scoutcraft at Camps Durrell and Becket," *Association Boys* 7 (December 1909): 315, as cited in Ward, *Organized Camping,* 44–45.

14. Henry W. Gibson, 1931 brochure, Camp Chimney Corners file, Boys' Work, box 7, YMCA.

15. Henry W. Gibson, "The History of Organized Camping (Part I)," *Camping* 8, no. 1 (January 1936): 14.

16. "Camp Dudley" (1907), CD.

17. Mary Gunn Brinsmade, as quoted in Eugene H. Lehman, "When and by Whom Was the First Camp Founded?" in Spalding's Athletic Library (Eugene

Lehman et al.), *Camps and Camping, for the Information and Guidance of Campers, Parents, Directors and Counsellors* (New York: American Sports Publishing, 1929), 40 (published annually; hereafter cited by date only).

18. See, for example, "Natural History Camp. Summer Camp for Boys" (1892), n.c. 8, NYPL-UNP.

19. George Bird Grinnell and Eugene L. Swan, eds., *Harper's Camping and Scouting: An Outdoor Guide for American Boys* (New York: Harper and Bros., 1911), 367.

20. "The Camp Conference, Secretary's Report, 1905–6," in "Early Years," Boys' Work, box 7, YMCA.

21. Arthur Walworth, *The Medomak Way: The Story of the First Fifty Years of an American Summer Camp for Boys* (Lancaster, N.H.: Bisbee, 1953), 31.

22. In 1919, for example, Surprise Lake Camp had only one adult leader for every thirty boys. "SLC—History—by Goldwasser," YMHA.

23. "Camp Chronicle," 11, no. 3 (December 1918): 11, SLHM.

24. In 1918, for instance, the Manhattan Girl Scouts at Camp Calemaco woke to the morning bugle, had elaborate rituals for raising and lowering the flag each morning and evening, and practiced group drill. See *The Golden Eaglet* (1918), GSUSA. See also Anna Worthington Coale, *Summer in the Girls' Camp* (New York: Century, 1919).

25. "Camp Champlain" (1920), 8, n.c. 1, NYPL-UNP. The Vermont camp's 1920 brochure promised that "while Champlain is not a military camp, it is conducted in a measure upon military lines. There is military drill twice a week, and the boys rise, assemble for meals and the various activities of Camp, and retire, at the sound of a bugle. This inculcates habits of obedience, promptness and regularity."

26. Camp Rotherwood brochure (1927), NYPL.

27. "What Is the Answer?" (editorial), *Camping* 4, no. 9 (June 1932): 1.

28. Julian Harris Salomon, "Changing Conditions in American Camping," *Camping* 12, no. 4 (April 1940): 3. Salomon was the non–Native American author of *The Book of Indian Crafts and Indian Lore* (New York: Harper and Row, 1928), among other books. He interpreted Indian customs at various camps, instructed in Indian Lore at Columbia University's Camp Leadership course, and worked with the Boy Scouts before joining the National Park Service.

29. E.L. to author, 8 May 1998.

30. Jay B. Nash, *Spectatoritis* (New York: Sears Publishing, 1932), 5. Nash was one of the original 1925 organizers of the Pacific Section of the Camp Directors Association. On his influence in the western camping movement, see Rosalind Cassidy, "Celebrating a Birthday," *Camping* 2, no. 8 (May 1930): 4.

31. John Dewey, *The School and Society* (1899; repr., Chicago: University of Chicago Press, 1915); and John Dewey, *Democracy and Education: An Intro-*

duction to the Philosophy of Education (New York: Macmillan, 1916). On Dewey and his role in progressive education circles, see Cremin, *Transformation of the School*. Dewey remained influential even as his later work moved away from educational theory and was sometimes critical of "child-centered" progressive education programs.

32. Dewey, *Democracy and Education*, 83.

33. On Kilpatrick, see Cremin, *Transformation of the School*, 215–220.

34. Blumenthal, *Group Work*, 66.

35. Ward, *Organized Camping*, 44–45.

36. One not atypical report, likely based on an acquaintance of but a few weeks, noted of a boy, "Though fairly intelligent and with a good sense of humor is obviously psychopathic." "Campers Reports, 1938," Camp Lehman, YMHA.

37. "Rosenfield's Kinacamps in the Colorado Rockies" (1931), 9, n.c. 10, NYPL-UNP.

38. "The Chronicle," Schroon Lake Camp, 1936–1937, SLHM.

39. Eliot made his oft-quoted statement at the meeting of the National Association of Directors of Girls' Camps, in Boston, 21 January 1922. The first mention of the speech appears in Spalding's Athletic Library, *Camps and Camping* (1922), 14.

40. The course was founded by Columbia University professor Elbert Fretwell and Maine camp director and former NADGC leader Eugene Lehman.

41. A series of monographs was published from 1930 to 1947 reporting on the George Williams College camp seminars, beginning with *Character Education* in 1930. Other volumes in the series considered camp standards and new practices in camping, including *Camping in a Democracy* (no. 7). On camp training programs nationwide, see, for instance, *Camping* 2, no. 7 (April 1930): 21. Only a small percentage of camp staff nationwide attended special training programs or had expertise in child psychology or social work.

42. Wilber I. Newstetter, *Wawokiye Camp, A Research Project in Group Work* (Cleveland: School of Applied Social Sciences, Western Reserve University, 1930).

43. Letter to Mr. Burritt, 14 June 1933, folder 269.1, box 42, CU-CSSC.

44. In 1925, only a third of the camps listed in the Children's Welfare Federation (CWF) survey offered organized recreation for the children; even fewer camps offered "nature work." These dismal statistics reflected a relatively untrained staff, the high camper-to-counselor ratio, and the notion that a trip to the country was in and of itself a satisfactory proposition. By 1927, under pressure from the CWF, these percentages rose to 72 percent and 63 percent, respectively. Children's Welfare Federation of N.Y.C.—Comm. on Convalescent and Fresh Air Care, *Report of Survey of Fresh Air Homes and Camps, Summer 1925–26*, NYPL.

45. Sharp noted that "conditions existing in many of these charity camps were of such a very low standard that they should not have been permitted to continue." Sharp, *Education and the Summer Camp,* 2.

46. R. F. to Gruenberg, 16 March 1953, in "CW: Letters of appreciation, 1938–53," carton 2, SL.

47. "Report of Rorschach Project—Second Trip, July 17 to Aug. 6, 1941," Camp Henry files, HSS.

48. Henry Wellington Wack, *The Camping Ideal: The New Human Race* (New York: Red Book Magazine, 1925), unpaginated.

49. Playground and Recreation Association of America, *Camping Out: A Manual on Organized Camping* (New York: Macmillan, 1927), 1.

50. Redbook Editorials, in reel 61, box 51, CU-LW.

51. William Heard Kilpatrick, introduction to Lieberman, *Creative Camping,* vi. Hedley Dimock and Charles Hendry, authors of the influential *Camping and Character* (1929), similarly described the log cabin at Camp Ahmek, the private Ontario boys' camp at the heart of their study, as both "in keeping with the pioneer traditions" and as a symbol of "a fresh, vigorous educational awakening." Dimock and Hendry, *Camping and Character,* frontispiece.

52. On the ambiguity of the frontier, see William Cronon, "A Place for Stories: Nature, History, and Narrative," *Journal of American History* 78, no. 4 (March 1992): 1347–1376. Historian Richard Slotkin speaks of the "Wild West" in similar terms, as "a mythic space, in which past and present, fiction and reality could coexist; a space in which history, translated into myth, was reenacted as ritual." Richard Slotkin, "Buffalo Bill's 'Wild West' and the Mythologization of the American Empire," in Amy Kaplan and Donald E. Pease, eds., *Cultures of U.S. Imperialism* (Durham, N.C.: Duke University Press, 1993), 166.

53. "The Children's Aid Society, Eighty-Seventh Annual Report for the year 1939," 11, CAS.

54. Miriam Ephraim, assistant director of the Jewish Cejwin camps, reminded a group of Jewish counselors-in-training in 1936 that "the Jew was part of the pioneers like any other ethnic group that came and settled here." "Surprise Lake Camp, Cold Spring, N.Y., Camp Counselors Training Course 1936," 18 August 1936, YMHA. The Habonim camps, run by the Young Poale Zionist Alliance from 1932 onward, explicitly conjoined the American pioneer past to hopes for an Israeli pioneer future. See David Breslau, ed., *Adventure in Pioneering: The Story of 25 Years of Habonim Camping* (New York: Shulsinger Bros., 1957).

55. David Glassberg makes a similar point in *American Historical Pageantry: The Uses of Tradition in the Early Twentieth Century* (Chapel Hill: University of North Carolina Press, 1990), 1.

56. Lieberman, *Creative Camping,* x.

57. Ibid., 15.

58. Surprise Lake Camp was typical of large organizational camps in charting

a middle course. In the 1930s, campers began to have a choice of activities during part of the day.

59. For example, in 1935, Camp Ramapo, a camp conducted near Rhinebeck by the Jewish Board of Guardians for "problem" boys, decided to experiment with "free choice," but the staff soon determined that the boys were flailing. Unsure of how to proceed, Ramapo staff returned to compulsory activities. "Surprise Lake Camp, Cold Spring, N.Y., Camp Counselors Training Course 1935," 8 August 1935, YMHA.

60. "Report of an Eastern Regional Conference for the Improvement of Y.M.C.A. Camping, May 8, 9, 10, 1931," 8, in file "The Guiding Hand, B," Boys' Work, box 7, YMCA.

61. Joshua Lieberman, "New Trends in Camping," in National Federation of Settlements, *Adventures in Camping* (New York: National Federation of Settlements, 1940), 3.

62. Ibid.

63. W. H. Jones, "Oldtimer Reviews Y.M.C.A. Boys' Camps," *Association Boys' Work Journal* 11, no. 2 (March 1938), in "Papers, 1921–1938," Boys' Work, box 11, YMCA.

64. Girl Scout accounts of Andrée Clark's life are ambiguous as to the cause of her death; she was evidently ill for several months beforehand.

65. Quoted in "The Story of Camp Andree Clark," in Camp and Camping, Camp Andree Clark—General, GSUSA.

66. On the early years of the camp, see Eveline Robertson to Miss Price, 11 January 1923, and "Camp and Camping, History, 1912–1953 (by Elin Lindberg)," in Camp and Camping, Camp Andree Clark—General, GSUSA. The camp attracted girls from across the nation, although most came from the Northeast. By 1928, twenty-eight states were represented. "Girl Scouts Continue to Win New Members," *New York Times,* 30 September 1928, "Camp and Camping—General," GSUSA.

67. "Developments in Girl Scout Camping," 30 July 1926, in "Camps and Camping—General," GSUSA. Troops of thirty-two girls, or four patrols, constituted a camp unit, but at times the term was used to refer to a group of eight.

68. Elsa G. Crosby (Assistant Director of Camp Andree) to Eveline Robertson, 31 August 1921, in Camp and Camping—Camp Andree Clark—First Session—1921, GSUSA.

69. "Macy—Training School for Leaders Notebook, 1926," GSUSA. The first two such Girl Scout camps were located at Camp Chapparal in Redwood State Park, California, and Camp Juliette Low in Cloudland, Georgia, in 1923. "Girl Scouts Continue to Win" and "History, 1912–1953," 15, GSUSA.

70. Alice Mary Kimball, "A Camp Where the Girls Boss," *The Outlook,* 11 June 1924, 234–235.

71. "Camp Andree—1923," 3, in Report by Camp Andree Camp Chiefs and

Councillors—1923," GSUSA. The camp's pioneer unit, known as Inisfree, generally attracted older and more experienced campers.

72. Camp Andree Reports 1935, GSUSA. In the late 1930s Allen also served as director of Camp Edith Macy and president of the American Camping Association.

73. See "Camp Survey," 31 August 1933, in Camp and Camping—Camp Andree Clark—Reports—1921–1933, GSUSA.

74. "First Experiment on Program Planning with Experienced Campers, Camp Andree, 1935," Camp Andree Experiment on Program Planning, 1935, GSUSA.

75. *Ye Andrée Logge 1922*, Camp Andree Clark Camp Folders, GSUSA.

76. Letter from Tip-Top to Mrs. Clark, 31 August 1921, in Camp and Camping—Camp Andree Clark—First Session—1921, GSUSA.

77. Katharine G. Ready, quoted in Camp Andree Reports 1927, GSUSA.

78. Camp Andree Reports 1928, GSUSA.

79. Camp Andree Reports 1938, GSUSA.

80. Dimock and Hendry, *Camping and Character*, 96.

81. Lieberman, *Creative Camping*, 7–8.

82. Ibid., 223–224.

83. Camp Andree Reports 1928, GSUSA.

84. Margaret Gibson, "Report—Camp Andree, 1921," GSUSA.

85. Douglas Haskell, "Initiative at Camps Is Rare," *Camping World* 2, no. 1 (January 1936): 8.

86. Lieberman, *Creative Camping*, 16.

87. "Camp Andree Inter-Divisional Meeting, Friday, January 20, 1939, 10:00 a.m.," in Camp Andree Clark Committee, 1937–46, GSUSA.

88. "Skeleton Outline of Aims, Objectives, and Evaluation of Adventures at Camp Andree—Summer 1938," Camp Andree Clark Committee 1937–46, in "Meetings/Conferences—Camp Andree Clark to Camp Committee 1934," GSUSA.

89. August Meier, "A Short History of Pioneer Youth Camp," 319, folder 19, box 3, August Meier Papers, NYPL-SCH.

90. Alexis Ferm to Mess. Meier and Gladstone, 20 August 1938, folder 13, box 3, August Meier Papers, NYPL-SCH. See also the final (anonymous) document produced by the committee, "A Short History of Pioneer Youth Camp," folder 13, August Meier Papers, NYPL-SCH.

91. Meier, "A Short History," 318, 459, folders 19 and 21.

92. Ibid., 446, folder 20.

93. Ibid., 194, folder 17.

94. Ibid., 264, folder 18.

95. Ibid., 278, folder 18.

96. Lieberman, *Creative Camping*, 136–139.

97. Meier, "A Short History," 296–297, folder 19.

98. Ibid., 278, folder 18.

99. Ibid., 446, folder 21.

100. Meier was the author of many books and edited collections concerning African American experience. His most influential works include August Meier, *Negro Thought in America, 1880–1915: Racial Ideologies in the Age of Booker T. Washington* (Ann Arbor: University of Michigan Press, 1963); August Meier and Elliott M. Rudwick, *From Plantation to Ghetto: An Interpretive History of American Negroes* (New York: Hill and Wang, 1964); Milton Meltzer and August Meier, *Time of Trial, Time of Hope: The Negro in America, 1919–1941* (Garden City, N.Y.: Doubleday, 1966); August Meier and Elliott Rudwick, eds., *The Making of Black America: Essays in Negro Life and History* (New York: Atheneum, 1969).

101. W. Barksdale Maynard, "Chocorua, Asquam, Pasquaney: Where Summer Camps Began" (master's thesis, University of Delaware, 1994), 41.

102. See, for example, *Echoes* 3 (11 August 1937), "Surprise Lake Camp, Echoes, Oct. 1936, Sept. 1938," YMHA.

103. Meier, "A Short History," 199, folder 17.

104. Ibid., 273, folder 18.

105. Ibid., 274, folder 18.

NOTES TO CONCLUSION

1. "CW: songs," carton 3, SL.

2. "CW: Valé (last talks), 1931–53," carton 3, SL.

3. Ethel Rose Mandel, Pasquaney Nature Club Diaries, 27 August 1914, vol. 3, NHHS.

4. "Where the New Brunswick Girl Scouts Have Been Spending Summer and Having an Elegant Time Living Out of Doors." *The Sunday Times*, circa 1918, "Camp Longwood," Camp and Camping, Miscellaneous Histories, GSUSA.

5. *The Mowglis Howl* 1, no. 1 (1907): 21, NHHS.

6. At Schroon Lake Camp, for instance, a typical banquet included raw vegetables and pickles, half a grapefruit, broiled salmon, "parisienne" potatoes, dinner rolls, Consommé Royale, roast stuffed spring chicken, string beans, corn on the cob, candied sweet potatoes, Waldorf Salad, vanilla ice cream with chocolate sauce, fresh fruit, stuffed dates, petit fours, and after-dinner mints. "The Chronicle," Schroon Lake Camp, 1936–1937 (1936 season), 31, SLHM.

7. The ritual by which campers voted for the most popular camper, the best built, and so on, was in place in 1895 at Camp Pasquaney. *White Birch* (Camp Pasquaney) 1, no. 10 (6 September 1899): 80, NHHS.

8. "Ward Manor—Historical Background," "Concerning the Island Camp," and "April 1936, Excerpt from Report to the Board of Managers of A.I.C.P.," box 70, CU-CSSC.

9. The prevalence of such sentiments among Surprise Lake campers suggests that the staff asked them to reflect on how they had changed for the better. Max Oppenheimer, "Report of the work done at Surprise Lake Camp during the summer of 1930," in "S.L.C., Reports Summer Camp 1905–1938," YMHA.

10. S. to Amy Faulkner, 26 August, circa 1940s, "CW: Letters of appreciation, 1938–53," carton 2, SL.

11. Estelle Nemeth, interview by Rose Miller, 18 January 1987, 34, William E. Wiener Oral History Library of the American Jewish Committee, NYPL-DOR; Estelle Nemeth, interview by author, 31 October 1998.

12. M. to "Mother and Dad," 25 August 1942, folder 91, carton 2, SL.

13. Hy Kampel, interview by author, 16 September 1998.

14. Mr. Sindelar to Miss Flood, 10 September 1930, "Overhill Cottage, 1930–1928 [*sic*]," box 43, CU-CSSC.

15. "Swimming and Dinner Table Most Popular at Camp Parsons" (reprinted from *The Villager*, 24 July 1941), Camp Herbert Parsons, Poughkeepsie, N.Y., in Greenwich House mf #2209, TM.

16. Adele Rose to author, 26 January 1998.

17. F. to "Mrs. G and Miss Faulkner," 16 July 1953, "CW: Letters of appreciation, 1938–53," carton 2, SL. Men evidently made similar trips; as *Dudley Doings* reported, "It is an interesting fact that many old Dudley boys pick out camp as one of the places to visit on their wedding trip. They want to show friend wife the camp they have been talking about these many years." "Annual Spring Number," 1928, CD. However, not all returning camp alumni felt welcome. When former Camp Lenore camper Diana Trilling stopped in to visit one summer as a young adult, she was surprised to realize that she was no longer an important "insider." Diana Trilling, "The Girls of Camp Lenore," *New Yorker* 72 (12 August 1996): 57–68.

18. Lydia Stoopenkoff to author, 28 November 1997.

19. Waziyatah girls, many of them from New York City and Philadelphia, came from wealthy families; the camp cost $400 and up in the 1920s, and $350 even at the height of the Depression. "CW: Specimens of mailings to parents, 1932–37," carton 4, SL.

20. W. to Gruenberg, 31 July 1935, "CW: letters of appreciation, 1926–36," carton 2, SL.

21. F. to Gruenberg, 16 March 1953, "CW: Letters of appreciation, 1938–53," carton 2, SL.

22. M. to Gruenberg, 9 September 1940, "CW: letters of appreciation, 1926–36," carton 2, SL.

23. B. to Gruenberg, 17 September 1941, folder 91, carton 2, SL.

24. N. to Gruenberg, 6 October 1944, "CW: Corresp. 1940–53," carton 2, SL.

25. Ellie Busman (nee Levin) to author, 21 March 1998.

26. E. L. to author, 8 May 1998.

27. "Camp Pok-O'-Moonshine in the Adirondacks" (1913), POM.

28. "Camp Mystic" (1926), n.c. 10, NYPL-UNP.

29. "Rosenfield's Kinacamps in the Colorado Rockies" (1931), n.c. 10, NYPL-UNP.

30. L. to Gruenberg, 21 August 1940, folder 99, carton 2, SL.

31. Olive Burt, "What Camp Did for My Child," *Parents* 9, no. 3 (March 1934): 27, 44.

32. One mother wrote to the staff of the YMHA's Surprise Lake Camp to praise its effect on her son: "His bureau drawer, since he came home from camp, has been so neat and tidy, that I cannot recognize it as his." Max Oppenheimer, "Surprise Lake Camp, Summer Season 1923, Administrator's Report," in "S.L.C., Reports Summer Camp 1905–1938," YMHA.

33. On young women's communities, see Helen Lefkowitz Horowitz, *Alma Mater: Design and Experience in the Women's Colleges from Their Nineteenth-Century Beginnings to the 1930s* (New York: Knopf, 1984); Lisa M. Fine, *The Souls of the Skyscraper: Female Clerical Workers in Chicago, 1870–1930* (Philadelphia: Temple University Press, 1990); and Angel Kwolek-Folland, *Engendering Business: Men and Women in the Corporate Office, 1870–1930* (Baltimore: Johns Hopkins University Press, 1994).

34. Former camper, quoted in Anna Worthington Coale, *Summer in the Girls' Camp* (New York: Century, 1919), 4. Coale was the director of Camp Tahoma.

35. "Surprise Lake Camp of the Educational Alliance and YMHA, Report, Winter Camp—Sept. 1942—June 1943, Summer camp, 1943, Cold Spring, New York," in Surprise Lake Reports, 1939–1943, YMHA.

36. On wartime camps, see, for instance, "News of Wartime Camping," *Camping* 14, no. 7 (December 1942): 12–13.

37. Directors to "Waziyatah Camper," 10 June 1942, "CW: Specimens of mailings to parents, 1938–53," carton 4, SL.

38. On childhood in the Second World War era, see William M. Tuttle Jr., *"Daddy's Gone to War": The Second World War in the Lives of America's Children* (New York: Oxford University Press, 1993).

39. See, for instance, *Camp Riverdale Stag and Eagle* 7, no. 3 (26 August 1943), file 19, box 2, AM.

40. Gerald P. Burns, *Program of the Modern Camp* (New York: Prentice-Hall, 1954), 17, estimated that at least four million children attended camps in 1951, well before most of the baby-boomers came of age to attend camps;

Robert McBride, *Camping at the Mid-Century* (Chicago: American Camping Association, 1953), 8–9, calculated that nonprofit agency camps served 2,750,000 children; private camps, 330,000; church camps, 200,000; and government-run camps, 60,000. The states with the most camps were New York, Pennsylvania, and California (California being a postwar upstart).

41. McBride, *Camping at the Mid-Century*, 1, 17. In 1959, the ACA estimated that five million children, or 12 percent of all U.S. children, would attend camp that year. Gerald J. Barry, "The Summer Camp Frenzy . . . How It's Growing More So and More Profitable," *Newsweek* 54 (13 July 1959): 70.

42. Wartime propaganda stressed the blessings of American democracy and the valuable contributions of Americans of all races. Wartime mobilization also restarted the migration of black Americans to northern cities, a process that had stalled during the Depression years. Moreover, soldiers from minority communities returned home after the war with a new sense of entitlement to the full benefits of American citizenship. On civil rights activism during the Second World War, see, for example, John Dittmer, *Local People: The Struggle for Civil Rights in Mississippi* (Urbana: University of Illinois Press, 1994), 1–18; Ronald Takaki, *Double Victory: A Multicultural History of America in World War II* (Boston: Little, Brown, 2000).

43. "Establishing Racial Good Will through Camping," *Camping* 17, no. 5 (May 1945): 9.

44. On postwar interracial camping, see Phyllis Palmer, "Recognizing Racial Privilege: White Girls and Boys at National Conference of Christians and Jews Summer Camps, 1957, 1974," *Oral History Review* 27, no. 2 (summer/fall 2000): 129–155.

45. Don Shellenberger, "An Exploration of Intergroup Relations in the Interracial Camp Setting" (unpublished manuscript, January 1962), 5–6, in "Camping Vignettes," Boys' Work, box 7, YMCA.

46. "Another Side of Integration," in "Camping Vignettes," Boys' Work, box 7, YMCA.

47. "Highlights of Camp Kern's History," Camp Kern, Boys' Work, box 7, YMCA.

48. Shellenberger, "An Exploration of Intergroup Relations," 16.

49. YWCA statistics are typical in this regard. In the late 1940s, almost all northern states' camps were integrated, the "border" states were mixed, and none of the southern camps were integrated. See "Information Regarding Y.W.C.A. Camps for Use by Community Division Staff" (20 December 1949), folder 3, box 82, YWCA; and "Report of Study of Intergroup Relations and Practices in Resident Camps for People Under Eighteen Years of Age," Committee on Camping, National Social Welfare Assembly, New York, 1953.

50. On race and postwar government aid, see Lizabeth Cohen, *A Consumers'*

Republic: The Politics of Mass Consumption in Postwar America (New York: Knopf, 2003).

51. Eugene A. Turner Jr., *100 Years of YMCA Camping* (Chicago: YMCA of the USA, 1985), 214.

52. Emory Bundy, quoted in "Young Men's Christian Association (YMCA) of Greater Seattle—Part 3: Readjustment, 1930–1980," essay 3100, HistoryLink .org website, http://www.historylink.org/essays/output.cfm?file_id=3100.

53. Sarah V. Estep, "What Inner-City Campers Taught Us," *Camping* 20, no. 5 (May 1968): 13.

54. Letter addressed "Dear Friend," 5 September 1971, YMCA Camping Firsts, and Dwight Call, "Not Knowing It Couldn't Be Done, They Did It," *Forum*, May 1974, 8–9, in Camp Leslie Marrowbone, Boys' Work, box 8, YMCA.

55. McBride, *Camping at the Mid-Century*, 28.

56. Elaine Tyler May, *Homeward Bound: American Families in the Cold War Era* (New York: Basic Books, 1988).

57. "Communist Indoctrination and Training of Children in Summer Camps," State of New York, Report of the Joint Legislative Committee on Charitable and Philanthropic Agencies and Organizations (Albany, N.Y.: Williams, 1956), 9, 22, 29.

58. June Levine and Gene Gordon, *Tales of Wo-Chi-Ca: Blacks, Whites and Reds at Camp* (San Rafael, Calif.: Avon Springs, 2002), xi, 168–186.

59. Frederick H. Lewis, "Camping Confronts an American Dilemma," *Camping* 26, no. 9 (December 1954): 12.

60. Kenneth Webb, "Camping for American Youth—A Declaration for Action" (Martinsville, Ind.: American Camping Association, 1962), 7–12. Kenneth and Susan Webb founded the Farm and Wilderness Camps in Plymouth, Vermont, in 1939.

61. Rising property taxes were part of the problem. Camp-intensive states like Maine and New York taxed camp properties as if they were fully developed, even though most were in use only a few months per year. See "To Pine Island Directors," 24 July 1979, folder 3, box 793, Pine Island Camp, UMO.

62. Dave Noland, "Hard Times among Summer Camps: Only the Fittest Survive," *New York Times*, 28 August 1977, 1 (section not listed), folder 1, box 793, Pine Island Camp, UMO. There were 270 Maine camps in 1969 and only 200 a decade later.

63. Turner, *100 Years*, 71.

64. Anne Fried, "Today's Counselors Are *Different*," *Camping* 41, no. 2 (February 1968): 8.

65. Letter to counselors, 1974 season, folder 12, box 793, Pine Island Camp, UMO. Camp directors picked their battles, officially prohibiting drug use for insurance purposes but often asking counselors to be discreet about their sexual

relationships with other staff members rather than trying to prevent such relationships from forming. On drug use at camps of the period, see Mike Schlesinger, "Pot Pills and People," *Camping* 42, no. 3 (March 1970).

66. Noland, "Hard Times."

67. One of the first authors to treat the "underside" of camp life was novelist Herman Wouk, in *The City Boy* (Garden City, N.Y.: Doubleday, 1952), and *Inside, Outside* (Boston: Little, Brown, 1985).

68. *The Simpsons,* episode 60 (1992).

69. American Camp Association, Media Center Camp Trends (February 2007), www.acacamps.org; David Koeppel, "Following in Small Footsteps: Children Go to Parents' Camp," *New York Times,* 15 August 2003, B2.

70. On *Bug Juice,* see Laurel Graeber, "Tomorrowland Was Never Like This," *New York Times,* 1 March 1998, TV3, 27, 33, 37.

71. Undated, unsigned letter in 1930 materials, "Clippings scrapbook," box 219, YWCA.

72. "Camp Mystic—1930s Adult Camp," folder 5, box 11, and "Mrs. Carl Akeley's Camp Mystic," folder 5, box 12, MRHS.

73. Althea Ballentine, interview by author, Alton, N.H., 15 December 2002.

74. Elin Lindberg, "Camp and Camping, History, 1912–1953," in Camp and Camping, History, 1912–1953, GSUSA.

75. Hortense Russell, "A Summary of a Few Working Principles of the Advisory Committee for Camp Andree Clark, a Center for Senior Girl Scouts," 4–39, in Camp and Camping, Camp Andree Clark—General, GSUSA.

76. Thomas Williford, "Tourism in the Adirondacks: Schroon Lake and the Jews" (unpublished manuscript, 1985), SLHM.

77. "Schroon–North Hudson Historical Society, 1983 Spring Newsletter," SLHM. In the mid-1960s, Eugene Moses and his wife, Betty, put the property up for sale. Classified ad, *New York Times,* 14 June 1964, F1.

78. Alfred Balch, "A Boy's Republic," *McClure's* 1 (August 1893): 254.

Index

Abbott, William, 65, 184
"Acting out," 143–50, 235; by camp counselors, 148–50, 161–62; camp staff toleration for, 161–62; pranks and, 146–47, 171, 252, 316n54; punishment for, 143–45, 150, 315n45; rule breaking in, 144–46, 148; social aggression and, 147–48, 316n62
Adams, Elizabeth Kemper, 152, 318n85
Adirondack tourism, 24, 185
Adirondack Woodcraft Camp, 65, 104, 122, 136, 184, 185, 187, 202, 277
Adolescence: camp attendance and, 109–10, 308nn37–39; concept of, 18, 27–28; counselor-in-training programs in, 110; girls and, 46, 127, 150, 294n113, 317n78; heterosexual attraction in, 152; same-sex intimacy in, 152–54; sexual maturation in, 150, 317n78; "teenage" culture of, 110, 308n41. *See also* Recapitulation theory
Adolescence, Its Psychology and Its Relation to Physiology, Anthropology, Sociology, Sex, Crime, Religion, and Education (Hall), 28, 288n29
Adults' aspirations: camp marketing to, 75–77, 301nn74–76, 302n77, 302n83; children's culture v., 13, 78, 136–43, 161–62; for summer camps, 2, 3, 7, 9–10, 13
Adventures in the Wilderness (Murray), 24, 287n22
African Americans: citizenship claims of, 211–12, 331n72; Great Migration of, 211; interracial camps, 58, 219, 267–70; New York City population ratios of, 211; racialized camp entertainment and, 203–7, 212, 223; summer camp employment of, 192, 213, 213–14, 218–

19; White Americans' ideas about, 193, 197, 212, 225, 326nn12–13, 327n24
African Americans at summer camps, 72–73, 220–22, 301nn62–63; Ku Klux Klan and, 186; local community relations with, 186, 272, 324n81, 325n83, 345n58; Negro Girl Scouts, 72, 221–22
Agrarian ideals, wilderness ideals v., 18, 23, 286n4
"Aids to Scouting" (Baden-Powell), 44
Akeley, Carl, 190, *190*, 326n7
Akeley, Mary Jobe. *See* Jobe, Mary
Allen, Hazel, 247
Amateur Circus Life (Balch, Ernest), 38, 291n71
America: camps' importance in, 2, 11–12, 191, 260; modernity and anxiety in, 25–26, 198
American Camping Association (ACA), 85; inclusiveness ideology of, 268, 344n43; postwar growth rates of, 267. *See also* Camp Directors Association (CDA)
American Indian League (AIL), 215
Americanization, camps and, 56–57, 59, 191
American Legion, 272, 345n58
American national character, outdoors impact on, 240–41, 338n49
American popular culture: Girl Scouts and, 181–83; summer camps and, 2, 11–12, 174–83, 265–66; summer camps' use of, 180–83
American postwar patriotism, racial integration and, 267–68
Amos 'n' Andy, 210
Amster, Cornelia, 141–42
Anthropology, exotic cultures of, 209, 330n63

347

John Martin's Book, children's magazine, 78
Junior Republic: George's camp model of, 53–54, 295nn141–43; Progressive Era reform and, 54

"Kehonka geese," 46, 98, 122–23
Kilpatrick, William Heard, 237, 241
Kneeland, Fred, 113, 309n48
Ku Klux Klan, 186, 206
Kunis, Rena, 156

Lake: Champlain, 42, 58; Cohasset, 187; Quinsigamond, 39–40; Wawayanda, 42; Wentworth, 46; Winnipesaukee, 47, 96. *See also* Newfound Lake; Squam Lake summer camps; Sylvan Lake
Langdon, William Chancy, 50–51
Latino/a campers, 72, 210, 219–20, 222
Laurel Falls Camp, 155
Lehman, Eugene, 76
Leisure: camp-learned swimming and, 115, 122; children's use of, 6, 12–13, 60, 235–36, 282n16; across gender lines, 52; heterosocial v. homosocial shift for, 152; spiritually restorative purpose of, 21–22, 168; youth culture focus on, 79, 302nn89–90
Lesbian staff members, 154–55, 319nn98–100
Levy, Henry, 178–79, 322n48
Lewis, Caroline, 182
Lewis, Frederick, 272, 345n59
Lieberman, Joshua, 140, 222, 226–29, 242–43, 251, 252, 333n118, 334nn2–3; Camp Andree impact of, 247–48, 250
Life Fresh Air Camp, 69, 239, 338n45
Little Darlings, camp image in, 275
Local community: African American summer camps' relations with, 186, 272, 324n81, 325n83, 345n58; Jewish-only camps' relations with, 186, 325n82; summer camps' relations with, 186–87
"Long Walk," as camps' extended hike, 119, 310nn64–65
Low, Juliette Gordon, 51, 182
Ludwig, Walter, 251, 253
Lurie, Alan, 143

Malay village, 209
Manabozho, 214, 331n78

Marriage, companionate ideal of, 79, 151–52
Masculinity, crisis of, 20–21, 287n16
Mason, Bernard, 208, 228, 330n58
Masturbation, 153–54, 318nn91–92
Mattoon, Laura, 46–47, 84, 97, 106, 109, 118, 155, 186, 277, 293n112, 294n118, 307n4, 310n61. *See also* Camp Kehonka
McWright, Leroy, 214
Mead, Margaret, 209
Meatballs, camp image in, 275
Meier, August "Augie": Pioneer Youth Camp memoir by, 251–55, 341n100
Meylan, George, 173–74, 321n32
Middle-class: birthrate decrease of, 27; children's position in, 27, 288n28; domestic ideal of, 26–27, 288n28
Middle-class values, charitable camps and, 55–56
Middleditch, Gertrude, 76–77
Minstrels. *See* Blackface minstrel shows
Modernity: anxiety about, 25–26, 198; camp as antidote to, 9–10, 176, 276–77, 284n25; camps' authenticity v., 165–74, 176, 209, 233–34, 321nn14–15, 321nn29–32
Mohegan tribe, 189
Moses, Eugene, 62, 64–66, 238, 278
Moses, Isaac, 61–62, 64–66, 67
Moss Lake Camp, 167–68, 202
Motion picture industry, camp industry v., 176, 322nn36–37
Motion pictures: *Camping* v. *Camp Life* on, 178, 322n48, 322n50; CDA's disapproval of, 178; summer camps and, 174–83, 322n48, 322n50
Movie nights: CDA's disapproval of, 178; at summer camps, 177, 179–80
Mr. Smith Goes to Washington, 265–66, 267, 274
Murray, William H. H. ("Adirondack"), 23–24, 44–45, 287n22
"Murray's Fools," 24
Muscular Christianity, 24–26, 46, 118, 288n24; social adjustment v., 238; summer camp influence of, 39, 71–72, 74; swimming and, 114, 309n52; women's characterization by, 46, 48; YMCA and, 25, 42, 288n25, 292n87
Museum of Natural History, 190

Pfaff, Robert, 202

Physical self-improvement: camp culture's goal of, 122–31; "normal" body focus in, 125; precamp physical and, 122–23; summer tans in, 193–96; weight gain/loss in, 124–25, 234, 274, 311n91

Pine Island Camp, 66, 217–18, 274

Pioneer iconography: camp types and relevance to, 241–42; children's democratic citizenship in, 242

Pioneering founder(s): of boys' camps, 37–38; of Boy Scouts, 44; of Camp Fire Girls, 49–50; of girls' camps, 46–48, 50, 294n118; of Girl Scouts, 51; of YMCA camps, 40–42

Pioneer nostalgia, 17–18, 20–21, 59, 241–42, 338n52

Pioneer Youth Camp, 74–75, 140, 151, 227, 234, 277; experimental summer camp of, 306n146; freedom and self-restraint in, 252–53; Great Depression and, 244–45; Lieberman's camp management model for, 226–28, 334nn2–3; Meier's memoir of, 251–55; pranks and "acting out" at, 252; as progressive camp, 74–75, 92, 242–43; progressive ideal learning at, 253; racial integration of, 219, 222, 269–70. *See also Creative Camping* (Lieberman); Lieberman, Joshua

Playground Association of America, 49, 55

Playgrounds, immigrant acculturation and, 55

"Playing Indian," 189, 191–92, 199, 200, 202–3, 217, 326n8, 327nn28–30, 328nn33–35; Blackface minstrel shows v., 207, 330n56; at Camp Dudley, 199, 200, 327n29; at Camp Mystic, 189, 197, 198, 200, 202; children's culture relation to, 208; girls' forms of, 201–2, 328n35; Hall's savage boy vision and, 201; recapitulation theory and, 208–9. *See also* Native American(s); The Woodcraft Indians

Plessy v. Ferguson, 58

Plume Trading and Sales Company, 214, 331n79

Poison ivy, 250

Polio, 70, 124, 311n87

Potok, Chaim, 70, 300n48

Powell, Herbert Preston, 329n46

Pranks, 146–47, 171, 252, 316n54

Precamp physical screening, 123

Primitivism, in camp culture, 191–92, 209, 326n8

Private camp(s): attendee estimates for, 63, 297nn6–7; charitable camps compared to, 56; counselor/camper ratio in, 67–68; counselors' compensation at, 65, 298n16; desegregation of, 268; economic vulnerability of, 66–67; fees charged at, 66, 298n22, 299n23; during Great Depression, 67, 299n29; for Jewish children, 61, 71, 72; number of, 62–63, 66, 297nn5–6; organizational camps compared to, 39–40, 46, 67–68, 73, 299n32; precamp physical screening for, 123; religious/ethnic founding of, 58, 60, 296n155; Squam Lake's earliest, 17–20, 35–36. *See also* Boy's camps, earliest; Girl's camps, earliest; Summer camp(s)

Private camp enrollment: camp director strategies for, 64–65, 66–67, 298nn13–15, 299n28; children's recruiting in, 80; finding new clients for, 65, 66–67; mass culture v. personal networks in, 63–64, 79–80, 92–93, 298n12. *See also* Camp enrollment

"Progressive" camps, 226–30, 242–45; Cold War communism, and fear of, 271–72, 345n57; progressive/radical ideals in, 92, 306n146. *See also* Camp Andree; Pioneer Youth Camp; Progressive ideal

Progressive education: Dewey's impact on, 237; Lieberman's camp model and, 226–27, 229, 243; Progressive Era reform v., 229–30, 335n8

Progressive Era camps: pride of, 232; regimentation in, 232–34

Progressive Era reform: focus of, 54–55, 245; Junior Republic ideal and, 54, 295n143; progressive education v., 229–30, 335n8; settlement-house movement and, 55

Progressive ideal: at Camp Andree, 246–50; camp directors' implementation of, 243–44; at Camp Edith Macy, 246–47, 339n69; in camp movement, 243–44; camp's tradition v., 249–51, 340nn85–87; freedom and self-restraint in, 252–53; Lieberman's camp model and, 226–27, 229, 243. *See also* Camp Andree;

About the Author

Leslie Paris is an assistant professor of history at the University of British Columbia.